Analyzing the
Distributional
Impact of Reforms

Analyzing the Distributional Impact of Reforms

A practitioner's guide to pension, health, labor markets, public sector downsizing, taxation, decentralization, and macroeconomic modeling

VOLUME TWO

EDITED BY
Aline Coudouel
Stefano Paternostro

THE WORLD BANK
Washington, D.C.

Cover design and typesetting by Circle Graphics

ISBN-10: 0821363484
ISBN-13: 978-0-8213-6348-5
eISBN: 978-0-8213-6349-2
DOI: 10.1596/978-0-8213-6348-5

Library of Congress Cataloging-in-Publication Data has been applied for

VOLUME TWO CONTENTS

BOXES

FIGURES

TABLES

Analyzing the Distributional Impact of Reforms

A practitioner's guide to trade, monetary
and exchange rate policy, utility provision,
agricultural markets, land policy, and
education

VOLUME ONE

EDITED BY
Aline Coudouel
Stefano Paternostro

Published in 2005 by the World Bank
ISBN 0-8213-6181-3

CONTENTS

ACKNOWLEDGMENTS

The preparation of this volume has benefited from invaluable contributions from many colleagues. We would like to acknowledge both written inputs and helpful comments provided for the entire project or for individual chapters from Luca Barbone, Mark Camden Bassett, Gordon Betcherman, Shiyan Chao, David Coady, Shanta Devarajan, Daniel Dulitzky, David Evans, Deon Filmer, Emanuela Galasso, Delfin S. Go, Markus Goldstein, Dave Gwatkin, Oleksiy Ivaschenko, Moataz Mostafa Kamel El Said, Vijdan Korman, Silvana Kostenbaum, Philippe Le Houerou, Jennie Litvack, Hans Löfgren, Antonio Nucifora, Martin Rama, Ana Revenga, George Schieber, Sudhir Shetty, Yvonne Sin, Quentin Wodon. Many chapters also benefited from comments received at various seminars held both inside and outside the World Bank. Cecile Wodon and Robert Zimmermann provided invaluable technical and editorial assistance.

ABOUT THE AUTHORS

Maurizio Bussolo, at the World Bank since 2003, works on quantitative analyses of economic policy and development, including studies of the links among trade, growth, and poverty. He has previously worked at the Organisation for Economic Co-Operation and Development, the Overseas Development Institute (London), and Fedesarrollo and the University of Los Andes (Bogotá). He holds a PhD in economics from the University of Warwick. He has published in international journals. His recent publications include *Globalization and Poverty: Channels and Policies* (Routledge, London 2005), which he jointly edited with Jeff Round, and *Structural Change and Poverty Reduction in Brazil: The Impact of the Doha Round*, with Jann Lay and Dominique van der Mensbrugghe.

David Coady is a technical assistance advisor to the Poverty and Social Impact Analysis Group in the Fiscal Affairs Department of the International Monetary Fund. His research interests include public economics and development economics. Recently, his research has focused on the evaluation of the targeting, financing, and impact of conditional cash-transfer programs. He has coauthored (with Margaret Grosh and John Hoddinott) *Targeting of Transfers in Developing Countries: Review of Lessons and Experience* (World Bank and International Food Policy Research Institute, Washington, DC 2004), which reviews the design and implementation of targeted transfer programs. Prior to joining the Fund, he was a research fellow at the International Food Policy Research Institute between 1998 and 2004 and a lecturer in economics at the University of London between 1992 and 1998.

Patrick J. Conway is professor of economics at the University of North Carolina at Chapel Hill. He has been on the faculty there since 1983. His research has focused on the international aspects of trade and finance with developing countries. He is the author of three books and many refereed journal articles. His current research interests include the impact of International Monetary Fund lending programs on developing-country welfare, the development of financial markets in transition economies, the welfare impact of exchange-rate depreciation in developing countries, and the impact on United States workers of U.S. textile and apparel imports.

Aline Coudouel is a senior economist with the Poverty Group at the World Bank. She leads the team working on poverty analysis, monitoring, and impact evaluation. She has been involved in the Poverty and Social Impact Analysis agenda in the World Bank since its inception, defining the approach and advising teams on its implementation for selected countries and reforms. She is one of the contributors to *A User's Guide to Poverty and Social Impact Analysis* (World Bank 2003). She is the coeditor (with Stefano Paternostro) of *Analyzing the Distributional Impact of Reforms*, volume one, on guidance for the PSIA in selected sectors (World Bank 2005), and coeditor (with Anis A. Dani and Stefano Paternostro) of *Poverty and Social Impact Analysis of Reforms: Lessons and Examples from Implementation* (World Bank 2006), a volume on operational experiences in implementing PSIA.

Klaus W. Deininger is a lead economist in the World Bank's Development Research Group. His main areas of interest are income and asset inequality and its relationship to poverty reduction and growth; access to land, land markets, and land reform, and their impact on household welfare and agricultural productivity; land tenure and the design and economic and social impact of measures aimed at increasing tenure security; and capacity building (including the use of quantitative and qualitative methods) for policy analysis and program evaluation.

Juan Jose Diaz is an associate researcher at the Group for the Analysis of Development, a Peruvian think-tank. His areas of interest include labor economics, the evaluation of social programs, and development. He has recently been working on research projects related to the effectiveness of nonexperimental evaluation methods of social programs, the evaluation of job-training programs in Peru, and the relationship between health care use and access to social security and private health insurance among the elderly in Mexico. He has served as consultant for the World Bank and the Inter-American Development Bank. He holds a PhD in economics from the University of Maryland.

B. Essama-Nssah is a senior economist with the Poverty Reduction Group at the World Bank, where he has been working on the development and application of simulation models for the study of the impact of economic shocks and policies on poverty and income distribution. He is the author of *Inégalité, pauvreté et bien-être social: Fondements analytiques et normatifs (Inequality, Poverty, and Social Well-Being: The Analytical and Normative Underpinnings*, De Boeck Université, Brussels 2000). He was a senior research associate with the Food and Nutrition Policy Program at Cornell University from 1990 to 1992. From 1984 to 1989, he was vice dean of the Faculty of Law and Economics and head of the Economics Department at the University of Yaoundé (Cameroon). He holds a PhD in economics from the University of Michigan.

Vivien Foster is a senior economist in the Infrastructure Economics and Finance unit at the World Bank. She specializes in infrastructure issues, including pricing, subsidies, regulation, private sector participation, and sector reform. She has more than 10 years' experience advising governments in Latin America on various aspects of infrastructure reform, particularly with regard to the water sector, and has also contributed to projects in Africa, Asia, and Eastern Europe. Her research has focused on the social impacts of infrastructure reform and the design of infrastructure subsidies. Before joining the Bank, she worked as an economic consultant with Oxford Economic Research Associates Ltd in the United Kingdom. She holds a Bachelor's degree from the University of Oxford, a Master's from Stanford University, and a PhD from University College London.

Kai Kaiser is an economist with the Public Sector Group at the World Bank. His current work focuses on public finance, decentralization, and the governance of service delivery. He was previously based in Jakarta during the unfolding of a major decentralization reform. He is now engaged in a research project to assess the impact of decentralization in Indonesia, including a series of governance and decentralization surveys meant to assess decentralized outcomes in public service delivery and accountability. He has also recently worked on decentralization reforms in Africa and South Asia.

Mattias K. A. Lundberg is an agricultural economist by training, but has focused more recently on issues of income distribution, impact evaluation, and health sector reforms. He is one of the contributors to *A User's Guide to Poverty and Social Impact Analysis* (World Bank 2003) and has recently completed a toolkit on "Public Expenditure Reviews in Human Development" for the World Bank. His published research includes papers on the impact on households of crises such as HIV/AIDS and flood exposure and on the relationship between income distribution and growth. He is currently on the staff of *World Development Report 2007*.

Alessandro Nicita is a consultant in the Development and Economic Research Group at the World Bank. His research focuses on issues related to international trade and development. His work has included the analysis of the effect of international trade policies on the exports of low-income countries, as well as the effect of trade policies on poverty and inequality. Most recently, he has been working extensively on the impact of World Trade Organization agreements and of the Doha Development Agenda on Least Developed Countries. He has authored several publications in the field of trade and development and collaborated on a number of World Bank reports. He holds a PhD in economics from the Université de Genève.

Pierella Paci is a lead economist in the Poverty Reduction Group at the World Bank. A labor economist by training, she has, since her arrival at the Bank, worked extensively in the area of poverty, the labor market, and gender. Before joining the Bank, she taught labor economics, econometrics, and public economics at a number of universities in the United Kingdom and published widely in the areas of labor economics, the economics of inequality and poverty, and the economics of gender. She has a Laurea in economics from the University of Rome and a PhD from the University of Manchester. Her regional experience is predominantly on Europe, the former Soviet Union and other transition economies, and Latin America.

Stefano Paternostro is a lead economist in the World Bank's Africa Region Human Development Group. From 2002 to 2005, he coordinated the World Bank Poverty Group's work on poverty and social impact analysis, developing and disseminating methodologies to assess impacts of policy reforms, producing *A User's Guide to Poverty and Social Impact Analysis* (World Bank 2003) and "Good Practice Note: Using Poverty and Social

Impact Analysis to Support Development Policy Operations" (World Bank 2004) and coordinating with external partners on operational issues. He is the coeditor (with Aline Coudouel) of the first volume on guidance for the PSIA in selected sectors, *Analyzing the Distributional Impact of Reforms* (World Bank 2005), and coeditor (with Aline Coudouel and Anis A. Dani) of *Poverty and Social Impact Analysis of Reforms: Lessons and Examples from Implementation* (World Bank 2006), a volume on operational experiences in implementing PSIA.

Caterina Ruggeri Laderchi is an economist in the Poverty Reduction and Economic Management unit for Eastern Africa at the World Bank, where she has been working on issues involving Ethiopia and Sudan. Her current efforts are focused on the integration of Millennium Development Goal strategies in government plans and Poverty Reduction Strategy Papers, poverty and distributional analysis, particularly in urban contexts, and impact evaluation and labor markets. Before joining the World Bank in 2003, she worked on poverty for the Human Development Report Office of the United Nations Development Program and on labor markets for the Directorate-General for Employment, Social Affairs, and Equal Opportunities, European Commission.

Anita M. Schwarz is a lead economist in the Human Development Department in the World Bank's Europe and Central Asia Region. She focuses on pensions. Previous to her current appointment, she was lead economist in the Bank's Social Protection Department, where she was team leader for the pensions work throughout the Bank. She was part of the research department team that produced *Averting the Old Age Crisis: Policies to Protect the Old and Promote Growth* (Oxford University Press 1994), the Bank's seminal initiation into the world of pension reform. She holds a doctorate in economics from the University of Chicago and was an assistant professor at the University of Delaware and at the Foreign Service Institute before joining the World Bank.

Erwin H. R. Tiongson is an economist in the Poverty Reduction and Economic Management unit of the World Bank Europe and Central Asia Region, where he currently works on issues related to poverty, labor markets, and public finance. Between 2003 and 2004, he was a member of the World Bank Poverty Group's PSIA team and provided technical contributions to various PSIA-related initiatives. Prior to joining the Bank, he was at the International Monetary Fund's Expenditure Policy Division, where he was involved in work on the efficiency and equity of public spending on education and health care in developing countries and transition economies.

Limin Wang is an economist on secondment to the World Bank from the Department for International Development (United Kingdom). She holds a PhD in economics from the University of Southampton, United Kingdom. Her research focuses on impact analysis of policy reforms, income inequality, labor market reforms, and determinants of health outcomes in developing countries. She has contributed to a series of academic publications and policy reports for the World Bank. Before joining the Bank in 1999, she was lecturer at King's College London and a research officer at the Suntory and Toyota International Centres for Economics and Related Disciplines, London School of Economics.

INTRODUCTION

The analysis of the distributional impact of policy reforms[1] on the well-being and welfare of various stakeholder groups, particularly the poor and vulnerable, has an important role in the elaboration and implementation of poverty reduction strategies in developing countries. In recent years, this type of work has been labeled Poverty and Social Impact Analysis (PSIA), and, increasingly, it is being applied to promote evidence-based policy choices and foster debate on the options in policy reform.

PSIA helps to realize the following tasks:

- analyze the link between policy reforms and the related poverty and social impacts
- consider trade-offs among reforms on the basis of the distributional impacts
- enhance the positive impacts of reforms and minimize the adverse impacts
- assess the risks involved in policy reform
- design mitigating measures and risk management systems
- build country ownership and capacity for analysis

PSIA is not a product in itself. Rather, it is an approach that may be used and prove useful in guiding the analysis of distributional impacts. The process begins with an ex ante analysis of the expected poverty and social impacts of policy reforms. This helps in the design of the reforms. Ideally, the approach then involves monitoring the results during the implementation of the reforms. Finally, where possible, ex post evaluations of the poverty and social impacts of the reforms are carried out. PSIA can be an especially important ingredient in the design and implementation of reforms that are expected to have large distributional impacts, are prominent in the policy agenda of governments, and are likely to provoke significant debate.

AVAILABLE RESOURCES

The World Bank has developed a series of resources over the past few years to help practitioners analyze the poverty and social impacts of reforms.[2]

First, *A User's Guide to Poverty and Social Impact Analysis*[3] introduces the main concepts underlying PSIA, presents major elements of good practice in PSIA, and highlights significant constraints on and operational principles of PSIA. The guide highlights key tools that practitioners may find useful in undertaking a PSIA of policy reforms. It does not aim to be comprehensive in coverage.

Second, as a complement to the user's guide, the World Bank has developed assistance through the identification of appropriate tools and techniques. A first volume, *The Impact of Economic Policies on Poverty and Income Distribution: Evaluation Techniques and Tools,*[4] is a compendium of existing techniques, the principles on which they are built, and illustrative applications. The techniques range from incidence analysis to tools linking microeconomic distribution to macroeconomic frameworks or models. A second volume, *Evaluating the Impact of Macroeconomic Policies on Poverty and Income Distribution using Micro-Macro Linkage Models,* is currently being prepared. This volume will present five approaches through which macro-counterfactual experiments can be modeled and linked to microeconomic data. The World Bank has also released a sourcebook of *Tools for Institutional, Political, and Social Analysis (TIPS) in Poverty and Social Impact Analysis,*[5] which has been produced in partnership with the Department for International Development (United Kingdom) and draws on a range of multidisciplinary tools to complement econometric analysis.

Third, the World Bank has produced the short "Good Practice Note: Using Poverty and Social Impact Analysis to Support Development Policy Operations,"[6] which provides advice to World Bank staff and their counterparts on promoting PSIA in countries and integrating it within development policy support operations as envisaged by the World Bank's Operational Policy on Development Policy Lending (OP 8.60).

Fourth, a book of case studies, *Poverty and Social Impact Analysis of Reforms: Lessons and Examples from Implementation,*[7] provides a detailed account of country experiences to date in implementing the PSIA approach, with a view to highlighting the spectrum of sectors and policy reforms to which PSIA can be applied and the range of analytical tools and techniques that have been used for PSIA, as well as the challenges being faced and the lessons being learned in carrying out this work on the ground. Each case largely deals with policy reforms in a single sector, such as agriculture, energy, utilities, education, social welfare, or taxation, but also includes practical guidelines on macroeconomic modeling.

WHY THE NEED FOR SECTOR-SPECIFIC GUIDANCE

While information is available on general approaches, techniques, and tools for distributional analysis, each sector displays particular characteristics. These have implications for the analysis of distributional impacts, including the types of impacts and transmission channels that warrant particular attention, the tools and techniques most appropriate, the data sources typically required, and the range of political economy factors most likely to affect the reform process.

Hence, as a complement to the resources listed above, each chapter in this volume provides an overview of the specific issues arising in the analysis of the distributional impacts of selected categories of policy and institutional reform. Each chapter also offers guidance on the selection of tools and techniques most appropriate for the reforms under scrutiny and supplies examples of applications of these approaches.

The individual chapters are meant to be indicative only; they do not attempt to cover issues for each selected type of reform in an exhaustive fashion. In addition, the chapters mainly focus on economic analysis.[8]

This is the second volume in a series. The first volume covers six key areas of policy reforms that are likely to have significant effects on distribution and poverty: trade, monetary and exchange rate policy, utility provision, agricultural markets, land policy, and education.[9]

OUTLINE OF THE VOLUME

Each chapter is organized around the transmission channels through which policy reforms may be expected to have an impact on populations. It provides an overview of the typical direction and magnitude of the expected impacts, the implementation mechanisms through which reforms are usually carried out, the stakeholders who are likely to affect or be affected by the reforms positively or negatively, and the methodologies normally used to analyze the distributional impacts. Each chapter describes and illustrates these points with examples of tools, methods, and applications, highlighting key theoretical and practical source materials. Each chapter also includes a bibliography.

This volume covers six crucial areas in which policy reform is likely to have significant effects on distribution and poverty: pensions, health care, the labor market, public sector downsizing, indirect taxation and public pricing, and decentralization. The final chapter supplies an overview of approaches to the modeling of macroeconomic shocks and policies.

A short synopsis of the most salient features of the individual chapters is presented below.[10]

Pension System Reforms

Anita M. Schwarz, the author of the first chapter, highlights that pension systems are designed to provide an income to those individuals who suffer a loss in earnings capacity through advanced age, the experience of a disability, or the death of a wage earner in the family. While, in some cases, the systems are designed to facilitate direct transfers from the government to particular target groups, the emphasis is, in most cases, on establishing a viable mechanism whereby the individual might insure himself now against the loss of earnings in the future.

The chapter begins with a review of mechanisms for supplying support for the elderly and disabled—namely, contributory versus non-contributory pension systems—and considers redistributive and social elements within these mechanisms.

The author notes that, while the primary goal of a pension system should be to ensure adequate, affordable, sustainable, and robust retirement incomes, most of the reforms are motivated by fiscal concerns. This arises partly because systems are rarely actuarially designed from the outset. Hence, the aging of populations, changes in the contributing labor force, poor system design, and poor administration often lead to systems that run deficits.

The chapter discusses the various types of pension system reforms and the distributional and social consequences of each type. Pension reforms may be grouped into at least four categories: parametric reforms that involve changes in the parameters of current pension systems, systemic reforms that involve the introduction of a new sort of pension system to replace or complement the existing system, regulatory reforms that involve changes in the investment regulations of funds having investible assets, and, finally, administrative reforms.

Since countries have very different systems, one should consider a few questions before analyzing the poverty and social impact of pension reforms: Are the elderly poor? What are the living arrangements of the elderly? How much income do the elderly need? What are the coverage rates of the systems? What is the fiscal status of the pension system now, and what will it be in the near future? Is the contribution rate affordable? The author also suggests that the benefit structure should be analyzed to assess the fairness of and the redistribution involved in the system. Three questions can be used as guidelines in the process, as follows: Are the benefits adequate? Are the pensions fairly provided? How redistributive is the pension system?

An important specificity is the fact that the distributional benefits of pension reforms will not be obvious in the short run since pension reforms usually take 30 to 40 years to unfold fully, given that acquired rights must be legally and, in some cases, constitutionally respected.

Health Sector Reforms

In the second chapter, Mattias Lundberg and Limin Wang aim to provide a guide for policy practitioners who wish to conduct an analysis of the impact of health reform or health policy changes on the welfare of households, especially poor households.

The authors discuss the rationale for and the types of reforms that are common in the health sector and highlight issues that are specific to the analysis of the sector. The scope of the health reforms implemented in developing countries varies substantially. It is useful, albeit rough and imprecise, to distinguish the reforms into those affecting the *supply side* and those affecting the *demand side* of the health sector, that is, those involving the financing, management, and provision of services on the one hand and, on the other hand, those involving the demand for and consumption of services. The vast majority of reforms have focused on the supply side.

In practice, reforms are generally not implemented independently or piece by piece. They are often ambitious and far reaching, comprising a broad range of different actions. This has implications for the analysis, since it is difficult convincingly to identify the impact of components of reform programs. There are also important factors outside the reforms themselves through which the impact of the reforms is experienced by the poor. In particular, the demand for services will greatly influence both the level and the efficiency of supply, and the perceived quality of services is a major determinant of the consumption of services.

Health reforms commonly include changes in health financing and changes in health system organization and management. Changes in financing may involve cost recovery and user charges for publicly provided services, community-based financing schemes, insurance schemes (social and private), and changes in public expenditure and allocation. Changes in system organization and management may entail decentralization (authority, responsibilities, and functions) and changes in the ownership of service provision and delivery (privatization or a public-private mix). The authors highlight two types of more commonly implemented reforms: community-based health financing and the decentralization of health services.

The authors also discuss the stakeholders in reforms, the transmission channels for the impact of reforms, and ways to choose the appropriate tools and methods in impact analysis. They focus on two quantitative tools in particular: conventional econometric welfare analysis (derived from a model of household welfare in which welfare or utility is determined by health status and the consumption of other goods and services) and the experimental method of randomized controlled trials.

Selected Labor Market Reforms

Employment is widely perceived as one of the most important channels through which the poor can move out of poverty. In making decisions on the implementation of labor market reforms, policymakers should therefore be fully aware of the potential direct and indirect impacts on the distribution of incomes of both individuals and households so that the full significance of the policies and reforms in terms of efficiency, equality, and poverty reduction may be adequately evaluated.

The goal of the chapter by Aline Coudouel and Pierella Paci is to provide policymakers with the tools they need to conduct such an assessment. The chapter focuses on three labor market policies: the minimum wage, employment protection legislation, and unemployment benefits. It describes possible reforms in these policies and the rationale behind the reforms. The authors also illustrate the channels through which the reforms may impact income distribution and poverty.

Labor market reforms have important potential impacts on income distribution and poverty via their effects on the level and distribution of wages and employment. In any examination of key transmission mechanisms, it is crucial to consider explicitly the *dual* dimensions of the economy and distinguish between the formal or covered sector, where the policies apply, and the informal or uncovered sector, where they either do not apply or are not enforced. On the whole, stricter, more binding policies result in higher wages for covered workers at the expense of employment in general and covered employment in particular. Thus, the overall impact of a reform depends on its combined effect on both the demand and the supply of labor in the covered sector and in other sectors of the economy. This effect differs according to the policies in place and current labor market conditions.

The authors then identify the stakeholders involved in each of the reforms analyzed and outline the tools of analysis and the main impacts of the reforms as identified in the empirical literature. Assessing the potential distributional impacts of labor market interventions and reforms in labor market institutions is not a simple task. This is due to a number of factors. Thus, in evaluating the potential impact of interventions and reforms on income distribution, one must distinguish between the distribution of earnings and the distribution of income. The former is defined at the level of individuals and by focusing only on employed workers. The latter is usually defined at the level of households and depends on the total labor income of all household members, plus income from other sources. Another element complicating the analysis is the fact that impacts are transmitted through both employment and earnings. Changes in policies will also typically affect not only the particular segment of the labor market to which the policy applies, but also the rest of the labor market outside these boundaries. Resolving the relevant issues therefore calls for broad analysis.

Public Sector Downsizing

This chapter provides an economic analysis of public sector downsizing operations and illustrates the analysis with examples of reforms during the 1980s and 1990s. Juan Jose Diaz presents the most common types of reforms: voluntary departure schemes, involuntary retrenchment schemes, contracting-out schemes, employee ownership, and privatization. The rationale for this sort of reform is to address the problem of a public sector characterized by public agencies and state-owned enterprises that are overstaffed, bureaucracies that are bloated, and public services that are inefficient.

One of the most recurrent challenges linked to this type of reform is the problem of adverse selection in voluntary separation schemes, which leads to the rehiring of essential staff, overcompensation, externalities of downsizing, and difficulties in the appraisal of financial and economic returns.

The author identifies key stakeholders in these reforms, their likely responses, and the dissemination channels of the impacts of the reforms. The financial costs of separation packages designed to compensate displaced workers may be substantial, and mass layoffs may generate significant social and political costs. Downsizing operations directly affect stakeholders other than separated workers, such as entire communities in the case of one-company towns, caterers and providers of services to state-owned enterprises, and final consumers and taxpayers.

The author concentrates on assessing the welfare losses among dismissed workers. These consist of the present value of the resulting change in earnings, the present value of the losses in nonwage benefits, and other intangible losses from separation. Downsizing may generate differential distributional impacts. Traditional rules of thumb used to compute severance compensations take into account only current wages and years of tenure in the public sector. Changes in welfare after dismissal are related to other observable characteristics that may serve as the basis for the design of a "just right" compensation package. In particular, the author suggests that a well-tailored downsizing operation may consider the education, geographic location, and gender of workers. Various studies also show that the just right severance compensation package outperforms more traditional rules of thumb on the grounds of both costs and fairness.

To help assess the consequences of various downsizing strategies on the computation of severance packages, the author refers to a computer application called the Downsizing Options Simulation Exercise that has been developed by the World Bank.

Indirect Tax and Public Pricing Reforms

It is common for governments in developing countries to influence the prices of goods and services using a range of policy instruments and institutional arrangements. These manipulations typically arise from the need to raise revenue, the desire to redistribute incomes toward the poor or toward politically important groups, the desire to provide protection for domestic producers, or the desire to affect the levels of supply or demand in related markets where prices cannot be readily controlled.

David Coady discusses three methodologies for addressing these issues: the general equilibrium approach, the limited general equilibrium approach, and the partial equilibrium approach. The general equilibrium approach allows for all commodity-demand and factor-supply responses and thus incorporates both the direct and the indirect welfare effects of reforms. The use of such models is particularly valuable in analyzing the distributional impact of reforms that involve significant changes in producer prices, for instance, trade liberalization. The limited general equilibrium approach typically focuses on a subset of price reforms or allows for only a subset of household responses, thereby incorporating only a subset of the indirect effects. The partial equilibrium approach focuses only on the direct effect of reforms on prices and household real incomes. Simple partial equilibrium analyses may provide valuable information on the likely magnitude of the impacts of tax and price reforms on household real incomes, as well as the distribution across households. They have relatively low resource costs in terms of data, time, and modeling requirements and may therefore be undertaken on a routine basis.

The chapter draws lessons from the empirical literature in categorizing reforms into three groups: tax reforms, trade liberalization, and reforms of public sector prices. Indirect tax reforms include the introduction of value-added tax systems in place of existing sales or excise taxes. Trade liberalization refers to reforms that replace taxes on international trade with taxes on domestic consumption (including the consumption of imported goods). Public sector pricing reforms include reforms that adjust prices controlled by the government.

The author points out that, typically, the introduction of a relatively broadbased value-added tax in place of a sales tax reduces the progressivity of a tax system. It does this by enlarging the tax base to include previously exempt goods and services that are usually relatively more important in the budgets of the poor or by reducing taxes on goods that are relatively more important in the budgets of higher-income households. He suggests that, given the substantial leakage of benefits to higher-income households and the potentially large efficiency costs, manipulating commodity taxes to soften the impact on poor households is a very blunt second-best approach to protecting the real incomes of the poor. In cases where price manipulations provide an effective approach to distribution (for example, low prices for agricultural goods that are both produced and consumed by rural households), a high efficiency cost is usually involved.

Decentralization Reforms

Decentralization may refer to a wide range of reforms, but it is possible to identify three principal types: deconcentration, delegation, and devolution. Kai Kaiser outlines three levels of analysis for a PSIA on decentralization depending on the institutional characteristics, the probable mechanisms of impact, and the likely available sources of information. At the first level, the focus is on the amount and distribution of public resources across places. At the second level, the analysis concerns the distribution of public resources across people, such as the poor and non-poor, given the prevailing institutional and governance arrangements within places. At the third level, the analysis investigates impacts on local governance and public service delivery. Assessing the distributional impacts of decentralization will typically require a considerable amount of subnational data.

Kaiser describes instruments and methodologies that offer valuable entry points for the analysis. Public expenditure reviews have helped in analyses of the aggregate level, composition, and operational efficiency of public expenditures. Through public expenditure tracking surveys, one strives to produce detailed analyses of the extent to which public resources actually reach localities and front-line service delivery points. Poverty mapping, using subnational fiscal data and other socioeconomic data, may be usefully combined to assess incidence across places. Front-line service delivery surveys may provide important insights into decentralized outcomes. Specialized surveys, including household and facility surveys, may also target dimensions of service delivery not usually found in standard household socioeconomic surveys, which normally supply evidence on basic service use and access, but not service quality. Institutional and governance reviews may serve as venues for describing the political economy of decentralization reforms.

Inherent in decentralization is the expectation that the outcomes are diverse across subnational jurisdictions. Hence, studies should attempt to gather evidence from a sufficiently large number of localities to be representative and at least indicative of national patterns. The author suggests that even the short-run evidence on decentralization is quite fragmented. One explanatory factor may be that decentralization efforts are, by design and manner of implementation, diverse and difficult to compare. Another issue is that the methodologies for establishing the direction and magnitude of distributional impacts have been idiosyncratic.

Macroeconomic Shocks and Policies

The importance of distributional issues in policymaking creates a need for empirical tools that can help assess the impact of economic shocks and policies, such as terms-of-trade shocks, fiscal adjustment, monetary policy, and trade liberalization, on the living standards of relevant individuals. B. Essama-Nssah reviews some of the modeling approaches that are currently available for the analysis of the impact of macroeconomic shocks and policies on poverty and income distribution. These approaches provide a framework that links a macroeconomic model to a model of the distribution of economic welfare at the individual or household level.

The approaches or specific models described in the chapter vary in the ways they specify the macroeconomy, the distribution of welfare, and macro-micro linkages. A first series of models focus only on income distribution, while the macromodel remains implicit. These models can be used in conjunction with assumptions about the response of the macroeconomy to shocks and policies. The models in this family include POVCAL and SimSIP, which are purely statistical, and PovStat, the maximum value or envelope model, and the household income and occupational choice model.

A second series involves embedding distributional mechanisms within a general equilibrium framework. While the standard representative household approach limits the analysis of the distributional impact of shocks and policies to their effects on representative socioeconomic groups, the extended representative household approach considers various socioeconomic groups as representative households. Within a general equilibrium framework, it is possible to account for various market and household behavioral adjustments induced by shocks or policies.

The third series adopts a modular approach in linking poverty and distributional outcomes to macroeconomic shocks and policies. These models have been influenced by an emerging approach known as Top-Down/Bottom-Up; they try to account for the feedback effects from the microlevel to the macrolevel and back until convergence is achieved. Within this class, the author focuses on the 123PRSP model (one country, two sectors, and three commodities); the poverty analysis macroeconomic simulator; a macro-micro simulation model that uses the investment savings–liquidity money framework for macroeconomic analysis; and the integrated macroeconomic model for poverty analysis framework, which links a dynamic computable general equilibrium model to unit record data.

The best approach to adopt depends on the problem at hand, the data, and other resource constraints.

NOTES

1. Here and throughout this book, the word reform is meant to encompass both policy and institutional changes.

2. Refer to http://www.worldbank.org/psia for further information. An electronic learning program (providing a self-paced introduction to PSIA approaches, tools, and methods) and a series of case studies that illustrate good practice are also available online and are included in the CD ROM in the case attached to the inside back cover of this volume.

3. Published by the Poverty Reduction Group and Social Development Department of the World Bank in 2003, the guide is available for download at http://www.worldbank.org/psia and included in the CD ROM attached to the inside back cover of this volume.

4. Edited by François Bourguignon and Luiz A. Pereira da Silva, the book was published by Oxford University Press in 2003. Visit http://www1.world bank.org/prem/poverty/psia/tools.htm for information. See also http://www.worldbank.org/psia for details about other tools and training materials.

5. More information is available at http://www.worldbank.org/tips.

6. Downloadable at http://www.worldbank.org/psia.

7. Edited by Aline Coudouel, Anis A. Dani, and Stefano Paternostro and published by the World Bank in 2006.

8. For more details on institutional, political, and social analyses, see http://www.worldbank.org/tips.

9. *Analyzing the Distributional Impact of Reforms: A Practitioner's Guide to Trade, Monetary and Exchange Rate Policy, Utility Provision, Agricultural Markets, Land Policy, and Education* (World Bank, 2005), edited by Aline Coudouel and Stefano Paternostro and available at http://www.worldbank.org/psia.

10. These chapters, updates, and further reference material are available at http://www.worldbank.org/psia.

Pension System Reforms

Anita M. Schwarz

Pension systems are designed to provide an income to those individuals who suffer a loss in earnings capacity through advanced age, the experience of a disability, or the death of a wage earner in the family. The systems are designed in some cases to facilitate direct transfers from the government to these particular target groups and may be evaluated as such, but, in most cases, the emphasis is on providing a mechanism whereby the individual might insure himself against the loss of future earnings.

Why are pension systems needed? In most traditional societies, families or communities care for individuals who reach old age, become disabled, or suffer the death of a wage earner. However, even in these instances, there are always individuals who do not have children to care for them or whose communities and families are too poor to supply adequate care or are otherwise unable or unwilling to do so. As societies modernize and people move from the communities in which they have been raised, community and family ties weaken and leave the elderly and disabled without an adequate safety net. Individuals may try to save, but, in the absence of secure financial markets, savings often take the form of real estate, livestock, or jewelry, all of which suffer from fluctuations in price and potential misfortunes due to disease, theft, or war. For these reasons, governments often take on the role of making some type of pension system available.

Even in developed countries, in which reasonably secure financial markets exist, governments frequently either support pensions directly or mandate the participation in pension plans furnished by employers or private pension providers. Two reasons are commonly cited for government involvement in old-age pension systems either as direct provider or as regulator and mandator. First, workers may suffer from "myopia" and not think about old age when they are young and healthy. By the time they begin to worry about old age, it may be too late for them to take adequate steps to provide for themselves. Second, workers may incur "moral hazard" by consuming as much as possible when young, with the expectation that society will care for them when they are old. The only way that governments can limit the costs of caring for the elderly is to require participation in a pension plan for those individuals who can afford it and then limit direct government transfers so that these go only to people who were too poor to be able to save during their working years.

What are the objectives of a pension system? First, a pension system tries to reduce poverty among the elderly. Second, a pension system tries to smooth consumption between the working years and the retirement years so that an individual does not suffer a huge drop in living standards when old age or disability reduces his or her earning ability.[1] While the first objective can be evaluated much like the objective of any other social program, the second is considerably different. In order for the second objective to be met, those people who earn more and consume more during their working years should continue to receive more and consume more during their retirement years. This feature makes pension systems unlike virtually all other forms of government expenditure. In the case of education spending, for example, ideally, there should not be a disparity in spending per pupil based on the income level of the pupil, or, if there is, the government should focus its spending on poorer pupils, with the rationale that government spending is meant to complement private spending on goods such as education. A similar argument could be made for health spending or spending on roads or electricity. Ideally, the government's spending should benefit all members of society equally or be targeted toward lower-income individuals.[2]

While the first pension-system objective, that of poverty reduction, may be financed through general revenues, consumption smoothing is typically financed by contributions from workers. Usually, workers make contributions based on their incomes and expect to receive pensions that are also based on their incomes.

However, the financing of pension systems through contributions that are calculated based on wages introduces a new set of problems from the point of view of poverty and social impact. It becomes close to impossible to collect and record contributions from workers who are not part of the formal sector. Determining income for groups such as farmers and the self-employed is difficult. Even in the United States, where the highly feared tax authorities collect social security contributions, compliance among the self-employed, excluding household employees, is estimated at less than 50 percent, while it stands at 96 percent for the rest of the population. The "informalization" of workers allows employers to avoid not only employment-related contributions and income taxes, but also compliance with unduly difficult labor regulations and standards. As a result, many workers in World Bank client countries are not covered under contributory pension systems.

Neither one of the two pension-system objectives—neither poverty reduction nor consumption smoothing—is necessarily to be preferred over the other; they simply represent separate societal priorities; countries place different emphases on these two objectives. Some countries, such as Australia, New Zealand, and, to a lesser extent, the United States, focus on poverty reduction more than consumption smoothing. New Zealand offers all individuals of a certain age a flat pension that is unrelated to previous income, while Australia offers a means-tested pension that provides some level of benefit to more than 75 percent of the elderly. But, even within contributory schemes, such as the one in the United States, a progressive benefit formula can result in a greater focus on poverty reduction relative to consumption smoothing. The average pension paid is around 40 percent of the relevant wages in the United States, but high-income individuals receive as little as 20 percent of their wage levels, while low-income individuals receive 100 percent of their previous wages. By contrast, countries such as Austria and Sweden strongly link contributions and benefits and achieve much higher rates of consumption smoothing.

Moreover, some countries choose to distinguish between these objectives by pursuing them using separate instruments. Social assistance programs, as part either of overall programs or of programs especially targeted at the elderly, may account for the bulk of poverty reduction, while the contributory system focuses on consumption smoothing. The French and German systems would fall in this category: the pension systems themselves are not expected to redistribute toward the poor, and old-age poverty relief is provided by other instruments. Other countries try to achieve both objectives using only one instrument. But trying to achieve both objectives through one instrument may create conflicts. Consumption smoothing implies that benefits should be tightly linked to contributions and therefore to income, with redistribution occurring across an individual's lifetime, but not among individuals. On the other hand, poverty reduction among the elderly clearly involves providing resources for the elderly poor. Within a contributory system, this usually implies that the resources come from the other contributors. But redistributing within the program weakens the link between contributions and benefits and can have a severely negative impact on the incentives for contribution compliance. Of course, mandating participation in a pension plan oriented toward consumption smoothing may prevent some myopic individuals from finding themselves in poverty in old age; so, the two objectives are interrelated up to a certain income level.

Given the possibility that more than one instrument may be used for old-age support, the pension system should not be viewed in isolation. The pension system may be merely one of many elements comprising the social safety net for elderly individuals. Each individual element need not incorporate the same level of redistribution since the pension system's objectives extend beyond redistribution. Therefore, it might be sensible to review all programs affecting the elderly population jointly rather than reviewing each individually. However, the task of this chapter is to look specifically at these issues with respect to pension programs and not at overall programs for the elderly even in the cases where social assistance programs are applicable to the elderly.

The remainder of the chapter is organized as follows. The next section reviews mechanisms for providing support for the elderly and disabled. The subsequent section considers redistributive and social elements within these mechanisms. The rationale for pension system reforms is examined thereafter. The types of pension system reform and the distributional and social consequences of each type are then explored. The impact of pension reform on stakeholders is assessed in the penultimate section. Finally, a checklist and toolbox for analyzing the poverty and social impacts of pension reforms are presented.

SUPPORT MECHANISMS FOR THE ELDERLY AND DISABLED

Contributory systems

The primary method for providing old-age support is contributory pension systems. Contributory pension systems are frequently described according to either the relevant financing mechanism or the benefit structure. Financing mechanisms are generally of two types: pay as you go or fully funded mechanisms. In pay as you go, current workers make contributions based on their current earnings. These contributions are immediately used to pay benefits for current recipients; the worker who is making the contribution only receives a promise from the government that it will pay benefits related to these contributions when the worker becomes eligible for a pension.[3] In what is known as fully funded pension systems, worker contributions are invested, rather than spent, and the investment earnings are an integral part of the benefits eventually paid. These investments can be managed by a monopolistic public agency or competitively, with participation by the private sector.

Benefit mechanisms are also of two types: defined-benefit mechanisms and defined-contribution mechanisms. Under the defined-benefit mechanism, the pension received is usually a function of income expressed as a percentage of income per year of contribution; it may also be defined in some other manner. The distinction is that the benefit provided is specified in some way. Should financing fall short, someone, typically either the government in a public plan or the employer in an employer-based plan, has the responsibility to provide the pension. Alternatively, under the defined-contribution mechanism, the contribution is specified as a percentage of wages, and rates are specified for employees, employers, and, potentially, the government, but the final pension is determined by the amount in one's pension account at the time of retirement, which includes both the contributions and the investment earnings on those contributions. Under this system, no specific benefit is promised; the pension is completely dependent on the money in the account, and there is no need for a guarantor of last resort.[4] Financial assets fully back the promise made in this case, which is simply a return of the money in the account.

In a strictly stylized world, the risk characteristics of these two types of pension systems would be considerably different, with governments or employers bearing the risk in defined-benefit systems, and workers bearing the risk in defined-contribution systems. However, in practice, these distinctions are quite blurred. The parameters in defined-benefit systems can change, substantially altering the nature of the benefit promised. Many Bank client countries find themselves unable to pay pensions on a timely basis, which imposes considerable risks on retirees during their most vulnerable years. Most defined-contribution systems, on the other hand, carry government guarantees of minimum pensions or are only one component in a broader pension strategy, whereby the other components mitigate the risks to the worker that are attributable to the defined-contribution arrangement.

Typically, defined-benefit systems are of the pay as you go sort, and defined-contribution systems are of the fully funded sort. It is possible for a defined-benefit system to be fully funded because the guarantor maintains sufficient financial assets to cover the liabilities in the plan. However, should investment returns fall in any particular year, the employer has the obligation to offset the lower returns by increasing his contribution. A hybrid defined-contribution, pay as you go system that is called notional accounts has been pioneered in the last decade. The key feature is that contributions are recorded and earn "notional" interest rates. The combination of contributions and notional interest earnings determine the pension benefit, much as in conventional defined-contribution systems. However, because the system is financed on a pay as you go basis and because there are no financial assets behind the accounts, the government must define the interest rate it will pay on the contributions. The system may run deficits, unlike in the case of a true defined-contribution system, and, if it does, the government is obliged to cover the deficits. As a result, the notional account system is not a true defined-contribution system, since, by defining both the contribution and the interest rate paid, the government has implicitly defined the benefits.

Noncontributory pension systems

Even where a contributory system exists, there will always be people who do not participate in the labor markets covered by the social security system, who do not participate sufficiently regularly to qualify for benefits, or whose low lifetime earnings leave them with even lower pension benefits. This is particularly true for the many informal sector workers in numerous Bank client countries. And, in many cases, groups of workers, such as the self-employed or farmers, are not covered by the national pension system because it is considered too difficult to assess income and collect contributions from these groups.

All of these groups are at risk of poverty in old age if they do not qualify for a contributory pension or if they qualify only for a small pension. As a result, most high- and middle-income countries with contributory systems also offer minimal benefits for those people who do not qualify. This benefit can take the form of a demogrant, whereby everyone above a certain age receives the benefit on the basis of a residency or citizenship requirement, as in countries as varied as Nepal and New Zealand, or it can be means tested, such that only those elderly with incomes below a certain level are eligible to receive the benefit. A few countries, such as New Zealand and, until 15 years ago, Australia, choose to offer only this type of demogrant or means-tested benefit in lieu of a contributory system.

The benefit in most cases is financed directly through general tax revenues. Both types of noncontributory systems tend to reduce poverty among the elderly. Obviously, the means-tested benefit is more well targeted toward the poor elderly, but, given the costs and complications involved with means testing, the potential changes to incentives, and the behavior of individuals trying to meet the qualifications, the demogrant approach may be a better solution in some countries. Some countries institute a demogrant, but then use other mechanisms to target resources more effectively away from higher-income individuals and toward lower-income individuals. New Zealand, for example, uses its progressive income tax to reduce the value of the demogrant to higher-income individuals. Similarly, some lower-income countries, such as Georgia and Nepal, ostensibly offer a demogrant, but the amount is so low that higher-income individuals are not interested in collecting it, and the systems are, to this extent, engaging in affluence testing rather than means testing.

Since the purpose of the noncontributory pension is clearly poverty reduction, with no attempt at consumption smoothing, some countries choose to integrate this social assistance for the elderly with the social assistance systems for the nonelderly, resulting in one national social assistance system. From a targeting perspective, such integration is ideal since resources flow to those most in need, regardless of age. However, from an administrative and social point of view, there may be arguments for separating the programs. Goals such as inducing working-age individuals to reenter the workforce are clearly not an issue in terms of the elderly; annual means testing may be necessary for working-age individuals whose situation can change dramatically from one year to the next, but less necessary for elderly individuals living alone or as part of a couple since their income situation is unlikely to improve in the future. Finally, elderly people who were not poor during their working lifetimes may feel especially stigmatized because they now must seek social assistance.

THE REDISTRIBUTIVE AND SOCIAL IMPACT OF PENSION SYSTEMS

Any social program that may involve expenditures in double-digit percentages of gross domestic product will have substantial impact on the economy in which it exists. Pension systems can affect poverty among the elderly. They can affect relationships between younger and elder cohorts, as well as family living arrangements. They also have a substantial impact on labor markets and employment, particularly if they are financed through contributory systems. They can impact national savings and the development of financial markets. They can affect the composition of government spending by squeezing out other types of spending. They can even affect the overall level of government spending. A huge body of literature exists on each one of these issues and would be impossible to summarize here.[5] However, it should be noted that much of this literature is derived from case studies and data on the United States and other countries of the Organisation for Economic Co-operation and Development. It is questionable whether all these results will apply equally across the board in the Bank's client countries.

This chapter focuses on the direct distributive impact of the pension system, ignoring secondary impacts arising through the economy. The distributive impact will depend on the type of pension system existing in the country.

The defined-benefit, pay as you go system

While the goal of a defined-benefit, pay as you go system is ostensibly to base benefits on contributions, thereby creating an institution that will allow individuals to smooth consumption over their lifetimes in the absence of a secure market institution, this type of pension scheme always has distributional implications within generations and across generations, some intentional, and others unintentional. Countries frequently try both to redistribute toward the poor and to provide a savings mechanism within these systems. However, there is a natural tension between redistribution in a contributory system and the provision to individuals of incentives to contribute by tying the benefits to contributions. There are also limits to how much true redistribution can be accomplished within a contributory system since the majority of redistribution occurs from one group of contributors to another. If coverage is low, both groups may already be receiving relatively similar incomes since they are more likely to belong to a narrow segment of the working population.

Intentional redistribution

Intentional redistribution in a defined-benefit scheme across a cohort takes place through at least three mechanisms. Most defined-benefit systems have a *minimum pension,* but individuals must contribute for a set period of time before they may receive this minimum pension. The minimum pension almost always involves some redistribution. Because of the minimum pension, workers at minimum wage who contribute for the minimum contribution period almost always receive higher pensions than the pensions they would have earned based on the formula. This, of course, leaves open the option that workers may game the system by contributing only enough to qualify for the minimum pension, but the poverty reduction objectives of pension systems have usually overridden these concerns. The higher the level of the minimum pension, the more the incentive issue begins to override the poverty reduction issue.

A second mechanism for redistribution results from a possibly *progressive benefits formula.* The United States is one of a few countries explicitly offering a benefits formula that provides a declining replacement rate as income goes up. Related to this approach, but usually less progressive, are schemes offering separate replacement rates for different groups of workers, usually by crediting more years of service per year of contribution. In Serbia, for example, women are given 15 percent more years of service credit over and above their years of contribution. In other countries, this special credit is given to particular occupations such as teachers or miners.

A third mechanism for explicit redistribution, more common than the second, is the *front-loaded benefit formula,* whereby the first 10–15 years of service are awarded higher benefit rates than are subsequent years. The thinking is that lower-income workers are more likely to interrupt their working careers, particularly in the formal sector, and are therefore unlikely to accumulate significant amounts of time in formal sector service. If the early years of contribution are rewarded more heavily, these workers will still be able to retire with reasonable pensions. As with minimum pensions, this design feature raises incentive issues; if people can earn reasonable pensions with only 10–15 years of contribution, why should they contribute throughout their careers? Nevertheless, countries continue to use this mechanism in the name of redistribution.

Unintentional redistribution

In addition to intentional redistribution, there are common design features within defined-benefit systems that have unintentional distributive consequences. One of the primary features is the *averaging period for wages* used to calculate the pensions. Pensions are expressed as a percentage of wages, but the wages may be defined as the last salary earned, as the average salary over the last five years, or as average wages over any period up to the lifetime average wage. If the averaging period is any period less than full career, then there is a redistribution involved. Individuals pay contributions on wages throughout their careers; if the pensions are not linked to the average career wage, then the pensions are not linked to the average contributions either. In addition, there is a systematic income-based bias to the extent that higher-income and more well educated workers generally experience more rapid wage growth, particularly toward the ends of their careers. Thus, the shorter the averaging period, the more redistribution there is in the system from future workers to current pensioners and the greater the redistribution toward higher-income pensioners who earn the highest wages at the ends of their careers.

A second issue is the *life-expectancy differential between income classes.* Higher-income individuals tend to live longer. This differential tends to make the defined-benefit scheme regressive, given that higher-income individuals will receive benefits for a longer period because of their longer life expectancy, resulting in a higher total benefit paid even if the monthly pension is identical.

A final issue is the *life-expectancy differential between men and women.* Defined-benefit schemes do not distinguish between the benefit rates paid to men and those paid to women even though women tend to receive the benefits for more years because of their longer life expectancy. As a result, there is an automatic redistribution from men to women implicit in the defined-benefit scheme. The common practice of allowing women to retire earlier with the same benefits only intensifies this redistribution.[6]

Intergenerational distribution

While the distributional consequences usually involve intracohort redistributions, the redistribution impact in defined-benefit schemes is larger between cohorts. Rarely are the schemes costed out in such a way that they are actuarially fair. Usually, a contribution rate is chosen, a benefit rate is chosen, and eligibility conditions are chosen. These parameters are almost never actuarially consistent. Since the schemes are normally set up when the countries are young, the parameters are often selected to maintain a balance between revenues and expenditures in the first years, with perhaps a small accumulated surplus. Because, at the start, many contributors are young, and few elderly are collecting benefits, contribution rates usually start low, and benefits are fairly generous. As a result, from the beginning, contributions rarely cover the future benefits to be paid out to these same contributors; the expectation is that the contributions of future generations will be used to pay the benefits of current workers. As long as population continues to grow rapidly, the scheme is viable, as all pyramid schemes would be. But, when the population of paying cohorts starts to stabilize in size or when it falls, huge deficits appear. Attempts to fix the fiscal deficits by raising contribution rates and reducing benefits exacerbate the intercohort redistribution problems.

Younger cohorts are asked to pay higher and higher contributions and receive fewer benefits; they are often required to postpone retirement, which also results in fewer benefits paid in total.

While there may be some justification for transferring income from one cohort to another, especially when particular cohorts are hard hit by wars, recessions, or a transition to a market economy, the redistribution system initiated under defined-benefit systems does not involve only a one-time transfer, but will result in undesirable and unexpected redistributions over time.

Even if the system were actuarially balanced at its introduction, changes in life expectancy and fertility will require continuous adjustments to maintain actuarial balance.[7] In countries where analyses have been carried out, the intercohort redistributions substantially overwhelm the intracohort redistribution, as shown in Figure 1.1 for the United States. Both panels in the figure show the internal rate of return in the social security system, the implicit rate of return that contributions made to the system would receive given the benefits that are provided by the system for two different cohorts, those retiring in 1960 and those retiring in 2005. While internal rates of return are higher for lower-income earners than they are for higher-income earners, the differences are not huge within the cohort of retirees in any particular year. The differences between those retiring in 1960, shown in the left-hand panel, and those retiring in 2005, shown in the right-hand panel, are far more pronounced than the differences within the cohort. Furthermore, the analysis represented in the figure does not take into account the mortality differences between low-income and high-income individuals and assumes that all individuals have the same life expectancy. When mortality differentials are included, the intracohort distribution almost disappears. And these results apply to the U.S. system, which is designed to be highly redistributive, with marginal benefit rates declining with income. Most defined-benefit systems do not incorporate even this element of redistribution and thus are unlikely to be positively redistributive. A more complete analysis of the U.S. system can be found in Steuerle and Bakija (1994).

The defined-contribution system

Little redistribution takes place in a pure defined-contribution system. At retirement, individuals get back their own contributions with the investment interest that these contributions have earned.

However, most systems are not pure defined-contribution systems; they contain an element of redistribution. Many systems, such as those

FIGURE 1.1 Comparison of Internal Rates of Return in a Social Security System over Time, United States, 1960 and 2005

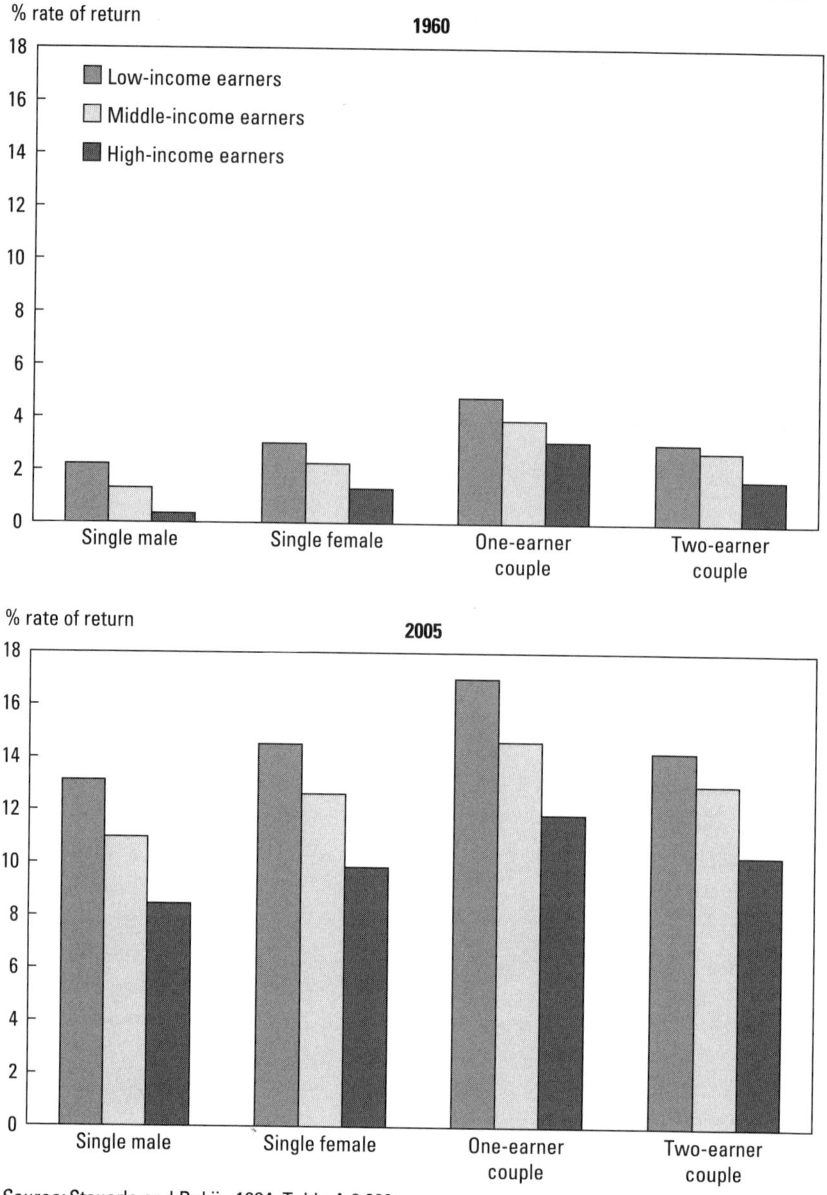

Source: Steuerle and Bakija 1994, Table A.9:290.

in Chile and Mexico, offer a *minimum pension guarantee* to workers, such that, after a given period of contribution, a minimum pension will be provided by the government. Other systems, such as those in Malaysia and Singapore, provide a guaranteed minimum rate of return, which can be redistributive depending on the level. If the minimum rate of return is high, it obviously redistributes from the guarantor, usually the government, to pensioners, but without regard to the income level of the pensioner. On the other hand, there are a few cases where the rate of return is virtually fixed ex ante, and, if the fund can earn better rates of return, then individuals lose by belonging to the fund, but, again, the loss is not dependent on income level.

A second redistributive element arises through the provision of *annuities.* An annuity is a mechanism for converting an account balance into a stream of periodic payments. Usually, an individual purchases an annuity from a life insurance company, which guarantees monthly payments as long as the individual or spouse lives. The payments can be adjusted upward periodically, often with inflation. As with defined-benefit pensions, if individuals are forced to buy annuities, higher-income individuals, who are typically longer-lived, gain at the expense of lower-income, shorter-lived individuals since the annuities are not priced differently for different income groups. Most countries (aside from those in Latin America) also require the use of unisex annuities when annuities are chosen. In unisex annuities, both men and women are in the same annuity pool, and there is no price differential. As with defined-benefit plans, unisex annuities result in a transfer toward women, who are, on average, longer lived than men.

Many countries do not require annuitization and set up *programmed withdrawals* as a benefit option, whereby an individual withdraws an amount from his account each month that is specified on an annual basis depending on the rate of return that the fund received on its investment earnings and the expected duration of the retirement. Upon the death of the individual, the balance in the individual's account is inheritable by whomsoever the individual specified. Under this approach, individuals take a risk that they will outlive the money in their accounts since they are not guaranteed payments for life, as under an annuity, but shorter-lived individuals have the option of leaving an inheritance rather than allowing the account to revert to the insurance company, which uses the money to cross-subsidize longer-lived individuals. Since lower-income individuals tend to die sooner than do higher-income individuals, the option of programmed withdrawals reduces the redistribution toward the rich.

A third, more indirect potential distributive element is linked to the *investment policy* of the pension fund. In some countries, assets, particularly when they are publicly managed, are invested largely in housing or in programs perceived to be socially beneficial (at the expense of lower rates of return to workers). In this case, there is a transfer from workers to the beneficiaries of the investment, and it is usually not a progressive transfer since it rewards those who are politically powerful and not those who are poor.

Voluntary or supplemental pensions

In defined-benefit and defined-contribution pensions, governments typically impose ceilings on the income that is subject to contributions, and the same ceiling is typically used in calculating benefits. The thinking is that, while governments want to promote poverty reduction and consumption smoothing among the elderly, they are generally not concerned with whether the super rich of the world have sufficiently smoothed their incomes. Since all requirements reduce individual freedom, a ceiling on the contribution requirement limits the impact to what is necessary to prevent old-age poverty and overcome myopia. The ceiling is often set at three to five times the average wage. Thus, the mandatory systems do not provide substantial consumption smoothing among higher-income individuals.

But governments would still like to provide incentives so that higher-income individuals save for consumption smoothing purposes. Governments do this by offering tax advantages for voluntary or supplemental savings. Typically, governments do not tax contributions made to voluntary pension systems or the returns the contributions earn; they tax only the benefits when these are received.[8] The policy represents an attempt by the governments to encourage long-term savings, which can then be invested and help stimulate growth in the economy. By and large, those people who take advantage of these schemes are higher-income individuals, resulting in tax reductions for these individuals. From a distributional standpoint, the policy can be worthwhile if the growth arising from the increased long-term savings helps the poor. However, the evidence generally suggests that higher-income individuals do not increase their savings in order to access these tax-advantaged retirement funds, but merely shift their savings from one instrument to another. In this case, the policy merely lowers the taxes on the rich without substantial improvements in growth or in lowering poverty. Thus, some countries impose limits on the amount of income that can earn tax advantages even if the income is saved through the pension system.

RATIONALE FOR PENSION SYSTEM REFORM

The primary goal of a pension system should be to provide adequate, affordable, sustainable, and robust retirement income.[9] Most Bank-sponsored reforms attempt to achieve all these goals.

However, the overwhelming reason for the Bank's involvement in pension reform issues is the fiscal implications, largely of defined-benefit systems, although sometimes also of social assistance benefits for the elderly. Since the systems are rarely actuarially designed from the outset, it is not surprising that, with the aging of populations, changes in the contributing labor force, poor system design, and poor administration, the systems begin to run deficits. Deficits within the pension system can be huge relative to overall gross domestic product and the overall deficits of a country. For example, in Brazil in the late 1990s, three-fourths of the government fiscal deficit of 8 percent of gross domestic product was directly attributable to social security, and, in Serbia, the fiscal deficit of the pension funds runs to 7 percent of gross domestic product. Such large deficits clearly create a drag on the entire economy.

These large deficits have huge distributional implications, particularly in countries with low labor force coverage. If only 5–10 percent of the labor force is part of the pension system, and the system is running deficits that need to be financed from general revenue, then money from all individuals who contribute to the general revenue is being transferred to the 5–10 percent of the population that is covered by the pension system, making even a progressively designed system potentially regressive. In the majority of Bank-client countries, coverage among the working-age population is below 50 percent; deficits in these pension systems clearly lead to regressive outcomes. Given the already huge intergenerational transfers that occur in these defined-benefit systems, the low coverage, combined with the financing of deficits from general revenue, pushes the cost of providing pensions not only on to younger cohorts covered under the system, but on to younger cohorts who are not even covered by the system, making the impact more regressive. As a result, much of the focus of the World Bank in pension reform is on reducing the fiscal deficits so that the pension system, if limited in coverage, is financed through contributions from that same limited population rather than through transfers from the broader population.[10]

Pension reform efforts have also attempted to increase coverage as a means of providing old-age security to a broader segment of the population, but most attempts at increasing coverage have not been successful. The one positive preliminary result has occurred in Mexico, where the government provides a flat contribution per day of worker contribution to the defined-contribution system, which amounts to approximately 5.5 percent of the minimum wage. The government contribution doubles the contributions going to the pension funds for low-income workers, which increases the incentive for low-income workers to contribute. Since this flat government contribution has been implemented, coverage among the lower three deciles of the income distribution has expanded.

But, because there are few successful examples, governments are turning to social assistance pensions as a means of providing support to elderly people who are not covered under contributory social security programs, rather than seeking to expand coverage. These social assistance programs are, in some cases, embedded within general social assistance, while, in other cases, they exist as stand-alone programs or are tied to the contributory pension system.

Countries running defined-contribution systems that might be earning poor investment returns also encounter trouble if substantial numbers of the elderly fall below the poverty line. Appropriate supervision and regulation of this type of pension fund and of voluntary pension systems need to be provided, along with flexibility in the investment of assets, so that the investment funds supply sufficient returns to workers making contributions. In some cases, governments see the pension fund reserves as a ready source of financing for whatever politically motivated investments they might desire. However, there is a trade-off between providing workers reasonable returns on their contributions and getting cheap financing for what might be socially laudable investment projects. Improvements in the functioning of capital markets may also be required before pension funds can provide adequate old-age support.

TYPES OF REFORM AND THE DISTRIBUTIONAL CONSEQUENCES

Since the primary reason, by far, for pension reforms has been to address the fiscal impact, the reforms have focused largely on improving fiscal deficits first. From a distributional standpoint, this is an appropriate focus given the incomplete coverage and the potential for regressive distribution from noncovered lower-income groups to covered higher-income groups. Any reform that lowers the fiscal deficit will be beneficial from a distributive perspective.

Pension reforms can be grouped into at least four different categories: parametric reforms, which involve changes in the parameters of current pension systems; systemic reforms, which involve introducing a new type of pension system to replace or complement the existing system; regulatory reforms, which involve changes in the investment regulations on funds having assets that can be invested; and administrative reforms.

Parametric reforms

Pension systems rely on three subgroups of parameters: contribution parameters, benefit parameters, and eligibility conditions for receiving pensions. Many parametric reforms involve changes in all three subgroups. Each of these parameter subgroups has a distributive impact among contributors and beneficiaries, and so do the reforms. The reforms also affect the fiscal sustainability of the pension system, and the fiscal sustainability affects the redistribution from outside the pension system to the contributors and beneficiaries of the pension system.

Contribution-revenue parameters apply both to the defined-benefit system and to the defined-contribution system, as well as voluntary systems. However, the impact on fiscal sustainability primarily occurs in defined-benefit systems. The parameters include the following:

- *Contribution rates.* Raising contribution rates clearly lowers the take-home salaries of workers and the net benefits that workers receive from the pension system. Rising labor costs may reduce or cause stagnation in the level of employment in the formal sector. These have a negative impact on workers, but may be necessary to maintain fiscal balance. Contribution rates above 15 percent are likely to have negative labor market impact.
- *Wages that are subject to contributions.* Raising the ceiling of the wages that are subject to contributions, another common measure, tends to be positively distributive in that higher-salaried workers pay more of their incomes into the pension fund, although, in the longer run, they will usually receive higher benefits, too. Thus, while there may be a positive redistributive effect in the short run, there will be little impact in the long run as the benefits for higher-income individuals rise, particularly if the higher, long-run benefits are not fiscally sustainable.

Benefit parameters include the following:

- *Accrual rate* (the rate of benefit per year of service). Lowering the accrual rate clearly makes pensioners worse off and lowers their net rate of return from the system, but, when the system runs deficits, it helps avoid transfers from younger cohorts and those people who are not covered by the system.

■ *Averaging period for wages.* The averaging period for wages should ideally be the full career, which best aligns the average contributions paid with the average benefits received. A shift toward full-career wages tends to be progressive since high-income workers gain if pensions are based on the final full year of salary.

■ *Revalorization of wages.* Wages should be revalued according to average wage growth in order to provide incentives for workers to contribute during their early years. This may be thought of as a means of providing a rate of return on contributions. The revalorization of wages to average wage growth is equivalent to giving workers a rate of return on their contributions that is equal to the wage growth. Lower revalorization could, theoretically, lead to greater fiscal sustainability, but usually results in more evasion since workers earn low rates of return on early contributions, and this undermines fiscal sustainability. This is among the variables that are least understood by individuals who are not pension professionals, but it has a huge impact on the actual benefits delivered by the pension system.

■ *Postretirement indexation of pensions.* The postretirement indexation of pensions should ideally be undertaken relative to inflation to protect the purchasing power of pensions during the retirement years. Lack of indexation results in the older elderly receiving substantially lower pensions and less protection than the younger elderly who might be able to work. Women, who generally live longer than men, are also disproportionately disadvantaged by a lack of indexation since their real pensions will fall over a greater number of years. Indexation to wage growth is essentially unaffordable for most countries and not justifiable from the perspective that the retiree does not need to increase his consumption over the course of his retirement, assuming that health expenditures are otherwise covered, regardless of how average wages change with respect to the pension. The postretirement indexation of pensions is an issue both in defined-benefit systems and in defined-contribution systems, as well as for noncontributory benefits.

■ *Minimum pension.* The level of the minimum pension is set too high in most countries, sometimes as high as or higher than the minimum wage. Given that workers at minimum wage make contributions from their wages, have families to support, and pay income taxes, while pensioners do not make contributions, have fewer family members to support, and usually pay no or fewer income taxes, it does not make sense to give pensioners more than the net wage they earned while they were working. Lowering the minimum pension might put some pensioners into poverty, but this has to be balanced against the goal of limiting out-of-system transfers and the goal of tying contributions to benefits in order to encourage individuals to contribute. The minimum pension affects both defined-benefit and defined-contribution systems, as well as noncontributory benefits, which are a form of minimum pension.

Eligibility conditions include the following:

- *Retirement age.* Ideally, the age of retirement should rise as life expectancy and the ability of the older population to work increase, restricting pension benefits to those people who are considered too old to work. An average of 15 years in retirement should be the goal of the pension system. In most cases, raising the age of retirement may reduce the number of lower-income individuals who collect pensions since their life expectancy is generally lower. However, benefits would be available to the survivors, who may be more numerous among lower-income individuals than the survivors of higher-income individuals, and the difference in life expectancy within the covered population, which is, itself, often only the higher-income classes in the country, may not be that great. Equalizing the retirement ages for men and women tends to be pro-women as it substantially raises the pension levels for most women. Changes in the retirement age affect both defined-benefit and defined-contribution systems, as well as noncontributory benefits and voluntary pension systems. In defined-benefit systems and for noncontributory pensions, changes in the retirement age improve fiscal sustainability, while, in the case of defined-contribution systems and voluntary systems, they raise the level of pensions.
- *Years of service required before receiving a pension.* Raising the years of service required before an individual may receive a full pension may similarly discriminate against lower-income individuals, who generally have shorter eligible working careers, but, again, the differences within the covered population may not be that great, and providing prorated pensions for shorter working careers may address this issue sufficiently.
- *Means testing.* In the case of noncontributory benefits, countries sometimes introduce means testing in order to reduce the fiscal costs or change the threshold for pension eligibility. Both these measures

reduce the numbers of people eligible for pensions, but balances this with lower fiscal costs, requiring fewer transfers from the working generations to the elderly.

A special note is warranted about reforms that represent a step toward a system of notional accounts or a point system. In some respects, these systems represent a new paradigm and therefore should be dealt with through systemic reforms. However, in other respects, they still involve liabilities for the government and can be mimicked through a combination of parametric reforms. In both systems, contributions are collected and recorded. In notional accounts, the actual contribution is recorded, and a notional interest rate is earned on the contributions. In the point system, individuals receive pension points each year depending on how long they have contributed and on the basis of the relevant wage; the points are then converted into a financial value at retirement. An implicit notional interest rate will equate the two, as will some combination of conventional defined-benefit parameters. Both systems tend to favor lifetime average income as the basis for determining pensions and closely link benefits and contributions, with the same distributional consequences as noted above. Notional accounts have the added feature that pensions are automatically reduced as life expectancy rises, suggesting that, as life expectancy increases, a larger and larger share of pensioners will receive only the minimum pensions if they do not postpone retirement. Most other parameters of these systems are identical to those of conventional defined-benefit systems, and their distributional impact is precisely the same.

In almost all cases, parametric reforms, particularly those in defined-benefit systems, will reduce the level of pensions and thus potentially put more elderly in poverty or require greater contributions from workers, also putting people at risk of poverty. These measures are nonetheless essential for maintaining the affordability and sustainability of the pension system. Without these measures, the pension system will pass its fiscal stress on to other sectors (squeezing out spending in other areas), encourage the use of inflation to cover deficit spending, or begin to accumulate arrears. None of these possibilities has positive social consequences. The accumulation of arrears is particularly detrimental since individuals who have reached old age and suddenly find themselves without pension benefits have few alternative means of support. Sustainability becomes even more of a social issue when coverage under the pension system is not complete and fiscal resources must be drawn from a broader population to cover pensions for the few, usually the higher-income few.

Furthermore, many common reform measures improve the distributional consequences of pension systems and often remedy unintentional negative effects. They may make pension systems fairer by more directly linking pensions to the contributions paid, and the perception of greater fairness can improve contribution compliance.

Systemic reforms

Many countries in the past 15 years have shifted from reliance on pure defined-benefit systems to defined-contribution systems or to mixed systems with both defined-benefit components and defined-contribution components. In the long run, the defined-contribution systems involve less redistribution, both positive and negative, than was inherent in the defined-benefit systems. They are also more able to contain the costs of the pension system, so that those individuals who pay will ultimately be beneficiaries of the system, and they are more able to reinstate the initial aim of smoothing consumption among individuals during their lifetimes. Since much of the redistribution within defined-benefit systems was often regressive, these changes should be positive. However, pure defined-contribution systems that are not accompanied by a safety net do not prevent the elderly, even those elderly who were middle income during their working years, from falling into poverty. Governments must provide a safety net, such as a minimum-pension guarantee, to protect workers against excessive fluctuations in capital markets. Governments that use both a defined-benefit component and a defined-contribution component normally allow the defined-benefit component to function as the safety net. However, the minimum-pension guarantee reintroduces an element of redistribution into the system, usually from the whole population to the covered minority, and breaks the link between contributions and benefits. Therefore, it needs to be designed to provide protection for workers, but not to be so generous that it distorts incentives or causes large-scale redistribution.

It should be noted, nonetheless, that a shift to a funded system involves transition costs since the government must continue to pay pensions to current pensioners and acquired rights to current workers when they retire even as workers begin to put part or all of their contributions into individual defined-contribution accounts. During this transition period, there is an increase in the regressiveness of the system because the government, through general revenue drawn from the whole population, pays pensions for the covered minority. However, this increase in regressiveness needs to be viewed as a temporary cost required to eliminate regressiveness in the system over the medium and longer term.

Other systemic changes include the introduction of a noncontributory benefit that tends to be positively redistributive as people who previously had no access to pensions are now provided with some benefits. The introduction of a voluntary pension system has redistributive consequences only through tax treatment (as noted elsewhere above).

Regulatory reforms to investment guidelines

Regulatory reforms rarely have direct distributional implications. However, improvements in regulation and supervision are positive steps in ensuring that the contributions that workers and their employers make will be available to them during retirement. Regulation and supervision can insure that less financially sophisticated consumers, typically with lower incomes, are treated as fairly as those with more financial knowledge. The demand for assets from pension funds can also spur development in capital markets, and this may add stability and depth to other financial-market transactions.

Administrative reforms

Administrative reforms focus on unifying multiple systems within a country, improving collection compliance, improving benefit service, individualizing databases, improving record keeping, and strengthening the eligibility criteria for disability, as well as aggregating contribution collection with tax collection.

The unification of systems involves a great deal more than the administrative process. Countries that have fragmented systems usually have separate benefit and contribution structures. During a unification, some groups clearly lose benefits. In a few cases, there are groups that gain benefits, but, to be affordable, the unification typically occurs at the level of the least generous scheme. Despite the presence of losing groups, not only does the unification improve the overall fiscal picture, but the defragmentation of the labor market results in a better allocation of labor and less uncertainty for all groups, which no longer have to fear the loss of pension benefits when faced with voluntary or involuntary job changes.

Improving benefit service usually not only improves service, but also reduces the ability of corrupt officials to take bribes to expedite payment, which the poor cannot afford, making benefits more equitably available to all income groups.

While all these improvements tend to enhance fiscal sustainability and the functioning of the pension system, it should be noted that many pension systems effectively function as quasi-social-assistance agencies so that anyone bold enough to present a pension claim will eventually be paid because the pension fund does not maintain sufficient records to check whether the individual has paid contributions. To the extent that these pensions reduce poverty and are being paid to individuals who have not contributed, poverty may temporarily increase. However, in the longer run, as contribution collections rise, the pension fund may be able to reduce the contribution rate, which would be an improvement for all workers. The government can then determine where to focus its poverty reduction efforts most effectively rather than paying out pensions only to individuals bold enough to present false documents to the authorities.

IMPACT OF PENSION REFORM ON STAKEHOLDERS

Stakeholders for pension reform include, of course, pensioners themselves, workers and their union representatives, and employers, as well as government agencies administering pensions and the Ministry of Finance. Pension reform typically takes place in the context of a deficitary pension system. The remedy for the deficit invariably involves reducing benefits. Clearly, pensioners and unions are not going to be in favor of these changes. Workers also frequently oppose reforms, but this is less understandable. In many cases, the pensions they have been promised are not going to materialize or are at risk if no changes are made. The changes might cut future benefits, but they generally increase the probability that benefits will be received, such that the expected value of the benefits may even be higher than before. But persuading workers and pensioners of the advantages of reforms that will be undertaken at a future time is a tough job and requires a politically powerful reform champion within government. For both pensioners and workers, reforms are usually phased in gradually so that no cohort faces an abrupt loss of benefits.

One issue that makes the reform of pension systems more difficult than the reform of other programs is the acquired rights of workers. Workers make contributions to the pension system in return for the promise of future benefits. Politically, it may be difficult to tell these same workers that the benefits they have already paid for are now going to be reduced. As a result, pension reforms usually have to be phased in slowly, with some grandfathering of existing contributors. The legal and constitutional status of these rights varies considerably. A few countries have ruled that workers who have begun work under a particular pension system with particular parameters have the right to continue working under the same parameters even if the pension regulations are changed. Other countries dictate that accumulated rights cannot be touched, but that all benefits earned after the enactment of reform will fall under the new system. Still other countries have ruled that the government can change any parameter of the pension system at any time. Specific details of worker rights are also sometimes written into a country's constitution, such as retirement age provisions in Brazil or the method of pension indexation in Uruguay.

Pension agencies may be either supportive of reforms or unsupportive, depending on how the reforms affect them. The unification of systems generally results in the shutting down of some administrative systems, with a potential loss of jobs or prestige. Similarly, transferring responsibility for contribution collection to tax authorities may result in a loss or reallocation of jobs. Breaking the monopoly power of public pension systems by introducing private pension funds may also be viewed negatively. Even at the ministerial level, since pension reforms are frequently undertaken to improve fiscal sustainability and involve collaboration with the Ministry of Finance, turf issues between the ministry in charge of pension programs, usually Labor or Social Affairs, and the Ministry of Finance may also surface. On the other hand, administrative reforms, which involve additional investment financing for the pension agency, are usually viewed quite positively.

Generally, Ministries of Finance view pension reforms quite positively and are very supportive. However, since the introduction of a mandatory, funded system usually involves spending fiscal resources in the short run, this particular type of reform may be problematic from the perspective of the Ministry of Finance. It is possible to adjust the design of the funded scheme in order to reduce costs. For example, the definition of the eligibility criteria for the new scheme—whether it is only open to new entrants, to people under the age of 30, under 40, under 50, or whatever age—will affect the number of people who join the new scheme and the extent of the loss of pension revenue as people put all or part of their contributions in their own individual accounts instead of contributing to the public pension system. Countries can also choose the portion of the contribution that goes to the individual accounts among those people eligible to join the new scheme; some countries have mandated that only 2 percentage points of a much larger contribution rate are allocated to the individual accounts, but allow the share to grow over time. The benefits offered to those who switch to the funded system from the public system may also be designed in a generous manner, which would encourage heavy switching, or in a less generous manner, which would discourage switching. Even the default option—what happens when people do not make choices—has an impact on who switches and to what. Finally, public information on the options available may make a big difference in managing switching decisions so that the result is fiscally feasible.

CHECKLIST AND TOOLS FOR ANALYSIS

Before analyzing the poverty and social impact of pension reforms, one ought to answer a few basic questions. Countries have made very different choices about the design of their pension systems, and coverage within the systems varies substantially as well. So, an initial stocktaking of the choices that a country has made will produce a more well-informed analysis.

Taking stock of the current system

1. *Are the elderly poor?* The first step is to determine how poor the elderly are. Several recent analyses suggest that the elderly are not uniformly poor in many Bank-client countries.[11] Pockets of poverty exist, but the elderly often live within extended families, which frequently means that poverty rates are no higher among them than the rates existing among the rest of the population. In countries where such cohabitation is common, the elderly who do live alone or as couples fall into one of two categories: (a) those elderly who have sufficient means and choose to live on their own,[12] and (b) those elderly who have no one to care for them. It is the latter group that is clearly at greater risk of poverty. The other case in which the elderly may become particularly vulnerable occurs when the adult children on whom the elderly were depending for old-age support disappear because of illness (such as AIDS), civil wars, or even extensive migration. These elderly are then left with few means of support. These results are very different from those in developed countries where the elderly depend for assistance in their old age more on public pension support than on the support of their own families.

   While it is useful to look at the pre- and posttransfer poverty positions of the elderly, it is important to recognize that pension arrangements have an impact on living arrangements. While many elderly would face poverty if their pensions were suddenly taken away, living arrangements might have changed in a way to accommodate the elderly if a pension system had not existed or had deteriorated over time. There are significant numbers of multigenerational households in countries in the Europe and Central Asia Region where the pension system no longer offers meaningful pensions. The extent of poverty among the elderly and the identification of pockets of poverty among the elderly will provide insights into whether scarce fiscal resources should be transferred to the elderly and also help identify the groups at which the resources should be targeted, particularly if thorough means testing is not feasible. This analysis needs to take place through examination of household surveys during a poverty assessment. Potential target groups that should be considered include widows, rural workers, the eldest of the elderly, and people with substantial health problems, but not all these groups are at risk of poverty in all countries.

2. *What are the living arrangements of the elderly? How much income do the elderly need?* In countries where cohabitation is common, the elderly who are part of larger households need far less income to avoid poverty than do the elderly who are living alone. However, the one consumption category that may require significant increases in expenditure for the elderly is health care. If the elderly are responsible for even a portion of their own health care expenses, the income requirements of the elderly go up significantly.

3. *What are coverage rates?* The third step in taking stock is to determine the percentage of the labor force that is actually covered and contributing to the pension system. Coverage rates as a percentage of the labor force vary from as low as 5 percent to as high as 95 percent. Coverage tends to vary by region and by income, with low coverage in poorer countries and in countries with newer systems. Coverage is thus typically lower in parts of Africa and Asia, though there are many exceptions. Uruguay, for example, which does not have a particularly high income, has a relatively high coverage rate of 80 percent.

   Coverage is important in terms of the degree of redistribution within a pension system. If coverage is high, redistribution within the pension system implies that overall redistribution occurs from the rich to the poor. If coverage is low, redistribution within the pension system may have little impact on overall redistribution, since whatever redistribution may be occurring is taking place between relatively high-income groups of individuals. The bigger concern in this case is the redistribution from outside the pension system to the covered elderly when the system runs deficits. Similarly, government contributions to a system may be positive if the coverage is high, particularly if these contributions are targeted, but may be highly regressive if coverage is low. While information on coverage can be gleaned from household surveys, there seems to be a systematic underreporting of coverage in such surveys. It is not clear whether this is a sampling issue or whether there is some other bias causing underreporting. Most pension agencies tend to have reasonable records of the number of contributors. A comparison of age- and gender-specific data with age- and gender-specific labor force data ought to provide a better picture of labor force coverage.

However, labor force coverage is only part of the picture. In many countries, coverage among the labor force is completely mismatched with the percentage of the elderly collecting pensions. In some cases, as in many countries in the Europe and Central Asia Region prior to transition, labor force participation was close to 100 percent, and everyone was covered. As a result, virtually all elderly qualify for a pension. But the high rates of unemployment that have accompanied the transition to a market economy and the privatization, downsizing, and closing of many state-run enterprises have led to declining formal labor force participation rates, and this will mean lower rates of coverage among the elderly in the future. By contrast, in parts of Africa, Asia, and Latin America, coverage among the elderly is much lower than is coverage among the labor force simply because many of today's elderly were rural farmers not working in covered occupations. Not only has coverage expanded over the last 30 years to include more groups of workers, but also changes in labor force composition have meant that more workers have entered covered categories relative to 30 years ago. Finally, poor system design can result in low coverage among the labor force, but high rates of coverage among the elderly. If people become eligible for benefits after only five years of contributions, as in Georgia, for example, individuals may choose to contribute for only five years and evade after that. As a result, labor force coverage of only one-ninth of the working-age population may result in complete coverage among the elderly, suggesting a fiscal issue, but not necessarily a lack of social protection for the elderly. The data on elderly coverage can be obtained directly from pension agencies. These agencies sometimes lack full data on contributors, but they usually have reasonable statistics on the persons to whom they pay benefits.

4. *What is the fiscal status of the pension system now, and what will it be in the near future?* If the pension system is running deficits, and coverage is low, then there are clearly transfers from outside the pension system to people within the system. These transfers are likely to be regressive

since the revenue collected at large by the government may include revenue from sources such as value-added taxes, which affect a segment of the population that is broader than the population share represented by persons who are beneficiaries of the pension system. Even if coverage is high, fiscal unsustainability suggests that the pension system will be squeezing fiscal resources. Governments respond very differently to fiscal deficits. Most governments, such as those in Brazil, Mexico, and Turkey, have responded to fiscal pressures in social security by running less-prudent macroeconomic policies and by squeezing other expenditures. Other governments, such as those in Argentina, Georgia, and Nigeria, have responded to fiscal pressures by not paying pensions and allowing arrears to pensioners to build up. While the first response has implications for other social expenditures, the second is perhaps worse in that pensioners who no longer have the capacity to work are suddenly denied pensions. Future payment of arrears is useless to the pensioner who dies before the payments are made. Fiscal deficits or prospective fiscal deficits also invariably lead to policy changes, since deficits are only sustainable for a limited time. Awareness of such deficits thus leads to uncertainty among pensioners and workers. The main idea of a pension system is to provide security when people are unable to work. Introducing a high degree of uncertainty to the benefit structure reduces the value of the pension system to workers.

One difficulty that arises in evaluating the financial results of the pension system pre- and postreform involves the increase in short-term deficits caused by the shift to a funded system. Deficits increase in the short term since the government has to cover pensions for the current elderly and the soon-to-be elderly, while younger workers put their contributions in their own individual accounts. Thus, taking a short-run view, it might appear that the reforms have made the situation worse. Even without a shift to a funded system, pension reforms are enacted so slowly that a major policy change may result in little fiscal change during the first five years.

The implicit pension debt in the pension system provides a truer picture of the impact of reform than do the short-run deficits because implicit pension debt measures the present value of the liabilities in the pension system. These alter immediately after the reform has been enacted, however long the pension reform takes to unfold, although changes that impact only new entrants will not affect the current implicit pension debt since there are no current liabilities with respect to people who have not yet entered the system.

The best tool for examining fiscal deficits and the implicit pension debt is the Bank's pension reform options simulation toolkit model (PROST), which has been available since 1997 and has been used for analysis on more than 80 countries. The model automatically outputs fiscal numbers and implicit pension debt both for current and for future years, as a well as a host of other information that will be valuable in understanding the poverty and social impacts of pension systems. PROST provides these numbers before and after reform to facilitate an understanding of the impact reform has on fiscal sustainability. The model also estimates the level to which contribution rates would have to rise to make the system durable, giving the user some sense of the risk involved in the pension system.

An example is shown in Figure 1.2 for the case of Turkey after the 1999 pension reform. Deficits in the future will still require substantial transfers from outside the system.

5. *Is the contribution rate affordable?* Contribution rates of around 15 percent of wages are required to provide reasonable pensions in demographically mature economies. Contribution rates higher than these

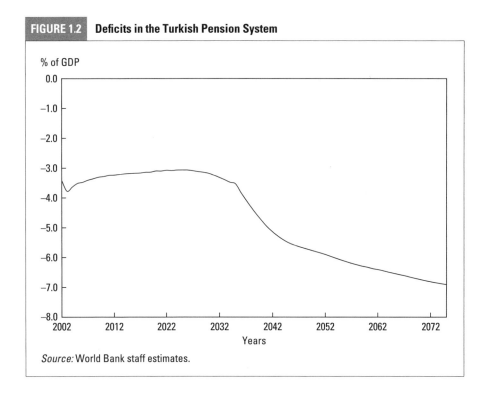

FIGURE 1.2   Deficits in the Turkish Pension System

% of GDP

Source: World Bank staff estimates.

impose high labor costs on the economy, encouraging informalization of the labor market and discouraging labor-intensive activities. In a geographically competitive world, high labor taxes also affect labor competitiveness, which, in turn, has an impact on employment.

Benefit structure: fairness and redistribution

1. *Are the benefits adequate?* The adequacy of benefits can be judged according to at least two very different criteria, each stemming from the two separate goals of the pension system. First, the level of the benefit should be compared with the poverty level to determine whether the benefit is sufficient to reduce poverty in old age. This needs to be evaluated both for new retirees and for individuals already in retirement since the absence of indexation can drive pension levels below the poverty line. The poverty evaluation should also be carried out for men and for women and over time. Particular attention should be paid to the level of the minimum benefit because many lower-income individuals will receive the minimum benefit, not the average benefit. However, it should be noted that pension benefits below the poverty line are not necessarily bad, especially if the pension is only one source of retirement income. If elders live with younger generations, even a pension below the poverty level may have significant poverty reduction impact.

   A similar analysis should be carried out relative to the average wage to determine how well the pension benefit performs relative to wage growth in the economy. Since pensions are typically indexed to inflation and not wage growth, the benefit usually falls relative to the average wage during a person's retirement period. A pension indexed to inflation may still be consumption smoothing since a person needs to smooth consumption over his own lifetime. Thus, inflation indexation will maintain the level of real pension benefits over the retirement period relative to real income during an individual's working years. Similarly, the analysis can be carried out for men and for women in each income group, taking into account the minimum pension, ceilings on benefits, and survivor benefits.

   The Bank's PROST model is also an excellent instrument for this analysis. Once the system characteristics have been entered for the fiscal analysis, all these measures of adequacy are automatically produced. There is also a module that allows the user to specify characteristics of individuals at one time with respect to gender, age at first employment, age at retirement, starting wage relative to the average for the cohort, wage growth relative to the average for the cohort, mortality rate relative to the average for the cohort, and work history. All these characteristics have an impact on the adequacy of the pension.

One issue that the Bank's model does not fully cover is the impact of taxation. At the very least, the adequacy analysis should compare net pension benefits with net wages. Typically, workers or unions consider gross replacement rates and complain that a 60 percent replacement rate of preretirement income is not adequate for pension benefits. But, if the contribution rate for a pension by the employee is 10 percent, the health-insurance contribution is 5 percent of wages, and income tax rates are 25 percent of wages, the 60 percent replacement rate for pension benefits represents 100 percent of net salary. Given the lower nutrition requirements and fewer number of dependents of the elderly, 100 percent of net salary represents an overly generous benefit. The output of PROST provides the overall information, but does not calculate the net salary since the tax structure may vary by individual, but this calculation can be easily performed in a separate spreadsheet.

2. *Are the pensions fairly provided?* Adequacy is not the only dimension upon which a particular benefit structure should be evaluated. Individuals and their employers make decisions about whether to join the pension system or not partly based on whether the system is perceived to be fair. Since people are being asked to make contributions in order to receive benefits, people need to feel that they are getting a reasonable deal from the pension system; otherwise, they will not want to participate, choosing to self-insure instead.

For example, pensions among men and women relative to the average wage in the economy will generally reflect the wage differences and work-history differences between men and women. Given the potentially large disparity between men's and women's wages, there can be a fairly large disparity in pensions as well. However, fixing the pension disparity through policy will weaken the link between contributions and benefits. If women receive relatively high benefits regardless of how much they contribute, they will contribute as little as possible. If, in order to redistribute toward women, men receive less relative to the amounts they have contributed, they will perceive the pension system as unfair and will tend to withdraw from the system as much as possible. Neither group will want to contribute, resulting in negative fiscal consequences for the system overall.

Fairness can be measured in at least two ways. One approach toward analyzing the fairness of a pension system involves calculating the *internal rate of return* inherent in the pension system for people in different income groups, cohorts, and genders. (The internal rate of return is the rate of return that will equalize the net present value of the benefits received with the net present value of the contributions paid.) This analysis may be carried out for a variety of people in different income groups, age groups, and gender groups, taking into account differences in the average age at first employment, differences in ages at retirement, differences in the growth path of wages experienced by different individuals, differences in the continuity of labor market participation, and differences in mortality across income groups.[13] The individuals should be representative of their income, age, and gender groups, but their careers may be either simulated or based on actual work histories. The goal would be to have a system based on either equal internal rates of return for different income groups, age groups, or gender groups or rates of return that are slightly higher for lower-income groups. The analysis can be carried out prior to reform and after reform to determine whether the internal rates of return have become more equitable or whether the inequality has increased.

A second, related tool takes the present value of the stream of benefits a person receives and subtracts the present value of the stream of contributions the person made, including an interest payment on the contributions, to determine the net transfer the individual receives from the pension system. This net transfer is usually normalized by dividing it by some variable such as the average wage. The resulting calculation can be interpreted as the equivalent of the person receiving or paying x additional average wages because of the person's participation in the pension system. As in the calculation of the internal rate of return, this approach takes into account contributions an individual makes, as well as the benefits received, but, unlike the calculation of the internal rate of return, it requires the user to define an appropriate interest rate. Since predetermining an interest rate may be difficult, many users prefer to rely on the similarly calculated internal rate of return. Furthermore, the tool can make interpretation difficult. If all pensioners receive benefits that are twice as high as their contributions, higher-income individuals will receive a net transfer that is higher in absolute monetary amounts since the pension benefits for higher-income individuals are higher than those for lower-income individuals. Do higher net transfers indicate a policy that is misaligned across income groups? Not necessarily, since consumption smoothing is one of the primary goals of pension systems. If the net transfer were to be normalized by the level of contributions for each group analyzed rather than by the average economy-wide wage (the typical normalization method), this tool could be useful for intra-cohort comparisons. The net transfer figure turns from positive to negative for the same cohorts for which the internal rate of return moves from above the market interest rate to below the market interest rate. The preference for one over the other largely reflects how comfortable a user is in defining an appropriate market interest rate.

Figure 1.3 provides an example of how analyses of adequacy and fairness may yield different results. Pre-reform, the Slovak Republic had an extremely redistributive system with relatively low ceilings on both contributions and benefits. As a result, the pension relative to the preretirement wage, shown in the right-hand panel, was extremely low for high-income women, but reasonable for average- and low-income women. The succession of reforms—first, a pay as you go reform, then the addition of a funded pillar, and then future reforms that will bring the pay as you go part to full sustainability—has managed to raise the benefit levels for high-income women, while maintaining or increasing the benefit levels for middle- and low-income women. However, while individuals might measure their pensions relative to their preretirement incomes as one indication of the adequacy of the pension, other measures of equity might gauge the amounts individuals pay relative to the benefits they receive, as shown in the left-hand panel. Even though high-income women were receiving pensions that were low relative to the women's preretirement wages, they were receiving rates of return on their contributions that were higher than those received by lower-income women, partly because of the longer life expectancy of higher-income women and partly because the pensions were based on wages earned toward the end of the career, where high-income individuals experience the most wage growth. The reforms have brought down rates of return among all income groups from the previous unsustainable levels and have tended to increase equality in the rates of return across income groups. Since funded systems tend to be more equitable in terms of rates of return than are unfunded systems, the heavier reliance on funded systems tends to produce more equality. However, the difference in life expectancy remains and still generates differences in the internal rates of return.

3. *How redistributive is the pension system?* Another tool looks at the extent to which a pension system is redistributive. Pension systems try both to redistribute income and to provide a mechanism for consumption

FIGURE 1.3 Pension Equity within a Cohort of Women, Slovak Republic

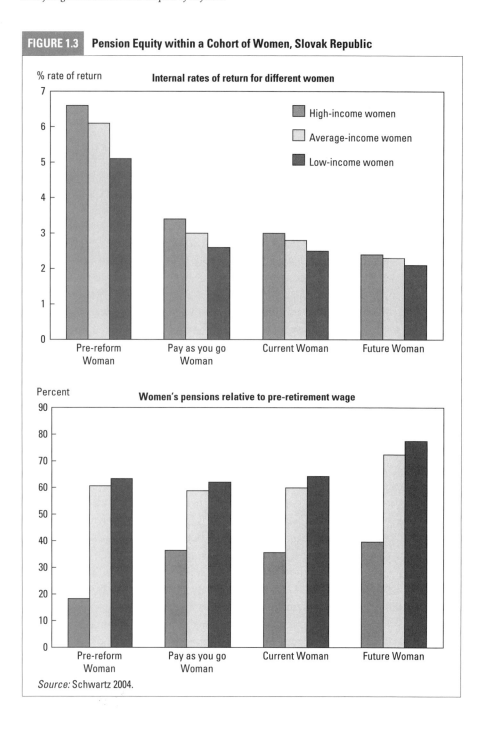

Source: Schwartz 2004.

34

smoothing. A tool recently developed by Whitehouse and Axia Economics and known as APEX models[14] graphs earnings against pension benefits. Earnings and pensions are both expressed as a percentage of average earnings for individuals earning from 0.3 average earnings to 5 average earnings. The results show the relationship between earnings and pension values. In some countries, because of flat-rate components, low ceilings on earnings-related benefits, and progressive benefit structures, benefits are virtually flat with respect to earnings. In other countries, there may be a flat initial benefit, followed by a link between earnings and pensions, but only until the ceiling on contribution earnings is reached, at which point the pension benefits become virtually flat again, but at a higher level than the case at low wages. Finally, a third group of countries shows a very strong earnings relationship with pensions through all income ranges.

The APEX tool adds a significant dimension to the internal rate of return analysis in that it looks at all pension benefits within a country, not merely the contributory benefits. It also allows the policymaker to think about the role of the pension in society. Is the pension meant to reduce poverty or is the pension meant to replace income? Countries with strong earnings-pension relationships are replacing income, while countries with more redistributive pensions are more oriented toward reducing poverty. The ceiling on contributions is a major determinant of this relationship and is not incorporated in the internal rate of return analysis, which only compares the benefits received with the contributions paid. The capping of contributions and benefits does not affect the internal rate of return. However, these ceilings, or caps, have significant impact on the role of the pension in society. The APEX analysis shows, for example, that countries such as Germany, Japan, and the United States, which have a strong earnings-related component, but low ceilings on contributions, have fairly redistributive programs compared with countries such as Finland, Italy, and the Netherlands, for instance. The APEX calculations also incorporate tax rates.

Examples of APEX graphs are shown in Figure 1.4. Countries make different choices about redistribution and consumption smoothing. But pension systems also evolve from the original designs. The APEX graphs are useful in identifying the choices that a country has made and asking the country itself whether the pension system fully reflects the role that it would want its pension system to fill.

But, as with all tools, there are limits to what each individual tool can show. The APEX methodology ignores the contribution side. Its

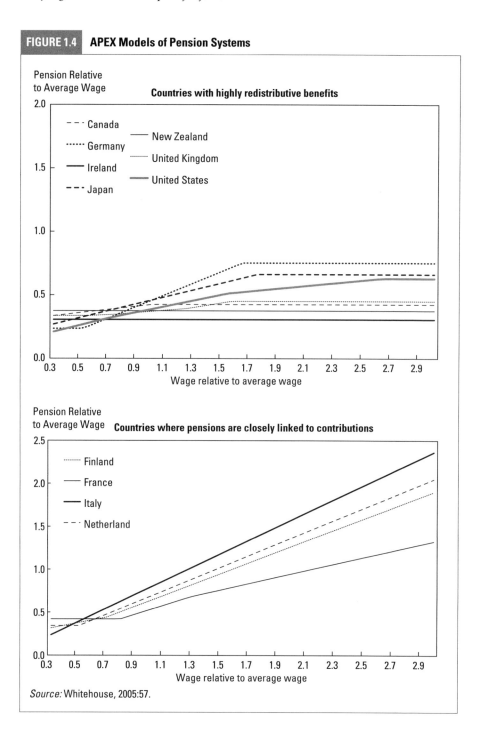

FIGURE 1.4   **APEX Models of Pension Systems**

Pension Relative
to Average Wage
Countries with highly redistributive benefits

- – – Canada
- ······· Germany
- —— Ireland
- – – Japan
- —— New Zealand
- ········ United Kingdom
- —— United States

Wage relative to average wage

Pension Relative
to Average Wage   **Countries where pensions are closely linked to contributions**

- ········ Finland
- —— France
- —— Italy
- – – Netherland

Wage relative to average wage

Source: Whitehouse, 2005:57.

focus is on relating pensions to earnings, not to contributions. To the extent that contributions are not directly linked to earnings, the results may differ from those shown by the internal rate of return analysis. For example, if contributions must be paid on a minimum wage, the extent of redistribution toward a worker earning less than the minimum wage is much lower according to the calculation of the internal rate of return than it is according to the APEX methodology. Similarly, if the maximum pension provided by the system is not strictly related to the contribution ceiling on earnings, the two tools will give different results. Finally, while the APEX tool shows the redistributive intent within the system, it does not specify the source of the redistributed funds. Internal rates of return can specify groups of contributors who are losing through the system and others who are gaining, but only if the system is fully self-financing. To the extent that the system runs a deficit and funds are injected from outside the system, neither internal rates of return nor APEX specifies who loses in the redistribution process. The APEX analysis has been completed for all countries in the Organisation for Economic Co-operation and Development and many countries in the Europe and Central Asia, Latin America and the Caribbean, and Middle East and North Africa Regions of the World Bank.

Benefit incidence analysis

Another tool frequently used to analyze expenditure items is benefit incidence analysis. The presence of consumption smoothing as a primary objective of many pension system designs suggests that traditional benefit incidence analysis is not an appropriate instrument for examining pension systems and pension system reforms. By design, people who earn more and contribute more should expect to receive higher benefits. Design issues, combined with the often low compliance among low-income earners, mean that pension expenditures are focused on higher-income individuals. But, unlike in other types of expenditures, this type of incidence inequality is not a negative in pension systems; it is an expected feature of pension system objectives. As long as the pension system is self-financing, expenditures skewed toward high-income individuals are fine.[15]

A second issue that complicates analysis of pensions systems is the typically contributory nature of systems. If one were to engage in benefit incidence analysis, the analysis would only be correct if it is carried out net of contributions, because contributions, unlike other taxes paid, are directly linked to the future services expected, the level of which may even be protected by law or the constitution. However, the work histories of a sample of individuals over their full life spans is usually beyond the scope of most benefit incidence analyses. The analysis becomes more complicated if pension system design parameters are introduced such as minimum pensions and changes in design parameters that occur over an individual's work and retirement history, as well as changes in life expectancy. Life events such as whether an individual marries and has children and the ages of the spouse and the timing of the children also affect the individual's benefits relative to contributions.

Table 1.1 is taken from a 2004 report on Mexico and shows that pension expenditures are concentrated on higher-income individuals.

Mexico has two federal pension systems. One pension system covers formal private sector workers, while the other pension system covers the civil service. Since few members of the bottom deciles contribute to either system, little of the pension expenditure goes to these individuals. This problem is worse in the civil service system, in which the expenditures mimic the income distribution of the group of civil servants rather than being in any way redistributive. (No sensible person would argue that

TABLE 1.1. Distribution of the Beneficiaries of Federal Public Expenditures on Pensions, Mexico, 2002

percentages

| Decile | Total | Public system for private sector workers | | Public system for federal civil servants | |
		Active workers	Pensioners	Active workers	Pensioners
1	0.9	0.9	1.4	0.2	0.0
2	1.7	3.3	2.2	1.2	0.0
3	4.7	6.2	5.4	1.9	3.2
4	6.7	7.8	8.2	4.7	3.1
5	7.2	11.1	8.9	4.9	1.6
6	9.6	11.3	10.3	7.8	6.7
7	11.7	12.6	12.9	11.5	8.1
8	15.8	14.1	15.5	14.9	16.8
9	17.9	15.4	17.1	23.6	19.8
10	23.9	17.3	18.0	29.2	40.6
Urban	95.0	93.4	94.5	91.4	97.9
Rural	5.0	6.6	5.5	8.6	2.1

Source: World Bank 2004: 39.

doctors and teachers should be drawn from the least-educated, lowest-income groups in order to equalize the distribution of pensions and wages within the civil servant system.) One could even contend that, in the case of civil servants, these pensions are not expenditures per se, but part of the compensation packages of teachers and health workers and thus should be included in the cost of education or health services rather than as a separate expenditure category.

CONCLUSIONS

Several critical points emerge in undertaking poverty and social impact analysis on pension systems and pension system reforms.

1. Pension systems are not a direct expenditure of the government, but provide a mechanism by which contributions can be made during working years and benefits can be received during retirement years. Thus, by nature, they are not transfer programs.
2. Benefit incidence analysis is not appropriate for the study of pension systems because it typically does not net out the contributions made over the employment careers of workers.
3. Pension systems attempt to reduce poverty during old age, but also try to smooth consumption between the working years and the retirement years. For this reason, it is anticipated that individuals who consume more during their working years will continue to consume more during their retirement years.
4. Many worthwhile pension reforms may result in poor distributional consequences in the short run. This is clearly the case when a shift is undertaken to a funded system, in which the government pays pension benefits to covered pensioners, while workers deposit their money into their individual accounts. However, this is a transition to a system in which the government will have limited liability for pension expenditures, freeing up future resources for more targeted assistance. Even in the case of parametric reforms that tie contributions more closely to benefits, those individuals who have not contributed will lose in the short run, though the fiscal improvements will free resources to cover those individuals who cannot contribute in the long run.
5. The distributional benefits of pension reform will not be obvious in the short run since pension reform usually takes 30 to 40 years to unfold fully, given that acquired rights must be legally and, in some cases, constitutionally respected.

6. Ideally, analysts should take a holistic approach to the welfare of the elderly in a particular country and should not focus solely on the distributional impact of a single instrument, the pension system.

NOTES

1. In fact, the International Labour Organization endorses a minimum standard of 40 percent of an individual's wage for 30 years of work. While the definition of an individual's wage is somewhat vague, it is clear that the standard is relative to some measure of one's own wage, not a minimum poverty level.
2. Unemployment insurance can have similar features in that the target benefit is related to one's income.
3. The pension agency may have reserve funds, in which case the system may be considered partially funded.
4. Typically, governments offer a minimum pension guarantee under a defined-contribution plan, but this design feature is similar to the role of a minimum pension in a defined-benefit plan and is only available to those who have fulfilled certain conditions.
5. The literature is extensive and includes Corsetti and Schmidt-Hebbel (1997), Diamond and Hausman (1984), Disney (1996), Gruber and Wise (1999), and Koitz (1988), among many others.
6. One might argue that this redistribution is corrected by the fact that men frequently leave widows and other survivors, while women do not. The pension to the man and his survivor is roughly equivalent in duration or may even be larger than the pension given to the longer-lived woman, who typically does not leave a survivor.
7. It should be noted that younger cohorts can be expected to live longer and therefore receive more benefits than their parents' generation, which might provide some compensation for having to pay higher contribution rates or for receiving lower benefits, but there is usually a lag between the change in the underlying demographics and the change in the policies, so that there is no automatic linkage to maintaining actuarial balance. Some cohorts receive net transfers; others lose.
8. Sometimes, governments tax contributions and make the pensions nontaxable. In a few cases, both contributions and benefits are exempt from tax. A systematic review of tax treatment can be found in Whitehouse (1999).
9. See Holzmann and Hinz et al. (2005).
10. It is certainly possible that the group of people covered by the pension system is identical to the group of people paying taxes, suggesting no increased regressivity from pension deficits. However, with the introduction of broad-ranging value-added taxes in a large number of countries, it is more likely that the tax base is broader than the coverage of the pension system.
11. Schwarz (2005); Kakwani and Subbarao (2005); Whitehouse (2000).

12. Evidence from developed countries suggests that independent living is a preferred state among the elderly, and, when income permits, the elderly choose to live alone. However, there may be a cultural element to these preferences.
13. The Bank's PROST model provides an automatic tool that can perform this analysis both before and after reform, but this analysis can be performed using simple spreadsheets as well.
14. See Whitehouse (2005).
15. The International Labour Organization and trade unions frequently argue in favor of tripartite financing, which is financing by employees, employers, and the government. This may be a reasonable policy in countries in which coverage is high, such as in the developed world, but, in countries with low coverage, this policy should be carefully evaluated, since it usually involves transferring general revenue only to those individuals who contribute, and these tend to be high-income individuals.

BIBLIOGRAPHY

Corsetti, G., and K. Schmidt-Hebbel. 1997. "Pension Reform and Growth." In *The Economics of Pensions: Principles, Policies and International Experience,* ed. S. Valdés-Prieto. Cambridge: Cambridge University Press.

Diamond, P., and J. Hausman. 1984. "Individual Retirement and Savings Behavior." *Journal of Public Economics,* 23 (1/2): 81–114.

Disney, R. 1996. *Can We Afford to Grow Older?* Cambridge, MA: The MIT Press.

Gruber, J., and D. A. Wise, eds. 1999. *Social Security and Retirement around the World.* Chicago: University of Chicago Press.

Holzmann, R., and R. Hinz et al. 2005. *Old-Age Income Support in the 21st Century: An International Perspective on Pension Systems and Reform.* Washington, DC: World Bank.

Kakwani, N., and K. Subbarao. 2005. "Aging and Poverty in Africa and the Role of Social Pensions." Sector Report, Human Development Department, Africa Region, World Bank, Washington, DC.

Koitz, D. 1988. *Social Security: Its Funding Outlook and Significance for Government Finance.* Washington, DC: Congressional Research Service.

Schwarz, A. M. 2004. "Slovak Republic: Pension Policy Reform Note." Sector Report, Human Development Department, Europe and Central Asia Region, World Bank, Washington, DC.

———. 2005. "Old Age Security and Social Pensions." Working Paper, Social Protection Department, Human Development Network, World Bank, Washington, DC.

Steuerle, C. E., and J. M. Bakija. 1994. *Retooling Social Security for the 21st Century: Right and Wrong Approaches to Reform.* Washington, DC: Urban Institute Press.

Whitehouse, E. 1999. "The Tax Treatment of Funded Pensions." Social Protection Discussion Paper 9910, Social Protection Department, Human Development Network, World Bank, Washington, DC.

————. 2000. "How Poor are the Old?: A Survey of Evidence from 44 Countries." Social Protection Discussion Paper 0017, Social Protection Department, Human Development Network, World Bank, Washington, DC.

————. 2005. *Pensions at a Glance: Public Policies across OECD Countries.* Paris: Organisation for Economic Co-operation and Development.

World Bank. 2004. "Mexico: Public Expenditure Review." Report 27894-MX, Latin America Economic Policy Sector, World Bank, Washington, DC.

2

Health Sector Reforms

Mattias Lundberg and Limin Wang

THE FUNCTION OF A PUBLIC HEALTH SYSTEM

The purpose of Poverty and Social Impact Analysis (PSIA) is to examine the distributional consequences of sectoral reforms. It is not a review of the impact of reforms on overall sectoral performance. However, the effect of health sector reforms on welfare among the poor and other groups is inextricably linked to the effect of reforms on sectoral performance. Reforms are intended to address a wide variety of problems and constraints in the sector and to achieve myriad and often conflicting objectives. Not all of these are explicitly intended to enhance equity, but they will all have distributional consequences.

As a prerequisite to examining health sector reforms, understanding what the health system is designed to do, how it can achieve its goals, and the context in which it operates is important. Although improved health is a goal in itself and is a requirement for economic growth, to expect that the health system can, on its own, achieve broader welfare or growth objectives is unreasonable. The health system should focus on improving health.

According to *World Health Report 2000* (WHO 2000a), national health systems have three fundamental objectives: (1) improving the health of the population they serve, (2) responding to people's expectations, and (3) providing financial protection against the costs of ill health. *World*

The authors gratefully acknowledge the comments and suggestions of Mark Camden Bassett, Shiyan Chao, Shanta Devarajan, David Evans, Deon Filmer, Dave Gwatkin, and George Schieber on this chapter.

Health Report 2000 goes on to suggest that the second and third goals are partly *instrumental,* that is, they contribute to the first goal.

Note that this list says nothing about how these objectives are to be achieved. There is nothing about health or public health that requires a particular mode of organization or delivery. This is distinct from the acknowledgment that certain components of health and health care are *public goods,* which (it is assumed) must be provided or at least encouraged by collective action.

To achieve these goals, health systems perform a number of general functions. Paraphrasing the *World Health Report,* these can be classified as: (1) governance and oversight, (2) investment and training, (3) finance and risk-pooling, and (4) service provision.

One can imagine many hundreds of things that health systems actually do, but they can reasonably be subsumed into these comprehensive categories of activities. This requires a broader view of health systems, such as described in both *World Health Report 2000* and *World Development Report 2004* (World Bank 2003a). Public health is not merely medical care, or human resources, or social insurance; similarly, it consists of more than vertical public campaigns targeted at specific diseases.

To understand the impact of health sector reforms, especially on poverty and welfare, one must ask how the proposed actions will influence the performance of the system and the system's ability to achieve its fundamental objectives. To make this a bit more concrete, it is important to ask, for example, not only whether a particular program (say, a program on insecticide-treated bed-nets) is achieving its objectives and not merely whether the program is pro-poor. It is important also to ask about the *opportunity costs* of the program: can the objectives of better public health and better health among the poor be achieved by other means? We can then ask whether the program is best designed to achieve its own objectives. In the current jargon, we must first ask whether we are "doing the right things" and then whether we are "doing them right."[1] It is also essential to have some idea of the *counterfactual:* what is likely to happen in the absence of any changes or intervention?

We must keep in mind that health is an input to human well-being, and human well-being is the goal of public policy. Health is instrumental, even (*pace* Amartya Sen) fundamental, but it is conceivable that, under certain conditions, welfare will be more enhanced by investments in items other than health. The concept of the counterfactual should therefore be broadened to encompass nonhealth alternatives. Even if one particular investment or policy is found to dominate others *within the sector,* it is possible that another nonhealth investment will increase living standards even more.

These alternative investments can cover items that also improve health, such as food, shelter, water, sanitation, and transport, but these are usually outside the purview of health ministries.

Thus, it is important to understand the broader context of health sector reforms. However, it is equally important to maintain the analytical focus on the distributional consequences of reforms. This chapter specifically aims to provide a guide for policy practitioners who wish to conduct an analysis of the impact of health reform or health policy changes on the welfare of households, especially poor households (thus, "poverty and social impact analysis").

At a minimum, analysis of proposed reforms in health must address the following questions:

- What is needed to enable the health sector to achieve its broader objectives?
- What is the potential welfare impact of the proposed reforms across socioeconomic groups?
- What can be done to avoid or minimize possibly adverse consequences of reforms?

The first of these questions addresses the design and context of reforms. Understanding the welfare consequences requires that we consider the main intended purpose of the reforms. What goals are the reforms intended to achieve, and how can the health system be organized to best achieve the goals? These questions are addressed in *World Development Report 2004*. The third question addresses the design of compensation mechanisms to mitigate the unintended adverse effects of policy changes. While there is little experience with designing mitigation mechanisms specifically for health reforms, more general guidance is provided in *A Sourcebook for Poverty Reduction Strategies* (Klugman 2002), especially Part 5, "Human Development" (pages 163–231) and "Technical Note" (pages 543–76), as well as in *A User's Guide to Poverty and Social Impact Analysis* (World Bank 2003b).

This chapter focuses on the second issue: the identification of the consequences of reforms for the poor and other groups. This information is clearly required for the design of mitigation programs, but mitigation should be considered a last-best alternative to designing reforms in order to achieve the best outcomes for all. The identification of impacts is also essential for designing effective reforms that enable the sector to achieve its overarching goal of enhancing public health.

This chapter proceeds as follows. First, we discuss the rationale for and the types of reforms that are common in the health sector. We then discuss the stakeholders and transmission channels for the impact of reforms. Finally, we turn to the technical aspects: analytical methods, assumptions, data requirements, and so on.

ISSUES SPECIFIC TO THE ANALYSIS OF HEALTH REFORMS

Before we begin, we must deal with a few aspects of reforms that are unique to the health sector. Some of these issues arise in other reforms, especially those dealing with public or quasi-public goods, such as education. But they are arguably more complex and more confounding in health reforms than in reforms in other sectors, and they are all vital to the analysis of the impact of reforms on welfare. These include the definition of equity, moral hazard and agency, asymmetric information and adverse selection, and other confounding factors.

Health care is not the same as health

One feature of health care that distinguishes it from other public goods and services is that the consumption of health care is only one input, albeit an important one, in the production of health. As Filmer, Hammer, and Pritchett (2000) demonstrate, the connection between public health spending and public health outcomes is rather tenuous. Health is produced in the household as a function of health care, nutrition, behavior, water, and myriad other factors. Wagstaff (1999) provides a figure to illustrate these links. He points out that not only do health outcomes vary across groups, but there is enormous inequality in the determinants of health outcomes as well (Figure 2.1).

When examining the impact of health reforms on health and welfare, one should understand that these other characteristics will inevitably get in the way of the path from policies to outcomes. It is equally important that we understand the interactions between the sectoral reforms and these confounding factors. Three main questions must be addressed, as follows:

- What effect will the reforms have on these other confounding factors?
- How will these confounding factors influence the impact of reforms on health?
- How will these confounding factors shape the process of reform?

The first of these questions is not intuitive. Reforms may have significant external (to the health sector) effects, positive and negative. For

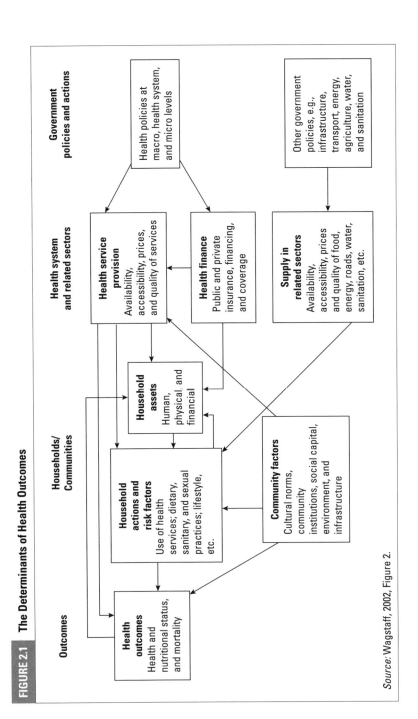

FIGURE 2.1   The Determinants of Health Outcomes

Outcomes

Health outcomes
Health and nutritional status, and mortality

Households/ Communities

Household assets
Human, physical, and financial

Household actions and risk factors
Use of health services; dietary, sanitary, and sexual practices; lifestyle, etc.

Community factors
Cultural norms, community institutions, social capital, environment, and infrastructure

Health system and related sectors

Health service provision
Availability, accessibility, prices, and quality of services

Health finance
Public and private insurance, financing, and coverage

Supply in related sectors
Availability, accessibility, prices and quality of food, energy, roads, water, sanitation, etc.

Government policies and actions

Health policies at macro, health system, and micro levels

Other government policies, e.g., infrastructure, transport, energy, agriculture, water, and sanitation

Source: Wagstaff, 2002, Figure 2.

example, reforms in the health sector may influence community institutions. There have been numerous experiments recently to harness community groups to monitor the performance of local public services (see, for example, Loewenson 2000). This may have the added effect of strengthening local capital and local institutions, which may then collectively bargain for (or informally provide) other services that incidentally enhance health, such as water and sewage connections.

The second question—on the influence of confounding factors on the outcomes of the reforms—is related to the issue of transmission channels. In this case, however, the transmission channels are primarily external to the sector and to the reforms. Clearly, enhanced access to health services will affect health care consumption and possibly health outcomes. That is the direct and intended impact. But this impact will differ across areas because of, for example, differing access to clean water. Health is not necessarily enhanced by the construction of clinics if the local drinking water is contaminated by sewage. There may be more subtle consequences as well: for example, the physiological impact of medical treatment may be affected by illnesses caused by pathogens in drinking water.

Finally, many nonhealth institutions, both private and public, will influence the implementation of reforms in the sector. These are external to the health sector proper, but will shape the process and impact of reforms. In Mozambique, for example, eight ministries are involved in health care finance and policy, six of which are actually providing health services. These include the ministries of public works, education, justice, and interior, as well as health.

Equity

Equity in health has been the subject of enormous discussion and literature. Here, some of the issues are mentioned that will arise in the context of any health reform. These can be crudely distinguished as *equity of what?* and *what equity?* These questions are not trivial: *World Health Report 2000* placed great emphasis on creating indexes of the equity of health finance and services (see the Statistical Annexes in the report), and these indexes have been remarkably controversial (for example, see Asada and Hedemann 2002; Wagstaff 1999). Here, the various concepts of equity are briefly described that are commonly used in health.

Equity in health care can be conceived in terms of *access, finance, expenditure,* and *outcomes,* and health policy has usually distinguished between *horizontal* and *vertical* equity, which have specific meanings in each case. Table 2.1 briefly describes these different terms as they are commonly used.

TABLE 2.1. Definition of Equity in Health Policy

		Concept of equity	
		Horizontal	Vertical
Dimension of equity	Access	Those with similar needs have similar access to services.	Those with greater needs have access to more care or more intensive care.
	Finance	Those in equal socioeconomic positions pay the same for care.	Wealthier households pay more than do poorer households.
	Expenditure	Those in equal socioeconomic positions or similar health receive the same value of publicly funded services.	Poorer households and households with more illness receive more than do wealthier, healthier households.
	Outcomes	All households experience similar health outcomes, regardless of socioeconomic status.	

Source: Compiled by the authors.

Horizontal equity generally refers to the distribution of costs and benefits across groups of similar socioeconomic or health status; vertical equity refers to the distribution of costs and benefits across groups of differing status. The underlying assumptions are that unequal health outcomes are unjust, that health services should be provided (or guaranteed) socially,[2] and that the distribution of costs and benefits should somehow be related to health and wealth status.[3] Note that there is one exception: in public health finance, equity is usually defined in terms of the ratio of payments to income; it is not necessarily defined as the ratio of payments to the consumption of health services. It is assumed that those who consume more health care are more ill and have greater need for health services.

Moral hazard

The common belief that health care payments need not be related to health care consumption presents a *moral hazard* on the part of the consumer. This can occur both ex ante and ex post. Ex ante moral hazard, that is, occurring prior to the need for health care consumption, leads individuals to engage in riskier behavior than they would do if they were required to bear the total cost of the health care. Ex post moral hazard, that is, following the appearance of the need for health care consumption, is manifest in the overconsumption of health care services or, in other words, the consumption of services even when the benefits are less than the total social cost. Health care is different from other public goods and services, such as education, since greater consumption is not always beneficial. There exists a point beyond which the net social returns to more use of health services are negative.[4] This is of greater concern in former socialist countries, in which overconsumption was common, but it may be troublesome also where publicly provided services are captured by a (presumably wealthier) minority.

Moral hazard can cause problems on the supply side as well, since doctors have no incentive to control costs. For instance, doctors working under a fee-for-service regime have an incentive to provide more services than the patients would choose to receive if they had complete information. This is also known as *supplier-induced demand.* It is not merely a theoretical concern, although the evidence is primarily from developed countries. Studies on China (Bumgarner 1992), France (Chiappori, Durand, and Geoffard 1998), the Netherlands (Hurst 1992), Taiwan (Cheng and Chiang 1997), and the United Kingdom (Dusheiko et al. 2003) find that fee-for-service reimbursement leads providers to increase the volume of services.

ASYMMETRIC INFORMATION

Moral hazard arises from the asymmetric distribution of information. Ex ante moral hazard occurs because an insurer (for example) cannot monitor the behavior of the people he insures. Asymmetric information causes, in addition to moral hazard, further problems in health care provision since the quality of care is generally unobservable. Moreover, the characteristics valued by the consumer of care are not necessarily related to the efficacy or medical quality of care. For instance, a patient might prefer a pleasant, but ineffectual doctor to an impolite, but effective one. In that case, the preferences of the patient and the public health authorities conflict.

The quality of care is unobservable partly because we cannot see clearly the effort that physicians and other providers expend in producing health care. Even if they show up for work (which is not always the case; see Chaudhury and Hammer 2003), it is difficult to monitor the attention providers give to patients. To use the economics jargon, the interests of the *principals* (the patients and the public health authorities) differ from those of the *agent* (the provider) who is hired to supply the services. The principals want greater health; the agents may want that, too, but they also want to avoid working long hours for low pay. This leads to lower levels and quality of service than the principals would like.

A good deal of research has gone into the design of incentives and payment schemes to minimize the difference between the interests of principals and agents, or, at least, to reduce the cost of controlling the agency problem. Since the agent's behavior is expensive to monitor, the principal must design a contract such that the provision of the services the principal wants is in the interest of the agent (Eggleston and Hsieh 2004; Hammer and Jack 2001; Jack 2001a; McGuire 2000).

This is not merely of academic interest, but has great impact on the distribution of services, since physicians may neglect poorer patients in favor of those who can pay, or may direct patients away from public services to alternative, fee-paying services. This issue of "dual practice" is rather controversial and has received considerable attention from reformers. On the one hand, dual-practice doctors can induce demand, reduce effort and quality in their public sector jobs, and steal other resources from public facilities to benefit their private practices. On the other hand, dual practice can be a way for the public sector to retain skilled doctors at low wages and for the doctors to target public services more effectively to those who cannot pay privately (Bir and Eggleston 2003; Ferrinho et al. 2004; Gruen et al. 2002).

The provision of health insurance and prepayment systems may be rendered inefficient or unsustainable by the problem of *adverse selection*. This refers to the observation that those who expect to have high health costs are more likely to seek insurance. The problem for insurance arises because the insurer cannot sort (and price-discriminate among) consumers according to health risks (or rather, that screening and monitoring are expensive), and high-risk consumers drive up the costs of care insurance.

HEALTH SECTOR REFORMS: MOTIVATION AND TYPOLOGY

Motivation

Health sector reforms have been a focus of policy debates in both developed and developing countries at least since the 1970s. In response to plainly deteriorating morbidity and mortality (for instance, see Bennett 1979), the Alma Ata Declaration of September 1978 established, among other points, that health is a fundamental human right and that people are entitled to take part in health care planning and implementation.

In principle, health sector policies in developing countries have emphasized equity and focused on delivering services to the poor, but, in practice, the basic goals of the Alma Ata Declaration have not been achieved in the intervening 25 years. According to some, the ideals have been abandoned; according to others, the ideals were unrealistic and unattainable in the first place (for example, see Hall and Taylor 2003).

In addition, recent research has demonstrated the weak links between public health policies and expenditures on the one hand and health services and outcomes on the other (see Filmer, Hammer, and Pritchett 2000 and *World Development Report 2004*). More money is clearly not sufficient and may not even be necessary to achieve better health outcomes. Surveys and case studies in low-income countries reveal a rather disappointing picture. Wagstaff (2000a) and Wang (2003) present data from more than 40 low-income countries in the 1990s showing that children in poor households had a much higher probability of dying before age 5 and that survival rates improved much less among these children than they did among children in more well off households.

Some of the reasons for continuing inequities and poor health outcomes are external to health policy. Thus, civil wars, natural disasters, and the AIDS crisis have overwhelmed public health services, and political commitment to the rhetoric of the Alma Ata Declaration has proven easier than committing the resources required to achieve the declaration's goals.

But some of the reasons for poor outcomes involve governance, capture, and mismanagement in the sector itself. Public spending intended for services to poor households has been captured by the non-poor (see Castro-Leal et al. 2000); large shares of limited public spending on health (about 1 percent of gross domestic product) have been devoted to curative services, which mainly benefit the more well off. Griffin (1992) found that the distribution of central government health resources to the provinces in many Asian countries was often inversely correlated with need as measured by infant mortality. Health programs that are designed specifically to benefit the poor (such as the expansion of primary health care) were not reaching the poor effectively. Poor children are much less likely to receive simple curative care such as oral rehydration salts, and they are much less likely to be immunized than are children from wealthier households (Gwatkin et al. 2000).

In a comprehensive review, the World Health Organization (WHO 2000a) categorized three generations of health sector reforms. As in many other areas, the first generation of reforms concentrated on cutting bloated budgets and encouraging the private sector.[5] The second wave of reforms emphasized public sector efficiency, human resource management, and decentralization. More recently, the approach has been to take a broader, "sectorwide" view to improve both service delivery and outcomes (see *World Development Report 2004*). This has meant that the aims of health reform have become—in principle, at least—more clearly defined and openly shared among policymakers and donor communities. The reforms reflect changes in thinking about health systems and their links to health outcomes, as well as to broader development objectives.

Very often, health system reforms are imposed from the outside. For example, in response to structural adjustment programs and imposed public sector reform, many African countries engineered partial changes in health system financing, such as the introduction of user fees. In Central America, the devolution of some management functions to district or regional health offices was a direct response to macroeconomic reforms because of fiscal crisis and government decentralization (Bossert 1998). These imposed reforms included the promotion of the private sector delivery of health services (mainly by nongovernmental organizations), which was often part of a nationwide privatization movement (McPake 1997).

Recent years have seen popular reaction against health sector reforms, with the common perception that reforms have adversely affected the provision of services, particularly for the vulnerable. The list of perceived failures associated with reforms has included inequity due to the introduction of user fees, the damage done to vertical immunization and family planning programs by decentralization, and the reduction of access to quality services by the poor caused by inadequately designed insurance schemes (Berman and Bossert 2000). In spite of this backlash, it is clear that continued reforms are essential both to enhance the performance of the sector and to expand coverage to poor and vulnerable groups (for example, see *World Development Report 2004*).

Typology of reforms

The scope of the health reforms implemented in developing countries varies substantially. It is useful, albeit crude and imprecise, to distinguish the reforms into those affecting the *supply side* and those affecting the *demand side* of the health sector, that is, those involving the financing, management, and provision of services on the one hand and, on the other hand, those involving the demand for and consumption of services. The vast majority of reforms have focused on the supply side. Table 2.2 presents a highly stylized selection of reforms and their potential consequences for welfare and poverty. These are not necessarily comparable: some are ambitious and comprehensive, and some are relatively minor.

The list is not exhaustive, nor is the taxonomy perfect, but it shows the majority of issues that will come up during health sector reforms. In the table, *supply-side* reforms include governance, organization, management, provider payments, human resources, and such issues. Primarily for convenience, the table combines *demand-side* issues with those dealing with *sources of funds* for the health sector. This chapter cannot deal with all these reforms in great detail, but the table does present a fairly representative

TABLE 2.2. Typology of Selected Health Sector Reforms

Reform	What is it?	What are the possible consequences for equity?	References
Supply-side reforms			
Community participation, monitoring, and governance	Local participation in the design of policy, health promotion and preventive care, resource mobilization, and resource allocation (service delivery), as well as monitoring to overcome agency problems.	Positive, in principle, with the caveats that local institutions are vulnerable to capture by local elites and that local revenue may be insufficient, inequitable, and unsustainable.	Brinkerhoff 2003; Cornwall, Lucas, and Pasteur 2000; George 2003; Johnston, Faure, and Raney 1998; Loewenson 2000.
Sectorwide approaches	Coordinated policy-setting among agencies, under government leadership; agreed milestones and targets; all supported by a medium-term expenditure framework.	Depends on the components of the reform program; successful sectorwide approaches have focused on constraints to the access and consumption of services; can improve coordination across ministries.	Foster and Mackintosh-Walker 2001; Jefferys and Walford 2003.
Defining and providing "essential packages" of services	Formalized in World Bank (1993); identifies most "cost-effective" interventions (defined by average costs); does not consider marginal costs.	May be effective for chosen interventions, but resources are often inadequate; does not deal with systemic constraints; may be rigid and unresponsive to local needs.	Enemark and Schleimann 1999; World Bank 1993.
Managing the "purchaser-provider split"	Separating the purchaser of care from the provider of care; in principle, this enables competition among providers and minimizes the incentive to oversupply care (and induce excess consumption).	The greater effect will be (in principle) on efficiency. The direct effect on distribution is neutral and depends on the extent to which the purchaser can target funding to pro-poor services or poor regions.	Gerdtham, Rehnberg, and Tambour 1999; Jack 2001a; McPake et al. 2003.

Decentralization	This is a vast topic, including transferring the management of service provision, policy formation, and revenue generation to local or regional authorities.	Mixed. Greater local responsiveness is positive, but requires local administrative capacity; may exacerbate regional inequality if institutions are weak and if revenue is based solely on local funding.	Atkinson and Haran 2004; Bossert 2000; Collins, Araujo, and Barbosa 2000; Gilson 1998; Jütting et al. 2004.
Human resource management, downsizing	This refers to reforms of human resource policy, as opposed to the impact of reforms on the health workforce. It includes training and deployment, as well as reducing the workforce. Arguably a sorely neglected issue in health reforms.	Positive when incentives can be designed to encourage greater delivery of services to the poor. Can be negative if morale and motivation are diminished. Careful consideration of working conditions and the interests of the workforce are essential. Implications of "dual practice" unclear.	Bir and Eggleston 2003; Dussault and Dubois 2003; Ferrinho et al. 2004; *Human Resources for Health*.
Resource allocation	The greater portion of health budgets are allocated to secondary and tertiary care, whereas the poor consume relatively more primary care.	Reorientation is generally pro-poor, but it is not sufficient; consumption among the poor is constrained by other factors, such as low quality.	Castro-Leal et al. 2000; Diderichsen 2004; Pearson 2002.
Pharmaceuticals policy and management issues and technical issues (for example, the cold chain)	The availability of medicines, especially vaccines, is often hampered by inadequate lines of supply to local clinics, as well as by leakage.	Expanding immunization coverage (for example, the expanded program on immunization) is generally positive.	Caines and Lush 2004; Fairbank et al. 2000; Grace 2003; Laing, Hogerzeil, and Ross-Degnan 2001; WHO 2000b.
Pharmaceuticals, trade-related aspects of intellectual property rights, and the World Trade Organization	Trade and patents are the subject of heated debate and are generally beyond the scope of the ministry of health in most countries.	Debatable. Advocates argue that patents increase barriers to treatment among the poor.	Bailey 2001; Druce 2004; Lanjouw 2002, 2004.

(continued)

TABLE 2.2. Typology of Selected Health Sector Reforms (*Continued*)

Reform	What is it?	What are the possible consequences for equity?	References
Regulation and support of private sector providers	The majority of care is provided by the private sector; most of the care consumed by the poor is private.	Monitoring is vital, but expensive, especially among unorganized individual providers. The poor often use informal or even illegal providers, who may play important roles, but require training.	Bennett, McPake, and Mills 1997; Kumaranayake et al. 2000; Mills et al. 2002; Smith, Brugha, and Zwi 2001.
Quality monitoring, control, enhancement	Poor consumers are affected at least as much by the quality of care as by the price.	There is considerable evidence that the poor will respond to quality enhancements even if prices also rise.	Collier, Dercon, and Mackinnon 2002; Montagu 2003; Mwabu, Ainsworth, Nyamete 1993; QAP and PAHO 2003.
Public-private partnerships	Engaging the private sector to provide the right mix of services to the target population; can include clinical care, as well as nonclinical services.	Can be positive if incentives are managed carefully.	Caines and Lush 2004; England 2002, 2004; Liu et al. 2004; Nieves, La Forgia, and Ribera 2000.
Payments to providers: incentive- and performance-based contracts	Using contingent contracts to pay providers; these are becoming popular, especially since the appearance of *World Development Report 2003* (World Bank 2002).	Can be positive if incentives are designed and managed carefully; can be used to deliver targeted or subsidized services.	Barnum, Kutzin, and Saxenian 1995; Bitrán and Yip 1998; Eggleston and Hsieh 2004; Jack 2001a; Lavadenz, Schwab, and Straatman 2001; Leonard 2000; Loevinsohn 2001, 2002; Maceira 1998.
Payments to providers: capitation	Population-based payments to providers; may be weighted by demographic characteristics and may specify the services to be provided.	Can increase access to services among the poor; must account for variations across communities; there is an incentive for cream-skimming and cost-cutting, since the provider's profit is the residual between his costs and the capitation grant.	Bitrán 2001; Bitrán and Yip 1998; Maceira 1998; Telyukov 2001.

Sources of revenue

General government revenue, taxes	From general government revenue such as income taxes, value-added taxes, duties, and so on; these may be earmarked for health care (for example, cigarette taxes).	Organisation for Economic Co-operation and Development evidence that tax-based systems are more progressive. The limited tax base in most countries is inadequate to fund adequate services; direct taxes can be progressive, but require functioning tax systems; indirect taxes are less progressive.	Bennett and Gilson 2001; Birdsall and James 1993; Wagstaff et al. 1999; World Bank 1993.
Prepayment schemes	General term for schemes including insurance that involve contributions ex ante; specifically, a scheme to pay in advance for services.	In principle, the schemes can protect participants from the financial consequences of care for catastrophic events; they may exacerbate differences between participants and nonparticipants.	La Forgia 1990; Maceira 1998; Schneider and Diop 2001; Schneider, Diop, and Bucyana 2000.
Medical savings accounts	These are not insurance; they are generally self-financing and do not pool risks.	No pooling, exclude nonparticipants; contributions may be (regressively) tax-deductible; will cause insurance premiums to rise.	Hanvoravongchai 2002; Hsiao 2001; Hurley 2001; Moon, Nichols, and Walls 1997; Nichols, Phua, and Prescott 1997.

Insurance and risk-pooling schemes

Formal sector, employment based	Can be privately or publicly managed; contributions usually paid through payroll deductions.	Excludes people not in the formal sector; cross-subsidization is possible, but difficult.	Abel-Smith and Rawal 1994; Jack 2001b; Kutzin 1997.

(*continued*)

TABLE 2.2. Typology of Selected Health Sector Reforms (*Continued*)

Reform	What is it?	What are the possible consequences for equity?	References
Covering the informal sector	Providing insurance to people outside formal employment. Extremely difficult to do either as a community-based or a provider-based scheme.	Evidence that programs are exclusive and not self-sustainable; they may best be added to poverty reduction programs or existing assistance schemes such as crop insurance.	Bennett, Creese, and Monasch 1998; Gumber 2002.
Social health insurance (broadbased)	Services are paid for through contributions to a health fund, most commonly through the payroll; enrollment can be mandatory.	Debatable: advocates argue that it provides self-sustaining, equitable protection; detractors argue that it exacerbates disparities between participants and nonparticipants, that it may not reduce out-of-pocket costs, nor increase access, that it requires "solidarity," managerial capacity, economic growth, and so on (Normand and Weber 1994).	Carrin, Desmet, and Basaza 2001; Gertler and Solon 2000; Jimenez 1987; Normand and Weber 1994.
Community health insurance (locally based)	Voluntary, nonprofit insurance scheme; pools resources and risks.	Promising, but mixed results: can provide greater access and financial protection, and local control may minimize moral hazard, but small financial and risk pool, and the poorest may still be excluded; requires external funding.	Atim 1999; Binam, Nkama, and Nkendah 2004; Criel, Van der Stuyft, and Van Lerberghe 1999; Jakab and Krishnan 2001; Preker et al. 2002a.

User fees	Hotly debated topic that may be missing the point; "free" does not mean affordable (there may be under-the-table payments), and demand is constrained by other factors, such as quality.	The poor are more price sensitive than the rich: most of the evidence suggests that user fees are regressive, but the poor are also more sensitive to other factors. User fees, plus better quality, can increase utilization.	Abel-Smith and Rawal 1992; Alderman and Lavy 1996; Arhin-Tenkorang 2000; Bitrán and Giedion 2003; Creese and Bennett 1997; Gertler and van der Gaag 1990; Gilson 1998; Gwatkin 2003; Khan 2005; Lawson 2004; Litvack and Bodart 1992; Nahar and Costello 1998.
Under-the-table payments	Payments required of clients and patients, in addition to official posted fees. These may be informal, negotiated at the point of service, or highly structured; they usually go directly to the provider rather than the facility.	Generally regressive. Both the levels and the uncertainty of prices discourage use of services among the poor. But there is evidence of better performance and higher utilization among providers who charge under-the-table payments.	Bloom, Han, and Li 2001; Chakraborty et al. 2002; Ensor 2004; Killingsworth 2002; Killingsworth et al. 1999; Lewis 2000; McPake et al. 1999; Vian et al. 2004.
Targeting: tariffs, fee waivers	Price discrimination: charging different prices to different groups; can be by *fiat* (decided by an administrator based on certain characteristics of the recipient) or by *self-targeting* (whereby the recipient decides whether to apply based on the characteristics of the good or service being provided).	Subject to type-I (incorrectly denied) and type-II (incorrectly accepted) errors; administrative targeting is expensive, requiring means testing and enforcement, but, in principle, it enables more resources to go to the poor (or other groups) than do untargeted benefits.	Bitrán and Giedion 2003; Bitrán and Muñoz 2000; Chaudhury, Hammer, and Murrugarra 2003; Gelbach and Pritchett 1995.

(continued)

TABLE 2.2. Typology of Selected Health Sector Reforms (*Continued*)

Reform	What is it?	What are the possible consequences for equity?	References
Vouchers	"Entitlements" to the purchase or receipt of specific services; has been used for general health services or specific goods (for example, treated bed-nets) for specific target groups (for example, sexually transmitted infection services for sex workers).	Generally positive; can be expensive to establish and maintain; impact partly depends on copayments; must deal with the issue of secondary markets; vouchers seem to perform better for specific goods and services rather than generally.	Bitrán and Giedion 2003; Ensor 2003; Ensor and Cooper 2004.
Other issues			
"Scaling up" of pilot programs	Many health policies are drawn from successful pilot programs, and a great deal of attention has been paid to the problems of replication and scaling up to nationwide levels.	Depends on the benefits and character-istics of the program; incentives and commitment are difficult to replicate; must be careful to consider increasing marginal costs.	Bertozzi et al. 2001; Johns and Baltussen 2004; Johns and Torres 2005; Wyss, Moto, and Callewaert 2001.

Source: Compiled by the authors.

selection of references—neutrally empirical, advocatory, or critical—to which the reader can refer for more information. Below, we highlight two of the most commonly undertaken reforms: decentralization and community-based health insurance.

In practice, reforms are generally not implemented independently or piece by piece. They are often ambitious and far reaching, comprising a broad range of different actions. This has implications for the analysis, since it is difficult convincingly to identify the impact of components of reform programs. Table 2.3 presents a few of these comprehensive reform

TABLE 2.3. Health Sector Reforms in Selected Countries

Country	Reform	Description
Zambia	Health financing and decentralization	Initiated in 1991–2; involved significant decentralization to district health-management teams and health boards, the introduction of user fees for publicly provided health services, and a nationally defined benefits package.
Colombia	Health financing and health delivery	Started in 1993; included the establishment of social insurance schemes designed to allow managed competition between public and private health insurance plans and the contracting of both public and private providers for service delivery.
Chile	Health financing, health insurance, and privatization of services	Started in early 1980s; involved the establishment of private insurance, the decentralization of primary health care, and user charges in public health facilities.
Czech Republic	Health insurance and privatization	Started in the early 1990s; covered the rapid privatization of state-owned public services, the creation of multiple state-linked and private health insurance funds, and the introduction of a new payment mechanism and regulation organization.
Hungary	Privatization, health insurance, and decentralization	Included the privatization of primary care, the introduction of a centralized social insurance system, and decentralization of health facility ownership to the municipal level.
China	Health financing and devolution (in a few localities)	Driven by economic reform; involved the decentralization of health services to local health centers, hospital financial autonomy, and the introduction of community medical schemes with three-tier financing (central, local government matching funds, and households).

Sources: Berman and Bossert 2000; Tang and Bloom 2000.

programs. The reforms in Chile, begun in the early 1980s, are typical of such ambitious and comprehensive restructuring efforts (de la Jara and Bossert 1995). This involved all the principal "control knobs" discussed by Hsiao (2000): the creation of a private insurance system funded largely through social insurance contributions, the decentralization of primary care facilities, the introduction of user charges and per capita payments, and new regulation regimes and new programs to alter health behavior and help address preventable conditions.[6]

Health reforms commonly include changes in health financing and changes in health system organization and management. Changes in health financing may involve cost recovery and user charges for publicly provided services, community-based financing schemes, insurance schemes (social and private), and changes in public expenditure and allocation. Changes in health system organization and management may entail decentralization (authority, responsibilities, and functions) and changes in the ownership of service provision and delivery (privatization or a public-private mix). Here, two types of the more commonly implemented reforms are highlighted: community-based health financing and the decentralization of health services.

Community-based health financing

Community-based health financing broadly covers financing schemes that have three key features: community control, voluntary membership, and prepayment for health care by community members (Hsiao 2004). It does not include compulsory regional or national social insurance plans. Community-based schemes have been implemented with increasing frequency since the early 1990s as a means to raise resources for health care, to overcome insurance market failures, and to promote the inclusion of the poor (Table 2.4).

In most low-income countries, the scope for raising public revenue to finance health services through general taxation is narrow.[7] The amount that can be allocated from the government budget to public health activities is limited, and providing primary health care to all is not sustainable through general government revenue alone. Other avenues, such as fees for service or some sort of prepayment, are required to raise the funds needed to provide care.

As noted in the section on issues specific to the analysis of health reforms, information problems lead to insurance market failures in both developed and developing countries so that health insurance is insufficient or even absent. Community-based health financing is seen by many

TABLE 2.4. Archetypal Community-Based Health Financing in Africa and Asia

Scheme	Example
Asia	
Cooperative health care	Financing and provision are integrated at the village level (for example, China's cooperative medical system)
Community-based third-party insurance	Insurance plan; the insured pay a significant copayment when using local health services (for example, Sichuan province, China)
Provider-sponsored prepayment	Insurance plan operated at local health facilities (for example, Dhaka health card program)
Africa	
Community health fund	Uses three financing mechanisms: user fees, insurance contributions, and government subsidies; decision about the use of funds is made at the subdistrict level (for example, Tanzania community health fund)
Village insurance scheme	Requires prepayment for essential drugs and the provision of primary health care at the village level (for example, the Abota system in Guinea-Bissau)
Community-financed health insurance	Provider-insurance model; management and health care are provided by hospitals (for example, Nkoranza insurance scheme in Ghana)

Sources: Hsiao 2004; Arhin-Tenkorang 2004.

as a powerful tool to extend health care coverage and financial protection to a larger number of low-income households in rural or poor urban localities by avoiding the problems associated, on the one hand, with comprehensive social insurance and, on the other, with private insurance.[8]

Evidence suggests that community-based financing is effective in mobilizing resources for health care provision among the poor and that it can spread risks and ease the burden associated with the high cost of illness. Still, such financing requires significant local capacity to implement and monitor, and it is usually not self-sustaining: the local financing pool is too small to provide sufficient revenue to operate the financing independently (see, for example, Bennett, Creese, and Monasch 1998). In addition, the poorest in the community are often excluded from the schemes, and wealthier households select themselves out, thus reducing the financing pool even further. It is important to note that, although community-based financing has gained in popularity and exposure, there is rather little evidence of the impact. In a review of 45 studies of such schemes, Jakab and Krishnan (2001) find many examples describing the design and intent of the schemes, but very few systematic reviews of outcomes.

Despite the limited amount of rigorous evidence of beneficial outcomes, there is no shortage of suggestions for the design of community-based financing schemes. Advocates have proposed numerous modifications to enhance sustainability and performance. These include (1) targeted subsidies for the poorest, (2) reinsurance to enlarge the effective size of the risk pool, (3) improved prevention interventions, (4) technical support to strengthen management capacity, and (5) strengthening links with formal financing and provider networks (Preker et al. 2002a, 2002b). In addition, community-based financing must take care to deal with (1) the levels of the insurance premium, (2) moral hazard and adverse selection, (3) "covariant risks" (the phenomenon that health problems are correlated within a population), (4) community participation, (5) the quality of care, (6) the referral system, and (7) cultural concepts of illness, among many other factors (Wiesmann and Jütting 2000). In addition, Jakab and Krishnan (2001) find that successful schemes take into account the nature of the incomes of the membership population, allowing members to pay premiums at irregular intervals and even through in-kind arrangements.

Community-based health financing is not a panacea. But broadbased social insurance is not a viable option for a typical poor country with a limited tax base and a small formal sector workforce, and private insurance is insufficient to provide for poor and vulnerable groups. Expanding health care to underserved populations will most likely require community participation in resource mobilization and in the management of care.

Decentralization of health services

Like community financing, decentralization comes in many forms. The term is applied to myriad diverse policies, from increasing hospital autonomy to local revenue generation. The impact of decentralization on the poor depends to a large extent on *what* is being devolved, *to whom,* and *under which circumstances.* The consequences of the decentralization of services are quite different from the consequences of the decentralization of revenues; empowering a local community group to monitor performance is different from entrusting medical training to a regional government; a large city will have a different set of management skills than a small rural council. It is also important to pay attention to the consequences of devolution for the management of the health system and the coordination of health policy, and it is important to be concerned about the people who are not in areas involved in the decentralization, as well as those who are in such areas.

Decentralization in health systems is justified on the basis that it will correct the information-related problems of agency and moral hazard discussed in the section on issues specific to the analysis of health reforms. In principle, local communities have better knowledge of local needs and conditions and can make better decisions if they are granted the authority to manage resources and organize and supply health services. Decentralization promotes accountability and participation among the local population, makes health service providers accountable to the local community, and boosts the responsiveness of the providers to the local demand for services. Decentralization is expected to improve the efficiency, equity, and quality of health service delivery and management.

Decentralization has been widely implemented in Latin America since the 1980s, in Africa since the 1990s, and elsewhere (China, Eastern Europe and Central Asia) more recently, but the ambitious goals presented above have only rarely been realized. A recent study of 19 country cases (Jütting et al. 2004) found that decentralization had "somewhat negative" or "negative" consequences for poverty and that all but one of the positive performers were middle-income countries.[9] The study concluded that "one has to be very cautious in promoting decentralisation for poverty reduction."

Decentralization will improve service delivery for the poor if the health system and other services and infrastructure are already performing well. When conditions are favorable, local participation and control may well be used to improve both the performance and targeting of services. But if there are problems with coordination and performance at the national level, decentralization may merely make things worse. Studies of the experience of rural China (Tang and Bloom 2000) and Nigeria (Khemani 2004) found that there is little enforcement or accountability at the local level. Decentralization will not, by itself, solve problems of governance. It is unlikely that local governments will function any better than national governments. If the national health system is performing poorly, local health systems are probably no better. Decentralization may simply reinforce local patronage systems (Brinkerhoff 2000).

In their review of country experiences, Jütting et al. (2004) present a list of the factors they found to be correlated with successful, pro-poor decentralization. These include:

- sufficient and stable local finances
- sufficient local human capital and managerial capacity
- political commitment at the national level

- donor support
- the free flow of information
- participation and accountability
- policy coherence, especially between the national government and donors

There is broad agreement that the constraints of poor governance and poor performance must be dealt with before attempting decentralization. Atkinson and Haran (2004) found that, in Ceará, Brazil, good management practices led to successful decentralization rather than vice versa.

> Any apparent association between decentralization and performance seems to be an artifact of the informal management, and the wider political culture in which a local health system is embedded strongly influences the performance of local health systems (Atkinson and Haran 2004: 822).

STAKEHOLDERS

One of the primary obligations of the health sector in any country and a major justification for reforms is that the system must be responsive to the needs of citizens. This is generally taken to mean the clients—actual and potential—of health services. A quick review of the literature, on the other hand, suggests that most of the focus has been on the "human resource" aspects of reform, that is, the impact of reform on health sector workers. There is even a professional journal devoted exclusively to this topic.[10]

Any policy change will affect different groups in different ways depending on their relationship to the sector, and reforms often reflect compromise among various stakeholders. It is important to understand that different stakeholders exercise different degrees of control and influence over the reforms.

Table 2.5 presents a list of stakeholders, distinguishing between those on the supply side and those on the demand side of health care. Again, the distinction is not perfect. Individuals can be both providers and consumers of services: employees of the local health ministry have children who need vaccinations and become ill. But it makes sense heuristically to consider these as two separate groups. The doctor who is ill becomes a patient. The household that consumes health services is concerned with efficiency when the time comes to pay taxes. Below, two categories of stakeholders are discussed in detail: health workers on the supply side and women on the demand side.

TABLE 2.5. Stakeholders in the Health Reform Process

Supply side	Demand side
International donor agencies	General population as consumers
National government	Women
Provincial government	Children and families
Central ministry of health	Elderly
Local ministry of health	Ethnic and racial minorities
Other ministries	Poor households
Public sector providers	Rural households
Private sector providers	Transhumant and migrant households
Informal practitioners	People living with HIV/AIDS
Drug companies	
Insurers, private and public	
General population as taxpayers	

Source: Compiled by the authors.

Health care workers

The attention paid to health workers in the design of reforms is not misplaced. As noted in the section on issues specific to the analysis of health reforms, one significant motivation for reform is to improve the efficiency of service provision, and the behavior of providers is one of the key determinants of productivity. In addition, the response of providers is probably the single most important ingredient in the success of reforms. So, it is necessary to understand not only the role of the workforce in providing services, but also to anticipate their response, to design incentives to encourage behavior that advances public health goals, and to engage the active support of the workforce in implementing the reforms.

Reforms must deal with the factors that motivate health sector workers. To some extent, workers in the sector are driven by a genuine desire to improve public health in general and the health of patients in particular.[11] Reforms that engage providers by promoting issues and policies that providers can "rally around" (Dussault and Dubois 2003) are more likely to succeed. But providers are discouraged by low wages, inadequate resources, poor working conditions, and the general lack of support from governments. Studies suggest that reforms have ignored these factors and that health sector workers resent being treated as "mere production tools" (Dussault and Dubois 2003). In spite of that rhetoric, health providers are not so different from the rest of us. Notwithstanding the anecdotal evidence, more money does matter to health workers (see, for example, the contracting studies cited in Table 2.2), but so do trust, autonomy, and professional recognition.

The unfortunate consequences for the poor of these human resource issues are well known, but difficult to resolve. There are few incentives in place to enhance service provision to poor, rural, or otherwise underserved communities. To improve the distribution of services, governments generally combine the carrot and the stick, that is, incentives and compulsion. The health system can provide supplements to wages or other financial incentives, funding for travel, or assistance to families. The government can also make certain services compulsory for medical graduates, as well as paying them more, as is the case in China, India, and Indonesia (Chomitz et al. 1997; *Hindu* April 7, 2005).

Reforms, especially those that introduce competition, tighten monitoring, or change payment regimes, will inevitably produce winners and losers. Successful reforms will require political strategies to address the concerns of different groups of providers. Reforms that threaten job security and incomes may lead—as they did in Zimbabwe—to strikes, theft, high turnover, and low morale among workers (Mutizwa-Mangiza 1998).

Finally, the AIDS epidemic is taking its toll among health workers. The perceived risk of contracting HIV is quite high among health workers, the demand for and complexity of care continue to outstrip the available resources, and workers are confronted daily with wards full of dying patients.[12] These factors contribute to stress and "burnout," leading to increased absenteeism and attrition (Aitken and Kemp 2003; Marchal, De Brouwere, and Kegels 2005; Tawfik and Kinoti 2003; World Bank 1997b). The human and financial demands of the AIDS crisis reduce the resources that might be otherwise available for expanded care for the poor.

Women as consumers of care

To some extent, treating women as a distinct and coherent category among consumers is to obscure enormous differences among women. Clearly, women can be disaggregated by health status, geography, caste and ethnicity, wealth, and myriad other factors. However, even if they do not always speak with one voice, they arguably share concerns and constraints in health care that are often neglected (Cornwall 2000). Men and women are often not treated equally even when they have common health needs, and, when their health needs are different, these differences are not addressed equitably (Mensch 1993; see also the papers cited in Lakshminarayanan 2003a).

There are few empirical studies of the impact of reform on women, especially poor women, and this section derives primarily from anecdotal evidence and advocacy. But there are some regularities, even among the anecdotes. One common concern is the effect of user charges on poor women. Although there is little robust evidence on the impact of user fees, women may have less disposable income and less control over purchasing decisions within households (Nanda 2002). Reforms that purport to increase access to care by poor women must take into account gender inequalities in purchasing power and decisionmaking.

Financial constraints are exacerbated where women do not have the right to travel alone or to be in the company of men, including health care providers, outside their immediate family. Where female health workers are not available, women may be forced to go without care. The opportunity costs of medical treatment may also be greater for a woman. If she becomes ill at harvest time, for example, there may be no one who will take her place in the fields or at home. The visit to a health worker might thus impose unacceptable burdens on the household (WHO 1998).

Women are the main health caregivers in the household. The first option for the treatment of children's diseases such as malaria is home treatment by the mother. The mother will buy over-the-counter medication, possibly on the advice of the shopkeeper, but lack of information can lead to ineffective treatment and accelerated drug resistance. A pilot study in Kenya found that training shopkeepers in appropriate drug use had a large impact on both the use and the adequate dosing of chloroquine (Marsh et al. 2004).

Women's health services have focused on the reproductive needs of women, especially contraception and safe childbearing, and the majority of studies on the impact of reforms on women have also focused on the consequences of reforms for reproductive health. These studies emphasize the importance of participation, openness, and flexibility in the reform process and in the management of health care, especially at the local level. They also emphasize the need to understand the constraints facing women and their consumption of health services (Futures Group International 2000; Lakshminarayanan 2003b; Langer, Nigenda, and Catino 2000).

TRANSMISSION CHANNELS

In this section, we examine the way households are connected to the health sector and the mechanisms through which the impact of reforms is felt by stakeholders. The PSIA guidebook (World Bank 2003b) lists five main transmission channels: labor markets, prices, assets, access to goods and services, and transfers and taxes. In health, there are a number of other factors through which the impact of reforms is experienced by the poor. First, because health is often publicly provided, some decision must be made on *which services* the public health system will supply. This includes determination of the "basic package" of services. Second, the demand for services will greatly influence both the level and the efficiency of supply. Third, the perceived quality of services is a major determinant of the consumption of services.

Table 2.6 presents a description of the major transmission channels. They are mostly supply side in that they transmit signals from producers to consumers. However, the links from those paying for services to those who produce services may be thought of as a demand-side transmission, and, in addition, the supply of services certainly responds to demand. The ultimate welfare impact of a reform depends also on how households and consumers respond to changes in policy, supply, prices, and so on. These channels do not operate in isolation: the effects of one (say, public-private interactions) will have an effect on others (for example, prices), and the distributional impact of reform can be transmitted through all of them.

Defining the service package is a major task for policymakers. This involves setting priorities based on information about the current burden of disease of the population and choosing the most cost-effective solutions. It depends on changes in available health financing, whether through fees for service, public health spending allocations, or insurance schemes. Changes in health financing, meanwhile, also have a direct impact on the incentives offered to service providers and on consumer behavior, which determines the level and distribution of health service provision and use. The ownership structure of service provision and delivery (private versus public, for instance) also has implications for health financing, as well as for the quality and equity of health services.

The health financing reform in Jamaica that involved a government-supported expansion of private insurance to the urban formal sector provides a useful illustration of these transmission channels (Gertler and Sturm 1997). The expansion of private insurance coverage can lead to a reduction in public health expenditure by inducing those who are better off to switch to private providers. The insurance scheme will lower the out-of-pocket price of health care at the point of use by smoothing payments across individuals and time, and it will reduce cost differentials between public and private providers. Both factors will encourage those covered by the insurance to opt out of public care in favor of private care. Indeed, Besley and Coate (1991) demonstrate theoretically that, in a quality-based separating equilibrium, individuals above some income level choose to purchase services from a higher-quality, higher-priced private sector,

TABLE 2.6. Health Reform Transmission Channels

Channel	Impact on the poor
Labor markets	Reforms will have an impact on workers in the health sector. Ideally, reforms will allow health workers to focus effort and resources on health care for the poor. But reforms will affect working conditions and motivation among workers. Some workers may be forced out if budgets are cut or if there is a drive for greater efficiency; rules against theft and opportunistic behavior, including dual private practice, may be tightened. In most countries, there will be little impact on general employment.
Public-private interactions	Reforms are often intended to strengthen the private sector and provide incentives for private provision to the poor. These incentives are difficult to design, and public services may be more easily targeted. Conversely, increased public provision of services may crowd out private provision. Better regulation and training of private sector (especially informal) providers will enhance the quality of services for the poor.
Finance and revenue	The cost of defined insurance contributions is clearly outweighed by the benefits from participating in an insurance plan. The same is true for local community insurance and prepayment plans. Self-insurance is far more expensive than almost any risk-sharing arrangement. Finance and payment mechanisms will, in turn, influence provider behavior.
Risk-sharing and insurance	Risk-sharing, whether through community or social arrangements, allows greater coverage (of people and services) at lower cost than self-insurance.
Transfers and taxes	Tighter targeting will increase type-I errors (false negatives); the general tax burden is usually borne by the middle and wealthy classes.
Package of services	What services are to be included, whether provided publicly or paid for publicly, has a significant impact on the welfare of beneficiaries. Different populations have different requirements: reproductive health, maternal and child health, treatment of infectious diseases, inpatient treatment, and so on, all have different constituencies. There is some discussion that the health system should provide insurance (that is, pay for services) rather than provide the services directly. This reduces, but does not eliminate, the pressure to define the package.
Prices	As noted in Table 2.2, the poor are more price sensitive than are the non-poor, and, so, all else being equal, they will consume more if user fees are reduced or eliminated. But all else is not equal: prices can be a signal of quality, and the poor are at least as sensitive to quality as to prices. In addition, opportunistic behavior among providers means that "free" services are not truly free.
Assets	Health sector reform will have no effect on asset values. To the extent that insurance is extended to cover the poor, the poor will have less need to liquidate assets to cover health expenditures.

(continued)

TABLE 2.6. Health Reform Transmission Channels (*Continued*)

Channel	Impact on the poor
Access to services	Access is here defined in terms of physical distance to providers. Distance and the time and cost required to cover distance can be more important than the price charged for services. Expanding services can have a great impact on consumption among the poor.
Quality	As noted in Table 2.2, the poor respond to quality, as well as to prices. Improvements in quality will encourage greater consumption of services.
Demand	Demand is key to the consumption of services and to health status. Understanding the determinants of demand and the constraints to greater consumption of services is an essential component in the design of pro-poor reforms.

Source: Compiled by the authors.

while individuals below that level of income opt for the lower-quality, lower-priced public sector.

Private insurance can also affect the distribution of the services provided. Public subsidies will shift away from curative care (consumed more by the wealthy) toward preventive care, which disproportionately benefits the poor. However, private insurance can have deleterious effects on public services. As households that are more well off opt out of the public system, the support for improving public services may be considerably eroded. When government initiatives to change health policy are politically motivated and heavily influenced by the interests of those who are more well off (as observed in many developing countries), policies such as the promotion of private insurance plans for the more well off may, in the long term, significantly worsen the welfare of poor households and increase inequities due to wider quality differentials between the private and the public services.

IMPLEMENTATION MECHANISMS

Two stages in the reform process are distinguished here: *policy formation* and *policy implementation.*

Policy formation

It is widely accepted that successful reforms are characterized by openness and consultation with the main stakeholders. Among the most obvious stakeholders are clients, but also public and private sector providers, including for-profit and nonprofit, charity, and nongovernmental-organization providers. This is because reforms are not merely technical blueprints, but are value laden and frequently conflict ridden (Gilson 1997). In other words, it is necessary to build collegial support for the reforms and to anticipate and deal with disagreements that might derail the reform process.

There must be coordination among international and bilateral donors and funders, as well as other ministries within the national government. This ensures that policies are consistent with medium-term plans, sectorwide approaches, the Poverty Reduction Strategy Paper, and the Poverty Reduction and Growth Facility.

There is often more talk about openness and consultation than there is actual openness, especially in the planning stage. In his study of participation in Tanzanian reforms, Semali (2003) found that, although the process of policy formation was supposed to follow the guidelines for consultation established in *World Development Report 1993* (World Bank 1993), the actual consultation consisted of meetings of Ministry of Health officials in Washington, a meeting of the "consultative group" of donors in Paris, and two workshops comprising ministry officials, donors, and the World Bank.[13]

Policies must also be internally consistent. For example, it is important that one set of policies does not encourage private sector providers to expand services, while another set of policies simultaneously discourages them from expanding. While this seems obvious on paper, sectoral policies can, in principle, be quite complex; to coordinate sectoral policies with those of, for instance, the tax authorities or policies regulating small businesses is even more difficult. In addition, the stated objectives of policy reform and the instruments proposed to achieve these objectives can appear to conflict, for instance, expanding private sector provision by tightening licensing restrictions (Gilson 1997).

Policy implementation

Successful reforms require a functioning and capable public sector at both the national and local levels. This again raises the unfortunate point that reforms—such as decentralization—cannot, in principle, be expected to solve problems of governance and stewardship.

Similarly, the reforms must define the responsibilities of all participants in the process. The government must have a clear conception of its role in the sector. This may simultaneously include the roles of policymaker, regulator, purchaser, and, possibly, provider of health services. On the other hand, the public sector need not actually supply the services.

The private sector dominates primary care provision in many countries, and many health ministries contract with private providers to deliver services to the poor (for example, Bangladesh, Mozambique, and Uganda).

The government must also have a firm commitment to achieving the goals set out by the reform process. This includes the will and ability to provide adequate funding. Policy statements and intentions are meaningless unless sufficient resources are allocated to fulfill the required tasks. Similarly, public expenditures and, more importantly, changes in sectoral institutions and structures must be supported by an appropriate legal and regulatory framework. For example, if the reforms are intended to encourage the participation of the private sector, the appropriate legal institutions should be established to define and protect both the rights and the responsibilities of private providers in health (Kumaranayake et al. 2000; Mills et al. 2002).

A number of studies have highlighted the importance of paying attention to the *process* of reforms and not merely the goals (Gilson 1997; Walt and Gilson 1994). It is not simply a matter of "knowing which direction to move in, but paying attention to how to get there: in essence, recognizing that policy implementation is as much a process as it is content" (Brinkerhoff 1996: 1395). Thus, it is important to develop a common understanding, to build consensus for the reforms, and to obtain input and support from a wide and inclusive selection of government people (including politicians), health providers, and civil society (Aga Khan Health Services 2004). This requires openness and consultation not only during the implementation, but during the process of policy formation as well.

TOOLS AND DATA FOR ANALYSIS

Once a potential set of reforms has been proposed to advance national health goals, a PSIA should aim to provide evidence to address the basic question posed at the beginning of this chapter: what is the potential welfare impact of the identified reforms across socioeconomic groups? In particular, how are disadvantaged households affected? As a requirement of PSIA, the identification of reform options is absolutely essential. In this section, we discuss how distributional analysis can be conducted on an identified policy change.

The choice of tools for analyzing the distributional impact on household welfare of health sector policy changes is determined by four basic considerations:

- the nature of the policy change
- the type of questions to be addressed

■ the available data

■ the constraints on time, resources, and analytical capacity

While the last two considerations are straightforward, the first two require some explanation. The policy itself will have an influence on the choice of analytical method. In general, health is not a tradable good, so it is usually not necessary to resort to economy-wide models with external accounts (such as computable general equilibrium models). On the other hand, if the reforms are broadly based, if they involve not only the health sector, but also other sections of the economy, some understanding of the link between health and (for instance) labor markets will be required. In addition, reforms will *always* have general equilibrium or multiplier effects, that is, any policy change will induce behavioral responses on both the supply side and the demand side. These responses, in turn, will affect each other: a change in finance policies will affect the demand for services, which will affect the supply of services, which will have further demand effects, and so on.

Second, the nature of the question to be asked will have an effect on the methods used. On one level, a policy analyst would like to examine the long-run consequences of reforms through all possible transmission channels and for all groups. But this will clearly not be possible in practice, nor is it necessarily desirable in all cases. In practice, the policy analyst may be interested in only one particular aspect of the reforms. For example, what are the direct effects of subsidized antiretroviral treatment on food consumption among households in which someone is infected with HIV? This very narrow question can be examined through econometric analysis of household expenditures. Nonetheless, the analyst must be aware that an approach that is too narrow might miss some important effects. In the case of antiretroviral medication, treatment may improve the health of the person with HIV to the extent that he can continue working or resume working, so that household income increases. Or the burden of caring for the ill household member will be diminished, so that other members of the household can increase the time they spend at school or in work. These factors might be missed by a narrowly defined and static econometric approach.

One can crudely distinguish the available analytical methods as *quantitative* and *qualitative*. A clear distinction between the two is not easy to draw, although Bamberger (2000) provides a useful summary of the methods in terms of the selection of units of analysis, the research protocol, and data collection. When time and data permit, a combination of the two methods (that is, "mixed" methods) is preferable. Qualitative methods can provide hypotheses to be tested by the quantitative methods, and the qualitative methods also supply a way of validating the results of the rather more abstract quantitative methods.

The following discussion centers on four topics: the choice of outcome indicators, data and sources, qualitative methods, and quantitative methods.

Choice of indicators

There are two factors to consider in the choice of indicators. Recalling the discussion in the section on issues specific to the analysis of health reforms, these can be thought of as "the distribution of what?" and "what distribution?" First, what dimension of outcomes are we interested in? Do we care about the distribution of health status or about the distribution of the financial burden of illness? Second, how do we measure the distribution of this outcome? The two issues are discussed here in turn.

The distribution of what?

How do we define and measure the changes in welfare among households or individuals because of health policy changes? Sen's (1984) capability approach has led to the recognition that welfare is multidimensional, so that human capital outcomes, such as those in health and education, are valid measures of welfare, as much as consumption and income. In the health literature, indicators such as child mortality, morbidity, life expectancy (often adjusted for disability), and self-reported health status are the most widely used.

Understanding the impact of health policy changes is complicated by a number of factors. First, as noted in the section on issues, health outcomes are determined by factors both inside and outside the health sector.[14] Second, health status is a lagging indicator of health investments and policies. The impact of health policy changes on health outcomes will only be manifest after some time even in the case of major policy changes. Third, self-reported health status indicators are often not independently reliable: they are determined partly by expectations and sensitivity to illness, which vary systematically with factors such as income. The poor are less likely than the more well off to report sickness. The poor are not healthier than the rich, but they are more likely to underreport, partly because they are less able to do anything about it (Schultz and Tansel 1997; Strauss and Thomas 1998).

These complications leave two options for analysis. The first is to choose a set of "proximate determinants" of health outcomes, that is, not health outcomes per se, but the factors that are closely (preferably causally) correlated with health outcomes. These include measures of the access to and utilization of health services, the incidence of public spending, and the degree of financial protection represented by various health financing programs. Second, the analysis can examine indicators of *process*. Since reforms are time consuming and since the impact of reforms will not be observed in health outcomes for even longer, choose indicators of the direction and progress made in the implementation of the reforms. Table 2.7 lists a range of possible indicators of both outcomes and process, but organized more thematically, that is, as measures of *access, quality, outputs and outcomes*, and *finance and sustainability*.

Again, this is not an exhaustive list, and some (especially the outcome variables) may be only tenuously related to the short-term consequences of reforms. In brief, *access* refers to the absence of barriers to receiving care, including prohibitive costs; *quality* refers both to the quality perceived by

TABLE 2.7. Indicators of Health Sector Reforms

Access	*Outputs and outcomes*
Proximity to services: distance, time, cost	Utilization
Primary services, hospital	Immunization coverage
Pharmacy, dispensary, drug shop	Supervised deliveries
Hours of service, primary care	Outpatient visits, inpatient days
Out-of-pocket service cost, inpatient and outpatient	Facility performance criteria
Medical and drug costs	Incidence, morbidity, and mortality
"Hotel" costs	Malaria
Fee schedule: targeted tariffs, waivers	HIV/AIDS
Under-the-table fees, gratuities	Diarrheal diseases
Waiting times for outpatient services	Maternal and postpartum health
Waiting lists for inpatient services	Malnutrition
	Demographic indicators
Finance and sustainability	Total fertility rate
	Crude birth and death rate
Household level	
Financial protection, household expenditures	*Quality*
Spending on regular and catastrophic care	
Sources of finance	Staff: number and qualifications
Share from taxes, fees for service, and so on	Availability of equipment and supplies
Incidence of payment for services	Protocols: whether they exist and are followed
Expenditures	Cleanliness
Out of pocket	Supervision
Insurance premiums and copayments	Client satisfaction
Insurance coverage	Client participation in governance, monitoring
Incidence of expenditures	

Source: Adapted from Hutton 2000, Table 1.

the clients and to the technical, medical quality of the care provided; *outputs and outcomes* are combined here and include the volumes of services provided (from the supply side) and population-level and household-level indicators; *finance and sustainability* also encompass both systemwide and household-level variables, including financial protection among households and sources of finance for the system.

What distribution?

The most commonly used measure of equity in public services is *benefit incidence,* that is, how much of a given benefit (or cost) accrues to which fraction or group within the population.[15] The usual practice is to rank the population by some welfare measure, such as income, and then ascertain the value of public benefit that each member of the population receives. Evaluation of the incidence of health care finance requires examination of all sources of health sector funding, not only the direct payments that are made exclusively for health care. In addition to out-of-pocket payments, health insurance contributions, and earmarked health taxes, the distributional burden of all direct and indirect taxes may be examined where these comprise a significant part of total health sector revenue.

Alternatively, one can calculate the *concentration index,* which is a summary measure describing benefit incidence. The advantage of the index is that one can also easily compute standard errors, which permit robust comparisons of statistically significant differences across classes of individuals or households.

One important advance is the computation of *marginal benefit incidence analysis.*[16] This is used to examine the distribution of the marginal costs and benefits of program expansion across different income groups. This is a more informative measure than average benefit incidence, since policy changes often involve the scaling up of existing programs. Recent research indicates that the benefits of public programs can be initially captured by the non-poor, but that the poor will benefit more as a program is expanded. For example, the rich may demand payoffs in return for their taxes to cover a social program's start-up costs, and only once the program has expanded (and the marginal costs of program expansion have been lowered) will it be politically feasible for the government to concentrate services in poor, remote areas (see Lanjouw and Ravallion 1999).

Data

The data required for the distributional analysis of health reform depend mainly on the nature and scale of the policy change, the question to be addressed, and the choice of methods. Lindelöw and Wagstaff (2003) offer a comprehensive review of the data sources commonly used in health analysis. Only a selection of the more widely available data are discussed here.

Demographic and Health Survey (DHS)

These surveys are among the most widespread sources for data on health status and policy. Funded by the U.S. Agency for International Development, nearly 200 of these household-level surveys have been collected since 1985 (see http://www.measuredhs.com). The DHS attempts to be comparable across countries and over time and includes a wide range of indicators, such as basic household characteristics, fertility, child nutrition and health status, access to environmental services (safe water, sanitation, and electricity), and utilization of basic health and education services. A typical DHS collects detailed information on reproductive history, educational attainment, knowledge about common childhood illnesses, HIV/AIDS, and sexually transmitted infections, as well as knowledge about the treatment of these illnesses. The DHS is useful for assessing health knowledge and practices, health status, and the consumption of health services.

One of the limitations of the DHS data is that they include only very little information on wealth and generally no information on income and expenditure. This information is traditionally used for measuring living standards and is essential for distributional analysis. A number of recent studies using DHS data have constructed a wealth index as a proxy measure of living standards in order to address distributional issues (see, for example, Filmer and Pritchett 1998).

The surveys and the methods are being continually updated and expanded; for example, surveys of providers are now being conducted. These facility-based provider surveys gather information on health service delivery, including quality, infrastructure, utilization, and availability, and can be linked to household surveys in order to identify relationships between behavior and outcomes on the household side and the supply of health services.

Living Standards Measurement Study (LSMS)

More than 50 LSMS surveys have been conducted in low-income countries to measure levels and changes in living standards. These are large and comprehensive household surveys that collect rich information on socioeconomic characteristics, especially on household consumption and income. They frequently include health modules to gather information on the health status of household members, service utilization, and access costs. The LSMS surveys that have an added health module are useful data sources for analyzing the impact of health policy changes (for example, user charges, health financing programs, or publicly financed health projects) on health demand, as well as for the distributional impact analysis of public spending.

For some, the LSMS and DHS datasets (which are narrow, but deep) can be combined with census data (which are broad, but shallow) to produce maps of poverty, health status, and access to services and infrastructure. The availability of such tools at the disaggregated level can be valuable in helping policymakers target poor localities accurately. Elbers, Lanjouw, and Lanjouw (2003) have developed a methodology to combine census and household-survey data to create reliable district-level poverty maps. An ongoing research project at Macro International (http://www.orcmacro. com) is exploring the possibility of replicating the methodology to produce maps on key health indicators. Similar work is being conducted elsewhere. Fujii (2003), for example, has developed anthropometric maps using DHS and census data on Cambodia.

Other household-level data sources

Other agencies conduct internationally comparable and valuable surveys, sometimes with a health focus. For example, the Multiple Indicator Cluster Surveys sponsored by the United Nations Children's Fund focus on women and children; about 50 country reports are available. Hundreds of other household surveys are conducted throughout the world every year, usually in an ad hoc fashion. There are periodic attempts to standardize and codify survey methods. The Paris 21 Initiative, for instance, was established by the United Nations to develop survey techniques and to build a "culture of evidence-based policymaking" (see http://www. paris21.org). The World Bank's Africa Household Survey Databank contains more than 400 surveys, and surveys are available for other regions as well.

Quantitative service delivery surveys and Public Expenditure Tracking Surveys

Quantitative service delivery surveys focus on the service facility and factors affecting quality of services. It is a technique for surveying service providers, resource availability, and performance. Public Expenditure Tracking Surveys measure problems in the budget execution process, such as leakage, delays, and the reallocation of resources, but they can also be used to examine incentives for service providers and the quality and quantity of services. These two are often linked, and the distinction between them is becoming smaller. About 30 of these two types of surveys had been carried out by the Bank and its clients as of early 2005 (see Dehn, Reinikka, and Svensson 2003).

Experimental and quasi-experimental data

Rigorous evaluation of the impact of a specific health intervention may require data collected from a policy experiment. This is because the impact of an intervention can be affected by factors that are impossible to disentangle exclusively through ex post evaluation. For example, a program may be put in a particular place for reasons that also affect the program's outcomes. If we were only to look at outcomes, we would be unable to determine the impact of the program and the impact of these other factors.[17]

Experimental analysis is complex and generally expensive; it requires both baseline and follow-up data, preferably including supply-side (health facility) and demand-side (household) surveys. However, surveys to analyze policy experiments generally use simpler instruments on smaller samples relative to the DHS or LSMS, especially if the intervention is a pilot program. See the section on quantitative methods hereafter for a more complete description of the method.

Qualitative data

Qualitative data differ from survey or experiment data because of the format of the data and the process through which the data are generated (see, for example, Chung 2000). For instance, focus-group interviews are often conducted during small meetings using open-ended questions about a specific topic. The information collected is often contextual and provides insights about the process and implementation of the reform program that are particularly valuable for confirming an evaluation based on experiment or survey data. See the section on analytical methods below for a more complete description.

National health accounts

National health accounts describe in great detail all the sources and uses of funds and other resources within the health system, private and public. These are an excellent source of information on the *functional* classification of the sources and the allocation of expenditures; they less often disaggregate the information by income or other household categories. National health accounts have so far been prepared for about 75 countries. Since 1999, the World Health Organization has been undertaking a systematic exercise to develop health expenditure data for all its 191 member states, based on the United Nations System of National Accounts (see WHO 2003).

Analytical methods

The methods used to examine the consequences of health reforms (or any reforms) are often distinguished as either *qualitative* or *quantitative*. In many ways, this is a false and unproductive dichotomy. *Faute de mieux,* we maintain this distinction and discuss a few of the methods in detail.

Qualitative methods

"Qualitative methods" generally refers to the use of case studies and in-depth, open-ended interviews and discussions to analyze the distributional impact of health reforms. The methods most commonly mentioned in the literature include social impact analysis, participatory beneficiary assessments, and stakeholder analysis. Each of these methods is described in *A User's Guide to Poverty and Social Impact Analysis* (World Bank 2003b).

One major strength of qualitative methods is that they provide a much deeper understanding of the processes underlying policy implementation, including the interactions among the various stakeholders, than can be elicited in a structured, impersonal questionnaire. This information is crucial for gauging the benefits and costs of a reform for different stakeholders. It can offer valuable insights into the reasons for the failure or success of a reform program in reaching the intended objectives. Findings from studies using this approach can also supply information that can be applied to improve the design of household surveys and interpret the results of quantitative analyses. It can also be employed to validate the outcomes of quantitative analysis.

For the analysis of the distributional impact of policy reform, these qualitative methods have a few limitations. First, they cannot *quantify* the welfare gains or losses due to a health policy change. Thus, they are not valuable as guides in the design of explicit compensation measures to mitigate any adverse impact (that is, the "willingness to pay" or "willingness to accept" a sum as equivalent to the welfare change caused by the policy). Indeed, very few empirical studies that use the qualitative method have touched upon the distributional aspect of reform. Two empirical examples of attempts to use qualitative methods to address equity issues are Bossert (2000), on the decentralization of health system organization in Bolivia, Chile, and Colombia, and Tang and Bloom (2000), on health service decentralization in rural China.[18] Second, findings from the qualitative approach are not usually generalizable; they are strongly dependent on local conditions (indeed, that is a strength of the method). This means that it is more difficult to apply the lessons learned in one case to another case and that any attempt to do so must carefully account for these differences in local conditions.

Table 2.8 summarizes several studies that have used qualitative tools to evaluate health reforms.

Quantitative methods

The majority of PSIA cases will involve some quantitative analysis. This is not to say that the information produced by these tools is always preferable to the information derived from the qualitative methods discussed above. In fact, the richest and most robust story will derive from *mixed methods*.[19] In this section, two of the quantitative methods are described that are commonly used to examine the distributional impact of health reforms. These are conventional econometric welfare analysis and experimental evaluation. These are illustrated in greater detail in *A User's Guide to Poverty and Social Impact Analysis* (World Bank 2003b).

The first method, *econometrics,* derives from a model of household welfare in which welfare (utility) is determined by health status and the consumption of other goods and services. Health outcomes, in turn, are modeled through a "production function," with individual, household, community, and other characteristics as inputs. Households maximize utility, subject to a budget constraint, by choosing the optimal combination of health services and other goods. From this solution can be derived a ("reduced-form") health-demand equation that can be estimated empirically as a function of prices and individual, household, and community characteristics.

A regression of the health-demand function using information commonly collected through household surveys and health-facility surveys provides an estimation of the marginal impact of policy changes. For example, the demand equation can be used to examine the impact of changes in user fees, improved access to health facilities, changes in quality, or any other *quantitatively measurable* policy change.

There are three main advantages to the econometric welfare approach. First, this method has a strong theoretical foundation, including

TABLE 2.8. Qualitative Analysis of Health Sector Reforms

Reform cases	Tools	Data sources	Examples	Comments
Expanding the role of the private sector	Stakeholder analysis, institutional and political analysis	Focus-group interviews	González-Rossetti and Bossert (2000) on Chile, Colombia, and Mexico	Identifies stakeholders, their interplay, their potential to influence the process, and the strategies used by reformers to pursue reforms.
Pharmaceutical policy reform	Political economy models	Case studies	Reich (1995) on pharmaceutical policy reform in Bangladesh, the Philippines, and Sri Lanka	Examines the political dynamics of health sector reform through a comparative study of pharmaceutical policy reform in three countries.
Decentralization of health services	Institutional analysis	Administrative data on public health facilities and utilization, focus-group interviews	Tang and Bloom (2000) on rural health service decentralization in China	Focuses on the impact of the devolution of health services on health service performance. The findings indicate that attempts to implement rapid decentralization without addressing the financial and institutional capacity of local governments can have negative consequences, as illustrated by the China case study.
Decentralization of health services	Stakeholder analysis	Focus-group interviews, case studies	Bossert (2000) on decentralization in Bolivia, Chile, and Colombia	The findings indicate that decentralization seems to improve utilization and equity in health expenditure over time in both Chile and Colombia. In Bolivia, the impact of decentralization depends on local institutional capacity.

Source: Compiled by the authors.

a clearly defined concept of welfare, which provides an analytical base for conducting distributional impact analysis. It is generally agreed what these methods measure, and the results are therefore comparable across studies and settings. Second, the method allows us to examine the *marginal* impact rather than the *average* impact of a policy change, that is, we can see the incremental value of the next dollar spent on a particular policy, rather than of the average dollar spent. This is important because there is no reason to believe that the impact of the next dollar will resemble the impact of an average dollar.[20] Third, this method can provide a basis for policy simulations of various reform scenarios. In other words, we can use these results to ask "what if?" for any number of changes to policy or social and environmental conditions. This can be extremely useful in designing policies and projecting the consequences of reforms.

The disadvantages to this approach revolve mainly around the fact that the reliability of the empirical results depends crucially on data quality and the correct specification of the health-demand function. Unfortunately, obtaining good data is difficult, and perfect data may be impossible to collect. Microbehavior is driven partly by nonmonetary costs and benefits, which are very hard to measure (Das and Hammer 2004). Analysis of the microlevel impact of health reforms therefore requires data that we cannot have or for which we must rely on imperfect proxies. In addition, the results are often driven by methods rather than by the data or by the question that needs to be answered. Different methods can yield different results. Please note that this does not mean that all econometric methods are equally suspect: differences may reflect problems in one method that can be corrected by another.

Addressing the misspecification of the health-demand function poses other formidable challenges to the analysis. The econometric evaluation of program impact suffers from the problems of *omitted variables* generally and *endogeneity* and *sample selection* problems specifically. For example, the impact of a child health intervention will depend on the motivation and behavior of the household in which the child lives. Children whose mothers are more able and willing to seek public health services and follow advice on the prevention of illness and disease are more likely to experience better child health outcomes. These households are also more likely to participate in government-promoted health programs. A naive evaluation runs the risk of ascribing to the intervention the benefits to the child of having a motivated mother. This problem would be minimized if we could measure the mother's motivation, but these variables (ability, knowledge, and willingness of mothers) are not directly observable.

These problems (omitted variables, sample selection, and measurement error) can yield misleading conclusions. Thus, the estimated coefficients of the health-demand function cannot be interpreted as a causal effect (that is, health policy changes generate changes in health outcomes); at best, they imply associations between the two sets of variables. Policy designs based on a misspecified health-demand function could produce serious, unintended welfare consequences. The push for introducing user fees to finance improvements in health services in developing countries in the 1990s provides a good illustration of the way invalid empirical results can bring about adverse welfare consequences. Box 2.1 presents a summary of studies on user fees and their impact on policy design.

Two econometric strategies can potentially correct the model-specification problem, but both are very data demanding. First, when panel data are available, taking the first difference of the demand function eliminates the time-invariant unobserved confounding factors. In practice, panel data are rare and expensive to collect, and they do not exist for many countries. Second, when selection into a program is unobserved, it is possible, in principle, to estimate the impact of the intervention using instru-

---

BOX 2.1 **Econometric Research on User Charges**

Early work on user charges was based on a regression framework of the health-demand function. This research found that prices were not an important determinant of demand, the relevant coefficients generally showing up as statistically insignificant or even positive in sign (Akin et al. 1984, 1986; Birdsall and Chuhan 1986; Heller 1982; Schwartz, Akin, and Popkin 1988).

Subsequent research indicated that the earlier results were mainly due to poor data quality and the misspecification of the estimation equation (Feldstein 1974; Gertler and van der Gaag 1988, 1990). More recent studies have found that prices are an important determinant of health demand in developing countries, with statistically significant negative price elasticities (Alderman and Gertler 1989; Cretin et al. 1988; Gertler, Locay, and Sanderson 1987; Mwabu 1986).

The policy implications and the potential welfare impact of user charges derived from the above two sets of research are clearly divergent. However, the understanding that the poor are price sensitive does not by itself imply that services should be provided free or at subsidized prices. The weight of empirical studies to date suggests that the benefits of subsidies will flow primarily to those who are better off rather than to the poor for whom the services are intended (Gwatkin 2003). Moreover, there is substantial evidence that consumers pay significant out-of-pocket charges for nominally "free" services (see, for example, Khan 2005).

mental variables. This requires the identification of a variable that determines the household's decision to participate in the program, but is not independently correlated with health outcomes. Valid instrumental variables are difficult to find. To some extent, good knowledge about program placement and implementation can help in identifying potential instrumental variables (see Baker 2000).

Table 2.9 presents a few examples of the use of quantitative econometric methods to simulate the impact of policies on health outcomes. This is clearly only suggestive: the list of references to this chapter and, indeed, most of the citations in Table 2.2 provide many examples of the use of quantitative econometric methods. Some of the studies presented in Table 2.9 are conducted ex ante, that is, prior to the introduction of policy changes, and some are conducted ex post, that is, following the policy changes. But they all share the same basic method, whereby demand parameters are derived econometrically, and then these are used to simulate the impact of the proposed policy change on behavior.

The search for solutions to the problems associated with cross-sectional econometric evaluation methods has led to the increased use of *experimental and quasi-experimental techniques,* especially to control for bias caused by nonrandom sample selection. These techniques are based on a simple comparison of differences between (usually two) subsamples drawn from the same population, one of which has received an intervention, while the other has not. In the scientific jargon, the first group is the *treatment* group, and the second is the *control.* The control group plays the role of *counterfactual,* permitting policy analysts to see what would have happened if the reform had not taken place.

There are two main strands to this literature, which can be distinguished by the underlying basis for the comparison between the treatment and control groups. In the first, the control group is selected ex post; in the second, the control and treatment groups are selected ex ante. Each is briefly described hereafter, and a few examples are presented.

The first method is often referred to as "quasi-experimental" evaluation and consists primarily of variants of *matching* methods. This involves creating the control group ex post, that is, from a sample that contains both treatment and control individuals (or households); one then selects the subsample of untreated individuals who most closely resemble the treated individuals. This is most commonly done by the method of *propensity-score matching* (see Cochrane and Rubin 1973; Rosenbaum and Rubin 1983). The propensity score is an estimate of the probability that any individual (treated or untreated) will receive the treatment, as a function of the individual's observed characteristics. Each treated individual is then matched

TABLE 2.9. Quantitative (Econometric) Studies of Health Sector Reforms

Case	Reference	Tools	Comments
Introduction of user charges in Peru	Gertler, Locay, and Sanderson 1987	Demand elasticities from the reduced-form health-demand function	The poorest two quintiles are more price sensitive than are other quintiles.
Distribution of government spending on education in India	Lanjouw and Ravallion 1999	Marginal benefit incidence analysis	Marginal incidence is significantly higher among the poor than it is among the non-poor, and marginal incidence among the poor is much higher than average incidence among the poor.
Determinants of health care demand in Uganda	Lawson 2004	Reduced-form health-demand functions for different segments of the population	Reducing travel time will increase the consumption of health care among all; reducing user fees will encourage consumption by women.
Placement of doctors in rural areas of Indonesia	Chomitz et al. 1997	Estimation of revealed preference and stated preference for location choices of physicians	Compensation and bonuses are likely to be more effective than compulsory postings, and more students from rural areas should be encouraged to train.
Social insurance in Hungary	Ravallion, van de Walle, and Gautam 1995	Simulations of the distribution of consumption over time	Cash benefits introduced to compensate for other policy reforms protected many from poverty, but promoted few out of poverty.
Community-based health insurance in Senegal	Jütting 2001	Estimation of the impact of participation on consumption and financial protection	Although the program reaches otherwise excluded people, the poorest in the communities are not covered.
Government subsidies for a health insurance program in Egypt	Yip and Berman 2001	Estimation of the impact of a school-based health insurance program on consumption and financial protection	The program increased visit rates and reduced out-of-pocket expenditures, especially among the poor, but only middle-income children benefited from the reduced financial cost.

Source: Compiled by the authors.

with one or more untreated individuals who are most closely similar based on the estimated propensity score. The control group is then the subsample of untreated individuals who are otherwise nearly identical (that is, "matched") to the treated individuals. The impact of the treatment can be seen as the difference in mean outcomes between the treated group and the matched, untreated control group.[21]

The main advantage of matching methods is that they can draw on existing datasets and are often more rapid and less expensive to implement.[22] The principal disadvantage of this method is that it may not completely solve the problem of selection bias: selection into the treatment group may be a function of unobserved characteristics. In addition, matching methods can be statistically complex, requiring considerable expertise in the design of the evaluation and in the analysis and interpretation of the results.

The second method involves experimental, randomized controlled trials. These studies require a sample of individuals equally eligible and willing to receive treatment. One subsample is randomly assigned to the treatment group, and the remainder is assigned to the control group, which does not receive the treatment. This is generally considered the most robust evaluation method. The random assignment process creates comparable treatment and control groups that are statistically equivalent to one another, given appropriate sample sizes. In principle, control groups generated through random assignment serve as a perfect counterfactual, free from the problems of selection bias that plague evaluations.

The benefits of this technique are the robustness and simplicity of the results: the impact of the intervention can be measured simply as the difference between the mean measured outcomes of the samples of the treatment group and the control group. Although experimental designs are considered the ideal approach to estimating project impact, there are several problems in practice:

- Randomization may be unethical or may be perceived as unethical.
- It can be politically difficult to provide an intervention for one group and not another.
- Nationwide programs or policy changes leave no room for a control group.
- Circumstances and the behavior of participants may change during the experiment: people move or may seek alternative treatment.
- Assignment may not be truly random: program administrators may exclude high-risk applicants to achieve better results.
- Experimental designs can be expensive and time consuming in certain situations, particularly in the collection of new data.

TABLE 2.10. Experimental and Quasi-Experimental Evaluations in Health

Case	Reference	Findings
Method: quasi-experimental, matching		
Privatization of water services in Argentina	Galiani, Gertler, and Schargrodsky 2005	Increase in connections was greater, and child mortality was significantly lower in privatized municipalities.
Water and sewerage provision in Ecuador	Galdo and Briceno 2004	Impact was significant on child mortality; among the poor, the decrease was significant only among households in which women had at least primary education.
Piped water in rural India	Jalan and Ravallion 2003	Drop was significant in diarrhea incidence and duration; among the poor, the decrease was significant only among households in which women had at least primary education.
Method: randomized controlled trial		
Deworming, health externalities, and education in Kenya	Miguel and Kremer 2001	Deworming led to more rapid growth and lower anemia among treated children and had significantly positive external effects among untreated children and neighboring nonparticipating schools.
Progresa (cash-transfer and incentive program) and health outcomes	Gertler 2000	Progresa increased consumption of primary care, lowered hospitalization, and improved health among both children and adults.
Deworming and child growth in Uganda	Alderman, Sebuliba, et al. 2004	Deworming led to more rapid weight gain among treated children.
Early childhood nutrition program in Uganda	Alderman, Britto, et al. 2004	Program significantly prolonged breastfeeding; increased consumption of milk, legumes, porridge, fruits, and vegetables; there was greater frequency of primary care visits and greater school enrollment.

Source: Compiled by the authors.

An important extension of these methods involves conducting the evaluation not on a static comparison of levels or outcomes between the treatment and control groups, but as the "difference in differences" between groups, that is, examining the difference in the *changes* in outcomes across groups. This will eliminate the influence of those unobserved characteristics that are time invariant (the characteristics that do not change during the period of the study).[23] This requires a baseline and follow-up surveys (panel data for comparisons across individuals).

Table 2.10 presents some examples of both experimental and quasi-experimental (matching) evaluations. They are primarily evaluations of specific interventions rather than large-scale multifaceted programs. That is not to say that these methods are not applicable to larger programs. Rigorous evaluation was key to the design of the Progresa program in Mexico and has been ongoing since before the program's launch in 1997. Fundamental to these types of evaluations, however, is the existence of a control group. Without external controls, it is only possible with these methods to conduct a "before and after" comparison within the treatment group itself. While some confounding unobservable characteristics may be controlled through instrumental variables, it is likely that the results will be biased by selection problems.

NOTES

1. In the literature on health sector reforms, it is common to equate these with *allocative* and *technical* efficiency, respectively.
2. Health care is seen as a *merit good,* that is, a good that we have decided is beneficial for people to consume, regardless of their own feelings in the matter. Health has *external effects,* that is, one person's health behavior and status affect the health and welfare of others.
3. See, for example, Wagstaff (2002) for a summary of inequality in the health sector.
4. The RAND health care experiment in the United States found that higher copayments reduced health care consumption, but had little impact on health, implying that people seek unnecessary care when the cost per visit is low (Newhouse and the Insurance Experiment Group 1993).
5. See, for instance, *World Development Report 1997* (World Bank 1997a).
6. Hsiao (2000) specifies a set of "control knobs"—financing, payment, organization, regulation, and consumer behavior—that capture the full range of health reforms.
7. Developing-country tax revenue is about 18 percent of gross domestic product, compared to 38 percent among countries of the Organisation for Economic Co-operation and Development (Tanzi and Zee 2001).
8. In addition to the references cited in Table 2.2, see Atim (1998) and Stinson (1982).
9. The exception was West Bengal.
10. *Human Resources for Health,* http://www.human-resources-health.com/.
11. It must be noted that these two goals are sometimes in conflict: what is good for any one particular patient may not be in the best public interest.

12. There is little evidence that the actual risk of HIV infection is higher among health workers. See Marchal, De Brouwere, and Kegels (2005).

13. Once this group had decided on a package of reforms, these were pilot tested, partly to gauge the reaction of communities to the proposed reforms.

14. The factors include better nutrition, mother's education, access to safe water and sanitation, access to electricity, and so on, in addition to health sector outputs such as immunization and basic health services.

15. For excellent introductions and instructions for these measures, see the technical notes, especially 7, 12, and 16, at http://web.worldbank.org/WBSITE/ EXTERNAL/TOPICS/EXTHEALTHNUTRITIONANDPOPULATION/ EXTPAH/0,,contentMDK:20216933~menuPK:460204~pagePK:148956~pi PK:216618~theSitePK:400476,00.html.

16. See Lanjouw et al. (2002); Lanjouw and Ravallion (1999); Younger (2003).

17. To make this a bit more concrete, imagine that a group of highly motivated parents lobby successfully for a child health intervention. Comparing the children who had received this intervention to a group of other children would conflate the beneficial consequences of the motivation of the parents on their children with the benefits of the intervention. The benefits of motivation are likely to be high, perhaps even higher than the benefits of the intervention itself. See Newman et al. (2002); Newman, Rawlings, and Gertler (1994).

18. Tang and Bloom (2000) indicate that rapid decentralization that does not address weaknesses in the financial and institutional capacity of local governments can have an adverse impact on the quality of health services, and poor areas are likely to be disproportionately affected. However, distributional issues are not explicitly analyzed. According to Bossert (2000), local stakeholders perceive that decentralization has improved service quality; but Bossert acknowledges that these findings are based on rather limited information.

19. See, for example, Bamberger (2000); Hentschel (1999); Rao and Ibanez (2003); and Woolcock (2001).

20. This is most clearly illustrated by the universal phenomenon of nonlinear costs. In a program to vaccinate 1 million children, for instance, the marginal cost of reaching the millionth child is likely to be much higher than the cost of reaching the thousandth child. Also see the discussion on marginal benefit incidence analysis in the section titled "What distribution?".

21. Becker and Ichino (1999) and Ravallion (2003) provide excellent explanations of the steps involved in the propensity-score-matching method.

22. This and the following three paragraphs draw on Baker 2000.

23. This includes factors such as the education of the parents of the included adults, ethnicity, religion, and place of birth, and other unobserved characteristics that might influence health behavior. However, the influence of unobserved individual characteristics that change during the study may be increased by differencing.

BIBLIOGRAPHY

Abel-Smith, B., and P. Rawal. 1992. "Can the Poor Afford 'Free' Health Services?: A Case Study of Tanzania." *Health Policy and Planning* 7 (4): 329–41.

———. 1994. "Employers' Willingness to Pay: The Case for Compulsory Health Insurance in Tanzania." *Health Policy and Planning* 9 (4): 409–18.

Aga Khan Health Services. 2004. "Health Facility Committees: The Governance Issue." Policy Brief 4, Best Practices in Community-Based Health Initiatives, Community Health Department, Aga Khan Health Services in Kenya, Nairobi.

Aitken, J.-M., and J. Kemp. 2003. "HIV/AIDS, Equity, and Health Sector Personnel in Southern Africa." Equinet Discussion Paper 12, Network for Equity in Health in Southern Africa, Harare, Zimbabwe.

Akin, J., S. C. Griffin, D. K. Guilkey, and B. M. Popkin. 1984. *The Demand for Primary Health Care in Developing Countries.* Totowa, NJ: Littlefield, Adams.

———. 1986. "The Demand for Primary Health Care Services in the Bicol Region of the Philippines." *Economic Development and Cultural Change* 34 (4): 755–82.

Alderman, H., P. Britto, P. Engle, and A. Siddiqi. 2004. "Longitudinal Evaluation of Uganda Nutrition and Early Child Development Program." Unpublished manuscript, World Bank, Washington, DC.

Alderman, H., and P. J. Gertler. 1989. "The Substitutability of Public and Private Health Care for the Treatment of Children in Pakistan." Living Standards Measurement Study Working Paper 57. World Bank, Washington, DC.

Alderman, H., and V. Lavy. 1996. "Household Responses to Public Health Services: Cost and Quality Trade-Offs." *World Bank Research Observer* 11 (1): 3–22.

Alderman, H., I. Sebuliba, J. Konde-Lule, and A. Hall. 2004. "Increased Weight Gain with Mass Deworming Given during Child Health Days in Uganda." Unpublished manuscript, World Bank, Washington, DC.

Arhin-Tenkorang, D. 2000. "Mobilizing Resources for Health: The Case for User Fees Revisited." CMH Working Paper Series WG3: 6, Commission on Macroeconomics and Health, World Health Organization, Geneva.

———. 2004. "Experience of Community Health Financing in the African Region." In *Health Financing for Poor People: Resource Mobilization and Risk Sharing*, ed. A. S. Preker and G. Carrin. Washington, DC: World Bank; Geneva: World Health Organization; Geneva: International Labour Office.

Asada, Y., and T. Hedemann. 2002. "A Problem with the Individual Approach in the WHO Health Inequality Measurement." *International Journal for Equity in Health* 1 (2). http://www.equityhealthj.com/content/1/1/2.

Asenso-Okyere, W. K., A. Anum, I. Osei-Akoto, and A. Adukonu. 1998. "Cost Recovery in Ghana: Are There Any Changes in Health Care Seeking Behavior?" *Health Policy and Planning* 13 (2): 181–88.

Atim, C. 1998. "Contribution of Mutual Health to Financing, Delivery, and Access to Health Care: Synthesis of Research in Nine West and Central African Countries." Technical Report 18, Partnerships for Health Reform Project, Abt Associates Inc., Bethesda, MD.

————. 1999. "Social Movements and Health Insurance: A Critical Evaluation of Voluntary, Non-Profit Insurance Schemes with Case Studies from Ghana and Cameroon." *Social Science and Medicine* 48: 881–96.

Atkinson, S., and D. Haran. 2004. "Back to Basics: Does Decentralization Improve Health System Performance?: Evidence from Ceará in North-East Brazil." *Bulletin of the World Health Organization* 82 (11): 822–32.

Bailey, M. 2001. "Priced Out of Reach." Briefing Paper 4, Oxfam International, Washington, DC.

Baker, J. L. 2000. *Evaluating the Impact of Development Projects on Poverty: A Handbook for Practitioners.* Directions in Development. Washington, DC: World Bank.

Bamberger, M. 2000. "Opportunities and Challenges for Integrating Quantitative and Qualitative Research." In *Integrating Quantitative and Qualitative Research in Development Projects,* ed. M. Bamberger, 3–36. Washington, DC: World Bank.

Barnum, H., J. Kutzin, and H. Saxenian. 1995. "Incentives and Provider Payment Methods." Human Resources Development and Operations Policy Working Paper 51, World Bank, Washington, DC.

Bassi, L. 1983. "Estimating the Effects of Training Programs with Nonrandom Selection." *Review of Economics and Statistics* 66: 36–43.

Becker, S. O., and A. Ichino. 1999. "Estimation of Average Treatment Effects Based on Propensity Scores." *The Stata Journal* 2 (4): 358–77.

Beegle, K. 1995. "The Quality and Availability of Family Planning Services and Contraceptive Use in Tanzania." Living Standards Measurement Study Working Paper 114, World Bank, Washington, DC.

Bennett, F. 1979. "Primary Health Care and Developing Countries." *Social Science and Medicine* 13A (5): 505–14.

Bennett, S., A. Creese, and R. Monasch. 1998. "Health Insurance Schemes for People Outside Formal Sector Employment." ARA Paper 16, Division of Analysis, Research, and Assessment, World Health Organization, Geneva.

Bennett, S., and L. Gilson. 2001. *Health Financing: Designing and Implementing Pro-Poor Policies.* London: Health Systems Resource Centre, Department for International Development.

Bennett, S., B. McPake, and A. Mills, eds. 1997. *Private Health Providers in Developing Countries: Serving the Public Interest?* London: Zed Books.

Berman, P. A., ed. 1995. *Health Sector Reform in Developing Countries: Making Health Development Sustainable.* Cambridge, MA: Harvard University Press; *Health Policy* 32 (1–3).

————. 1997. "National Health Accounts in Developing Countries: Appropriate Methods and Recent Applications." *Health Economics* 6 (1): 11–30.

Berman, P. A., and T. J. Bossert. 2000. "A Decade of Health Sector Reform in Developing Countries: What Have We Learned?" Paper prepared for the Data for Decision Making Project Symposium, "Appraising a Decade of Health Sector Reform in Developing Countries," Washington, DC, March 15.

Bertozzi, S. M., B. Aracena, L. Cahuana, A. Corcho, K. Rely, and V. Zurita. 2001. "Study on Costs of Scaling-Up Health Interventions for the Poor in Latin-American Settings: Final Report." Working Group 5, Commission on Macroeconomics and Health, World Health Organization, Geneva.

Besley, T., and S. Coate. 1991. "Public Provision of Private Goods and the Redistribution of Income." *American Economic Review* 81 (4): 979–84.

Bhushan, I., S. Keller, and B. Schwartz. 2002. "Achieving the Twin Objectives of Efficiency and Equity: Contracting Health Services in Cambodia." ERD Policy Brief 6, Economics and Research Department, Asian Development Bank, Manila.

Binam, J. N., A. Nkama, and R. Nkendah. (2004). "Estimating the Willingness to Pay for Community Health Prepayment Schemes in Rural Areas: A Case Study of the Use of Contingent Valuation Surveys in Central Cameroon." Unpublished manuscript, Institute of Agricultural Research for Development, Farming Systems, Economy and Rural Sociology Division, Yaoundé, Cameroon. http://www.csae.ox.ac.uk/conferences/2004-GPRaHDiA/papers/4h-Binam-CSAE2004.pdf.

Bir, A., and K. Eggleston. 2003. "Physician Dual Practice: Access Enhancement or Demand Inducement?" Working Paper 2003-11, Department of Economics, Tufts University, Boston.

Birdsall, N., and P. Chuhan. 1986. "Client Choice of Health Treatment in Rural Mali." Unpublished manuscript, Population and Rural Resources Department, World Bank, Washington, DC.

Birdsall, N., and E. James. 1993. "Health, Government, and the Poor: The Case for the Private Sector." In *The Epidemiological Transition: Policy and Planning Implications for Developing Countries,* ed. J. N. Gribble and S. H. Preston. Washington, DC: National Academy Press.

Bitrán, R. 2001. "Paying Healthcare Providers through Capitation in Argentina, Nicaragua, and Thailand: Output, Spending, Organizational Impact, and Market Structure." Major Applied Research 2, Technical Paper, Partnerships for Health Reform Project, Abt Associates Inc., Bethesda, MD.

Bitrán, R., and U. Giedion. 2003. "Waivers and Exemptions for Health Services in Developing Countries." Social Protection Discussion Paper 0308, Social Protection Unit, Human Development Network, World Bank, Washington, DC.

Bitrán, R., and C. Muñoz. 2000. "Targeting Methodologies: Conceptual Approach and Analysis of Experiences." Partnerships for Health Reform Project, Latin America and Caribbean Regional Health Sector Reform Initiative. http://www.lachsr.org/documents/targetingmethodologiesconceptualapproachandanalysisofexperiences-EN.pdf.

Bitrán, R., and W. C. Yip. 1998. "A Review of Health Care Provider Payment Reform in Selected Countries in Asia and Latin America." Major Applied Research 2 Working Paper 1, Abt Associates Inc., Bethesda, MD.

Bloom, G., L. Han, and Xiang Li. 2001. "How Health Workers Earn a Living in China." *Human Resources for Health Development Journal* 5 (1–3): 25–38.

Blundell, R., and M. Costa-Dias. 2000. "Evaluation Methods for Non-Experimental Data." *Fiscal Studies* 21 (4): 427–68.

Blundell, R., M. Costa-Dias, C. Meghir, and J. van Reenen. 2000. "Evaluating the Employment Impact of Mandatory Job-Search Assistance: The UK New Deal Gateway." Unpublished manuscript, Institute for Fiscal Studies, London.

Bossert, T. J. 1998. "Analyzing the Decentralization of Health Systems in Developing Countries: Decision Space, Innovation, and Performance." *Social Science and Medicine* 47 (10): 1513–27.

———. 2000. "Decentralization of Health Systems in Latin America: A Comparative Analysis of Chile, Colombia, and Bolivia." Latin America and the Caribbean Health Sector Reform Initiative Working Paper, Harvard School of Public Health, Boston.

Brenzel, L. 1993. "Selecting an Essential Package of Health Services Using Cost-Effectiveness Analysis: A Manual for Professionals in Developing Countries." Population and Human Resources Sector, Population, Health, and Nutrition Department, World Bank, Washington, DC; Data for Decision Making Project, Department of Population Studies and International Health, Harvard School of Public Health, Boston.

Brinkerhoff, D. 1996. "Process Perspectives on Policy Change: Highlighting Implementation." *World Development* 24: 1395–401. Quoted in Gilson (1997).

———. 2000. "Democratic Governance and Sectoral Policy Reform: Tracing Linkages and Exploring Synergies." *World Development* 28 (4): 601–15.

———. 2003. *Accountability and Health Systems: Overview, Framework, and Strategies.* Bethesda, MD: Abt Associates Inc.

Bumgarner, J. R., ed. 1992. *China: Long-Term Issues and Options in the Health Transition.* World Bank Country Study. Washington, DC: World Bank.

Caines, K., and L. Lush. 2004. "Impact of Public-Private Partnerships Addressing Access to Pharmaceuticals in Selected Low- and Middle-Income Countries: A Synthesis Report from Studies in Botswana, Sri Lanka, Uganda, and Zambia." Initiative on Public-Private Partnerships for Health, Global Forum for Health Research, Geneva.

Carrin, G., M. Desmet, and R. Basaza. 2001. "Social Health Insurance Development in Low-Income Developing Countries: New Roles for Government and Non-Profit Health Insurance Organizations." In *Building Social Security: The Challenge of Privatization.* International Social Security Series, vol. 6, ed. X. Scheil-Adlung, 125–53. London: Transaction Publishers.

Cassels, A., and K. Janovsky. 1996. "Reform of the Health Sector in Ghana and Zambia: Commonalities and Contrasts." SHS Paper 11, WHO/SHS/CC/96.1, Division of Strengthening of Health Services, World Health Organization, Geneva.

Castro-Leal, F., J. Dayton, L. Demery, and K. Mehra. 2000. "Public Spending on Health Care in Africa: Do the Poor Benefit?" *Bulletin of the World Health Organization* 78 (1): 66–74.

Chakraborty, S., R. Gatti, J. Klugman, and G. Gray-Molina. 2002. "When is 'Free' Not So Free?: Informal Payments for Basic Health Services in Bolivia." Unpublished manuscript, World Bank, Washington, DC.

Chaudhury, N., and J. S. Hammer. 2003. "Ghost Doctors: Absenteeism in Bangladeshi Health Facilities." Policy Research Working Paper 3065, World Bank, Washington, DC.

Chaudhury, N., J. S. Hammer, and E. Murrugarra. 2003. "The Effects of a Fee-Waiver Program on Health Care Utilization among the Poor: Evidence from Armenia." Policy Research Working Paper 2952, World Bank, Washington, DC.

Cheng, S., and T. Chiang. 1997. "The Effect of Universal Health Insurance on Health Care Utilization in Taiwan." *Journal of the American Medical Association* 278: 89–93.

Chiappori, P. A., F. Durand, and P. Y. Geoffard. 1998. "Moral Hazard and the Demand for Physician Services: First Lessons from a French Natural Experiment." *European Economic Review* 42 (3–5): 499–511.

Chomitz, K. M., G. Setiadi, A. Azwar, N. Ismail, and Widiyarti. 1997. "What Do Doctors Want?: Developing Incentives for Doctors to Serve in Indonesia's Rural and Remote Areas." Policy Research Working Paper 1888, World Bank, Washington, DC.

Chung, K. 2000. "Issues and Approaches in the Use of Integrated Methods." In *Integrating Quantitative and Qualitative Research in Development Projects,* ed. M. Bamberger, 37–46. Washington, DC: World Bank.

Cochrane, W., and D. Rubin. 1973. "Controlling Bias in Observational Studies." *Sankyha* 35: 417–46.

Collier, P., S. Dercon, and J. Mackinnon. 2002. "Density versus Quality in Health Care Provision: Using Household Data to Make Budgetary Choices in Ethiopia." CSAE Working Paper 2002-17, Centre for the Study of African Economies, Oxford University, Oxford.

Collins, C., J. Araujo, and J. Barbosa. 2000. "Decentralizing the Health Sector: Issues in Brazil." *Health Policy* 52: 113–27.

Cornwall, A. 2000. "Beneficiary, Consumer, Citizen: Perspectives on Participation for Poverty Reduction." SIDA Studies 2, Swedish International Development Cooperation Agency, Stockholm.

Cornwall, A., H. Lucas, and K. Pasteur, eds. 2000. "Accountability through Participation: Developing Workable Partnership Models in the Health Sector." *Institute of Development Studies Bulletin* 31 (1).

Creese, A., and S. Bennett. 1997. "Rural Risk-Sharing Strategies." In *Innovations in Health Care Financing.* Proceedings of a World Bank Conference, March 10–11, 1997, ed. G. Schieber. Washington, DC: World Bank.

Cretin, S., E. Keeler, A. Williams, and Y. Shi. 1988. "Factors Affecting Two Town-Countryside Differences in the Use of Health Services in Two Rural Counties in Sichuan." Unpublished manuscript, Rand Corporation, Santa Monica, CA.

Criel, B., P. Van der Stuyft, and W. Van Lerberghe. 1999. "The Bwamanda Hospital Insurance Scheme: Effective for Whom?, A Study of Its Impact on Hospitalisation and Utilisation Patterns." *Social Science and Medicine* 48 (7): 879–911.

Das, J., and J. S. Hammer. 2004. "Which Doctor?: Combining Vignettes and Item Response to Measure Doctor Quality." Policy Research Working Paper 3301, Public Services, Development Research Group, World Bank, Washington, DC.

Deaton, A., and J. Muellbauer. 1980. *Economics and Consumer Behavior.* Cambridge: Cambridge University Press.

Dehn, J., R. Reinikka, and J. Svensson. 2003. "Survey Tools for Assessing Performance in Service Delivery." Unpublished manuscript, World Bank, Washington, DC.

Deininger, K., and P. Mpuga. 2004. "Economic and Welfare Effects of the Abolition of Health User Fees: Evidence from Uganda." Policy Research Working Paper 3276, Rural Development, Development Research Group, World Bank, Washington, DC.

de la Jara, J. J., and T. J. Bossert. 1995. "Chile's Health Sector Reform: Lessons from Four Reform Periods." *Health Policy* 32 (1–3): 155–66.

Demery, L. 2003. "Analyzing the Incidence of Public Spending." In *The Impact of Economic Policies on Poverty and Income Distribution: Evaluation Techniques and Tools,* ed. F. Bourguignon and L. Pereira da Silva, 41–68. Washington, DC: World Bank; New York: Oxford University Press.

Demery, L., S. Y. Chao, R. Bernier, and K. Mehra. 1995. "The Incidence of Social Spending in Ghana." PSP Discussion Papers 82, Poverty and Social Policy Department, World Bank, Washington, DC.

Diderichsen, F. 2004. "Resource Allocation for Health Equity: Issues and Methods." Health, Nutrition, and Population Discussion Paper, World Bank, Washington, DC.

Diop, F., A. Yazbeck, and R. Bitrán. 1995. "The Impact of Alternative Cost Recovery Schemes on Access and Equity in Niger." *Health Policy and Planning* 10: 223–40.

Druce, N. 2004. "Access to Medicines in Under-Served Markets." Overview Paper, Health Systems Resource Centre, Department for International Development, London.

Dusheiko, M., H. Gravelle, R. Jacobs, and P. Smith. 2003. "The Effects of Budgets on Doctor Behaviour: Evidence from a Natural Experiment." Discussion Paper 2003/04, Department of Economics, University of York, York, United Kingdom.

Dussault, G., and C.-A. Dubois. 2003. "Human Resources for Health Policies: A Critical Component in Health Policies." *Human Resources for Health* 1 (1). http://www.human-resources-health.com/content/1/1/1.

Eggleston, K., and C.-R. Hsieh. 2004. "Health Care Payment Incentives: A Comparative Analysis of Reforms in Taiwan, Korea and China." Working Paper 2004-2, Department of Economics, Tufts University, Boston.

Egypt, Ministry of Health and Population, Department of Planning. 1995. "National Health Accounts for Egypt." Data for Decision Making Project,

Department of Population Studies and International Health, Harvard School of Public Health, Boston.

Elbers, C., J. Lanjouw, and P. Lanjouw. 2003. "Micro-Level Estimation of Poverty and Inequality." *Econometrica* 71 (1): 355–64.

Enemark, U., and F. Schleimann. 1999. "Financing Health Services in Poor Countries: Feeding a White Elephant?" Discussion Paper 1, Danish International Development Agency, Copenhagen.

England, R. 2002. *Contracting and Performance Management in the Health Sector: Some Pointers on How to Do It.* London: Health Systems Resource Centre, Department for International Development.

———. 2004. *Experiences of Contracting with the Private Sector: A Selective Review.* London: Health Systems Resource Centre, Department for International Development.

Ensor, T. 2003. *Consumer-Led Demand Side Financing for Health and Education: An International Review.* Oxford, United Kingdom: Oxford Policy Management.

———. 2004. "Informal Payments for Health Care in Transition Economies." *Social Science and Medicine* 58 (2): 237–46.

Ensor, T., and S. Cooper. 2004. "Overcoming Barriers to Health Service Access: Influencing the Demand Side." *Health Policy and Planning* 19 (2): 69–79.

Fairbank, A., M. Makinen, W. Schott, and B. Sakagawa. 2000. "Poverty Reduction and Immunizations: Considering Immunizations in the Context of Debt Relief for Poor Countries." Abt Associates Inc., Bethesda, MD. http://www.gaviftf.info/forum/bb2/7-21_hipc.pdf.

Feldstein, M. 1974. "Econometric Studies of Health." In *Four Frontiers of Quantitative Economics,* vol. 2, ed. M. Intriligator and D. Kendrick, 377–442. Amsterdam: North-Holland.

Feng, X. S., S. L. Tang, G. Bloom, M. Segall, and X. Y. Gu. 1995. "Cooperative Medical Schemes in Contemporary Rural China." *Social Science and Medicine* 41 (8): 1111–18.

Ferrinho, P., W. Van Lerberghe, I. Fronteira, F. Hipólito, and A. Biscaia. 2004. "Dual Practice in the Health Sector: Review of the Evidence." *Human Resources for Health* 2 (14). http://www.human-resources-health.com/content/2/1/14.

Filmer, D., J. S. Hammer, and L. Pritchett. 2000. "Weak Links in the Chain: A Diagnosis of Health Policy in Poor Countries." *World Bank Research Observer* 15 (2): 199–224.

———. 2002. "Weak Links in the Chain II: A Prescription for Health Policy in Poor Countries." *World Bank Research Observer* 17 (1): 47–66.

Filmer, D., and L. Pritchett. 1998. "Estimating Wealth Effects without Expenditure Data or Tears: With an Application to Educational Enrollments in States of India." Policy Research Working Paper 1944, Development Research Group, Poverty and Human Resources, World Bank, Washington, DC.

Foster, M., and S. Mackintosh-Walker. 2001. "Sector Wide Programmes and Poverty Reduction." Centre for Aid and Public Expenditure Working Paper 157, Overseas Development Institute, London.

Fujii, T. 2003. "Maps of Anthropometric Indicators: Using Cambodia DHS and Census." Unpublished manuscript, Agricultural and Resource Economics, University of California, Berkeley, CA.

Futures Group International. 2000. "Health Reform, Decentralization, and Participation in Latin America: Protecting Sexual and Reproductive Health." Policy Project, Futures Group International, Washington, DC.

Galdo, V., and B. Briceno. 2004. "Evaluating the Impact on Child Mortality of a Water Supply Project and Sewerage Expansion in Quito, Ecuador." Unpublished manuscript, Office of Evaluation and Oversight, Inter-American Development Bank, Washington, DC.

Galiani, S., P. J. Gertler, and E. Schargrodsky. 2005. "Water for Life: The Impact of the Privatization of Water Services on Child Mortality." *Journal of Political Economy* 113 (1): 83–120.

Gelbach, J. B., and L. H. Pritchett. 1995. "Does More for the Poor Mean Less for the Poor?: The Politics of Tagging." Policy Research Working Paper 1523, World Bank, Washington, DC.

George, A. 2003. "Accountability in Health Services: Transforming Relationships and Contexts." HCPDS Working Paper Series 13 (1), Harvard Center for Population and Development Studies, Cambridge, MA.

Gerdtham, U.-G., C. Rehnberg, and M. Tambour. 1999. "The Impact of Internal Markets on Health Care Efficiency: Evidence from Health Care Reforms in Sweden." *Applied Economics* 31 (8): 935–45.

Gertler, P. J. 1998. "On the Road to Social Health Insurance: The Asian Experience." *World Development* 26 (4): 717–32.

———. 2000. "Final Report: The Impact of Progresa on Health." Unpublished manuscript, International Food Policy Research Institute, Washington, DC.

Gertler, P. J., L. Locay, and W. C. Sanderson. 1987. "Are User Fees Regressive?: The Welfare Implications of Health Care Financing Proposals in Peru." *Journal of Econometrics* 36 (1–2) (supplement): 67–88.

Gertler, P. J., and O. Solon. 2000. "Who Benefits from Social Health Insurance?: Evidence from the Philippines." NBER Working Paper XXX, Haas School of Business, University of California at Berkeley, Berkeley, CA.

Gertler, P. J., and R. Sturm. 1997. "Private Health Insurance and Public Expenditures in Jamaica." *Journal of Econometrics* 77 (1): 237–57.

Gertler, P. J., and J. van der Gaag. 1988. "The Willingness to Pay for Social Services in Developing Countries." Living Standards Measurement Study Working Paper 45, World Bank, Washington, DC.

———. 1990. *The Willingness to Pay for Medical Care: Evidence from Two Developing Countries.* Baltimore: Johns Hopkins University Press.

Gilson, L. 1997. "Implementing and Evaluating Health Reform Processes: Lessons from the Literature." Major Applied Research 1 Working Paper 1, Partnerships for Health Reform Project, Abt Associates Inc., Bethesda, MD.

———. 1998. "In Defense and Pursuit of Equity." *Social Science and Medicine* 47 (12): 1891–96.

González-Rossetti, A., and T. J. Bossert. 2000. "Enhancing the Political Feasibility of Health Reform: A Comparative Analysis of Chile, Colombia, and Mexico." Data for Decision Making Project and the Latin American and Caribbean Health Sector Reform Initiative, Department of Population Studies and International Health, Harvard School of Public Health, Boston.

Gorter, A. 2003. "Competitive Vouchers for Health." Background paper, Instituto CentroAmericano de la Salud, Managua, Nicaragua; World Bank, Washington, DC.

Grace, C. 2003. "Equitable Pricing of Newer Essential Medicines for Developing Countries: Evidence for the Potential of Different Mechanisms." Unpublished manuscript, London Business School, London.

Griffin, C. C. 1992. *Health Care in Asia: A Comparative Study of Cost and Financing.* World Bank Regional and Sectoral Studies. Washington, DC: World Bank.

Gruen, R., R. Anwar, T. Begum, J. R. Killingsworth, and C. Normand. 2002. "Dual Job Holding Practitioners in Bangladesh: An Exploration." *Social Science and Medicine* 54 (2): 267–79.

Gumber, A. 2002. "Health Insurance for the Informal Sector: Problems and Prospects." Working Paper 90, Indian Council for Research on International Economic Relations, New Delhi.

Gumber, A., and V. Kulkarni. 2000. "Health Insurance for the Informal Sector: Case Study of Gujarat." *Economic and Political Weekly,* September 30: 3607–13.

Gwatkin, D. R. 2003. "Free Government Health Services: Are They the Best Way to Reach the Poor?" Unpublished manuscript, World Bank, Washington, DC.

Gwatkin, D. R., S. Rutstein, K. Johnson, R. P. Poande, and A. Wagstaff. 2000. "Socioeconomic Differences in Health, Nutrition, and Population." Health, Nutrition, and Population Discussion Paper, Health, Nutrition, and Population Family, Human Development Network, World Bank, Washington, DC.

Hall, J. J., and R. Taylor. 2003. "Health for All Beyond 2000: The Demise of the Alma-Ata Declaration and Primary Health Care in Developing Countries." *Medical Journal of Australia* 178 (1): 17–20.

Hammer, J. S. 1993. "The Economics of Malaria Control." *World Bank Research Observer* 8 (1): 1–22.

Hammer, J. S., and W. Jack. 2001. "The Design of Incentives for Health Care Providers in Developing Countries: Contracts, Competition, and Cost Control." Policy Research Working Paper 2547, World Bank, Washington, DC.

Hanvoravongchai, P. 2002. "Medical Savings Accounts: Lessons Learned from International Experience." EIP/HFS/PHF Discussion Paper 52, World Health Organization, Geneva.

Heller, P. 1982. "A Model of Demand for Medical and Health Services in Peninsular Malaysia." *Social Science and Medicine* 16: 267–84.

Hentschel, J. 1999. "Contextuality and Data Collection Methods: A Framework and Application to Health Service Utilisation." *Journal of Development Studies* 35 (4): 64–94.

Hindu (Chennai, Madras, India). 2005. "Law on Service in Rural Areas for Doctors Likely," April 7. http://www.hindu.com/2005/04/07/stories/2005040708310400.htm.

Hope, R. L. 2003. "Paying in Potatoes: Community-Based Health Insurance for the Rural and Informal Sector." *The Lancet* 362 (938): 827–29.

Hsiao, W. C. 2000. "Inside the Black Box of Health Systems." Program on Health Care Financing, Harvard School of Public Health, Boston.

————. 2001. "Commentary: Behind the Ideology and Theory, What is the Empirical Evidence for Medical Savings Accounts?" *Journal of Health Politics, Policy and Law* 26 (4): 733–37.

————. 2004. "Experience of Community Health Financing in the Asian Region." In *Health Financing for Poor People: Resource Mobilization and Risk Sharing*, ed. A. S. Preker and G. Carrin. Washington, DC: World Bank; Geneva: World Health Organization; Geneva: International Labour Office.

Human Resources for Health (various). http://www.human-resources-health.com/.

Hurley, J. 2001. "Medical Savings Accounts in Publicly Financed Health Care Systems: What Do We Know?" Research Working Paper 01–12, Centre for Health Economics and Policy Analysis, McMaster University, Hamilton, Ontario, Canada.

Hurst, J. W. 1992. "The Reform of Health Care: A Comparative Analysis of Seven OECD Countries." OECD Health Policy Studies 2, Organisation for Economic Co-operation and Development, Paris.

Hutton, G. 2000. "Indicators for Monitoring Health Sector Reform and the Sector-Wide Approach." Presentation at Sector-Wide Approach in Health Conference, "Moving from Policy to Practice," Royal Tropical Institute, Amsterdam, November 27–28.

INEI (Instituto Nacional de Estadística e Informática). 1986. "Encuesta nacional de nutrición y salud, ENNSA" (Survey of Nutrition and Health), National Statistics Institute, Lima.

Jack, W. 2001a. "Purchasing Medical Care: A Conceptual Framework." Unpublished manuscript, Georgetown University, Washington, DC.

————. 2001b. "Health Insurance Reform in Four Latin American Countries: Theory and Practice." Policy Research Working Paper 2492, World Bank, Washington, DC.

Jakab, M., and C. Krishnan. 2001. "Community Involvement in Health Care Financing: A Survey of the Literature on the Impacts, Strengths, and Weaknesses." Health, Nutrition, and Population Discussion Paper, September, Health, Nutrition, and Population Family, Human Development Network, World Bank, Washington, DC.

Jalan, J., and M. Ravallion. 2003. "Does Piped Water Reduce Diarrhea for Children in Rural India?" *Journal of Econometrics* 112 (1): 153–73.

Jefferys, E., and V. Walford. 2003. "Mapping of Sector Wide Approaches in Health." Institute for Health Sector Development, London.

Jimenez, E. 1987. *Pricing Policies in the Social Sectors: Cost Recovery for Education and Health in Developing Countries.* Baltimore: Johns Hopkins University Press.

Johannesson, M. 1995. "The Relationship between Cost-Effectiveness Analysis and Cost-Benefit Analysis." *Social Science and Medicine* 41 (4): 483–89.

Johannesson, M., and M. Meltzer. 1998. "Some Reflections on Cost-Effectiveness Analysis." *Health Economics* 7 (1): 1–7.

Johns, B., and R. Baltussen. 2004. "Accounting for the Cost of Scaling-Up Health Interventions." *Health Economics* 13 (11): 1117–24.

Johns, B., and T. T. Torres. 2005. "Costs of Scaling-Up Health Interventions: A Systematic Review." *Health Policy and Planning* 20 (1): 1–13.

Johnston, T., S. D. Faure, and L. Raney. 1998. "The World Bank and the Health Sector in Mali." Report 18112, World Bank, Washington, DC.

Jütting, J. 2001. "The Impact of Community-Based Health Financing on Financial Protection in Africa: Case Study Senegal." Unpublished manuscript, Health, Nutrition, and Population Family, Human Development Network, World Bank, Washington, DC.

Jütting, J., C. Kauffmann, I. McDonnell, H. Osterrieder, N. Pinaud, and L. Wegne. 2004. "Decentralisation and Poverty in Developing Countries: Exploring the Impact." Working Paper 236, Development Centre, Organisation for Economic Co-operation and Development, Paris.

Khan, S. H. 2005. "Free Does Not Mean Affordable: Maternity Patient Expenditures in a Public Hospital in Bangladesh." *Cost Effectiveness and Resource Allocation* 3 (1). http://www.resource-allocation.com/content/3/1/1.

Khemani, S. 2004. "Local Government Accountability for Service Delivery in Nigeria." Development Research Group, World Bank, Washington, DC.

Killingsworth, J. R. 2002. "Official, Unofficial, and Informal Fees for Health Care." Draft Discussion Note 13, Third Health Sector Development Technical Advisory Group Meeting, "Health Care Financing in the Western Pacific Region," Manila, February 17–19.

Killingsworth, J. R., N. Hossain, Y. Hedrick-Wong, S. Thomas, A. Rahman, and T. Begum. 1999. "Unofficial Fees in Bangladesh: Price, Equity, and Institutional Issues." *Health Policy and Planning* 14 (2): 152–63.

Klugman, J., ed. 2002. *A Sourcebook for Poverty Reduction Strategies.* 2 vols. Washington, DC: World Bank.

Kremer, M. 1995. "Research on Schooling: What We Know and What We Don't (A Comment on Hanushek)." *World Bank Research Observer* 10 (2): 247–54.

Kumaranayake, L., S. Lake, P. Mujinja, C. Hongoro, and R. Mpembeni. 2000. "How Do Countries Regulate the Health Sector?: Evidence from Tanzania and Zimbabwe." *Health Policy and Planning* 15 (4): 357–67.

Kutzin, J. 1997. "Health Insurance for the Formal Sector in Africa: 'Yes but . . .'." Current Concerns ARA Paper 14, Division of Analysis, Research, and Assessment, World Health Organization, Geneva.

La Forgia, G. M. 1990. *Health Services for Low-Income Families: Extending Coverage through Prepayment Plans in the Dominican Republic.* Bethesda, MD: Health Financing and Sustainability Project, Abt Associates Inc.

Laing, R. O., H. V. Hogerzeil, and D. Ross-Degnan. 2001. "Ten Recommendations to Improve Use of Medicines in Developing Countries." *Health Policy and Planning* 16 (1): 13–20.

Lakshminarayanan, R. 2003a. "Gender and Health Sector Reform: An Annotated Bibliography." Unpublished manuscript, International Women's Health Coalition, New York.

———. 2003b. "Decentralisation and its Implications for Reproductive Health: The Philippines Experience." *Reproductive Health Matters* 11 (21): 96–107.

Langer, A., G. Nigenda, and J. Catino. 2000. "Health Sector Reform and Reproductive Health in Latin America and the Caribbean: Strengthening the Links." *Bulletin of the World Health Organization* 78 (5): 667–76.

Lanjouw, J. O. 2002. "Intellectual Property and the Availability of Pharmaceuticals in Poor Countries." Working Paper 5, Center for Global Development, Washington, DC.

———. (2004). "Drug Patents: Taking the Poorest Out of the Fight." *Milken Institute Quarterly Review.* http://are.berkeley.edu/~lanjouw/milken.pdf.

Lanjouw, P., M. Pradhan, F. Saadah, H. Sayed, and R. Sparrow. 2002. "Poverty, Education, and Health in Indonesia: Who Benefits from Public Spending?, Volume 1." Policy Research Working Paper 2739, World Bank, Washington, DC.

Lanjouw, P., and M. Ravallion. 1999. "Benefit Incidence, Public Spending Reforms, and the Timing of Program Capture." *World Bank Economic Review* 13 (2): 257–73.

Lavadenz, F., N. Schwab, and H. Straatman. 2001. "Decentralized and Community Health Networks in Bolivia." *Pan-American Journal of Public Health* 9 (3): 182–89. (In Spanish).

Lawson, D. 2004. "Determinants of Health-Seeking Behaviour in Uganda: Is it Just Income and User Fees that are Important?" Unpublished manuscript, University of Manchester, Manchester, United Kingdom.

Leonard, K. L. 2000. "Moral Hazard in Health Care: An Empirical Investigation in Rural Cameroon." Unpublished manuscript, Department of Economics, Columbia University, New York.

Lewis, M. 2000. "Who Is Paying for Health Care in Eastern Europe and Central Asia?" Europe and Central Asia Region, Human Development Sector Unit, World Bank, Washington, DC.

Lindelöw, M., and A. Wagstaff. 2003. "Health Facility Surveys: An Introduction." Policy Research Working Paper 2953, Public Services, Development Research Group, World Bank, Washington, DC.

Litvack, J. I., and C. I. Bodart. 1992. "User Fees Plus Quality Equals Improved Access to Health Care: Results of a Field Experiment in Cameroon." *Social Science and Medicine* 37 (3): 369–83.

Liu, X., D. R. Hotchkiss, S. Bose, R. Bitrán, and U. Giedion. 2004. *Contracting for Primary Health Services: Evidence on Its Effects and Framework for Evaluation.* Bethesda, MD: Partners for Health Reform*plus* Project, Abt Associates Inc.

Loevinsohn, B. 2001. "Contracting for the Delivery of Primary Health Care in Cambodia: Design and Initial Experience of a Large Pilot Test." Manuscript, World Bank, Washington, DC.

————. 2002. "Practical Issues in Contracting for Primary Health Care Delivery: Lessons from Two Large Projects in Bangladesh." World Bank, Washington, DC.

Loewenson, R. 2000. "Participation and Accountability in Health Systems: The Missing Factor in Equity?" Equinet Discussion Paper 1, Network for Equity in Health in Southern Africa, Harare, Zimbabwe.

Maceira, D. 1998. "Provider Payment Mechanisms in Health Care: Incentives, Outcomes, and Organizational Impact in Developing Countries." Major Applied Research 2 Working Paper 2, Partnerships for Health Reform Project, Abt Associates Inc., Bethesda, MD.

Marchal, B., V. De Brouwere, and G. Kegels. 2005. "Viewpoint: HIV/AIDS and the Health Workforce Crisis, What are the Next Steps?" *Tropical Medicine and International Health* 10 (4): 300–4.

Marsh, V. M., W. M. Mutemi, A. Willetts, K. Bayah, S. Were, A. Ross, and K. Marsh. 2004. "Improving Malaria Home Treatment by Training Drug Retailers in Rural Kenya." *Tropical Medicine and International Health* 9 (4): 451–60.

McFadden, D. 1981. "Econometric Models of Probabilistic Choice." In *Structural Analysis of Discrete Data with Econometrics Applications,* ed. C. Manski and D. McFadden, 114–78. Cambridge, MA: The MIT Press.

McGuire, T. G. 2000. "Physician Agency." In *Handbook of Health Economics,* ed. A. J. Culyer and J. P. Newhouse, 461–536. Amsterdam: Elsevier Science.

McPake, B. 1997. "The Role of the Private Sector in Health Care Provision." In *Private Health Providers in Developing Countries: Servicing the Public Interest?,* ed. S. Bennett, B. McPake, and A. Mills. London: Zed Books.

McPake, B., D. Asiimwe, F. Mwesigye, M. Ofumbi, L. Ortemblad, P. Streefland, and D. Turinde. 1999. "Informal Economic Activities of Public Health Workers in Uganda: Implication for Quality and Accessibility of Care." *Social Science and Medicine* 49: 849–65.

McPake, B., F. J. Yepes, S. Lake, and L. H. Sanchez. 2003. "Is the Colombian Health System Reform Improving the Performance of Public Hospitals in Bogotá?" *Health Policy and Planning* 118: 182–94.

Mensch, B. 1993. "Quality of Care: A Neglected Dimension." In *The Health of Women: A Global Perspective,* ed. M. Koblinsky, J. Timyan, and J. Gay. Boulder, CO: Westview Press. Cited in WHO (1998).

Miguel, E., and M. Kremer. 2001. "Worms: Education and Health Externalities in Kenya." *Econometrica* 72 (1): 159–217.

Miller, K., R. Miller, I. Askew, M. C. Horn, and L. Ndlovu, eds. 1998. "Clinic-Based Family Planning and Reproductive Health Services in Africa: Findings from Situation Analysis Studies." Population Council, New York.

Mills, A., R. Brugha, K. Hanson, and B. McPake. 2002. "What Can Be Done about the Private Health Sector in Low-Income Countries?" *Bulletin of the World Health Organization* 80 (4): 325–30.

Montagu, D. 2003. "Accreditation and Other External Quality Assessment Systems for Healthcare: Review of Experience and Lessons Learned." Health Systems Resource Centre, Department for International Development, London.

Moon, M., L. M. Nichols, and S. Walls. 1997. "Winners and Losers under Medical Savings Accounts." *Spectrum* 70 (1): 26–29.

Murray, C. J. L., A. D. Lopez, C. D. Mathers, and C. Stein. 2001. "The Global Burden of Disease 2000 Project: Aims, Methods and Data Sources." Research Paper 01.1, Harvard Burden of Disease Unit, Center for Population and Development Studies, Cambridge, MA.

Mutizwa-Mangiza, D. 1998. "The Impact of Health Sector Reform on Public Sector Health Worker Motivation in Zimbabwe." Major Applied Research 5 Working Paper 4, Partnerships for Health Reform Project, Abt Associates Inc., Bethesda, MD.

Mwabu, G. 1986. "Health Care Decisions at the Household Level: Results of a Rural Health Survey in Kenya." *Social Science and Medicine* 22 (3): 315–19.

Mwabu, G., M. Ainsworth, and A. Nyamete. 1993. "Quality of Medical Care and Choice of Medical Treatment in Kenya: An Empirical Analysis." *Journal of Human Resources* 28 (4): 838–62.

Nahar, S., and A. Costello. 1998. "The Hidden Cost of 'Free' Maternity Care in Dhaka, Bangladesh." *Health Policy and Planning* 13 (4): 417–22.

Nanda, P. 2002. "Gender Dimensions of User Fees: Implications for Women's Utilization of Health Care." *Reproductive Health Matters* 10 (20): 127–34.

Newhouse, J. P., and the Insurance Experiment Group. 1993. *Free for All? Lessons from the RAND Health Insurance Experiment.* Cambridge, MA: Harvard University Press.

Newman, J. L., M. Pradhan, L. B. Rawlings, G. Ridder, R. Coa, and J. L. Evia. 2002. "An Impact Evaluation of Education, Health, and Water Supply Investments by the Bolivian Social Investment Fund." *World Bank Economic Review* 16 (2): 241–74.

Newman, J. L., L. B. Rawlings, and P. J. Gertler. 1994. "Using Randomized Control Designs in Evaluating Social Sector Programs in Developing Countries." *World Bank Research Observer* 9 (2): 181–201.

Nichols, L. M., K. H. Phua, and N. M. Prescott. 1997. "Medical Savings Accounts for Developing Countries." In *Innovations in Health Care Financing.* Proceedings of a World Bank Conference, March 10–11, 1997, ed. G. Schieber. Washington, DC: World Bank.

Nieves, I., G. M. La Forgia, and J. Ribera. 2000. "Large-Scale Government Contracting of NGOs to Extend Basic Health Services to Poor Populations in Guatemala." World Bank, Washington, DC.

Normand, C., and A. Weber. 1994. *Social Health Insurance: A Guidebook for Planning.* Geneva: World Health Organization.

Pearson, M. 2001. "Demand Side Financing for Healthcare." Unpublished manuscript, Health Systems Resource Centre, Department for International Development, London.

————. 2002. "Allocating Public Resources for Health: Developing Pro-Poor Approaches." Health Systems Resource Centre, Department for International Development, London.

Preker, A. S., G. Carrin, D. Dror, M. Jakab, W. C. Hsiao, and D. Arhin-Tenkorang. 2002a. "Health Care Financing for Rural and Low-Income Populations: The Role of Communities in Resource Mobilization and Risk Sharing." Background report, Commission on Macroeconomics and Health, World Health Organization, Geneva.

————. 2002b. "Effectiveness of Community Health Financing in Meeting the Cost of Illness." *Bulletin of the World Health Organization* 80 (2): 143–50.

QAP (Quality Assurance Project) and PAHO (Pan American Health Organization). 2003. "Maximizing Quality of Care through Health Sector Reform: The Role of Quality Assurance Strategies." Working draft, Quality Assurance Project, Bethesda, MD. http://www.qaproject.org/pubs/PDFs/PAHO.pdf.

Rannan-Eliya, R. P., C. Blanco-Vidal, and A. K. Nandakumar. 1999. "The Distribution of Health Care Resources in Egypt: Implications for Equity, An Analysis Using a National Health Accounts Framework." Data for Decision Making Project, Department of Population Studies and International Health, Harvard School of Public Health, Boston.

Rao, V., and A. M. Ibanez. 2003. "The Social Impact of Social Funds in Jamaica: A Mixed-Methods Analysis of Participation, Targeting, and Collective Action in Community-Driven Development." Policy Research Working Paper 2970, World Bank, Washington, DC.

Ravallion, M. 2003. "Assessing the Poverty Impact of an Assigned Program." In *The Impact of Economic Policies on Poverty and Income Distribution: Evaluation Techniques and Tools*, ed. F. Bourguignon and L. Pereira da Silva, 103–22. New York: Oxford University Press.

Ravallion, M., D. van de Walle, and M. Gautam. 1995. "Testing a Social Safety Net." *Journal of Public Economics* 57 (2): 175–99.

Reich, M. R. 1995. "The Politics of Health Sector Reform in Developing Countries: Three Cases of Pharmaceutical Policy." *Health Policy* 32 (1–3): 47–77.

Rosenbaum, P. R., and D. B. Rubin. 1983. "The Central Role of the Propensity Score in Observational Studies for Causal Effects." *Biometrika* 70 (1): 41–55.

Sandiford, P., A. Gorter, and M. Salvetto. 2002. "Vouchers for Health: Using Voucher Schemes for Output-Based Aid." Public Policy for the Private Sector, Viewpoint 243, World Bank, Washington, DC.

Schmeer, K. 2000. "Stakeholder Analysis Guidelines." In *Policy Toolkit for Strengthening Health Sector Reform*, ed. S. Scribner and D. Brinkerhoff, 2: 1–43. Bethesda, MD: Abt Associates Inc., Bethesda, MD.

Schneider, P., and F. Diop. 2001. *Impact of Prepayment Pilot on Health Care Utilization and Financing in Rwanda: Findings from Final Household Survey*. Bethesda, MD: Partners for Health Reform*plus* Project, Abt Associates Inc.

Schneider, P., F. Diop, and S. Bucyana. 2000. "Development and Implementation of Prepayment Schemes in Rwanda." Technical Report 45, Partnerships for Health Reform Project, Abt Associates Inc., Bethesda, MD.

Schultz, T. P., and A. Tansel. 1997. "Wage and Labor Supply Effects of Illness in Côte d'Ivoire and Ghana." *Journal of Development Economics* 53 (2): 251–86.

Schwartz, J., J. Akin, and B. M. Popkin. 1988. "Price and Income Elasticities of Demand for Modern Health Care: The Case of Infant Delivery in the Philippines." *World Bank Economic Review* 2 (1): 49–76.

Semali, I. A. J. 2003. "Understanding Stakeholders' Roles in the Health Sector Reform Process in Tanzania: The Case of Decentralizing the Immunization Program." PhD dissertation, University of Basel, Basel, Switzerland. http://pages.unibas.ch/diss/2003/DabsB_6803.pdf.

Sen, A. 1984. "Poor, Relatively Speaking." In *Resources, Values, and Development*, ed. A. Sen. New York: Basil Blackwell.

Smith, E., R. Brugha, and A. Zwi. 2001. "Working with Private Sector Providers for Better Health Care: An Introductory Guide." Options and London School of Hygiene and Tropical Medicine, London.

Stinson, W. 1982. *Community Financing of Primary Health Care*. Washington, DC: American Public Health Association.

Strauss, J., and D. Thomas. 1998. "Health, Nutrition, and Economic Development." *Journal of Economic Literature* 36 (2):766–817.

Tang, S., and G. Bloom. 2000, "Decentralizing Rural Health Services: A Case Study in China." *International Journal of Health Planning and Management* 15 (3): 189–200.

Tanzi, V., and H. Zee. 2001. "Tax Policy for Developing Countries." *Economic Issues* 27, International Monetary Fund, Washington, DC.

Tawfik, L., and S. N. Kinoti. 2003. "The Impact of HIV/AIDS on Health Systems and the Health Workforce in Sub-Saharan Africa." Unpublished manuscript, Support for Analysis and Research in Africa Project, Office of Sustainable Development, Bureau for Africa, U.S. Agency for International Development, Washington, DC.

Telyukov, A. 2001. "Guide to Prospective Capitation with Illustrations from Latin America." Abt Associates Inc., Bethesda, MD.

Thomason, J. A., W. C. Newbrander, and R.-L. Kolehmainen-Aitken, eds. 1991. "Decentralization in a Developing Country: The Experience of Papua New Guinea and Its Health Service." Pacific Research Monograph 25, National Centre for Development Studies, Australian National University, Canberra.

van de Walle, D. 2002. "The Static and Dynamic Incidence of Vietnam's Public Safety Net." Policy Research Working Paper 2791, Public Services, Development Research Group, World Bank, Washington, DC.

van de Walle, D., and K. Nead, eds. 1995. *Public Spending and the Poor: Theory and Evidence*. Baltimore: Johns Hopkins University Press.

Vian, T., K. Gryboski, Z. Sinoimeri, and R. Hall Clifford. 2004. "Informal Payments in the Public Health Sector in Albania: A Qualitative Study." Partners for Health Reform*plus* Project, Abt Associates Inc., Bethesda, MD.

Wagstaff, A. 1999. "Measuring Equity in Health Care Financing: Reflections on (and Alternatives to) the World Health Organization's Fairness of Financing Index." Policy Research Working Paper 2550, World Bank, Washington, DC.

―――. 2000a. Presentation to London Meeting on Health and Equity, Department for International Development, London. Cited in Bennett and Gilson (2001).

―――. 2000b. "Socioeconomic Inequalities in Child Mortality: Comparisons across Nine Developing Countries." *Bulletin of the World Health Organization* 78 (1): 19–29.

―――. 2002. "Poverty and Health Sector Inequalities." *Bulletin of the World Health Organization* 80 (2): 97–105.

Wagstaff, A., and E. van Doorslaer. 2002. "Catastrophe and Impoverishment in Paying for Health Care: With Applications to Vietnam, 1993–98." Unpublished manuscript, World Bank, Washington, DC.

Wagstaff, A., E. van Doorslaer, H. van der Burg, et al. 1999. "Equity in the Finance of Health Care: Some Further International Comparisons." *Journal of Health Economics* 18 (3): 263–90.

Walsh, J. A., and K. S. Warren. 1979. "Selective Primary Health Care: An Interim Strategy for Disease Control in Developing Countries." *New England Journal of Medicine* 301 (18): 967–74.

Walt, G., and L. Gilson. 1994. "Reforming the Health Sector in Developing Countries: The Central Role of Policy Analysis." *Health Policy and Planning* 9 (4): 353–70.

Wang, L. 2003. "Determinants of Child Mortality in LDCs: Empirical Findings from Demographic and Health Surveys." *Health Policy* 65 (3): 277–99.

Whitehead, M., G. Dahlgren, and T. Evans. 2001. "Equity and Health Sector Reforms: Can Low-Income Countries Escape the Medical Poverty Trap?" *The Lancet* 358 (9284): 833–36.

WHO (World Health Organization). 1998. "Gender and Health: A Technical Paper." World Health Organization, Geneva. http://www.who.int/docstore/frh-whd/GandH/GHreport/gendertech.htm.

―――. 2000a. *The World Health Report 2000: Health Systems, Improving Performance.* Geneva: World Health Organization.

―――. 2000b. *How to Develop and Implement a National Drug Policy.* 2nd ed. Geneva: World Health Organization.

―――. 2003. *Guide to Producing National Health Accounts.* Geneva: World Health Organization.

Wiesmann, D., and J. Jütting. 2000. "The Emerging Movement of Community Based Health Insurance in Sub-Saharan Africa: Experiences and Lessons Learned." *Afrika Spectrum* 2/2000: 193–210.

Woolcock, M. 2001. "Social Assessments and Program Evaluation with Limited Formal Data: Thinking Quantitatively, Acting Qualitatively." Social Development Briefing Note 68, World Bank, Washington, DC.

World Bank. 1993. *World Development Report 1993: Investing in Health.* New York: Oxford University Press.

―――. 1997a. *World Development Report 1997: The State in a Changing World.* New York: Oxford University Press.

―――. 1997b. *Confronting AIDS.* Baltimore: Johns Hopkins University Press.

————. 2002. *World Development Report 2003: Sustainable Development in a Dynamic World.* New York: Oxford University Press.

————. 2003a. *World Development Report 2004: Making Services Work for Poor People.* New York: Oxford University Press.

————. 2003b. *A User's Guide to Poverty and Social Impact Analysis.* Washington, DC: Poverty Reduction Group and Social Development Department, World Bank.

Wyss, K., D. D. Moto, and B. Callewaert. 2001. "Improving Health Outcomes of the Poor: Constraints to Scaling Up Health Interventions, Country Case Study, Chad." Working Group 5, Commission on Macroeconomics and Health, World Health Organization, Geneva. (In French).

Xu, K., D. Evans, K. Kawabata, R. Zeramdini, J. Klavus, and C. Murray. 2003. "Household Catastrophic Health Expenditure: A Multicountry Analysis." *The Lancet* 362 (9378): 111–17.

Yazbeck, A. S., and M. Wenner. 1994. "Social Financing in Niger." Major Applied Research Working Paper 15. Health Financing and Sustainability Project, Abt Associates Inc., Bethesda, MD.

Yip, W., and P. A. Berman. 2001. "Targeted Health Insurance in a Low-Income Country and Its Impact on Access and Equity in Access: Egypt's School Health Insurance." *Health Economics* 10 (3): 207–20.

Younger, S. D. 2003. "Benefits on the Margin: Observations on Marginal Benefit Incidence." *World Bank Economic Review* 17 (1): 89–106.

3

Selected Labor Market Reforms

Aline Coudouel and Pierella Paci

Overall, in recent years, the policy advice of bilateral and multilateral donors to policymakers in developing countries has been centered on reducing the degree of government intervention in the functioning of the labor market and on increasing the liberalization of labor market institutions. Underpinning this advice is the traditional neo-classical assumption that the laissez-faire approach ensures the highest social welfare by promoting labor market efficiency and job creation.

However, this view has long been challenged by those who see in the many market failures in the labor markets of developing countries the need for a more active role for labor market policies. A number of non-competitive theoretical frameworks question the efficiency of unregulated markets, provide a rationale for different types of labor market interventions, and, in combination with the *Theorem of Second Best*,[1] challenge the view that liberalization always leads to increased efficiency. In addition, the strongest criticism of the laissez-faire approach is based on considerations of equity and on poverty reduction objectives on the grounds that the outcomes of unregulated, competitive labor markets are not necessarily consistent with the social justice objective. The different definitions of social justice or *equity* preclude any simple answer to this question (Barr 1993). However, the claim becomes much easier to assess when the focus is on poverty and on income distribution. The argument here is that labor market interventions reduce inequality in labor incomes by (1) maintaining earnings at the lower end of the income distribution above the level at which they would have been in an unregulated market, and (2) reducing the vulnerability of earnings.

Employment is widely perceived to be among the most important channels through which the poor can move out of poverty. This is mainly for two reasons. First, labor is the most abundant asset of the poor, and, second, what distinguishes the poor from the non-poor is labor incomes: labor force status is repeatedly found to be a critical determinant of household welfare in developing countries. Thus, among other studies, the recently released "Pro-Poor Growth in the 1990s: Lessons and Insights from 14 Countries" (World Bank 2005) highlights employment as a crucial link between growth and poverty reduction; it identifies labor market regulations and segmentation and the links between the investment climate and employment as priority areas for pro-poor growth strategies. Yet, access to jobs is not sufficient; the existence of so many *working poor* underlines the importance of the availability of jobs that offer some degree of security and pay *decent* wages.

From this arises the essential role of labor market policies designed to improve job security and guarantee a decent wage for the most vulnerable workers. However, this potential role would clearly be significantly reduced if the security of decent labor incomes for some was achieved at the cost of reduced employment opportunities and more inadequate working conditions for others. This raises important challenges for policymakers, such as: (1) how to design a package of labor market policies that reconcile the right of workers to secure and decent wages—which is essential for reducing poverty and labor market vulnerability—with the overall objective of widening employment opportunities; (2) how to implement any necessary reform of the existing package of interventions; (3) how to quantify the potential distributional impact of any such reform; and (4) how to minimize the welfare costs to those people who would lose out from these changes.

These are important issues for development as, contrary to expectations, the developing world generally tends to have relatively rigid labor laws governing the relationship between employers and employees. This is evident in Figure 3.1, which presents four indexes of labor market rigidity, ranging from 0 to 100, from least to most rigid. The indexes are as follows:

- the difficulty of hiring index, which is based on the legality of part-time and fixed-term contracts and their applicability
- the rigidity of hours index, which is based on the rules that govern the hours of work (maximum, treatment of night-shift work, overtime, and so on), the policy toward work leaves, and the minimum wage

FIGURE 3.1 Selected Indexes of Labor Market Rigidities across Regions

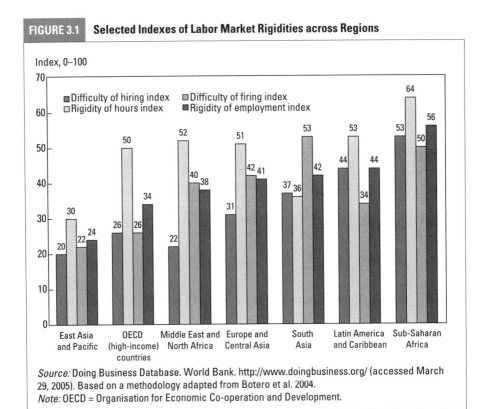

Source: Doing Business Database. World Bank. http://www.doingbusiness.org/ (accessed March 29, 2005). Based on a methodology adapted from Botero et al. 2004.
Note: OECD = Organisation for Economic Co-operation and Development.

- the difficulty of firing index, which is based on the grounds allowed for firing, the firing procedures in place, the firing notification requirements, the size of severance payments, and whether the right to job security is enshrined in the country's constitution
- the rigidity of employment index, which is a synthesis of the three indexes above

Figure 3.1 shows that, with the exception of the East Asia and the Pacific Region, formal labor markets in all regions exhibit labor market rigidity that is greater than the average for the countries of the Organisation for Economic Co-operation and Development (OECD). The greater rigidity is particularly evident in firing restrictions and employment regulation. The rigidities are especially substantial in Sub-Saharan Africa, where all the indexes are in excess of 50, and hiring and firing are twice as difficult than they are in the OECD countries. At the other end of the spectrum are the East Asian countries, which have, on average, much less stringent laws.

However, it may be misleading to derive conclusions about the overall degree of the rigidities of the labor market from the findings shown in Figure 3.1. This is because the coverage of these laws and their level of implementation vary considerably from country to country partly as a reflection of the size and structure of the informal sector. Indeed, for most, labor market policies only apply to a subset of the workforce, namely, those people in the formal sector. As shown in Table 3.1, the size of this subset varies considerably across regions and countries, but it represents over 40 percent of gross domestic product in Africa and Latin America and 35 percent in the transition countries of Europe and Central Asia. In addition, in countries with weak implementation capacity, large pockets of unprotected employment persist even in the formal sector.

This suggests that labor market legislation directly affects employment conditions only for a relatively small percentage of the workforce in the developing world. Nevertheless, it is likely to affect the incomes and the vulnerability to poverty of a much larger part of the population than the small percentage covered by the policy. Indeed, evidence has emerged that conditions prevailing in the formal sector have indirect effects on the informal sector by, for example, raising the average wage in both sectors. More importantly, the degree of intervention prevailing in the formal sector may represent a barrier to job creation in general and to the employment of new workers in particular. It may also affect the size and structure of the informal sector: informality may be more widespread, and the gap between the formal and informal sectors may be larger in economies with more highly regulated labor markets.

TABLE 3.1. Average Size of the Informal Economy in Terms of Value Added, by Region, 2000

Region	Value added (% gross domestic product)	Countries covered (number)
Africa (including North Africa)	41.0	23
Latin America and the Caribbean	41.0	18
Middle East and Asia	29.0	26
Central and Eastern Europe and Central Asia	35.0	23
Western European OECD	18.0	16
North America and Pacific OECD	13.5	4

Source: Schneider and Klinglmair 2004.

Thus, labor market policies and policy reforms are an important determinant of income distribution and poverty incidence even in countries where the relative importance of the covered sector in the overall labor market is small. This is because of the indirect effect of the policies and the reforms on the rest of the economy. Indeed, when the focus is on improving overall social welfare and reducing poverty, labor market interventions may act as a double-edged sword by protecting the income levels and security of those covered by the policies, the *insiders,* while increasing the vulnerability of the rest of the population, the *outsiders,* who may face increasing barriers to employment and have access only to jobs in the uncovered sector of a typically *dual* labor market.[2] For this reason, any reform of the prevailing labor market is unlikely to be Pareto neutral. It will leave some members of society worse off, while improving the living standards of others and will therefore have an important distributional impact. Who the winners and losers will be will depend on a number of factors, ranging from the type and direction of the reforms—that is, more intervention versus increased liberalization—to the characteristics of the labor and output markets.

In deciding on the implementation of these policies and reforms, policymakers should thus be fully aware of the potential direct and indirect impacts on the distribution of income at both the individual and the household levels so that the full significance of the policies and reforms in terms of efficiency, equality, and poverty reduction can be adequately evaluated.

The objective of this chapter is to provide policymakers with the tools they need to conduct such an evaluation. The chapter first describes a variety of labor market policies, focusing on three of these policies. It then describes possible reforms of these policies and the rationale behind the reforms. The subsequent section illustrates the channels by which the reforms may impact income distribution and poverty. The following section identifies the stakeholders involved in each of the reforms analyzed. Finally, the tools of analysis and the main impacts of the reforms as identified in the empirical literature are outlined.

The chapter is not intended as a full-scale analysis of the pros and cons of particular labor market policies and reforms, but more simply as a guide to the comprehensive evaluation of potential distributional impacts. Thus, the attention is on the possible effects on income inequality and the incidence of poverty rather than on the efficiency of the system or the existence of a trade-off between efficiency and equity considerations.[3]

LABOR MARKET POLICIES

The types of labor market policies implemented in countries are many and varied. In the interest of maintaining a tight focus, the analysis in this chapter is limited to the potential distributional impacts of reforms in three areas of labor market policy that are of particular relevance to developing countries, namely, the minimum wage, employment protection legislation, and unemployment benefits.

The chapter neglects other types of labor market policies and reforms[4] and the potential interactions of these reforms with the conditions prevailing in other areas of the labor market.[5] In addition, the analysis takes a partial-equilibrium approach and does not deal with the issue of possible interactions between, on the one hand, capital and product market institutions and reforms and, on the other, the reforms of labor market interventions; nor does it address the potential impact of labor market reforms on the competitiveness of a country vis-à-vis its neighbors. These are important limitations because the status and the sequencing of reforms in product and labor markets are clearly interrelated, and the changes in labor costs brought about by reforms may have important second-round effects on labor market outcomes and income distribution, as shown by the examples in Box 3.1. However, the decision to focus on only three types of labor market policies and to analyze these three in isolation from other reforms both within and outside the labor market is dictated by the need to keep the task within manageable dimensions.

BOX 3.1   Labor Market Reforms Do Not Happen in a Vacuum

Recent empirical literature on economic liberalization has unveiled a number of interactions among labor market reforms, their impact, and the conditions prevailing in other markets. For example:

- Evidence from South Asia points to the importance of industrial policies in determining the impact of labor market reforms.
- Trade liberalization appears to have led to the expansion of the informal sector in Colombia until a major labor market reform also increased the flexibility of the labor market (Goldberg and Pavcnik 2003).
- Soaring minimum wages and labor costs in Indonesia are believed to have eroded the country's competitivity (Agrawal 1995).
- Analyses of European countries show that the effects of shocks depends on the nature of institutions. Shocks have a larger and more persistent effect in countries with poor labor market institutions, and a similar shock has differentiated effects on unemployment when labor market institutions differ (Blanchard and Wolfers 1999).

The minimum wage

Minimum wage legislation sets a lower bound to the wages paid to individual workers. The conceptual definition is very simple, but the scale, eligibility, and policy design differ considerably from country to country. The majority of countries opt for a single national minimum rate set on an hourly, daily, weekly, or monthly basis. Beyond the single national wage, a reduced or subminimum rate is sometimes applied for some groups of workers, notably, youth, the unskilled, or the long-term unemployed; for most workers, subminimum rates sometimes exist de facto, because special employment programs allow employers to pay lower wages for young workers. In other countries, minimum wage premiums are sometimes used that are related to worker characteristics. For example, the minimum wage may rise according to worker experience, worker qualifications, or worker family status.

In addition, different minima may be set for different regions, occupations, or industries. This is particularly common in Latin America. For example, in Argentina, there are dozens of minimum wages set for agricultural workers, while one minimum wage is set for all other economic activities (World Bank 2006), and, in Mexico, wages are set separately for three regions and 88 occupations (Gindling and Terrell 2004a). Countries also vary in the process they adopt to set the minimum wage. The government sets it unilaterally in some countries. In others, it is the result of negotiations between representatives of workers and firms. In a number of countries, it is indexed to price inflation. The available information on selective features of minimum wage policies across countries is summarized in Table 3A.1 in the annex to this chapter.

Such diverse approaches make international comparisons of minimum wages difficult. Nevertheless, cross-country comparisons can be made by measuring the value of the minimum wage relative to some measure of average wage (the *Kaitz index*). Maloney and Mendez (2003) provide estimates for the Kaitz index for most Latin American countries. They find a large variance across countries. Argentina, Bolivia, Brazil, Chile, Mexico, and Uruguay represent the lower bound (with a Kaitz index around 20–25 percent), while El Salvador, Honduras, Paraguay, and Venezuela are among the countries with the largest values (with estimates around 50–60 percent). The evidence for African countries is less readily available. Jones (1998) finds that, in Ghana, the Kaitz index for manufacturing workers fell from 50 percent in the early 1970s to around 20 percent in the early 1990s.

Employment protection legislation

Employment protection legislation refers to the set of norms and procedures to be followed when hiring or dismissing workers. The legislation typically obliges employers to give workers a monetary compensation in case of early termination of permanent contracts and imposes procedures to be followed in case of individual or collective layoffs.[6] It also imposes constraints on the type and length of the available contracts, for example by limiting the use of temporary contracts.

Typically, the legislation governs *severance payments* and *advance notice*. A *severance payment* is a monetary transfer to a worker in case of firm-initiated layoff. The payment may include compensation for unjustified dismissal, seniority premiums, and compensation for wages forgone during any legal process if the worker brings an action against the firm,[7] and so on. An *advance notice* is a specific period of time allowed to the worker before a layoff can be implemented. Firms typically either provide notice and keep the workers during the notice period or provide a compensation equivalent to the wages that would have been earned during the notice period. When workers continue on the job during the notice period, their level of effort is likely to be reduced, which translates into an extra cost for the employer. In addition to mandatory payments, some firms and sectors also have collective agreements that specify other requirements. These components of the legislation can be conceived of as *monetary transfers* similar in nature to wages.

Another aspect of the legislation is the *administrative procedures* that must be followed. In most countries, the employer is required to discuss layoff decisions with the representatives of the workers. In some countries, dismissals must be approved by authorities (for example, India), and, in most countries, the legislation distinguishes between *individual* and *collective dismissals*. Within individual dismissals, a distinction is usually made between economic dismissals and disciplinary dismissals (often not covered by the legislation). The procedures for collective dismissals apply to large-scale restructuring and typically impose tighter administrative burdens in the form of prolonged consultations with worker representatives. The legislation may also govern the distribution of legal costs if workers contest dismissals by initiating court proceedings. These components of the legislation can be conceived of as "*taxes*" since they correspond to payments to third parties.

The multifaceted character of the legislation throughout the world makes international comparisons of the nature and comprehensiveness of the legislation difficult. However, several synthetic measures of the rigidity of the legislation exist. International comparisons of two of these indicators are illustrated in Figure 3.2. The figure shows the *difficulty of firing index,* which ranges from 0 (least rigid) to 100 (most rigid), and the *firing costs* expressed in weeks. Figure 3.2 indicates that firing existing workers is far more difficult in the developing world than in OECD countries. Firing is two times more difficult in South Asia and Sub-Saharan Africa than in the OECD. Firing costs are also much higher in developing countries than in OECD countries. In South Asia, they are over twice those in the high-income countries of the OECD.[8] A more complete breakdown of the values of synthetic indicators of the strictness of employment protection legislation by country and region are provided in Table A3.2 in the annex to this chapter.

Unemployment benefits

The objective of unemployment benefits is to provide income to individuals during spells of unemployment. Typically, the systems function as insurance schemes, whereby the amount and duration of the benefit are based on the worker's employment history, past contributions to the system, and most recent wage (unemployment insurance). Some schemes

FIGURE 3.2 **An International Comparison of Selected Indicators of Employment Protection Legislation**

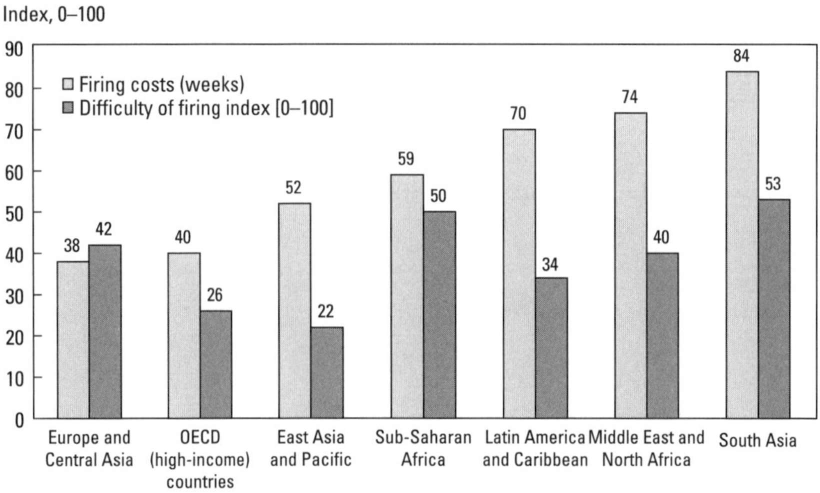

Source: Doing Business Database. World Bank. http://www.doingbusiness.org/ (accessed March 29, 2005). Based on a methodology adapted from Botero et al. 2004.
Note: OECD = Organisation for Economic Co-operation and Development.

also include a component that is independent of the worker's profile and (usually) provides flat benefits to individuals with long unemployment spells or who are below a certain income level (unemployment assistance). In most developed economies, unemployment benefits are combined with other transfers designed to supplement income for individuals who are out of work, such as early retirement schemes, invalidity pensions, and social assistance benefits. In addition, alternative ways of supporting the income levels of the unemployed while increasing their reemployment opportunities have recently been tried by a number of countries. These policies, commonly referred to as active labor market policies, vary substantially in their characteristics and in the degree of their success both as safety nets and as a means of reemployment. Vodopivec and Raju (2002) offer an extensive review of alternative systems of income support for the unemployed and an evaluation of the relative merits.

Several key features characterize an unemployment benefit system. Among these are the level of payments, the duration of the payments, and the eligibility requirements. To deal with the size of the benefit and the length of time during which the benefit is provided, the OECD tabulates a "summary measure of benefit generosity," defined as the average replacement rate during the first two years of unemployment for an "average production worker" having sufficiently long seniority to be offered the benefits up to their maximum duration. Another useful indicator is the coverage rate, that is, the fraction of the unemployed population receiving benefits. This measure depends on the duration of the benefits and the characteristics of unemployment (in particular, the share in unemployment represented by those individuals who typically do not benefit from the system because of a lack of work experience).

The potential interaction between different policies

The three policies highlighted in this chapter interact in interesting ways. This is particularly true of the unemployment benefit and employment protection legislation because the effects of the benefit are likely to differ depending on how flexible the legislation is, and, to a degree, the legislation and the benefit can substitute one for the other. However, in order to maintain a tight focus, this chapter does not address the topic.

TYPES OF REFORMS AND THE RATIONALE OF REFORM

The rationale for labor market intervention has traditionally been based on the argument that the market for labor is a very special type of market because of its nature and the fact that it deals in people rather than goods. This makes issues of equity particularly important and also makes the occurrence of market failures more likely and worrisome. In the view of many, this implies that an unregulated labor market would lead to outcomes that are inequitable and inefficient and that some form of intervention is required to increase the efficiency of the labor market and enhance the equity of its outcomes. However, many other people believe that the acceptance of this argument has caused labor markets to become excessively regulated in numerous wealthy and less wealthy countries and that this has led to outcomes that are neither efficient nor equitable. Based on these two competing views, calls for reform have focused on the implementation or strengthening of interventionist policies or on their weakening. For the most part, this has led only to marginal changes designed to alter the coverage or the generosity of systems.

Reforms of the minimum wage

In addition to the setting or elimination of a minimum wage, reforms in the area of the minimum wage are typically of two types: those that either increase or decrease the average value of the wage threshold and those designed to introduce subminimal wage floors for particular groups of workers (such as the unskilled, youth, or the long-term unemployed) or locations or regions (areas of high unemployment or poor areas). The main rationale for a generalized increase in the minimum wage is the need to ensure a *living wage* to all workers and concerns about excessive wage inequalities. In such a context, the introduction or increase of a minimum wage acts as an instrument for redistributing income within a formal labor market characterized by large numbers of "working poor."[9]

On the other hand, a reduction in the average minimum wage or in the minimum wage of specific types of workers is advocated when the existing level of the relevant minimum wage appears to act as a barrier to employment either across the board or among workers characterized by particularly low productivity, typically youth, the unskilled, or the long-term unemployed. The introduction of regional variations in the minimum wage may also be advocated in a context of differences in the cost of living across regions or systematic differences in labor demand or skill levels across parts of a country.

Thus, these contrasting proposals reflect two different views of the impact of the minimum wage and of minimum wage reforms. One view stresses the *redistribution dimension* of the minimum wage, while the other view stresses the *quantity crowding out* dimension. These two different views also reflect the key transmission mechanisms of the minimum wage, as described in more detail below.

Reforms of employment protection legislation

The range of possible reforms in employment protection legislation is large, but the reforms are mostly linked to concerns about long-term unemployment and large pockets of unemployment among specific groups, typically the young and women. Any legislative initiative that induces a change in the regulations on individual or collective dismissals can be considered a reform in employment protection legislation. Furthermore, since the rigidity and enforcement of the legislation depend also on the way the judicial system applies and interprets the legislation, changes in the functioning and organization of the judicial system are also an important factor in legislative reforms.

One may distinguish between radical and marginal reforms. *Radical reforms* typically refer to changes in the regulations that apply to all jobs (for example, changes in the level of severance payments, the length of the required advance notice, the definition of fair dismissal, court procedures and the burden of proof, collective dismissal procedures, and so on). *Marginal reforms* refer to changes that apply only to newly created jobs. These include changes in the regulations on temporary or atypical contracts (for instance, interim contracts) and so on.

As shown in Table 3.2, by far the most popular reforms in employment protection legislation in Europe since 1985 have been marginal ones. Each country has, on average, undertaken one reform every other year, and the reforms have reduced or increased protection in equal shares.[10] The numerous reforms have led to an expansion in contractual types and a growth in the number of both fixed-term and unstable jobs, as well as permanent and still heavily protected positions. This has increased the dualism in European labor markets, making them more segmented not only with respect to insiders and outsiders, but also with respect to various sorts of outsiders.

TABLE 3.2. Employment Protection Legislation Reforms in Europe since 1985

	Increasing protection	Decreasing protection	Total
Structural reforms	7	4	11
Marginal reforms	59	53	112
Total	66	57	123

Source: Social Reforms Database. Fondazione Rodolfo DeBenedetti. http://www.frdb.org (accessed February 5, 2003).

Reforms in unemployment benefits

The main reforms in unemployment benefits consist of changes in the duration of benefits, in entitlements, and in replacement rates. The reforms are often designed to realize policies to encourage labor market activity and labor force participation or to increase the incentives for unemployed individuals to take up jobs. In addition, a number of countries have also recently been experimenting with alternative ways to support the income levels of the unemployed, while increasing their reemployment opportunities. These policies, commonly referred to as active labor market policies, vary substantially in their features and in the degree of their success as safety nets and as a means to boost reemployment.

An analysis of reforms in unemployment benefits in the European Union since 1987 shows that reforms in basic benefit systems are numerous, with an average of two reforms in each country every three years. Most of these reforms have aimed at augmenting benefits, but have only entailed marginal changes (that is, phasing in new beneficiaries rather than changes in existing entitlements) or have increased the rewards for labor market participation by altering the incentive structure. Finally, reforms have typically taken place during phases of economic growth and have often involved simple changes in administrative rules, for example, requiring more frequent visits to an employment office before one is eligible to receive benefits or rewriting the definition of "suitable job offer." This reflects the fact that the implementation of administrative reforms during economic growth is often less controversial than changes in benefit levels.

To avoid the opposition of people already covered by the system, more radical reforms to benefit systems are typically implemented little by little via marginal adjustments in benefits and a gradual narrowing of entitlements. Benefit reforms therefore usually "grandfather" existing entitlements by exempting those individuals who are receiving benefits at the time of the reform and allowing for the new rules to be phased in. An important exception is represented by the case of the former planned economies of Central and Eastern Europe, where fiscal constraints and the need to set right the perverse incentive structure that prevailed before the transition led to dramatic reforms, which, in some instances, severely reduced benefits and halved the maximum duration of benefits (Boeri 2000).

There are three main reasons for carrying out reforms in unemployment benefits. The first relates to the observed positive correlation between the duration of a benefit and the *duration of unemployment.* Exits from unemployment are found to respond strongly to the benefit-entitlement period (the exit rate increases as workers near the end of their entitlements). A second reason relates to the effects of benefits on *unemployment levels.* More generous benefit systems tend to be associated with higher unemployment rates because of longer unemployment and because of a dampening effect on entries into the workforce. A third reason for benefit reforms is the *fiscal cost* of the benefit system that, in conjunction with other nonemployment benefits, may account for a significant proportion of social spending.

The argument for implementation and strengthening of labor market interventions

From an efficiency perspective, the arguments for significant intervention in the labor market focus on the existence of different causes of *market failure.* First, the efficient working of a market under laissez-faire conditions requires full information flows. However, the substantial degree of heterogeneity among workers and jobs makes information flows highly complex and the costs of acquiring and updating information extremely high, leading to the use of infrequently updated stereotypes that distort decisionmaking and may put some groups systematically at a disadvantage, that is, either by being discriminated against in employment decisions or by being paid less than their marginal value product. Second, the presence of externalities may distort the relationship between individual utility-maximizing objectives and the overall objective of maximizing social welfare. A third potential source of market failure may arise when product market monopolies, trade unions, or a labor market monopsony cause the relationship among productivity, real wages, and employment to be distorted, leading to inefficiency in resource allocations.[11] Finally, the failure of markets for goods, services, and resources to perform efficiently may distort the operation of demand and supply.

Box 3.2 provides examples of the different categories of labor market failures discussed above. It is important to note that these are not mutually exclusive. On the contrary, they may interact to generate widespread market failures. This is particularly evident in the case of unemployment insurance.

An additional argument for labor market intervention derives from the fact that contracts for employment are more likely to be incomplete than are contracts prevailing in goods and output markets because of the "idiosyncratic" character of labor as a factor of production. Indeed, contracts involving the exchange of labor have dimensions other than duration and terms of employment that cannot be easily quantified or communicated, such as attentiveness, effort, and creativeness. Since these

BOX 3.2   Examples of Types of Market Failures in the Market for Labor

The following are examples of the four prevailing types of failures of the market for labor in developing countries.

1. *Asymmetric information.* In many situations, information is available asymmetrically in the labor market. This is a particular problem in markets with less effective reputation effects, that is, markets characterized by small firms, mobile workers, and informal contractual arrangements.
   - Firms may find that it is expensive to discover the true characteristics of applicants, and job-seekers may find that it is difficult to discover the true characteristics of job offers.
     - Off-the-job search is inefficient.
   - Employees may be unable to obtain full information on job-security arrangements in their current jobs.
     - They may make inefficient decisions about training and job-seeking.
   - Firms may conceal their difficult financial situations in order to prevent new job-seeking and departures by their most valuable workers.

2. *Externalities.* There are many examples of externalities in this area.
   - In deciding whether or not to close a branch, firms are unlikely to internalize the costs to local workers or to the government in the form of lost tax revenues and increased benefit payments.
   - In deciding whether or not to accept jobs, unemployed job-seekers are unlikely to take into account the costs of their refusal for firms or for the government.
   - If firms or workers are prepared to internalize these costs, free-riders who have failed to do so may nevertheless share in the resulting benefits.
     - Private decisionmaking in the unregulated labor market is inefficient because it does not internalize these costs.

3. *Monopoly power* may result from a number of factors both in the labor market and the product market and affect both demand and supply.
   - The existence of technologies idiosyncratic to a particular firm means that skills obtained through on-the-job training cannot be transferred to other employers. This makes labor turnover costly.
     - Virtually all employees and firms possess some degree of monopoly power.
     - Labor mobility is restricted; the labor market is not competitive, and wages may not clear.
   - Trade unions or monopolistic behavior may lead to similar distortions in the wage and employment equilibrium.

4. *Absence of markets for goods and services* may distort the operation of both the demand side and the supply side of the labor market.
   - The investment decisions of individuals may be distorted by the inability of workers to realize the value of their human capital in the same way they sell their financial assets.
     - There will be underinvestment in education and training.
   - The inability to obtain full insurance against redundancy because of the risk of moral hazard may distort interfirm mobility.

dimensions are not specified in the contract, they cannot be enforced, and the agency problem results. Thus, contracts need to be designed to increase the incentives for workers to behave in a manner that is consistent with the interest of employers, that is, supply-acceptable levels of effort and so on, or, more technically, "no shirking." These incentive mechanisms may involve piece-rate systems of pay or internal promotion that may distort the operation of market forces, leading to the development of internal labor markets and requiring intervention.

Finally, Keynes argued that, in the context of a more aggregate approach toward labor contracts, competitive labor markets are prone to coordination problems, resulting in aggregate market failures and persistent aggregate unemployment. These difficulties derive from the fact that contracts are negotiated at regular, but potentially long intervals and in terms of money wages. Meanwhile, worker demands are motivated in terms of real wages, and the offers of firms are motivated by labor costs. This means that any adjustments will be achieved through employment rather than wages. More recently, the "new growth theory" has expressed concerns about the ability of unregulated labor markets to produce optimal growth performance because of the failure of private employers to internalize the full development benefits of the existence of a trained and educated labor force.

However, the argument most often used to justify labor market interventions is the one based on *equity*. Many question the capacity of an unregulated labor market to produce an outcome that is socially acceptable given the fact that the trade in individual labor is involved. The various definitions of social justice or equity preclude any simple response (Barr 1993). Nonetheless, calls for equity become much easier to address when the focus is on poverty reduction since employment at a "decent" wage is widely perceived as the most important channel through which the poor can move out of poverty. It is also somewhat easier to evaluate the impact of policies on earning distribution and on earnings variability. This is because labor market policies, for the most part, are designed to reduce inequalities in labor incomes by maintaining earnings at the lower end of the income distribution above the level at which they would have been in an unregulated market, as well as to minimize income vulnerability in the light of possible dismissal, unemployment, and so on.

The argument for less labor market intervention

In recent years, the policy advice of bilateral and multilateral donors to policymakers in developing countries has been centered on reducing government intervention in the labor market and increasing the liberalization of labor market institutions. Underpinning this advice is the conviction that, despite the clear potential for market failures and the active role labor market policies can play in promoting a more equitable distribution of incomes and in reducing poverty, labor markets across the world tend to be overregulated. This overintervention may result in significant efficiency costs that lead to a trade-off between efficiency and equity. Furthermore, some have argued that, in the name of equity and fairness, excessive intervention may ultimately hurt those very groups it is designed to protect: the vulnerable and the poor. This can happen in a number of ways.

At the simplest level, overintervention may result in excessive government expenditure, and the imposition of taxes to finance this expenditure will reduce efficiency. Taxes will distort key relative prices, such as those between work and leisure on the supply side and those between labor and capital on the demand side. These distortions cause labor market behavior to deviate from that consistent with economic efficiency by, for example, discouraging formal employment, reducing employment potential, or generating growth in the uncovered, untaxed informal sector at the expense of the formal one. Similarly, interventions in the minimum wage or through employment protection legislation, by prohibiting employment under certain conditions, reduce the freedom of choice of workers and employers. When excessive, they may prevent the signing of mutually beneficial labor contracts, which would have important implications for the overall level and distribution of welfare. In addition, enforcement of these policies requires resources that could be used more directly for wealth creation.

STAKEHOLDERS AND THE POLITICAL ECONOMY OF REFORM

It is clear that any type of reform is likely to have important distributional effects because of the differential impact on the welfare of various groups in society; some groups may benefit, while others will likely lose out. However, the losers and the winners will be specifically determined by the type of policy and the nature of the reform.

The minimum wage

One important difference between reforms of the minimum wage and reforms of other labor market institutions is that the former mostly affect the bottom of the income distribution in contrast to, for example, changes in the structure of unemployment benefits, which directly affect all workers. Indeed, the main winners from a rise in the minimum wage are those workers who thereby enjoy a wage increase. Meanwhile, the losers are those people who lose their formal jobs because of the related reduction in employment. Typically, both groups are *unskilled workers in the formal sector.* The opposite is true for a reduction in the minimum wage. Finally, the expectation is that the introduction of differentiated minima for groups or regions facing particularly high risks of unemployment will benefit workers from these groups or regions. In the case of the introduction of subminimal wages for selected groups, the policy may disadvantage other workers at the same level of productivity because employers would tend to replace more expensive workers with those at the subminimal wage.

In addition, *workers slightly above the minimum wage* are also likely to be (or to be afraid of being) affected by reforms because they risk being replaced by workers at the minimum wage. Indeed, they would benefit from a rise in the minimum wage if this reform results in the elimination of the least skilled (the employment effect) since it would increase their marginal value and hence their wages. On the other hand, they would suffer from a reduction in the minimum wage, since it might bring less-skilled workers into the market, and they might lose their jobs. Hence, semiskilled workers might support an increase in the minimum wage, although they do not benefit directly from such an increase.

Workers in the informal sector are also likely to be indirectly affected because the minimum wage may come to represent a "fair wage" and hence a binding constraint on employers in the informal sector who need to attract labor and minimize labor turnover. Some *employers* are likely to lose from reforms that increase the minimum wage, but the extent of the loss will partly also depend on their ability to elude the increase via an increase in shadow activity or other subtle methods to lower the effective hourly wage without violating the statutory minimum (for example, by extending working hours or reducing training schemes).

Reforms that decrease or increase the minimum wage are relatively simple to implement and have no direct *fiscal implications.* The administration of the minimum wage is also rather simple, and this limits the need for a sizable enforcement agency.

Employment protection legislation

Insider workers hired under permanent contract in the covered sector are those for whom the bulk of employment protection legislation applies directly. They are likely to suffer from radical reforms that soften the legislation since this might increase the chance they will lose their jobs. Thus, radical reductions in the scope of the legislation are generally difficult to implement because successful reforms typically need the approval of the median voter, who is likely to be an insider worker protected by the legislation. This might explain part of the resilience of job-security provisions and the difficulty of implementing radical reform once the institutions are in place. In such a context, marginal reforms seem to be the only politically viable option since they do not affect the median voter. A toughening of the legislation reduces the probability of exiting employment for those currently employed, but also increases the difficulty of finding a new job if one is lost. This produces a sense of insecurity among protected workers, who tend to exert pressure to maintain a high level of protection. Since protected workers tend to have greater political power than outsiders, they will typically oppose any diminution in the legislation.

The *outsiders,* on the other hand, include workers in the informal, uncovered sectors, the unemployed, and workers with fixed-term contracts. For them, a relaxing of the legislation usually has a positive impact in that it increases the hiring rate and, hence, the chance of these people to enter employment as insiders. However, these groups are unlikely to have sufficient political power to bring about the required reforms, and poorer, marginalized workers (youth, women, the unemployed, the discouraged) will tend to become more marginalized.

Finally, *capital owners and shareholders* are likely to benefit from a relaxing of the legislation, both marginal and structural, because strict legislation is akin to a tax on capital since it forces capital to be allocated to low-productivity jobs.

Unemployment benefits

More generous unemployment benefit systems tend to redistribute from less exposed workers to more exposed workers and from the employed to the unemployed. However, the extent to which different groups will gain or lose depends on the strength of the various effects.

Under strong wage effects (when adjustments in the labor market occur through wage compression rather than through employment reduction), *insider workers* are more likely to suffer from reductions in benefits. Consequently, employed workers oppose reforms and may benefit from strong support from unions. Conversely, currently *unemployed individuals* may be more prone to accept benefit cuts because they may realize potential increases in job-finding rates. The progressivity of unemployment benefits is also important. *Skilled workers* may support reductions in strongly progressive systems (or oppose the extension of progressive systems) since they do not benefit so much from these systems. For instance, they might oppose the introduction of a flat rate. Finally, when reforms have a strong active labor market policy content, both employed and unemployed individuals might be winners. Indeed, these policies increase the welfare of outsiders (by increasing expected job-finding rates), while reducing payroll taxes earmarked for unemployment benefits. They may also increase the wages of insiders. Overall, surveys in Europe eliciting the preferences of individuals for benefits (Boeri, Börsch-Supan, and Tabellini 2001) find that the demand for benefits is stronger among unemployed individuals than it is among all employees.

Unions often oppose reforms that reduce the generosity of benefit systems. This is partly because unions typically represent a relatively unskilled segment of the workforce and because unions are sometimes directly involved in the management of benefit systems.

The political economy of reform

Since both intervention and the lack of it have the potential of leading to inefficient and inequitable outcomes, the desirability of labor market intervention depends crucially on the nature and characteristics of the policy. Some policies and intervention designs lead to improvements in efficiency and equity, while others result in a trade-off between the two dimensions, and still others represent a definite worsening in both dimensions. Consequently, it is not possible to evaluate the need for a reform and the potential impact of a reform on poverty and growth without a careful evaluation of the impact on labor market efficiency and income distribution.

Moreover, even in cases in which such an evaluation dictates a particular reform, the actual implementation of the change is never simple for reasons of political economy. This is because the reform is unlikely to be "Pareto neutral" due to its differential impact on the welfare of various groups in society; some groups will benefit, and others are likely to lose out. The magnitude and direction of these benefits and losses will depend crucially on the type of policy under revision and on the details of the reform.

One concern derives from the consideration that a government's decisions on these and other matters may reflect more its overwhelming desire to be reelected rather than the objective of maximizing social welfare. This has two important negative implications. The first might be called short-"termism," whereby policies aiming at long-term social welfare gains that take more than one election cycle to become fully realized are less likely to be implemented than those aiming at a more immediate impact. An example of policies that risk being neglected would be a policy designed to match school education, skill training, and labor market employment.

On the other hand, governments will tend to favor policies that, while suboptimal in terms of welfare impact, may produce tangible gains, but generate costs that are so widely diffused that they are not perceived as costs or are so perceived only by groups or individuals who have little voice and limited political power. Examples of this type of intervention are provided by minimum wage legislation and employment protection legislation.

An example of a highly popular policy with insubstantial or negative welfare impact is the practice of subsidizing the purchase of shares in newly privatized companies. Meanwhile, depending on the prevailing political economy conditions, interventions that have great potential impact, such as improving information flows in the labor market, may be neglected by governments since the benefits are widely dispersed and unlikely to have an important influence on the popularity of the government.

A final rationale for the introduction of and support for interventions that are inefficient is provided by the theory of regulation. The analysis of Peltzman (1976) emphasizes that: (1) regulation confers benefits on certain market participants by providing subsidies or restricting competition; (2) in a static model, by doing this, regulation redistributes wealth toward particular groups; and (3) these groups try to retain or strengthen the regulation by providing political or financial support to sympathetic politicians. Excessively high levels of minimum wage or overly strict employment protection legislation provide good examples of policies that can be introduced and retained despite their potentially negative impact on social welfare.

IMPACT PATHWAYS

Reforms of the labor market have important potential impacts on income distribution and poverty via their impacts on the level and distribution of wages and employment. On the whole, more binding and stricter policies result in higher wages for covered workers at the expense of employment in general and covered employment in particular. Thus, the overall effect of a reform depends on its combined effect on the demand and the supply of labor in the covered sector and in other sectors of the economy. This effect differs across policies and labor market conditions. In any examination of key transmission mechanisms, it is crucial explicitly to consider the *dual* dimension of the economy and distinguish between the formal or covered sector, where the policies apply, and the informal or uncovered sector, where they either do not apply or are not enforced.[12]

The minimum wage

The overall effects of changes in the minimum wage on income distribution and poverty depend on the characteristics of the labor market.

Effects on the level and the distribution of wages in the covered sector

Minimum wage legislation involves establishing a floor for wages so that the equilibrium wage cannot drop below this floor. The expectation is that the introduction of minimum wage legislation or an increase in the minimum wage will, ceteris paribus, result in a compression in wage distribution and a reduction in wage inequality in the formal sector since it boosts the wages of the lowest-paid workers above the unregulated market equilibrium. Conversely, a reform designed to reduce the minimum wage across the board or among selected groups of workers is expected to increase earnings inequality.

However, evidence suggests that the effect of changes in the minimum wage are not limited only to workers at the lower end of the wage distribution. Indeed, a rise in the minimum wage may lead to a shift in the wage distribution and an increase in average wages, and part of this increase may be enjoyed by workers with earnings higher than the minimum wage. If this is the case, any reduction in wage inequality may be considerably less than anticipated.

Effects on the level of employment in the covered sector

In a perfectly competitive labor market, the imposition of a minimum wage above the equilibrium wage—or an increase in the value of the minimum wage—would generally reduce employment through a reduction in labor demand along an upward-sloping labor supply. Workers whose marginal value product is below the minimum wage are forced out of employment; classical unemployment arises and can only be reabsorbed by lowering the minimum wage. If, in addition, the increase in the minimum wage results in an overall increase in wages, the reform will lead to a generalized reduction in employment across the earnings distribution. The extent of this reduction and the overall change in labor incomes received by workers in the covered sector depend on the elasticity of labor demand (at constant output). Across the world, this typically varies between −0.15 and −0.75, with an average of −0.45 (Hamermesh 1993).

On the other hand, if a labor market or any of its segments are dominated by a single employer, the monopsonist, then the impact of an increase in the minimum wage may be very different. The reason for this conclusion is that the monopsonist can affect the equilibrium wage by deciding on the volume of hiring. If labor supply grows with wages, the monopsonist will have an incentive to restrict hiring in order to benefit from low wages. In this context, a rise in the minimum wage is perfectly consistent with a rise in employment. Thus, for a sufficiently low level of starting wage, an increase in the minimum wage could be accompanied by an increase in employment. However, above some specific threshold, the traditional negative relationship sets in. This result is very important. However, three caveats are in order:

- Pure monopsony situations are very uncommon; they may occur in specific geographic areas where labor mobility is low and the number of firms is small.
- An increase in the minimum wage acts positively on employment only when the initial level of wages is low (below the competitive wage); this is not common in most real-life markets.
- The impact on employment of a rise in the minimum wage depends on the elasticity of labor supply; labor supply has little elasticity on average.

Over the last 10 years, a number of papers have studied various imperfect models in which an upward-sloping supply curve at the firm level may arise, implying that the basic monopsony model may become relevant. When imperfect information is pervasive, workers may have an interest in refusing job offers when the wage is too low, since they may get better offers later on. A firm must then choose a wage level that will allow it to attract a sufficient number of workers to meet its needs (Burdett and Mortensen 1998; Masters 1999). This mechanism ensures a monotonic relationship between the wage and the size of firms. Other scholars have proposed variants of the monopsony model grounded in the theory of "efficiency wages." Manning (2004) summarizes and reviews this research in detail.

The introduction of a subminimal wage among categories of workers characterized by particularly low average productivity (youth) or a high variation in productivity levels (women) has an impact on these workers that is equivalent to that of a generalized reduction in the minimum wage, that is, it will increase employment among them unless the monopsonist model applies. However, the increase in employment among these workers may be achieved at the expense of a reduction in employment among other workers, and the overall effect on aggregate employment is uncertain.

It appears that no systematic evaluation of the impact of reductions in the minimum wage exists. However, experimental evidence suggests that the effects of changes in opposing directions in the minimum wage are not symmetrical and that the positive effect of a reduction in the minimum wage on employment may be much smaller than the negative effect of an increase of equal proportion in the minimum wage. This is because the existence of the minimum wage results in a permanent increase in reservation wages that does not fully adjust downward when the level of the minimum wage is reduced (Falk, Fehr, and Zehnder 2005).

The impact on wages and employment in the uncovered sector

In most developing countries, there is a substantial informal sector, and, in large pockets of the formal sector, minimum wage legislation is not applied. This does not mean that these sectors are unaffected by minimum wage reforms since there are important spillover effects between the two sectors. The standard theoretical argument is that, following an increase in the minimum wage, sector wages that are not covered will fall because redundant workers will move into employment in the uncovered sector, and employment in this sector will rise (Gramlich 1976; Mincer 1976; Welch 1976).[13] However, if an increase in the minimum wage in the formal sector leads firms in the informal sector to raise their average wage to keep attracting good workers or because of "fair remuneration considerations," an increase in the minimum wage can lead to an increase in informal sector wages (the lighthouse effect) or a drop in employment.

The effect on participation, job-seeking, and unemployment

In the context of a labor market that is supply constrained, the expected impact of the minimum wage may be somewhat different given the existence of endogenous labor market participation and endogenous search effort on the part of the unemployed. One can think of the decision to participate in the labor market as the solution to the trade-off between the value of being an unemployed job-seeker and the value of being engaged full time in home production. In this situation, the increase in the potential benefits of employment generated by the increase in the minimum wage may lead to an increase in labor force participation and a shift in labor supply that increases employment among the low paid. In addition, if the new minimum wage exceeds the reservation wage, the intensity of the job search by the unemployed and their exit rate from unemployment may rise. Thus, the supply-side effects of the introduction of a new, higher minimum wage may combine to increase employment and reduce unemployment.

The effect of minimum wage reforms on income distribution and poverty

In evaluating the potential impact of minimum wage reforms on income distribution, it is important to distinguish between earnings distribution and income distribution. The former is defined at the level of the individual and by focusing only on employed workers. The latter is usually defined at the level of households and is calculated according to the total labor income of all household members, plus income from other sources.

An increase in the minimum wage can have both a positive and a negative effect on inequality in household incomes. First, a rise in incomes at the lower end of the income range among the formally employed typically reduces inequality in individual earnings. However, it might also result in less employment among the low-paid workers for whom the minimum wage is binding or in the transfer of some of these workers to the uncovered, less-well-paid informal sector. This could increase inequality in labor incomes both at the individual level and at the household level, especially if workers on the minimum wage live in households with a high proportion of low-skilled, potentially low-paid individuals. The overall direct effect on income inequality depends on labor market conditions, demographics, and household composition.

These effects are compounded by the indirect changes in the sector not covered. If labor is mobile across sectors, then the standard covered-uncovered adjustment mechanisms operate, and an increase in the minimum wage leads to an increase in earnings inequality. Yet, the impact is reduced if the lighthouse effect comes into play, since a higher minimum wage leads to an increase in wages in both the covered market and the uncovered market. In this case, the overall impact on the distribution of household income will depend on the employment dynamics between the covered sector and the uncovered sector, as well as the impact of the reform on the two segments of the labor market.

Reforms of the minimum wage are also expected to have a typically ambiguous impact on the *poverty rate*.[14] An increase in the minimum wage, for example, will typically raise the earnings of low-paid workers who maintain their jobs, and, ceteris paribus, this will bring the poverty rate down if these individuals are the lone earners within their households and if all low-paid earners within households maintain their employment at the prereform level. However, the increase is also likely to reduce employment in the covered sector, and this will result in lower labor income at the household level if any wage earners lose their jobs because of the policy or are forced to transfer to the lower-paying, uncovered sector. This may increase the vulnerability to poverty of households that are close to the poverty line (Brown 1999). However, evidence in developed countries suggests that a large proportion of earners on the minimum wage are second or third earners in households that are well above the poverty line. This substantially reduces the potential impact of minimum wage reforms on the incidence of poverty.

Employment protection legislation

There are four transmission mechanisms through which reforms in employment protection legislation can affect the distribution of incomes and the incidence of poverty.

Impact of reforms on hiring, firing, and employment levels

Hiring and, especially, firing are the key standard mechanisms of any reform in employment protection legislation because such legislation tends to increase the cost to firms of initiating a worker separation. Thus, the most direct effect of legislative reform is a change in the rate of firings since the reform affects the tendency of firms to hoard labor—to hold onto marginal jobs—and delay the timing of labor adjustments. However, legislative reform also has an obvious indirect effect on hiring because firms, at the hiring stage, will attempt to anticipate future costly adjustments because of adverse shocks. Strict legislation will therefore reduce the incentive for firms to hire additional workers. The combination of direct and indirect effects suggests that strict legislation will reduce turnover (hiring and firing), while any reform that reduces the stringency of the legislation will lead to an increase in turnover among firms. The effects on the stock of employment are more ambiguous. In equilibrium, hiring and firing among firms offset each other. In this case, the existence of legislation has no clear effect on the average employment level. The key transmission mechanism of employment protection legislation does not imply a reduction in average employment, but rather an effect on the flows of employment.[15]

The transmission mechanism described above can be easily applied to the case of radical reforms, but, when reforms are marginal, the situation is more complicated. This is illustrated by a reform that increases the availability of fixed-term contracts, a typical marginal reform in OECD countries during the 1990s.[16] The availability of temporary contracts will certainly raise the incentive for firms to hire new workers on a temporary basis. In addition, it will increase the incentive for firms to wait until the expiration of temporary contracts before implementing reductions in personnel. This suggests that a marginal reform in the labor market can lead to the formation of a dual labor market, wherein a stock of protected workers hired under a complete legislative regime of employment protection exists alongside a fringe of workers hired under temporary contracts, and that this dual labor market acts as a buffer against labor market shocks (Blanchard and Landier 2002).

The workings of the key transmission mechanism depend crucially on the behavior of wages and on the use of taxes versus transfers. The baseline transmission mechanism functions smoothly if wages do not adjust in response to changes in employment protection legislation and if a reform relates to a tax component of the legislation. The situation becomes more complicated if wages can adjust, especially in the case of legislation involving transfers.

Wage-bargaining

Another important transmission mechanism involves the effect of employment protection legislation on the *threat point* of wage-bargaining for insider workers. The existence of such legislation reduces a firm's threat point in the bargaining over the wages of insiders because insiders are protected by the legislation against dismissal in case a wage agreement is not reached. As a result, the existence of the legislation leads to higher wages for insider workers.

The key issue is what happens to the wages of outsiders. Most wage-bargaining models predict the emergence of a two-tier regime, whereby the wages of outsiders are reduced because of the legislation. In other words, workers on temporary contracts partly prepay, in the form of lower wages, the future cost of employment protection legislation. The size of the prepayment will depend on whether the legislation provides for a firing tax or a severance payment.

In the case of severance payments, the prepayment is full, so that the expected cumulative wage bill obtained by hiring an outsider is constant. This is the well-known neutrality result of the existence of severance payments and wage flexibility, originally identified by Lazear (1990). It is an important benchmark result, since it suggests that, when employment protection legislation takes the form of a transfer and wages are sufficiently flexible, the legislation is neutral. In the case of firing taxes, the prepayment is never full, so that the predictions obtained by the standard mechanism apply. To sum up this transmission mechanism: employment protection legislation induces a reduction in the wages of outsiders and an increase in the wages of insiders. In addition, when the legislation provides for a transfer, the effect of wage-bargaining is so important that the legislation is neutralized. The neutrality disappears, however, as soon as wages become rigid or if the legislation provides for a tax rather than a transfer.[17]

The effort of workers and labor productivity

Another transmission mechanism revolves around the impact of employment protection legislation on worker productivity. Since such legislation increases job security, it automatically reduces the incentive of workers to make any extra effort and, thus, in turn, reduces labor productivity. While it is true that an increase in job security can certainly lead to an increase in the propensity of workers to shirk, one needs to bear in mind the difference between economic dismissal and disciplinary dismissal; legislative provisions typically govern only economic dismissals, that is, dismissals that are not caused by a shortcoming of the workers (Ichino and Riphahn 2005). If a clear distinction exists between economic and disciplinary dismissals, the potential for an increase in shirking is substantially reduced. In addition, many have argued that the greater job tenure that derives from employment protection legislation may in fact foster an increase in productivity via the higher incidence of job-specific training and greater company loyalty among workers.

Capital-labor substitution and capital allocation

Employment protection legislation may also have an impact on the prevailing technology. This mechanism was originally discussed by Caballero and Hammour (1998), and it is best understood from the perspective of a sort of putty-clay technology.[18] In the short run, capital is largely fixed and installed, and capital-labor substitution is low. In the long run, however, firms have a much more flexible technological menu at their disposal and can select different capital-labor ratios. This suggests that more encompassing employment protection legislation may have different effects in the short and long run. In the short run, an increase in legislative coverage may result in a tax on existing capital in ways that cause a greater share of the surplus to be captured by labor. The situation is different in the long run. Since employment protection legislation acts partly as a tax on labor, firms have an incentive to invest in labor-saving technologies, leading to an increase in the capital-labor ratio.

Finally, the passage of stricter legislation tends to reduce the reallocation of capital from ailing sectors to expanding sectors. In a sense, this is in the nature of a sclerotic market; it suggests that, in a country with strict legislation, capital is not allocated efficiently. This may have an obvious impact on the average productivity of the economy and may also affect the growth process.

Unemployment benefits

Reforms of the system of unemployment benefits can impact labor market outcomes through various channels.

Impact on unemployment duration and incentives for job-seeking

Generous, long-term benefit entitlements may provide an incentive for longer spells of unemployment; cross-country evidence demonstrates the existence of this positive association (Boeri, Layard, and Nickell 2001). Thus, a reduction in unemployment benefits is advocated as a way of reducing the duration of spells of unemployment. However, some studies suggest that causality might work the other way: in cases of high long-term unemployment, governments might be pressed to increase the duration of benefits. For instance, changes in the duration of unemployment benefits in some parts of the United States tend to follow upon increases in the duration of unemployment (Card and Levine 2000). This means that the negative effects of benefits on the duration of unemployment may be overstated.

Thus, most benefit systems are designed to discourage recipients from using the system for the maximum duration. For instance, unemployment insurance benefits typically decrease in value over time, and there may be limits on the maximum duration of unemployment assistance benefits or conditions may be imposed in terms of the time or effort spent job-seeking. New policies also provide incentives to increase search efforts by imposing restrictions and conditions on the receipt of unemployment benefits. Finally, assistance in job-seeking is often provided to encourage more active searches. On the other hand, eligibility for unemployment assistance that is based on means-testing at the household level can create strong incentives for other members of the household to leave employment or limit their searches (because their incomes may increase the average household income above the eligibility income threshold).

Reforms reducing the generosity of unemployment benefits (or raising the rewards of labor market participation) provide incentives for the unemployed to increase the intensity of their job searches. Furthermore, evidence supports the positive effect on employment and on earnings of the provision of assistance in job hunting. Evidence also points to the cost savings arising from the increased flows of people from unemployment to employment generated by the imposition of job-seeking requirements. Finally, penalties on individuals refusing to take up suitable job offers seem to be rather effective in a few selected countries (the Netherlands for example).

Impact on the level and type of employment

The implementation of an increase in wage subsidies through variable contribution rates among employers for different types of workers may also affect employment and wages, depending on the elasticity of labor demand and supply.[19] A reduction by 21 percent in employer contributions in Belgium for the wages of unskilled workers is expected to increase employment among low-skilled workers by almost 7 percent. Estimates for France and the Netherlands point to similar increases.[20]

Linking benefits to past contributions reduces the incentive to evade payroll contributions and provides an incentive for workers to stay in the formal sector. Since these workers would likely require a higher wage in the informal sector, this also provides an incentive to firms to remain active in the formal sector to avoid paying higher wages.

TOOLS OF ANALYSIS AND THE FINDINGS

Natural experiment is the best empirical methodology for assessing the distributional effects of labor market reforms. This methodology consists of exploiting exogenous changes in the economic environment of certain agents to compare their reactions to those of otherwise similar agents who have not undergone the changes. The influential work of Card and Krueger (1994) on the effect of the minimum wage represents a key illustration of this methodology. However, the opportunity for carrying out studies based on this technique is rarely at hand, and, for the most part, researchers have to find other ways of assessing the impact of labor market reforms.

Computable general equilibrium models can also be useful, but they have to depend on an underlying structure of the labor market in a way that is consistent with the complex effects of the regulation in question. There are two key features that should be kept in mind, particularly if one is dealing with a complex dual labor market in a developing country. First, the analyst should pay special attention during the modeling of both the formal-covered sector and the informal-uncovered sector of the economy. Second, a model based on a simple two-sector conception of perfect competition is hardly appropriate for assessing the effects of reforms that may have considerably different impacts under different labor market conditions, say, the impact of a reform of the minimum wage in a context of monopsonistic price setting. The literature does not yet seem to provide a good example of complex labor markets that could be used as reference points.

For the most part, the empirical literature focuses on

- evaluating the impact on one particular link in the chain of reactions described above (that is, employment or the wage level), without much consideration of the transmission channels of the impact (that is, the full distributional impact)
- the impact of the implementation of a particular policy rather than the potential effects of reforms in the current system

The review that has been undertaken of methodologies and findings for this chapter covers the existing evidence and treats the implementation or removal of a policy as a type of reform that causes a labor market to become more regulated or less regulated. The findings on each of the transmission channels and on the overall impact on income distribution and poverty are summarized below.

Minimum wage

Over the last 10 years, an extensive amount of research on the employment effect of the minimum wage has emerged, mainly in response to the results of the empirical studies carried out by Card and Krueger (1995). Furthermore, the growing availability of microdata for developing countries has permitted a deepening understanding of the minimum wage in dual markets. Most of the empirical literature analyzes total employment from the perspective of the effects of the introduction of or increase in the minimum wage. Some also focuses on the impact of changes in the subminimal wage on the employment of youth. On the basis of the available evidence, it is not clear that an increase in the minimum wage leads, on average, to substantial job losses. However, the increase may contribute to a shift from formal to informal employment.[21]

Effects on the level of employment

Card and Krueger (1994, 1995) studied the impact of increases in the minimum wage in New Jersey in 1992 and in California in 1988, taking

Pennsylvania, a state where the minimum wage did not change, as a control. Using a difference-in-difference estimator, they found that, after the minimum wage was raised from $4.25 to $5.05 in New Jersey, the level of employment in fast-food establishments rose more quickly in New Jersey than it did in Pennsylvania. They concluded that an increase in the minimum wage may lead to a rise in employment if the wage is sufficiently low at the outset, as it was in New Jersey. (In the literature on development, no evidence derived from natural experiments has been discovered on changes in the minimum wage.)

The research by Card and Krueger generated a vivid debate along two dimensions. The first dimension was the interpretation of the results, for example, whether consumers of fast food can be considered representative of the population as a whole, since it may well be that persons earning minimum wages are typical consumers of fast food. The second dimension of the debate revolved around the fact that the original Card and Krueger study was based on data gathered through telephone interviews and not on administrative data. However, despite the arguments and counterarguments exchanged between Neumark and Wascher (2000) and Card and Krueger (1994), the results of the earlier study seem to have been confirmed.

In the absence of access to the natural experiment methodology, the large majority of empirical studies adopt a methodology that consists of highlighting the aggregate correlation between variations in employment and the minimum wage, while controlling for the other factors that might affect employment. These studies make use of the evolution over time of the minimum wage, as well as differences in the level of the minimum wage across industries and geographic regions. The estimates vary from country to country. Large negative effects are found in Colombia (Bell 1997), Ghana (Jones 1998), Morocco (Agenor and El Aynaoui 2003), and Puerto Rico (Castillo-Freeman and Freeman 1992), while the impact appears to be insignificant in Indonesia and Mexico (Bell 1997; Rama 1996). Carneiro (2004) also finds evidence of a significant reduction in formal sector employment and a shift toward employment in the low-paying informal sector. It is clear that, in this type of study, too many variables are often left out of the analysis, and the coefficients should not be interpreted as robust evidence, but simply as important country-specific correlations.

Data at the level of firms are becoming available in developing countries and are often used to estimate the impact of the minimum wage on labor demand. Studies typically use these data on the formal manufacturing sector and regress employment at the level of firms on a set of controls (such as the prices for other factors and value added, if available), a minimum wage dummy, and employment lags to allow for dynamic adjustment.[22] The estimates of the impact vary across countries. The effect of the minimum wage appears large and negative in Colombia (Bell 1997; Maloney and Mendez 2003), but small or negligible in Costa Rica and Mexico. In Indonesia, the sharp increase in the minimum wage registered between 1990 and 1996 appears to have reduced employment in small domestic firms, but not in larger ones, foreign or domestic. Meanwhile, the impact on total employment was found to be positive in Brazil, but was the result of a composition effect between hours and jobs; the total number of hours increased, but the number of jobs fell.

Estimates of the impact also vary across *groups of workers.* The job losses resulting from an increase in the minimum wage in Brazil and Mexico seem to have particularly affected marginal groups such as women, youth, and low-skilled workers. It is supposed that this impact depends on the level of the minimum wage relative to the wages of these groups (World Bank 2006). In Chile, an increase in the minimum wage appears to have reduced employment opportunities among youth and the unskilled and, thus, especially unskilled youth, while promoting the employment of skilled and older workers (Montenegro and Pagés 2003). The minimum wage also appears to be responsible for much of the increase in long-term unemployment among the unskilled population in Bulgaria and Lithuania (Rutkowski 2003a, 2003b). Similarly, experience in Mexico suggests that the erosion of the minimum wage in the 1990s boosted employment among women (Feliciano 1998). Some countries also experimented with subminimal wages for apprenticeship, which seems to have improved employment opportunities for young graduates in Chile (Gill, Montenegro, and Domeland 2002).

While most of these studies use data on the formal sector, there are at least three studies that use the same methodology to look at the employment effects of changes in the minimum wage in the *informal sector* (Lemos 2004a for Brazil; Gindling and Terrell 2004a for Costa Rica; Jones 1998 for Ghana). Using microdata for Brazil, Lemos finds evidence of adverse employment effects in both the formal sector and the informal sector, challenging standard two-sector models. Her results are consistent with a sizable lighthouse effect. Similar effects are also found by Gindling and Terrell for Costa Rica who, perhaps surprisingly, also discovered evidence that the minimum wage compresses wage distribution in the informal sector more than in the formal sector. Yet, no wage effect of the minimum wage was found for the self-employed. In contrast, Jones (1998) found that the effects of the minimum wage in the informal sector in Ghana appear consistent with the standard mechanism of the traditional two-sector model.

Individual longitudinal data make it possible to follow the labor market histories of persons whose wages are at or close to the minimum wage. Recent studies in this area find that changes in the minimum wage have a significant impact on employment among these workers. Nevertheless, there is no agreement over the direction of these changes. Abowd et al. (1999) found that, in France, an increase of 1 percent in the minimum wage reduces the employment probability of workers on minimum wage by 1.3 percent among men and 1.0 percent among women. In the United States, a reduction by 1 percent in the minimum wage increases the employment probability of affected workers by 0.4 percent among men and 1.6 percent among women. Portugal and Cardoso (2001) found different results using the same type of methodology. They exploited legislative changes in the minimum wage in Portugal in 1987. The minimum wage was raised by 50 percent for adolescents aged 16 to 18 and 33 percent for youths 18 and 19. They found that the hikes had a dampening effect on hiring, but that those young people who found jobs had a greater tendency to keep them. In other words, Portugal and Cardoso observed fewer departures from employment, and this partly offset the fall in hiring.[23] Using longitudinal data from three contrasting individual data sets, Stewart (2004) found that the introduction of the minimum wage in the United Kingdom had an insignificant effect on the employment probability of low-wage workers.[24] Indeed, overall, the minimum wage appeared to have potentially significant effects on the probability of being hired or of losing a job. However, it does not invariably have a positive effect on the probability of job loss among the population affected by the minimum wage.

Effects on the wage level, the average wage, and wage distribution

Empirical evidence suggests that the introduction of or increase in the minimum wage has considerable spillover effects on the level of wages of workers further up the earning distribution. For instance, studies in Brazil, Colombia, and Mexico show that a 10 percent increase in the minimum wage results in a 1–6 percent increase in average wages (World Bank 2006). This appears to be caused by the fact that the minimum wage seems to be used as a more general unit of account or "numeraire," for instance in quoting wages or monetary contracts in general, and, hence, the minimum wage influences wages throughout the earnings distribution. For example, in Bolivia, the effects of a change in the minimum wage have echoed up the wage distribution; 60 percent of the rise has been transferred to wages around the minimum wage, and 38 percent to wages around four times the minimum wage (Maloney and Mendez 2003). In Indonesia, a doubling of the minimum wage led to an estimated 10 percent increase in average wages (Rama 1996).

However, empirical evidence from Latin America suggests that some groups of workers benefit disproportionately from increases in the minimum wage and that this has important distributional implications. For example, analyses in Brazil and Mexico suggest that minimum wage increases benefit men more than women throughout the wage distribution. A 10 percent increase in the Mexican minimum wage led to a 10–36 percent increase in men's wages, but only to a 0–10 percent increase for women (World Bank 2006). Similarly, in Mexico, adults with wages around the minimum wage are found to benefit more from minimum wage increases than do the young in the same earnings category.

The minimum wage appears also to operate somewhat in the informal sector in many countries of Latin America, including Brazil, Chile, Colombia, Ecuador, El Salvador, Guyana, Mexico, Nicaragua, Panama, Paraguay, Peru, Venezuela, and Uruguay (World Bank 2006). In Brazil, there is evidence that the minimum wage has a strong influence on the informal labor market and acts as a "voluntary" reference wage. Over 20 percent of wage adjustments in the informal sector were exactly equal to the minimum wage adjustment after the launching of the Real Plan, September 1994 to May 1995 (Amadeo, Gill, and Neri 2002). In Costa Rica, the minimum wage compresses the wage distribution in the informal sector more than in the formal sector, but does not have wage effects among the self-employed (Gindling and Terrell 2004a). Similarly, there does not seem to be evidence of a strong lighthouse effect among the self-employed in Bolivia; this might be related to the fact that the self-employed may adjust their earnings frequently to avoid inflation erosion (Maloney and Mendez 2003).

The effect of minimum wage reforms on income distribution and poverty

One way of assessing whether the minimum wage is actually enforced is to plot the earnings of individuals as a histogram. The position and shape of the histogram provide information on the extent of compliance with the minimum wage. If there had been no government intervention in the labor market, one would expect the wage distribution to be relatively smooth, reflecting the underlying distribution of skills among workers. On the other hand, if employers actually enforce the minimum wage, workers who would have earned less than the minimum are no longer employed, and the distribution is truncated. The fact that some workers have lost their jobs should create a spike in the wage distribution that is relatively close to the legally imposed minimum. If there is no spike or if the spike lies significantly to the right or the left of the minimum wage, the data indicate that the minimum wage is having little "bite." This empirical methodology is often used to provide a first assessment of the impact of a minimum wage. Most studies on developing countries *find evidence of a spike* in the wage distribution that corresponds to the minimum wage. This is a first, visual effect of the ability of the minimum wage to compress the earnings distribution. This effect appears to occur in most developing countries in Latin America and in some transition economies.[25]

Particularly interesting is the search for a wage spike in the informal sector. Since the minimum wage is not binding in that sector, one would expect to find no spike, but, if the lighthouse effect is relevant, one may find a spike in the wage distribution also in the informal sector. The lighthouse effect is precisely what Lemos (2004a) finds in her study of the impact of the minimum wage in the formal and informal sectors of the Brazilian economy. Similar results have also been found in other Latin American countries (World Bank 2006).

The overall impact of a reform on earnings inequality seems to depend on the initial level of the minimum wage. In Latin America, increases in a high minimum wage have been found to boost inequality, while increases in a relatively low minimum wage reduce inequality (World Bank 2006). The decrease in the real minimum wage in Brazil and Mexico in the 1990s has been blamed for a large share of the increase in overall inequality. Thus, the decrease was responsible for 4.8 percent of the increase in inequality in the formal sector and 18.4 percent in the informal sector in Brazil (Rodrigues and Menezes-Filho 2004). Similarly, a study of 121 countries over the period 1970–2000 shows that the minimum wage (relative to per capita income) tends to worsen income inequality (Calderón, Chong, and Valdés 2004).

On the other hand, empirical research in the United States generally concludes that the minimum wage reduces wage inequality (Brown 1999) and that an increase in the minimum wage also reduces wage inequality. DiNardo, Fortin, and Lemieux (1996) and Lee (1999) suggest that the fall in the real value of the minimum wage contributed significantly to rising wage inequality in the United States in the 1980s. DiNardo, Fortin, and Lemieux (1996) look at the evolution of the distribution of wages between 1979 and 1988 and find that the fall in the minimum wage explains one-quarter of the rise in the standard deviation in the distribution of men's wages and 30 percent of the standard deviation for women. Lee (1999), for his part, estimates that the shrinking minimum wage over this period explains 70 percent of the increase in the ratio of average fifth-decile wages to average first-decile wages.

Evidence from the United States suggests that the net effect of a minimum wage increase on *poverty* is very small; only 4.1 percent of the group was lifted out of poverty, while 3.9 percent of the previously non-poor fell into poverty as a result of the policy (Neumark and Wascher 1997). One possible explanation lies in the fact that earners of the minimum wage are typically distributed across the broader population (including in middle-income households) rather than only in low-income households. Hence, some of those who lose their jobs might live in households that have other substantial sources of income that can help maintain the newly unemployed individuals within the non-poor household. Similar results have also been obtained through a simulation exercise in the United Kingdom that used data from the family-expenditure survey and Polimod, a tax-benefit microsimulation model (Sutherland 2001). Findings from this simulation suggest that the minimum wage is not an efficient method for targeting poverty in the United Kingdom because it benefits the same proportions of the poor and the non-poor. In addition, poverty rates appear not to be very sensitive to the level of the minimum wage, and the introduction of the minimum wage appears to have only a small impact on the overall poverty rate, a potential reduction of only 1.2 percent.

For the minimum wage to have a significant impact on poverty, it needs to be higher than the subsistence minimum for wage earners and their dependents. However, the minimum wage provides for the basic needs of one worker, plus one dependent in only 7 of the 17 countries in a study on Latin America and the Caribbean (World Bank 2006). A look at both the increased wages among those household members who kept their jobs and the fall in earnings among those who lost theirs reveals that the increase in the minimum wage had some impact on wage poverty rates in Colombia, but not in Brazil (Arango and Pachon 2003). A disaggregation among the poor, who represent a large share of the population in these countries, shows, however, that the poorest do not benefit. Rather, the main beneficiaries are households near the poverty line. The poorest 25 percent in Colombia are not helped at all, which might be because the wage and unemployment effects cancel each other out or because the minimum wage laws do not have effects on this part of the population. In Brazil, the bottom 30 percent of the income distribution actually experiences wage losses, while poor households in higher brackets do not benefit. These results are confirmed by Carneiro (2004), who suggests that the shift of employment from the formal sector to the informal sector following the increases in the minimum wage in Brazil from 1982 to 2002 was largely responsible for the rise in poverty over that period. Similarly, evidence from Indonesia suggests that increases in the minimum wage may have worsened the poverty situation there (Mason and Baptist 1996).

In contrast, an analysis in four African, five Asian, and thirteen Latin American countries shows that the minimum wage does reduce poverty as measured by headcount, the poverty gap, or calorie intake. These effects are similar in the various regions, though they are more marked for urban poverty relative to rural poverty. However, since the minimum wage is also associated with higher unemployment, the reduction in poverty may be offset by losses in efficiency over the long term (Lustig and McLeod 1996).

Employment protection legislation

Assessing the impact of a specific reform in employment protection legislation is not easy. In the absence of evaluations using natural experiments, most empirical regularities are revealed through cross-country comparisons rather than through full-fledged policy evaluation. Researchers have used statistical methods to compare the effects of a reform on treatment groups of workers, as well as control groups. This is always done using microdata on firms and workers. A good example is the work of Kugler (2000, 2004) on the Colombian reform. The identification strategy of this type of analysis consists of exploiting the change over time in labor market legislation, together with the variability in coverage across groups. While such studies broadly confirm the empirical regularities, they provide much sounder economic analyses. Another example of this type of study is Acemoglu and Angrist (2001).

Effect on employment levels

According to the theoretical wisdom, the overall effect of employment protection legislation on employment should be limited. Indeed, stricter legislation is expected to reduce labor turnover, which would translate into higher employment rates during periods of recession (since firms cannot adjust their labor force downward) and lower employment rates during periods of expansion (since firms do not adjust for fear of subsequent recessions). Hence, the net impact of reforms is likely to vary according to economic cycles.

Evidence from cross-country time-series data on OECD countries tends to find that stricter employment protection legislation has either a negative or an insignificant impact on employment. Similarly, the effect on unemployment is ambiguous. However, evidence based on disaggre-

gated data for single countries, which permit the capture of more variations in regulatory policies, suggests that job-security regulations have a
negative effect on employment.[26]

In Peru, the use of severance payments is found to have a negative
effect on the level of employment, and labor demand appears to adjust
more slowly to economic cycles. Between 1987 and 1990, a 10 percent
increase in dismissal costs reduced long-run employment rates by an estimated 11 percent, keeping wages constant (Saavedra and Torero 2000,
2003). Evidence from Argentina also points to a negative relationship
between employment protection legislation and employment, with a
10 percent increase in dismissal costs, leading to a 3 to 6 percent decrease
in employment rates (Mondino and Montoya 2003). Overall, the
country-specific evidence from Latin America consistently points to a
negative impact on average employment rates by employment protection
legislation, although a cross-sectional analysis of time-series data on a
pool of countries does not yield robust results (Heckman and Pagés
2003). Similarly, in South Africa, 39 percent of large manufacturing
firms reacted to stricter legislation by reducing the level of hiring or substituting capital for workers, which suggests that the legislation had a
negative impact on employment levels.[27] An equally strong negative relation emerges in Croatia, where excessive legislative controls have been
identified as the only major reason for high levels of unemployment
(Rutkowski 2003c).

In the longer term, legislation may have an impact on the type of
technology that firms select. An increase in legislative controls could, in
the long run, lead firms to invest in labor-saving technologies, thereby
raising the capital-labor ratio and lowering employment. This phenomenon seems to be confirmed by a comparison of France and the United
States in the 1980s and 1990s (Caballero and Hammour 1998). Capital-
labor ratios are larger in France than they are in the United States, and
the evolution of profit shares is consistent with this finding (Blanchard
1997). The evidence from South Africa presented in Table 3.3 also points
to substitution, with 39 percent of large manufacturing firms responding
to stricter legislation by replacing workers by capital.

Effects on employment flows

Overall, radical reforms in employment protection legislation affect the
cost for firms of the worker separations the firm may initiate. A first direct
effect is that strict legislation pushes the firms to hold on to marginal jobs
and delay labor adjustment (that is, they hoard labor). Stricter legislation
also leads firms to anticipate more costly labor adjustments in the future

TABLE 3.3. Cumulative Employment Response of Firms in the Greater Johannesburg Metropolitan Area to the Stricter Labor Policies of 1995–9, 1999

percentage share of firms

	Large manufacturing	Large tourism	Large information technology
Hire fewer workers	39.2	25.9	7.0
Substitute capital machinery for workers	38.9	7.3	14.0
Hire more temporary than permanent workers	41.6	27.9	14.0
Rely more on subcontracting	33.5	27.8	19.0
Improve labor relations	29.6	26.0	9.0
Increase labor productivity	11.9	18.7	—

Source: Chandra and Nganou 2001.

in response to adverse shocks, which reduces their incentive and propensity to hire. This suggests that stricter legislation reduces turnover (hiring and firing) within firms and increases the duration of unemployment. As a result, any reform that reduces the stringency of employment protection legislation should induce an increase in turnover within firms. This assessment is strongly supported by empirical studies in OECD countries. For instance, Scarpetta (1996) finds that the effect of strict legislation is more severe on long-term unemployment than on average unemployment.

The reduction in the costs of firing in Peru since 1991 through fewer job-security regulations, the introduction of temporary contracts, and changes in the severance payment regime has led to a growth in turnover, especially in the formal sector, among blue-collar workers and temporary workers (Saavedra and Torero 2000, 2003). Similarly, the introduction of fixed-term contracts and employment trial periods in Argentina led to a sharp increase in labor turnover, increasing hazard rates during trial periods by 40 percent, without an offsetting decrease in long-term employment (Hopenhayn 2001).[28] In Colombia, a loosening of regulations in 1990 increased the dynamism of the labor market by raising entry and exit rates into and out of unemployment, especially in the formal sector and among large firms (Kugler 2000).

Effects on types of employment

Marginal reforms can have an impact on types of employment. For instance, a reform in employment protection legislation that increases the availability of fixed-term contracts will increase the incentive for firms to hire new workers on temporary contracts and wait to lay off employees until the expiration of temporary contracts. Hence, such marginal reforms can lead to the establishment of a dual labor market wherein a stock of protected workers hired under a full employment protection regime is accompanied by a fringe of flexible workers hired on temporary contracts. These temporary contracts thus act as a sort of buffer to shocks in the output market (Blanchard and Landier 2002).

The use of temporary contracts varies across countries, but it is substantial in some cases. For instance, in Spain, the share of workers hired on temporary contracts is now as high as 30 percent (Dolado, García-Serrano, and Jimeno 2002). The share of temporary contracts in formal salaried employment in Lima rose from under 20 percent in 1991 to 44 percent in 1997 after the red tape and restrictions on temporary contracts were reduced (Saavedra and Torero 2000). In Argentina, the rise in hiring on temporary contracts was associated with a substitution away from longer-term employment (Hopenhayn 2001). In Colombia, growing employment turnover following a relaxation of employment protection legislation resulted in greater reliance on temporary contracts, as well as less job security for permanent workers (Kugler 2000). Evidence on large firms, especially manufacturing firms, in the metropolitan area of Johannesburg also points to a shift to temporary contracts as a result of the passage of stricter legislation in 1995–9, as shown in Table 3.3. More generally, the introduction of strict legislation in India and Zimbabwe appears to have been followed by a substantial decline in the demand for employees, with a clear causality relation, at least in the case of India (Fallon and Lucas 1991).

Effect on the demographic structure of employment

Similarly, stricter legislative regimes can increase the marginalization of outsiders. While average employment is not necessarily directly affected by strict legislation, stricter employment protection legislation tends to be associated with fewer jobs for newcomers to the labor market (youth, low-skilled workers, women, and so on). This can be explained partly by the fact that the value of severance payments rises with wages and with seniority, making it more expensive for firms to dismiss older or more well paid workers. For instance, in the OECD and in Latin America, more stringent legislation is found to increase youth unemployment more than average unemployment (Heckman and Pagés 2000 and Scarpetta 1996). The evidence for differentiated impacts on men and women is less uniform. Heckman and Pagés (2000) find that stricter legislation is associated with lower employment rates among women in the OECD, but with higher employment rates among women in Latin America. Evidence from Chile suggests that stricter regulations reduce the employment opportunities of the young and the unskilled (thus, especially unskilled youth). It also finds that stricter regulations may force some workers, particularly women and the unskilled, out of wage employment and into self-employment (Montenegro and Pagés 2003).

Effect on formal employment

To the extent that different employers are subject to different rules (either because of their formal or informal status, or because of their sector), reforms in employment protection legislation can influence the sectoral distribution of employment. In India, stricter employment protection (in favor of workers) is found to decrease registered manufacturing output and employment (firms are registered in the formal sector once they reach a certain size) and increase unregistered (informal) manufacturing output, with no net effect on total output (Besley and Burgess 2004). Marquez (1998) finds that, in Latin America, more stringent protection is associated with a larger percentage of self-employed workers. Overall, however, the evidence is still mixed on this effect both in the OECD and in Latin America (Heckman and Pagés 2000).

Effects on unemployment

While the evidence suggests that stricter protection legislation has a negative effect on employment, the evidence concerning unemployment is ambiguous. Some workers appear to leave the labor market altogether because of reduced employment opportunities.[29] For example, the increased flexibility in hiring and firing introduced in Colombia is estimated to have decreased the unemployment rate by between 1.4 and 1.7 percent from the late 1980s to the early 1990s, a period of economic expansion. However, in contrast, the greater flexibility may also explain part of the surge in the unemployment rate during the late 1990s, a period of economic recession (Kugler 2000). A study of the effect of the 1990 Bolivian reform shows that the duration of unemployment decreased as a result of more relaxed legislation and that exit rates from unemployment into formal employment (especially into large firms) rose more than exit rates into informal employment (Kugler 2004).

Effects on wages

While it is difficult to isolate the effect of employment protection legislation on wages, most of the empirical work on wage determinants among temporary workers finds unexplained wage differentials. In other words, for a given tenure, education, gender, occupation, and experience, temporary workers receive lower wages. Such residual differentials are consistent with the prepayment effect outlined above (OECD 2002).

Effect on productivity

Employment protection legislation increases job security and can therefore be expected to reduce the incentive for workers to take extra effort, which, in turn, reduces labor productivity. This applies as long as the cost of supervision is excessive so that the risk of disciplinary dismissal is limited. The effect of reforms also ultimately depends on the actual enforcement of the reform. For instance, the effectiveness of legislation depends partly on how the norms are interpreted by the courts.

In an indirect way, stricter legislation reduces the reallocation of human capital from ailing sectors to expanding sectors, resulting in an inefficient allocation of labor. More relaxed legislation may allow for a better allocation of workers among firms since the cost of experimentation with new, potentially better matched workers is lower. This may have an impact on average productivity in the economy and on growth.

Strict legislation will also likely hamper the speed at which economies adjust to shocks. Estimates based on 60 countries for the 1980s and 1990s show that, in countries where the rule of law is well established (that is, better enforcement), a shift from a low level of job security (20th percentile of the distribution in the 60 countries) to a high level of job security (80th percentile) cuts the speed of adjustment to shocks by one-third and reduces annual productivity growth by about 1 percent. In contrast, such a shift in countries with poorer enforcement does not have much impact on productivity growth (Caballero et al. 2004).

Effect on poverty

To the extent that reforms in employment protection legislation have an impact on types of employment and relative wages, they can be expected to have an impact on poverty if the people who are affected are living near the poverty line. The evidence is scarce on this type of impact. Besley and Burgess (2004) find that, in India, stricter legislation tends to reduce the size of the formal or registered manufacturing sector, which affects the urban poor. They estimate that poverty would have been 11 percent lower (that is, 520,000 fewer poor) in the state of West Bengal if the state had not passed stricter legislation. Conversely, poverty would have been 12 percent higher (that is, 640,000 more poor individuals) in the state of Andhra Pradesh if the state had not relaxed the relevant legislation.

Unemployment benefits

In the absence of evaluations of the impact of unemployment benefits based on natural experiments, the most solid empirical evaluations of the impact of the benefits and the relevant reforms have been produced through microeconometric studies. An alternative method of assessing benefit reform at the aggregate level is to use difference-in-differences techniques to compare labor market performance in reforming and non-reforming countries before and after the policy changes.

Effects of increasing the length and generosity of unemployment benefits

A key predictor related to the baseline transmission mechanism revolves around the links between the generosity of unemployment benefits and *long-term unemployment,* which is measured as the share in all the unemployed of those who have been unemployed for more than one year. Cross-country tabulations display a positive association between the maximum duration of unemployment benefits and long-term unemployment (Boeri, Layard, and Nickell 2001).[30] However, several recent studies suggest that the causality may run the other way: governments in countries with a higher incidence of long-term unemployment are subject to pressure to increase the maximum duration of benefits. Indeed, in the United States, regional variations in the maximum duration of benefits tend to occur in parallel with increases in the duration of unemployment in some states (Card and Levine 2000). Indeed, Lalive, van Ours, and Zweimueller (2002) show that this policy endogeneity may lead one significantly to overstate the negative effects of benefits on the duration of unemployment. The microeconomic literature can deal more effectively with these "policy endogeneity" problems. It suggests that the duration of unemployment benefits has a strong effect on the flows from unemployment to employment. The literature draws on so-called duration analysis (Kiefer 1988) and points to the negative effects of the duration of benefits on unemployment outflows even when controlling for regional characteristics and cyclical conditions (Atkinson and Micklewright 1991; Krueger and Meyer 2002). Similarly, the reduction in the possible duration of unemployment benefits undertaken in Slovenia in 1998 appears to have had a significant positive effect on the exit rate out of unemployment to employment and to other categories of activity (Van Ours and Vodopivec 2005a, 2005b).

Overall, there is little doubt that generous unemployment benefits increase the duration of unemployment. Nonetheless, estimates of the effects of benefit generosity on unemployment duration should be viewed with caution. The role played by policy endogeneity suggests that these estimates may be more fruitfully viewed merely as upper bounds to the elasticity of unemployment outflows with respect to benefit generosity.

The argument centered on the key transmission mechanism holds that greater benefit generosity is correlated with potential reductions in the *employment rate* of groups exhibiting elastic labor supply (via the effects on the incentives for job-seeking) and groups represented by unions (via the effects of unions on labor demand). In accordance with these predictions based on the key transmission mechanism, estimates of aggregate employment and unemployment equations (Nickell 1997; Blanchard and Wolfers 1999; Scarpetta 1999) point to the existence of a mild, but statistically significant and positive effect of the generosity of unemployment benefits on unemployment. This conclusion seems also to apply to the transition countries of Europe and Central Asia (Alam et al. 2005).

Evidence supplied through surveys of individuals and households suggests that the reservation wage of job-seekers is positively affected by unemployment benefit receipts (as predicted by the above argument based on the transmission mechanism), and this puts upward pressure on *wages*.[31] Estimates of earnings functions also find that the effect of unemployment benefits on wages is positive, although many different channels could generate this result.

Effects of employment on conditional incentives

Evidence related to both the earned income tax credit in the United States (Eissa and Hoynes 1998) and the working family tax credit in the United Kingdom (Blundell and Hoynes 2001) indicates that the programs have lowered employment rates among married women with working spouses. The most relevant example in Europe—at least in terms of take-up rates— is the Dutch SPAK measure (see Doudeijns, Einerhand, and Van de Meerendonk 2000), which allows employers to reduce their contributions on low wages.[32] The amount of the reduction declines as the wage rises, and the reduction ceases to be available at 115 percent of the statutory minimum wage. Evaluations based on general equilibrium models of the Dutch economy (De Mooij, Graafland, and Bovenberg 1998) have predicted a total increase in employment of between 1 and 5 percent among the low skilled. Evaluations of similar programs in Belgium and France report significant effects on employment. On the basis of individual data on firms, Crépon and Deplatz (2001) estimate the number of jobs created at between 255,000 and 670,000. Sneessens and Shadman-Metha (2001) estimate that, in Belgium, a cut of 21 percent in employer contributions for unskilled jobs may increase total employment of the unskilled by 6.7 percent. All these estimates are based on different estimates of demand and supply elasticities.

Effects of employment activation policies

The jury is still out on which employment activation policies work and which do not. However, there is a consensus that different categories of individuals—youth, married women returning to the labor market, the long-term unemployed—respond more readily to different activation policies. The experimental evidence on activation policies is confined, regrettably, mostly to the United States, and nonexperimental evidence exists for the United States and some European countries. Nevertheless, for the most part, the picture that emerges is quite consistent and, at a minimum, allows some policies to be ruled out because they are not effective.[33]

A key result is that employment activation policies should be different for people receiving unemployment insurance and people receiving unemployment assistance. This is partially caused by differences in the average characteristics of the two groups of recipients.[34] Recipients of unemployment assistance include many older individuals with long unemployment spells whose employability is questionable. The evidence on how these individuals might be helped is disappointing because no strategy seems effective. To avoid wasting human and financial resources, it is therefore important to test the willingness of these individuals actively to seek work. Hence, the best strategy for recipients of unemployment assistance may be to promote slots in active labor market programs, such as training programs, and, if necessary, subsidized jobs or job-creation schemes; however, expectations should not be boosted. The strategy should be understood mainly as a screening device. A job-seeker's refusal to participate might be discouraged by providing for reductions in the duration of unemployment assistance or outright elimination of the benefit.

Australia has experimented the most with policies aimed at helping the long-term unemployed. The Australian New Start allowance for the long-term unemployed emphasized "activity agreements," which funded paid work experience or unpaid volunteer work proposed by the recipient. This was part of a "case management" approach involving greater administrative oversight of the long-term unemployed and more frequent interviews with the public employment service. The strategy proved costly, and the results were far from encouraging. In 1996, the approach was scaled back by the new Labor government, and the intervention was increasingly decentralized to private and not-for-profit organizations, with premiums for the placement of older workers.

Empirically, activation policies for women returning to the labor market have been found to be the most successful, especially when they take the form of assistance in job-seeking, counseling, and training directed at facilitating an immediate return to employment. Successful policies for other groups of unemployment assistance beneficiaries with limited labor market experience, such as unemployed youth, have proved elusive. In particular, there is evidence that training per se has very little effect on this group; constant monitoring and testing of employment activity are crucial.

For the young unemployed, the most effective scheme would seem to be the British New Deal, which is the most articulated effort to deal with this problem to date. Key features of the New Deal are (1) the combination of lump-sum wage employment subsidies and assistance in job-seeking and on-the-job training; (2) the screening during the initial four-month gateway period to separate out individuals who tend to be unemployable and minimize deadweight costs; and (3) a division of the young unemployed into two groups according to age and the duration of the unemployment spell.

Unemployment insurance recipients are individuals who experience relatively short unemployment spells and whose employability (or lack thereof) must generally still be assessed. Activation strategies aimed at these individuals therefore rely less heavily on employment activation and more on assistance in job-seeking and testing, which have proved to be among the most effective instruments.

Effects of job-seeking requirements

Evidence demonstrates the usefulness of job-seeking assistance among women and recipients of benefits who have recently become unemployed. Over and above the effects of financial incentives, the Canadian Self-Sufficiency Project and the Minnesota Family Investment Project in the United States (both targeted at welfare recipients) were designed specifically to test the *incremental* effects of policies aimed at an early reintegration into employment, primarily assistance in job-seeking, then short-term training and job counseling. The incremental effects of these policies on employment seem large: up to a 7 percentage point increase in employment rates in the case of the Self-Sufficiency Project and nearly a 10 percentage point increase in the case of the Minnesota Family Investment Project. There are also positive effects on earnings. Although these estimates should be interpreted as upper bounds, assistance in job-seeking and related activities are starting to be regarded as cost effective.

Other experiments conducted in cooperation between several states and employment services in the United States have achieved considerable cost savings by augmenting job-seeking requirements. Thus, in Switzerland, the United Kingdom, and the United States, individuals must now fill out a minimum number of job applications in a given period (usually determined case-by-case by the public employment service). Experimental evidence (mainly from the state of Maryland) shows that job counseling has a substantial effect on outflows from unemployment to jobs. Significantly, most of the increase in exits from unemployment occurred shortly before a compulsory four-day training workshop on job hunting, which represented a rise in the opportunity costs of drawing unemployment benefits. Attendance at the workshop itself did not have a significant effect on outflow rates. In other words, it was the "help and hassle" approach involved in the initiative that stimulated exits from unemployment, rather than the job-hunting training scheme per se.

CONCLUSIONS

Assessing the potential distributional impacts of labor market interventions and reforms in labor market institutions is not a simple task. This is due to a number of factors.

First, in evaluating the potential impact of interventions and reforms on income distribution, one must distinguish between the distribution of earnings and the distribution of income. The former is defined at the level of individuals and by focusing only on employed workers. The latter is usually defined at the level of households and depends on the total labor income of all household members, plus income from other sources.

At least in the case of the policies described in this chapter, the difficulty arises from the fact that the empirical evidence suggests that labor market policies protect the prospective earnings of workers in the sectors that are covered at the expense of employment opportunities in that sector and earning levels in the rest of the economy, that is, the sectors that are not covered, whether formal or informal. As long as such an imbalance exists between earnings and employment opportunities in the covered sector, the risk is that labor market policies may lead to greater inequality and more poverty. This is particularly true in the case of labor market policies that are not directly targeted at low-income earners, but it also applies to policies designed to protect the most vulnerable workers, such as workers at minimum wage.

An increase in the minimum wage can have both a positive and a negative effect on inequality in household incomes. First, an increase in the incomes at the lower end of the range of the formally employed typically tends to reduce inequality in individual earnings. However, it might also result in a reduction in employment among low-paid workers, for whom the minimum wage is binding, or in the transfer of some of these workers to the uncovered, lower-pay informal sector. This could increase inequality in labor incomes both among individuals and at the household level, especially if workers at the minimum wage live in households with a high proportion of low-skilled, potentially low-pay individuals. The overall direct effect on income inequality depends on labor market conditions, demographics, and household composition. The effects are also compounded by indirect changes in the uncovered sector. If labor is mobile across sectors, then the standard covered-uncovered adjustment mechanisms will come into play, and an increase in the minimum wage will lead to an increase in earnings inequality.[35] In this situation, the overall impact on the distribution of household incomes will depend on the employment dynamics operating between the covered and uncovered sectors, as well as on the impact of the reform on the two segments of the labor market.

Similarly, reforms of the minimum wage are also expected to have a typically ambiguous impact on the *poverty rate*. An increase in the minimum wage, for example, will usually boost the earnings of low-paid workers who maintain their jobs, and, ceteris paribus, this will bring the poverty rate down if the individuals are the only income earners within their households or if all low-paid earners within households maintain their employment at the prereform level. However, the increase in the minimum wage is also likely to reduce employment in the covered sector, and this will result in lower labor incomes among households if any wage earners in the households lose their jobs as a result of the policy or are forced to transfer to the lower-paying uncovered sector. This may increase the vulnerability to poverty of households that are close to the poverty line.

Thus, the impact of labor market policies and reforms of these policies on the distribution of household incomes and on poverty depends crucially on the existence of a trade-off between labor market protection and employment, that is, a trade-off between intervention and efficiency. This is not as clear cut as the advocates of liberalization would like one to believe. The arguments presented in this chapter show that both intervention and the lack of intervention may lead to inefficient and inequitable outcomes.

The desirability of a particular sort of labor market intervention therefore depends crucially on the type and characteristics of the policy.

Some policies and intervention designs generate improvements on both efficiency and equity grounds; others result in a trade-off between efficiency and equity, and still others lead to a definite worsening in both areas. Similarly, it is unwise to argue in favor of or against a particular reform without careful evaluation of the potential impact of the new policy on labor market efficiency, income distribution, and poverty.

This chapter has provided the tools required to conduct such an evaluation by (1) identifying the main channels through which the redistributive and poverty impacts of three labor market policies—the minimum wage, employment protection legislation, and the unemployment benefit—affect earnings and household incomes and (2) reviewing the existing empirical evidence on the magnitude and direction of the impacts of these policies on each link in the chain. The evidence points to a number of cases in which the labor market interventions analyzed here may have negative effects on income equality and may increase poverty rather than reducing it. However, this is clearly not the case across the board. This leaves policymakers faced with the challenge of designing interventions that strike the right balance between reducing income inequality and curbing poverty on the one hand, while continuing to protect the living standards of workers. This can only be done effectively by mastering the factors that lead to the existence of tensions between labor market interventions and employment. It requires policies that are at once pro-growth and pro-equity. Some of the innovative policies introduced recently by a number of countries in Central Europe and Latin America to maintain the incomes of the unemployed seem to answer this challenge. Among these are conditional transfer programs and employment activation programs.

NOTES

1. The theory of the second best assumes that, if one of the conditions necessary to achieve Pareto optimality is missing, then the "second best" position can only be reached by departing from all the other Paretian conditions. Pareto efficiency is defined as the efficiency of a market that is unable to produce more from the same level of inputs without reducing the output of another product.
2. The insider-outsider theory, developed by Lindbeck and Snower (1989), argues that existing workers, *insiders,* enjoy a relatively advantageous position and expropriate rents from their employers thanks to the high barriers to employment faced by unemployed and entrant workers, the *outsiders.* However, in this chapter, "insiders" is used to refer to the workers covered by labor market regulations, and "outsiders" is used to refer to the unemployed

or to those people working in uncovered jobs in the formal or the informal sectors. This distinction is somewhat better defined than that between formal and informal employment.

3. The focus of the chapter is on statutory regulations and interventions. This is so despite the fact that, in many countries, these types of policies have been replaced through voluntary negotiations and agreements between labor and managers; these act in a way very similar to the mandatory steps described. The voluntary agreements are not explicitly analyzed here.

4. Other types of labor market institutions and regulations that are not analyzed here include labor unions, labor standards, wage-setting laws (other than minimum wages), collective bargaining, the constraints imposed in the context of privatization (for example, no retrenchment), pensions, active labor market programs (such as public works), the public sector's role in the labor market, training and retraining programs, microfinance and unemployment lending, and payroll taxes.

5. For instance, Scarpetta (1996) finds that the size of the impact of strict employment protection legislation on unemployment depends on the wage-bargaining system. Such interactions are not systematically reviewed here.

6. For an extensive review of different types of employment protection legislation and the relative advantages, see Betcherman, Luinstra, and Ogawa (2001).

7. This can represent a substantial cost when the period is long. For instance, prior to the 1999 reforms in Brazil, more than 6 percent of all salaried workers (about 2 million workers) filed lawsuits every year, and the average dispute took almost three years. (This was cut in half by the reforms; see World Bank 2002.) The number of cases and the length of court hearings vary greatly in the OECD. Up to 20 percent of layoffs become subjects of court proceedings in France, with an average dispute lasting over a year (OECD 2004).

8. Of course, these laws only formally apply to workers in the formal economy, which often represents a very small share of the total number of workers.

9. The *working poor* are those workers who are employed full time and, nevertheless, appear to be living close to the poverty line.

10. Fondazione Rodolfo DeBenedetti, http://www.frdb.org.

11. Labor market monopsony refers to the situation wherein a dominant employer is, in essence, a single "buyer" of labor services in a particular segment of the labor market. Under this condition of demand-side monopoly, the monopsonist employer pays lower wages and employs less labor than would employers in the case of perfect competition.

12. This distinction is somewhat sharper than that between formal and informal labor markets as highlighted by the theory of labor market duality.

13. This prediction requires that labor mobility be perfect between the two sectors.

14. The poverty rate is usually measured as the proportion of individuals whose *incomes* are less than a threshold value referred to as the *poverty line*.

15. The best description of this mechanism is contained in the work of Bentolila and Bertola (1990) and Bertola (1999). Ljungqvist (2002) studies

this transition mechanism through a variety of models and finds that it is quite robust.

16. Spain is the most prominent example in this respect. There, the share of workers hired on temporary contracts is now as high as 30 percent (Dolado, García-Serrano, and Jimeno 2002).

17. See Garibaldi and Violante (2002).

18. So called from the properties of putty and clay. Putty can be molded as one might wish before it is baked, but, through baking, putty becomes hardened clay, and the shape can no longer be altered.

19. When the elasticity of labor demand is larger than that of labor supply, the employment effect will be larger than the earnings effect.

20. Crépon and Deplatz (2001); De Mooij, Graafland, and Bovenberg (1998); Doudeijns, Einerhand, and Van de Meerendonk (2000); European Commission 1999; Sneessens and Shadman-Metha (2001).

21. See, for example, Carneiro (2004) on Brazil.

22. Note that this type of equation is econometrically identified only if the firm is a price-taker in the labor market, so that the monopsonistic model does not apply. To insure proper identification, these studies often use a lagged value for the minimum wage.

23. Note that this result is coherent with the prediction of the monopsony model, since it confirms the greater attachment of youth to their jobs when wages improve.

24. The three data sets used were the labor force surveys, the British household panel survey, and the matched new earning surveys for the period after 1999.

25. See Maloney and Mendez (2004) and Eriksson and Pytlikova (2004).

26. For a summary and discussion, see Addison and Teixeira (2003) and Heckman and Pagés (2003).

27. Firms in service industries, particularly in tourism, also reduced their hiring, as is evident in Table 3.3.

28. Additional examples are summarized in Heckman and Pagés (2000).

29. See Heckman and Pagés (2003) for a summary of the evidence.

30. The best example is probably offered by transatlantic differences in unemployment rates. These differences can be almost entirely explained by the differences in long-term unemployment rates. Meanwhile, unemployment benefits in Europe are significantly more generous than those in the United States.

31. The reservation wage is the lowest wage at which a job-seeker would consider a job offer.

32. SPAK is short for *Specifieke Afdrachtskorting* (specific tax rebate).

33. For a detailed review of the evidence on this issue, see Betcherman, Olivas, and Dar (2004).

34. Unemployment assistance covers workers who have been unemployed for a long time and the other individuals without occupation, such as youths with no or limited labor market experience, mothers returning to the labor mar-

ket after exhausting maternity protection, disabled individuals, and older, long-term unemployed who have exhausted unemployment assistance. Unemployment insurance covers other unemployed workers who have accumulated enough contributions to be eligible for unemployment benefits.

35. The potential negative impact is reduced if there is a lighthouse effect, since a higher minimum wage leads to an increase in wages in the market, whether covered or uncovered.

BIBLIOGRAPHY

Abowd, J., F. Framarz, T. Lemieux, and D. Margolis. 1999. "Minimum Wage and Youth Employment in France and the United States." In *Youth Employment and the Labor Market,* ed. D. Blanchflower and R. Freeman, 427–72. Chicago: University of Chicago Press.

Acemoglu, D., and J. Angrist. 2001. "The Consequence of EPL: The Case of the Employment Disability Act." *Journal of Political Economy* 109 (5): 915–57.

Addison, J., and P. Teixeira. 2003. "The Economics of Employment Protection." *Journal of Labor Research* 24 (1): 85–129.

Agenor, P. R., and K. El Aynaoui. 2003. "Labor Market Policies and Unemployment in Morocco: A Quantitative Analysis." Policy Research Working Paper 3091, World Bank, Washington, DC.

Aghion, P., and B. Hermalin. 1990. "Legal Restrictions on Private Contracts Can Enhance Efficiency?" *Journal of Law, Economics, and Organization* 6 (2): 381–409.

Agrawal, N. 1995. "Indonesia: Labor Market Policies and International Competitiveness." Policy Research Working Paper 1515, World Bank, Washington, DC.

Alam, A., M. Murthi, R. Yemtsov, E. Murrugarra, N. Dudwick, E. Hamilton, and E. Tiongson. 2005. "Growth, Poverty, and Inequality: Eastern Europe and the Former Soviet Union." Washington, DC: Europe and Central Asia Region, World Bank.

Amadeo, E. J., I. S. Gill, and M. C. Neri. 2002. "Assessing the Impact of Regulations on Informal Workers in Brazil." In *Crafting Labor Policy: Techniques and Lessons from Latin America,* ed. I. S. Gill, C. E. Montenegro, and D. Domeland, 67–95. New York: Oxford University Press.

Arango, C., and A. Pachon. 2003. "Distributive Effects of Minimum Wages on Household Incomes: Colombia 1997–2002." Unpublished manuscript. Banco de la Republica (Colombia) and World Bank. Cited in World Bank (2006).

Atkinson, A. B., and J. Micklewright. 1991. "Unemployment Compensation and Labor Market Transitions: A Critical Review." *Journal of Economic Literature* 29 (4): 1679–1727.

Barr, N. 1993. *The Economics of the Welfare State.* Oxford: Oxford University Press.

Bell, L. A. 1997. "The Impact of Minimum Wages in Mexico and Columbia." *Journal of Labor Economics* 15 (3): S102–35.

Bentolila, S., and G. Bertola. 1990. "How Bad is Eurosclerosis." *Review of Economic Studies* 57 (3): 381–402.

Bertola, G. 1999. "Microeconomic Perspectives on Aggregate Labor Markets." In *Handbook of Labor Economics,* ed. O. Ashenfelter and D. Card, Vol. 3C, Part 12, Chapter 45, 2985–3028. Amsterdam: Elsevier Science, North-Holland.

Besley, T., and R. Burgess. 2004. "Can Labor Market Regulations Hinder Economic Performance?: Evidence from India." *Quarterly Journal of Economics* 119 (1): 91–134.

Betcherman, G., A. Luinstra, and M. Ogawa. 2001. "Labor Market Regulation: International Experience in Promoting Employment and Social Protection." Social Protection Discussion Paper 0128, Social Protection Department, Human Development Network, World Bank, Washington, DC.

Betcherman, G., K. Olivas, and A. Dar. 2004. "Impacts of Active Labor Market Programs: New Evidence from Evaluations with Particular Attention to Developing and Transition Countries." Social Protection Discussion Paper 0402, Social Protection Department, Human Development Network, World Bank, Washington, DC.

Blanchard, O. 1997. "The Medium Run." *Brookings Papers on Economic Activity* 1997 (2): 89–158, The Brookings Institution, Washington, DC.

Blanchard, O., and A. Landier. 2002. "The Perverse Effects of Partial Deregulation: Fixed Duration Contracts in France." *Economic Journal* 112 (480): F214–44.

Blanchard, O., and P. Portugal. 2001. "What Lies behind the Unemployment Rate: Comparison of U.S. and Portugal." *American Economic Review* 91 (1): 993–1008.

Blanchard, O., and J. Tirole. 2003. "Contours of Employment Protection Reform." Working Paper Series 03-35, Department of Economics, Massachusetts Institute of Technology, Cambridge, MA.

Blanchard, O., and J. Wolfers. 1999. "The Role of Shocks and Institutions in the Rise of European Unemployment: The Aggregate Evidence." NBER Working Paper 7282, National Bureau of Economic Research, Cambridge, MA.

———. 2000. "The Role of Shocks and Institutions in the Rise of European Unemployment: The Aggregate Evidence." *Economic Journal* 110 (462): 1–33.

Blundell, R., and H. Hoynes. 2001. "Has In-Work Benefit Reform Helped the Labor Market?" NBER Working Paper 8546, National Bureau of Economic Research, Cambridge, MA.

Boeri, T. 2000. *Structural Change, Welfare Systems, and Labor Reallocation.* Oxford: Oxford University Press.

Boeri, T., A. Börsch-Supan, and G. Tabellini. 2001. "Would You Like to Shrink the Welfare State?: The Opinions of European Citizens." *Economic Policy* 16 (32): 7–50.

Boeri, T., J. I. Conde-Ruiz, and V. Galasso. 2003. "Protecting against Labor Market Risk: Employment Protection or Unemployment Benefits?" CEPR Discussion Paper 3990, Centre for Economic Policy Research, London.

Boeri, T., R. Layard, and S. Nickell. 2001. "Welfare-to-Work and the Fight against Long-Term Unemployment." Research Report 206, Department for Education and Skills, London.

Boeri, T., and K. Terrell. 2002. "Institutional Determinants of Labor Reallocation in Transition." *Journal of Economic Perspectives* 16 (1): 51–76.

Botero, J., S. Djankov, R. La Porta, F. Lopez-de-Silanes, and A. Shleifer. 2004. "The Regulation of Labor." *Quarterly Journal of Economics* 119 (4): 1339–82.

Brown, C. 1999. "Minimum Wages, Employment, and the Distribution of Income." In *Handbook of Labor Economics,* ed. O. Ashenfelter and D. Card, Vol. 3B, Part 8, Chapter 32, 2101–63. Amsterdam: Elsevier Science, North-Holland.

Burdett, K., and D. Mortensen. 1998. "Wage Differentials, Employer Size, and Unemployment." *International Economic Review* 39 (2): 257–73.

Caballero, R., K. Cowan, E. Engel, and A. Micco. 2004. "Effective Labor Regulation and Microeconomic Flexibility." NBER Working Paper 10744, National Bureau of Economic Research, Cambridge, MA.

Caballero, R., and M. Hammour. 1998. "Jobless Growth: Appropriability, Factor Substitution, and Unemployment." Carnegie-Rochester Conference Series on Public Policy 48: 51–94, Elsevier, New York.

Calderón, C., A. Chong, and R. Valdés. 2004. "Labor Market Regulations and Income Inequality: Evidence for a Panel of Countries." Research Department Working Paper 514, Inter-American Development Bank, Washington, DC.

Cameron, L. A., and V. Alatas. 2003. "The Impact of Minimum Wages on Employment in a Low-Income Country: An Evaluation Using the Difference-in Differences Approach." Policy Research Working Paper 2985, World Bank, Washington, DC.

Card, D., and A. Krueger. 1994. "Minimum Wage and Employment: A Case Study of the Fast-Food Industry in New Jersey and Pennsylvania." *American Economic Review* 84 (4): 772–93.

———. 1995. *Myth and Measurement: The New Economics of Minimum Wage.* Princeton, NJ: Princeton University Press.

Card, D., and P. Levine. 2000. "Extended Benefits and the Duration of UI Spells: Evidence from the New Jersey Extended Benefit Program." *Journal of Public Economics* 78 (1–2): 107–38.

Carneiro, F. G. 2004. "Are Minimum Wages to Blame for Informality in the Labour Market?" *Empirica* 31 (4): 295–306.

Castillo-Freeman, A. J., and R. B. Freeman. 1992. "When the Minimum Wage Really Bites: The Effects of the U.S.-Level Minimum Wage on Puerto Rico." In *Immigration and the Work Force: Economic Consequences for the United States and Source Areas,* ed. G. J. Borjas and R. B. Freeman, 177–211. Chicago: University of Chicago Press.

Chandra, V., and J. P. Nganou. 2001. "Obstacles to Formal Employment Creation in South Africa: Evidence from Recent Firm Surveys." Paper presented at the Development Policy Research Unit and Friedrich Ebert Foundation

Conference, "Labor Markets and Poverty in South Africa," Johannesburg, November 15–16.

Crépon, B., and R. Deplatz. 2001. "Une nouvelle évaluation des effets des allégements des charges sociales sur les bas salaires." *Economie et Statistique* 348 (8): 2001–8.

Daveri, F., and G. Tabellini. 2000. "Unemployment, Growth, and Taxation in Industrial Countries." *Economic Policy* 15 (30): 47–104.

De Mooij, R. A., J. Graafland, and A. L. Bovenberg. 1998. "Tax Reform and the Dutch Labor Market in the 21st Century." CPB Report 1998 (2): 19–24, Bureau for Economic Policy Analysis, The Hague.

DiNardo, J., N. M. Fortin, and T. Lemieux. 1996. "Labor Market Institutions and the Distribution of Wages, 1973–1992: A Semi-Parametric Approach." *Econometrica* 64 (5): 1001–44.

Dolado, J. J., C. García-Serrano, and J. F. Jimeno. 2002. "Drawing Lessons from the Boom of Temporary Jobs in Spain." *Economic Journal* 112 (480): 270–95.

Doudeijns, M., M. Einerhand, and A. van de Meerendonk. 2000. "Financial Incentives to Take Up Low-Paid Work: An International Comparison of the Role of Tax and Benefit Systems." In *Policy Measures for Low Wage Employment in Europe*, ed. W. Salverda, C. Lucifora, and B. Nolan, 43–66. Cheltenham, United Kingdom: Edward Elgar.

Eissa, N., and J. B. Hoynes. 1998. "The Earned Income Tax Credit and the Labor Supply of Married Couples." NBER Working Paper 6856, National Bureau of Economic Research, Cambridge, MA.

Eriksson, T., and M. Pytlikova. 2004. "Firm-Level Consequences of Large Minimum-Wage Increases in the Czech and Slovak Republic." *Labor* 18 (1): 75–103.

European Commission. 1999. "Energy in Europe: Economic Foundations for Energy Policy." The Shared Analysis Project, European Commission, Brussels.

Falk, A., E. Fehr, and C. Zehnder. 2005. "The Behavioral Effect of Minimum Wages." CEPR Discussion Paper 5115, Centre for Economic Policy Research, London.

Fallon, P. R., and R. E. B. Lucas. 1991. "The Impact of Changes in Job Security Regulations in India and Zimbabwe." *World Bank Economic Review* 5 (3): 395–413.

Feliciano, Z. M. 1998. "Does Minimum Wage Affect Employment in Mexico?" *Eastern Economic Journal* 24 (2): 165–80.

Fields, G. S. 2005. "A Guide to Multisector Labor Market Models." Social Protection Discussion Paper 0505, Social Protection Department, Human Development Network, World Bank, Washington, DC.

Forteza, A., and M. Rama. 2000. "Labor Market Rigidity and the Success of Economic Reforms across More than a Hundred Countries." Policy Research Working Paper 2521, World Bank, Washington, DC.

Freeman, R. B. 1996. "The Minimum Wage as a Redistributive Tool." *Economic Journal* 106 (436): 639–49.

Garibaldi, P., and G. L. Violante. 2002. "Firing Tax and Severance Payment in Search Economies: A Comparison." CEPR Discussion Paper 3636, Centre for Economic Policy Research, London.

Gill, I. S., C. E. Montenegro, and D. Domeland, eds. 2002. *Crafting Labor Policy: Techniques and Lessons from Latin America.* New York: Oxford University Press.

Gindling, T. H., and K. Terrell. 2004a. "Minimum Wages and the Wages of Formal and Informal Sector Workers in Costa Rica." William Davidson Institute Working Papers Series 2004–647, William Davidson Institute, Stephen M. Ross Business School, University of Michigan, Ann Arbor, MI.

———. 2004b. "Minimum Wages, Inequality, and Globalization." IZA Discussion Paper 1160, Institute for the Study of Labor, Bonn.

Goldberg, P. K., and N. Pavcnik. 2003. "The Response of the Informal Sector to Trade Liberalization." *Journal of Development Economics* 72 (2): 463–96.

Gramlich, E. 1976. "Impact of Minimum Wages on other Wages, Employment, and Family Incomes." *Brookings Papers on Economic Activity* 1976 (2): 409–51, The Brookings Institution, Washington, DC.

Hamermesh, D. S. 1993. *Labor Demand.* Princeton, NJ: Princeton University Press.

Heckman, J., and C. Pagés. 2000. "The Cost of Job Security Regulation: Evidence from Latin American Labor Markets." NBER Working Paper 7773, National Bureau of Economic Research, Cambridge, MA.

———. 2003. "Law and Employment: Lessons from Latin America and the Caribbean." NBER Working Paper 10129, National Bureau of Economic Research, Cambridge, MA.

Hopenhayn, H. 2001. "Labor Market Policies and Employment Duration: The Effects of Labor Market Reform in Argentina." Research Network Working Paper R–407, Inter-American Development Bank, Washington, DC.

Ichino, A., and R. T. Riphahn. 2005. "The Effect of Employment Protection on Worker Effort: A Comparison of Absenteeism during and after Probation." *Journal of the European Economic Association* 3 (1): 120–43.

Jones, P. 1998. "The Impact of the Minimum Wage Legislation in Developing Countries where Coverage is Incomplete." Working Paper 98–2, Institute of Economics and Statistics, Oxford, United Kingdom.

Kiefer, N. M. 1988. "Economic Duration Data and Hazard Functions." *Journal of Economic Literature* 26 (2): 646–79.

Krueger, A., and B. Meyer. 2002. "Labor Supply Effects of Social Insurance." NBER Working Paper 9014, National Bureau of Economic Research, Cambridge, MA.

Kugler, A. 2000. "The Incidence of Job Security Regulations on Labor Market Flexibility and Compliance in Colombia: Evidence from the 1990 Reform." Research Network Working Paper R–393, Inter-American Development Bank, Washington, DC.

———. 2004. "The Effect of Job Security Regulations on Labor Market Flexibility: Evidence from the Colombian Labor Market." In *Law and Employment:*

Lessons from Latin America and the Caribbean, ed. J. Heckman and C. Pagés, 183–228. Chicago: University of Chicago Press.

Lalive, R., J. C. van Ours, and J. Zweimueller. 2002. "The Effect of Benefit Sanctions on the Duration of Unemployment." IEW Working Paper 110, Institute for Empirical Research in Economics, University of Zurich, Zurich, Switzerland.

Lazear, E. 1990. "Job Security Provisions and Employment." *Quarterly Journal of Economics* 105 (3): 699–726.

Lee, D. 1999. "Wage Inequality in the United States during the 1980s: Rising Dispersion or Falling Minimum Wage?" *Quarterly Journal of Economics* 114 (3): 977–1023.

Lemos, S. 2004a. "The Effects of the Minimum Wage across the Formal and Informal Sectors in Brazil." IZA Discussion Paper 1089, Institute for the Study of Labor (IZA), Bonn.

———. 2004b. "Are Wage and Employment Effects Robust to Alternative Minimum Wage Variables?" IZA Discussion Paper 1079, Institute for the Study of Labor, Bonn.

Lindbeck, A., and D. Snower. 1989. *The Insider-Outsider Theory of Unemployment.* Cambridge, MA: The MIT Press.

Ljungqvist, L. 2002. "How Do Lay-Off Costs Affect Employment?" *Economic Journal* 112 (482): 829–53.

Lustig, N., and D. McLeod. 1996. "Minimum Wages and Poverty in Developing Countries: Some Empirical Evidence." Brookings Discussion Papers in International Economics 125, The Brookings Institution, Washington, DC.

Maloney, W. F., and J. N. Mendez. 2003. "Measuring the Impact of Minimum Wages: Evidence from Latin America." NBER Working Paper 9800, National Bureau of Economic Research, Cambridge MA.

———. 2004. "Measuring the Impact of Minimum Wages: Evidence from Latin America." In *Law and Employment: Lessons from Latin American and the Caribbean,* ed. J. Heckman and C. Pagés, 109–30. Chicago: University of Chicago Press.

Manning, A. 2004. *Monopsony in Motion: Imperfect Competition in Labor Markets.* Princeton, NJ: Princeton University Press.

Marquez, G. 1998. "Proteccion al empleo y funcionamiento del Mercado de trabajo: una aproximacion comparative." Unpublished manuscript, Inter-American Development Bank, Washington, DC. Cited in Heckman and Pagés (2000).

Mason, A. D., and J. Baptist. 1996. "How Important are Labor Markets to the Welfare of the Poor in Indonesia?" Policy Research Working Paper 1665, World Bank, Washington, DC.

Masters, A. 1999. "Wage Posting in Two-Sided Search and the Minimum Wage." *International Economic Review* 40 (4): 809–26.

Mincer, J. 1976. "Unemployment Effects of Minimum Wages." *Journal of Political Economy* 84 (4): 87–104.

Mondino, G., and S. Montoya. 2004. "The Effect of Labor Market Regulations on Employment Decisions by Firms: Empirical Evidence for Argentina." In *Law and Employment: Lessons from Latin America and the Caribbean,* ed. J. Heckman and C. Pagés, 351–99. Chicago: University of Chicago Press.

Montenegro, C. E., and C. Pagés. 2003. "Who Benefits from Labor Market Regulations?: Chile 1960–1998." NBER Working Paper 9850, National Bureau of Economic Research, Cambridge, MA.

Neumark, D., and W. Wascher. 1997. "Do Minimum Wages Fight Poverty?" NBER Working Paper 6127, National Bureau of Economic Research, Cambridge, MA.

———. 2000. "Minimum Wages: A Case Study of the Fast Foods Industry in New Jersey and Pennsylvania; Comment." *American Economic Review* 90 (5): 1362–96.

Nickell, S. 1997. "Unemployment and Labor Market Rigidities: Europe versus North America." *Journal of Economic Perspectives* 11 (3): 55–74.

Nickell, S., and R. Layard. 1999. "Labor Market Institutions and Economic Performance." In *Handbook of Labor Economics,* ed. O. Ashenfelter and D. Card, Vol. 3C, Part 12, Chapter 46, 3029–84. Amsterdam: Elsevier Science, North-Holland.

OECD (Organisation for Economic Co-operation and Development). 1998. "Making the Most of the Minimum: Statutory Minimum Wages, Employment, and Poverty." *OECD Employment Outlook 1998,* Chapter 2, 31–77, Organisation for Economic Co-operation and Development, Paris.

———. 2002. *OECD Employment Outlook 2002,* Organisation for Economic Co-operation and Development, Paris.

———. 2004. *OECD Employment Outlook 2004,* Organisation for Economic Co-operation and Development, Paris.

Peltzman, S. 1976. "Toward a More General Theory of Regulation." *Journal of Law and Economics* 19 (2): 211–40.

Portugal, P., and A. R. Cardoso. 2001. "Disentangling the Minimum Wage Puzzle: An Analysis of Job Accession and Separation from a Longitudinal Matched Employer-Employee Data Set." CEPR Discussion Paper 2844, Centre for Economic Policy Research, London.

Rama, P. 1996. "The Consequences of Doubling the Minimum Wage: The Case of Indonesia." Policy Research Working Paper 1643, World Bank, Washington, DC.

Riboud, M., C. Sánchez-Parámo, and C. Silva-Jáuregui. 2002. "Does Eurosclerosis Matter?: Institutional Reform and Labor Market Performance in Central and Eastern European Countries in the 1990s." Social Protection Discussion Paper 0202, Social Protection Department, Human Development Network, World Bank, Washington, DC.

Rodrigues, E. A. S., and N. A. Menezes-Filho. 2004. "Minimum Wage and Inequality in Brazil and Mexico, 1981–2000: A Semiparametric Approach." Research Department, Banco Central do Brasil, and Department of Economics,

University of São Paulo. http://www.bcu.gub.uy/autoriza/peiees/jor/2004/iees03j3290804.pdf.

Rutkowski, J. 2003a. "Rapid Labor Reallocation with a Stagnant Unemployment Poor: The Puzzle of the Labor Market in Lithuania." Labor and Employment Working Paper 2946, World Bank, Washington, DC.

———. 2003b. "Why is Unemployment so High in Bulgaria?" Labor and Employment Working Paper 3017, World Bank, Washington, DC.

———. 2003c. "Does Strict Employment Protection Discourage Job Creation?: Evidence from Croatia." Labor and Employment Working Paper 3104, World Bank, Washington, DC.

Saavedra, J., and M. Torero. 2000. "Labor Market Reforms and Their Impact on Formal Labor Demand and Job Market Turnover: The Case of Peru." Research Network Working Paper R-394, Inter-American Development Bank, Washington, DC.

———. 2004. "Labor Market Reforms and their Impact over Formal Labor Demand." In *Law and Employment: Lessons from Latin America and the Caribbean,* ed. J. Heckman and C. Pagés, 131–82. Chicago: University of Chicago Press.

Saint Paul, G. 2000. *The Political Economy of Labor Market Institutions.* Oxford: Oxford University Press.

Scarpetta, S. 1996. "Assessing the Role of Labor Market Policies and Institutional Settings on Unemployment: A Cross-Country Study." *OECD Economic Studies* 26 (1): 43–98, Organisation for Economic Co-operation and Development, Paris.

———. 1999. "Labor Market Reforms and Unemployment: Lessons from the Experience of the OECD Countries." Research Department Working Paper 382, Inter-American Development Bank, Washington, DC.

Schneider, F., and R. Klinglmair. 2004. "Shadow Economies around the World: What Do We Know?" Working Paper 0403, Department of Economics, Johannes Kepler University of Linz, Linz, Austria.

Sneessens, H., and F. Shadman-Metha. 2001. "Chocs asymétriques et persistance du chômage: Wallonie et Flandre comparées." IRES Discussion Paper 2001–024, Institut de Recherches Economiques et Sociales, Université Catholique de Louvain, Louvain, Belgium.

Stewart, M. B. 2004. "The Impact of the Introduction of the UK Minimum Wage on the Employment Probabilities of Low-Wage Workers." *Journal of the European Economic Association* 2 (1): 67–97.

Stigler, G. J. 1946. "The Economics of Minimum Wage Legislation." *American Economic Review* 36 (3): 358–65.

Sutherland, H. 2001. "The National Minimum Wage and In-Work Poverty." Microsimulation Unit Discussion Paper MU0102, Department of Applied Economics, University of Cambridge, Cambridge.

Van Ours, J. C., and M. Vodopivec. 2005a. "How Changes in Benefits Entitlement Affect the Duration of Unemployment." Center Discussion Paper 2005–30, Tilburg University, Tilburg, The Netherlands.

Van Ours, J. C., and M. Vodopivec. 2005b. "Changes in Benefit Entitlement and Job Finding: The Slovenian Experiment." http://europa.eu.int/comm/economy_finance/events/2005/bxlworkshop0305/doc11en.pdf.

Vodopivec, M., and D. Raju. 2002. "Income Support Systems for the Unemployed: Issues and Options." Social Protection Discussion Paper 0214, Social Protection Department, Human Development Network, World Bank, Washington, DC.

Welch, F. 1976. "Minimum Wage Legislation in the United States." In *Evaluating the Labor Market Effects of Social Programs*, ed. O. Ashenfelter and J. Blum, 1–38. Princeton, NJ: Princeton University Press.

World Bank. 2002. "Brazil Jobs Report." Sector Report 24480-BR, Latin America and the Caribbean Region, World Bank, Washington, DC.

———. 2005. "Pro-Poor Growth in the 1990s: Lessons and Insights from 14 Countries." Report, Operationalizing Pro-Poor Growth Research Program, World Bank, Washington, DC.

———. 2006. "Minimum Wages in Latin America and the Caribbean: The Impact on Employment, Inequality, and Poverty." Draft manuscript, Latin America and the Caribbean Region, World Bank, Washington, DC.

Characteristics of the Minimum Wage in Selected Countries

TABLE 3A.1. Characteristics of the Minimum Wage in Selected Countries

Country	Minimum wage–setting procedure	Coverage: scope
Europe and Central Asia		
Albania	The national minimum wage rate is set in an order of the government.	The national minimum wage rate applies to all workers.
Bulgaria	The government sets the national minimum wage rate by decree.	The national minimum wage rate applies to all workers and employees.
Cyprus	There is no national minimum wage. The government sets minimum wage rates for selected low-wage occupations. These minimum rates are adjusted yearly.	Only workers in the occupations specified by the government.
Czech Republic	The government stipulates the national minimum wage rate in an official decree. It also sets 12 minimum tariff rates for different grades. The minimum wage is adjusted yearly.	The Labor Code applies to all employees except those who work for a company registered in the Czech Republic, but work and reside in a foreign country. Employees of a company with foreign capital interest may be excluded if the government specifies a regulatory framework that governs them.
Estonia	The minimum wage and the procedures to amend it are set by the government based on a bipartite agreement between worker and employer organizations.	The minimum wage rate applies to all workers employed under an employment contract.
Hungary	The minimum wage rate is determined by the government. The National Labor Council is consulted during the process, and minimum wage rates are subject to its agreement.	Minimum wage regulations apply to all, including public service officials otherwise exempt from the Labor Code. They apply also to employees of Hungarian employers working abroad, but not to foreign employers and their employees working in Hungary.
Latvia	Minimum wage rates are determined by the government.	The Labor Law of 2001 covers all employees and employers.
Lithuania	The government determines minimum wage levels according to the recommendations of a tripartite council.	Regulations apply to all workers employed in Lithuania or posted abroad by their employers. They do not apply to foreign employers who post employees to Lithuania.

Coverage: variations in minimum wage, by categories	Level(s)[a]
• The government may establish a lower minimum wage rate for young workers to facilitate their entry into the workforce.	PPP$195.27 per month.
• During an apprentice's training period, which cannot exceed six months, the wage may not be less than 90% of the minimum wage. • Piece-rate workers.	PPP$213.02 per month.
• The minimum wage order applies to shop assistants, clerks, nursing aids, and child-care workers. • A minimum wage rate that is slightly lower than the regular rate applies during the first six months of employment with a new employer.	US$618.00 per month for the first six months. US$657.60 per month after the first six months.
• When employers do not sign a collective agreement with trade unions, they must pay their employees at least the minimum tariffs for the grade of the employees. • Employees between 18 and 21 years of age are entitled to 90% of the minimum wage for a six-month period. Employees under 18 are entitled to 80% of the minimum wage. • Employees with partial disability pensions are entitled to 75% of the minimum wage. Employees with full disability pensions and disabled juveniles without pensions are entitled to 50% of the minimum wage.	PPP$466.48 per month.
	PPP$384.75 per month.
• The Labor Code provides that separate rates may be set for a specific field or area. In fact, no separate rates have been set. • Minors, disabled employees, and part-time employees may receive less than the minimum wage only if a derogation is issued by the National Labor Council. No such derogation has been issued.	PPP$420.80 per month.
• A separate minimum hourly rate is established for workers under 18 years of age.	PPP$335.61 per month.
• The legislation provides that specific wage rates may be set for categories of employees and different branches of the economy. In fact, no specific rates have been set.	PPP$313.73 per month.

(continued)

175

TABLE 3A.1. Characteristics of the Minimum Wage in Selected Countries (*Continued*)

Country	Minimum wage–setting procedure	Coverage: scope
Poland	The Tripartite Commission negotiates minimum wage levels by July 15 every year based on the government's proposal. If the commission does not reach a consensus, the government sets the minimum wage, which cannot be lower than what it proposed to the commission. The minimum wage is adjusted yearly, unless forecasted inflation is above 5% (adjusted twice a year).	The minimum wage applies to all employees in full-time employment.
Romania	The government sets a national minimum wage rate following consultations with social partners.	The Labor Code applies to all Romanians working in Romania or overseas if employed by a Romanian employer (unless the legislation of the host country is more favorable), and to foreigners working in Romania for a Romanian employer.
Russian Federation	The federal government establishes a national minimum wage rate. The Labor Code provides for social partnership involving mutual consultations on guarantees of employee labor rights and improvements to labor laws in general.	The national minimum wage applies to all nonqualified workers in an employment relationship.
Slovenia	The government sets the minimum wage rate by special regulation in accordance with a tripartite pay policy agreement. The Economic and Social Council of Slovenia is frequently the forum at which minimum wage negotiations take place.	The minimum wage applies to all employees in the private sector with no exception. All employers must pay a wage that is at least equal to the minimum wage.
Slovakia	The government sets the minimum wage rate by special regulation following the recommendation of social partners. The minimum wage is adjusted yearly.	The Labor Code applies to all employees, including those working for foreign employers, unless otherwise stipulated. Employees posted to another EU member state are governed by that state's regulations provided their stay exceeds one month and work exceeds 22 days in the year.

Coverage: variations in minimum wage, by categories	*Level(s)*[a]
• First-time entrants to the labor market may receive less than the minimum wage rate. As of the end of 2005, remuneration for first-time entrants could not be less than 80% of the minimum wage for the first year and 90% for the second year of employment. • Other categories—For employees working on a part-time basis the amount of minimum wage is reduced proportionally to the actual number of hours worked.	PPP$448.86 per month.
	PPP$224.02 per month.
• States may establish regional minimum wage rates that are higher than the national minimum wage. Regional minimum wage rates are subject to the consent of the federal government.	PPP$59.47 per month.
	PPP$818.16 per month.
• If there is no collective agreement, the employer must pay a minimum wage according to the difficulty of the position, ranging from once to twice the minimum wage. • Juveniles between 16 and 18 years of age receive 75% of the minimum wage. Juveniles under 16 receive 50% of the minimum wage. • Employees with partial-disability pensions receive 75% of the minimum wage, while those with full-disability pensions and disabled persons under 18 receive 50% of the minimum wage.	PPP$376.01 per month.

(continued)

177

TABLE 3A.1. Characteristics of the Minimum Wage in Selected Countries (*Continued*)

Country	Minimum wage–setting procedure	Coverage: scope
Turkey	Minimum wage rates are set by the Minimum Wage–Setting Board. The rate is supposed to be adjusted every two years. In practice, rates have been adjusted every 6 to 12 months.	The provisions of the Labor Act concerning the minimum wage apply to all employees.
Africa Angola	The minimum wage is set by decree of the Council of Ministers based upon the proposal made by the minister of protection, labor, and finance.	All workers are covered by minimum wage regulations. The government may exclude workers covered by a collective agreement signed within six months preceding the issue of the decree setting the minimum wage.
Botswana	Minimum wage rates are set by sector. The minister of labor must consult the Minimum Wage Advisory Board when adjusting or setting rates for trade or industry that may require a statutory minimum wage rate, but is not obliged to accept the board's recommendations. Additionally, the minister must publish a notice in the Official Gazette announcing the intention to alter rates before any adjustment is made. In practice, the rates are adjusted each year.	Minimum wage rates apply only to workers in the sectors set forth in the Employment Act, 1982. Unless the minister of labor issues a specific regulation, government officials are not covered by any minimum wage rate order.
Burkina Faso	The government determines one minimum wage rate for nonagricultural workers and one minimum wage rate for agricultural workers after receiving the opinion of the Labor Advisory Commission.	Minimum wage provisions apply to all workers except those employed in public administration and apprentices.
Cape Verde	There is currently no minimum wage in Cape Verde.	
Chad	The 1996 Labor Code provides for minimum wages to be determined in agreement with organizations representing employers and workers. In practice, minimum wage rates have not been adjusted since 1994.	The minimum wage applies to all workers.

Coverage: variations in minimum wage, by categories	Level(s)[a]
• There is a lower minimum wage rate for workers younger than 16 years of age. The minimum wage rate is currently TL378,000,000 per month (US$251.85) for employees younger than 16.	PPP$590.93 per month for employees 16 years of age and above.
• The legislation provides that the minimum wage rates may be set by sector or by territorial region. However, as of 2003, only one national minimum wage rate had been established.	US$50 per month.
• The minister of labor sets minimum wage rates for night watchmen. • The minister of labor may establish minimum wage rates for building and construction; exploration and quarrying industry; garage and motor trade; road transport industry; hotel, catering, and entertainment trade; manufacturing, service, and repair trade; and wholesale and retail distribution trade. • Disabled persons to whom a wage order applies or their prospective employers may apply for a permit authorizing them to be paid less than the minimum wage rate.	PPP$0.86 per hour for night watchmen. PPP$1.02 per hour for workers in trades set forth in the Employment Act other than the retail distribution trade.
• Piece-rate workers must receive wages that are proportional to those that would be received by a full-time worker.	PPP$0.89 per hour for agricultural workers. PPP$0.97 per hour for nonagricultural workers.
• Minimum wage rates vary according to occupation and seniority. • Separate minimum wage rates have been established for agricultural workers and nonagricultural workers. • Workers between 14 and 18 years of age who are not working under a contract of apprenticeship may not receive less than 80% of the relevant minimum wage rate. • The amount paid to a piece-rate worker must be proportional to what a worker paid per hour would receive for the same work.	PPP$171.45 per month for nonagricultural workers. PPP$173.06 per month for agricultural workers.

(continued)

179

TABLE 3A.1. Characteristics of the Minimum Wage in Selected Countries (*Continued*)

Country	Minimum wage–setting procedure	Coverage: scope
Gabon	The government sets a national minimum wage rate. It may also set minimum wage rates for certain professions if collective agreements do not provide minimum rates. The National Wage Committee must meet at least once every three years.	The minimum wage applies to all workers.
Ghana	The national daily minimum rate of remuneration is determined by the National Tripartite Committee.	Before the Labor Act of 2003, regulations did not apply to part-time workers, piece workers, sharecroppers, sea-going personnel who are not wage earners, and apprentices. In the absence of any revocation, these exemptions are assumed to apply.
Guinea-Bissau	The government sets the minimum wage rates by decree following consultation with social partners. This consultation takes place within the Social Dialogue Council (Conselho Permanente de Concertação Social), a tripartite advisory body. There are two national minimum wage rates: one for agricultural workers, and one for nonagricultural workers.	The minimum wages apply to all salaried workers, except domestic workers and public servants. Public servants are covered by a separate wage-setting system.
Lesotho	Minimum wage rates are set according to occupations in wages orders issued by the minister of labor on the basis of recommendations and proposals of the Wages Advisory Board. The Wages Advisory Board must examine the rates annually.	The minimum wage applies to all workers. Workers whose occupation is not specified in the wages orders must be paid at least the rate for unskilled laborers.
Madagascar	The government sets a national minimum wage rate and a wage scale for nonagricultural workers and agricultural workers based on recommendations of the National Employment Council.	The Labor Code applies to all workers whose employment contract was entered into in Madagascar.

Coverage: Variations in minimum wage, by categories	Level(s)[a]
• Workers paid on a piece-rate basis must be paid at a rate that a worker of average capabilities working normally would be paid.	PPP$111.35 per month.
• The minister of labor may issue a permit excluding a person affected by some type of infirmity, physical injury, or disability from the legislative provisions concerning minimum wage.	PPP$7.69 per day.
• The law provides that different national minimum wages can be set by sector. • An employee under the age of 16 shall be paid no less than 60% of the national minimum rate. An employee between the age of 16 and 18 shall be paid a rate not less than 80% of the national minimum rate. A minor with more than six months of employment in the same activity shall be paid the full minimum rate.	PPP$25.00, plus one bag of rice per month.
• Minimum wage rates have been established for the following occupations: drivers; hammer mill operators; junior clerks; machine operators; machine attendants; messengers; receptionists; shop assistants; telephone operators; ungraded artisans; unskilled laborers; waiters; trainee weavers and sewing machine workers; watchmen; domestic workers; and copy-typists. • Workers employed by small businesses whose occupation is not specified in a wages order must be paid at least the minimum wage rate for small businesses, which is lower than the rate for unskilled laborers.	PPP$105 per month for domestic workers. PPP$210.5 per month for workers in small businesses. PPP$310.50 per month for unskilled laborers. PPP$595.50 per month for drivers.
• Wage rates are set on a wage scale that allows for rates to vary in accordance with level of seniority and professional category. • Rates paid to piece workers must be such that an average worker working at a normal rate receives the same wage as workers being paid according to the time worked.	PPP$70.4 per month for nonagricultural workers. PPP$80.63 per month for agricultural workers.

(continued)

TABLE 3A.1. Characteristics of the Minimum Wage in Selected Countries (*Continued*)

Country	Minimum wage–setting procedure	Coverage: scope
Mauritius	There is no national minimum wage. The minister of labor sets minimum wage rates for workers in the private sector in industry-wide remuneration orders on the basis of recommendations from the National Remuneration Board; he may accept, reject, or amend the recommendation. The Pay Research Bureau establishes wages for public sector workers. Each year, on July 1, the wages of private sector workers are adjusted for increases in the cost of living.	Minimum wages have been established for 29 industries and occupations in the private sector. Workers in other industries or occupations have no statutory minimum wage rate.
Mozambique	Minimum wage rates are set by consensus by the Labor Advisory Commission with the participation of social partners. Agreements are announced by the government. If no agreement proves possible, the government sets the minimum wage rates.	A minimum wage rate is determined for agricultural workers, and another for workers in industry, trade, and other activities.
Namibia	There is no national minimum wage. Minimum wage rates may either be set by the government in wage orders or in collective agreements. All minimum wage rates are currently set in collective agreements. Adjustments to the rate in the agricultural sector should be discussed on an annual basis.	Minimum wage rates apply to agricultural workers in a collective agreement and workers in the mining and construction sectors.
Nigeria	A national minimum wage is determined by the government. In 2000, when the national minimum wage rate was updated, an ad hoc tripartite committee was formed to facilitate discussions on the new rate.	National minimum wage rates do not apply to: establishments employing fewer than 50 workers, part-time workers, workers paid on a commission or piece-rate basis, workers in seasonal employment such as agriculture, and workers in merchant shipping or civil aviation.
São Tomé and Principe	The government sets the minimum wage rate.	The minimum wage rate applies to all workers. However, the legislation does allow different sectoral minimum wages.

Coverage: variations in minimum wage, by categories	Level(s)ᵃ
• Apprentices or trainees in public transport; printing; catering; block making, construction, and stone crushing; electrical, engineering, and mechanical workshops; furniture workshops; newspapers and periodicals; and tailoring have a special rate. • Workers between 15 and 18 years of age receive lower rates in the sugar, livestock, field crop and orchards, and tea industries. • A disabled worker or prospective employer may apply for a reduced minimum wage rate. • Certain remuneration orders provide that the minimum wage rate for workers paid on a piece-rate basis must be 10% higher than the minimum wage rate for workers paid on a monthly basis.	PPP$39.40 per week for unskilled workers in export-processing zones. PPP$378.46 per month for unskilled workers in the printing industry (first year).
	PPP$166.8 per month for agricultural workers. PPP$232.00 per month for civil service, industry, and services workers. PPP$76.36 per month.
• Persons who have an infirmity or physical disability may be paid less than the national minimum wage rate provided their employers have been granted an exemption by the minister of labor.	PPP$117.77 per month.
• An employee under the age of 16 years shall be paid at least 50% of the relevant national or sectoral minimum rate. An employee between the age of 16 and 18 shall be paid at least 60% of the relevant national or sectoral minimum rate.	US$23.50 per month. US$25.70 per month for civil servants.

(continued)

TABLE 3A.1. Characteristics of the Minimum Wage in Selected Countries (*Continued*)

Country	Minimum wage–setting procedure	Coverage: scope
Senegal	There are national minimum wage rates for nonagricultural workers and agricultural workers. In addition, minimum wage rates higher than these rates can be set by joint committees for sectors covered by collective agreements.	The minimum wage rates for agricultural and nonagricultural workers apply to all workers.
South Africa	A dual system of minimum wage–setting has been established. The government may set rates for certain sectors in sectoral determinations, following recommendations of the Employment Conditions Commission. In addition, minimum wage rates may be determined in collective agreements. Most of the sectoral determinations predetermine increases (or link them to the consumer price index) for the subsequent three years.	The Basic Conditions of Employment Act applies to all employees and employers, except members of the National Defense Force, the National Intelligence Agency, and the Secret Service, unpaid volunteers working for charitable organizations, and persons employed on sea vessels. Sectoral determinations may not apply to workers already bound by collective agreements.

East Asia and the Pacific

Country	Minimum wage–setting procedure	Coverage: scope
Cambodia	The Ministry of Labor sets a guaranteed minimum wage based on recommendations made by the Labor Advisory Committee.	The Labor Code applies to all professional, charitable, and educational enterprises. It does not apply to judges; permanent public servants; members of the police, army, military forces, air and maritime transportation personnel (governed by a separate statute); and domestic workers.
China	The government is responsible for implementing a system of regional minimum wage rates; there is no national minimum wage rate. Standards are stipulated by provincial, regional, and municipal governments and reported to the State Council for consent. They are adjusted at least once every two years.	The provisions concerning minimum wages apply to enterprises, private nonenterprise entities, individual industrial and commercial households, and the laborers who have formed a labor relationship with them.

Coverage: variations in minimum wage, by categories	Level(s)[a]
• Workers paid by the piece and working for at least two weeks must receive at least 90% of the applicable minimum wage.	PPP$0.82 per hour for agricultural workers. PPP$0.94 per hour for nonagricultural workers.
• Sectoral determinations have been established for domestic workers, contract cleaning workers, private security workers, farm workers, wholesale and retail workers, welfare workers, and engineers. • Minimum wage rates vary by region. • In the wholesale and retail sector, a specific minimum wage rate is stipulated for trainee managers and trainees. Also, employees who perform commission work must receive at least two-thirds of the applicable minimum wage.	PPP$280.39 per month for farm workers. PPP$514.31 per month for general assistants in the wholesale and retail sector.
• As of October 2003, minimum wage rates had only been set for the textile, garment, and shoe manufacturing industries. • Minimum wage rates may vary regionally. • Workers on a probation period (one to three months) may receive a minimum wage slightly lower than the regular rate. • Piece-rate workers must be paid by the hour at least the amount guaranteed to a worker earning the minimum wage.	US$45 per month for regular workers in the textile, garment, and footwear sector.
• Different minimum wage rates may be set in each province and within the separate administrative areas of each province. All of China's 39 provinces, regions, and municipalities are subject to minimum wage legislation.	PPP$104.80 per month in certain towns in Jiangzxi region. PPP$350.21 per month in Shanghai city.

(continued)

TABLE 3A.1. Characteristics of the Minimum Wage in Selected Countries (*Continued*)

Country	Minimum wage–setting procedure	Coverage: scope
Fiji	There is no national minimum wage in Fiji. The government may establish Wages Councils for groups of workers if no collective bargaining mechanism is in place. Wages Councils make wage regulation proposals to the minister of labor who may enact the proposal as an order. Minimum wages for sectors of the workforce not covered by Wages Councils are determined in collective agreements.	Only workers in sectors covered by Wages Councils are entitled to statutory minimum wage rates.
Indonesia	The governor of each province sets minimum wage rates for the respective province or regency. The Law on Manpower Affairs provided that a National Wage Council, Provincial Wage Councils, and District/City Wage Councils should be established to develop a national wage system. Minimum wages are reviewed by each province on a yearly basis.	All workers are covered by minimum wage regulations except for domestic workers. The legislation provides for exceptions for companies unable to pay minimum wage rates.
Korea, Republic of	The minister of labor sets the national minimum wage each year, following the Minimum Wage Council's proposal. If the minister of labor does not agree with the wage proposal, but two-thirds of the Council support it, the minister must adopt the proposal. The minister of labor publishes the rate proposals, and representatives of workers or employers may raise objections within 10 days of publication.	The minimum wage applies to all workers, except domestic workers and businesses using only relatives living together. An employer may obtain permission to exclude certain workers from minimum wage provisions in cases of disability, probation (a maximum of three months), training, or for workers engaged in surveillance or intermittent work.
Lao PDR	The Labor Act of 1994 states that the government or other relevant body will establish minimum wage rates for each region.	The Labor Act applies only to workers in the formal sector. The Act does not apply to civil servants employed in state administrative and technical services, national defense, or public order.

Coverage: variations in minimum wage, by categories	Level(s)[a]
• Rates are set for the building, civil, and engineering trade; wholesale and retail trade; hotel and catering trade; road transport; mining and quarrying industries; saw milling and logging industry; printing trades; garment industry; and manufacturing industry. • All apprentices are entitled to minimum hourly rates in accordance with the number of years of apprenticeship completed. • A few industries have set separate rates for workers under 18. • A disabled worker, employer, or prospective employer may apply for a reduced minimum wage rate to apply to the worker. • The minimum wage is increased by 25% for casual workers.	PPP$1.31 per hour for learners in the garment industry. PPP$2.16 per hour for workers in printing trades.
• Many provinces have set a basic minimum wage that applies to all sectors. However, provinces are entitled to set separate minimum wages for each sector on the basis of agreements between corporate organizations and worker unions or labor federations. • Workers on probation must be paid the minimum wage. • Piece-rate workers, contractors, and freelancing daily workers are covered if they are employed for one month or more.	PPP$113.88 per month in East Java. PPP$255.06 per month in the province of Jakarta.
• Separate minimum wage rates may be set for seamen. • Workers under the age of 18 employed for less than six months should receive 90% of the applicable minimum wage rate. • Workers with a disability may be excluded from minimum wage protection. • Piece-rate workers must receive hourly wage rates equivalent to the minimum wage rate. The Minimum Wage Act stipulates that a separate minimum wage rate may be determined for piece workers. No decrees in this regard have yet been made. • The legislation also applies to contractors, for whom the minimum wage rate shall be determined according to a certain unit of output or achievement.	PPP$674.74 per month.
• Workers on a probationary period must receive at least 90% of the applicable minimum wage (for a maximum of one or two months). • Workers may only be paid on a piece-rate basis if the government or relevant body has not established a minimum wage rate for a specific region, or if the employer allows workers to bring and do supplementary work outside their labor unit.	PPP$46.19 per month.

(continued)

TABLE 3A.1. Characteristics of the Minimum Wage in Selected Countries (*Continued*)

Country	Minimum wage–setting procedure	Coverage: scope
Malaysia	There is no national minimum wage. The government may establish Wages Councils for certain nonunionized sectors of the workforce not covered by collective agreements. These councils submit wage regulations proposals, which the government may choose to enact in a wage regulation order.	Wages Councils have been established for certain nonunionized sectors of the workforce not covered by collective agreements. Casual workers or someone employed other than for the purposes of the employer's business are excluded from minimum wage protection.
Papua New Guinea	A Minimum Wages Board may make determinations on minimum wages, which must be approved by the head of state. Currently, one national minimum wage rate has been established. Minimum wages may also be set in registered awards and common rules. A 1992 determination states that future determinations should be made following negotiations between employers and employees, which has not happened to date.	The minimum wage applies to all employees and employers.
Philippines	Regional Tripartite Wages and Productivity Boards determine minimum wage rates applicable in their regions, provinces, or industries subject to the guidelines set by the National Wages and Productivity Commission. In addition, the secretary of labor and employment may establish the minimum wage rate for home workers and those employed in cottage industries. Wage orders should be determined whenever conditions in the region so warrant, but no sooner than 12 months after issuance of rates by the boards, unless particular circumstances warrant it.	The provisions do not apply to domestic workers, home workers carrying out needlework, or workers in cottage industries. A minimum wage rate for domestic workers is provided separately. Retail or service establishments with fewer than 10 workers may apply to be excluded from the requirements.
Solomon Islands	The minister of labor may set minimum wage rates. The minimum wage may be abated by way of a collective agreement if the commissioner for labor provides a written permit for such abatement.	The minimum wage provisions apply to all workers except domestic workers and seamen.

Coverage: variations in minimum wage, by categories	Level(s)[a]
• Minimum wage rates are set for workers in the catering and hotel sector and for stevedores, cinema workers, and shop assistants. • For shop assistants, two regions have been identified with different rates, and specific minimum wages rates have been set for apprentices. • Workers in the catering and hotel sector and shop assistants receive different minimum wage rates if between 14 and 16 or 16 and 18. • An employer or prospective employer of a disabled person may apply for a reduced minimum wage to the relevant Wages Council.	PPP$94.98 per month for cinema workers. PPP$153.19 per month for shop assistants in certain urban districts.
• New entrants to the workforce between 16 and 21 years of age are entitled to 75% of the national minimum wage rate.	PPP$28.12 per week.
• Domestic workers are covered by specific wage rates. • The regional boards set minimum wage rates for at least two categories: agricultural and nonagricultural workers. There are also specific rates for hospital workers in 7 regions; retail/service workers in 12 regions; cottage workers in 10 regions; and school workers in 3 regions. • Apprentices receive at least 75% of the applicable minimum wage for the first six months. • Disabled workers receive at least 75% of the minimum wage. • Workers paid by output must not receive less than the applicable minimum wage.	PPP$8.24 per day for retail and service workers in selected areas. PPP$21.41 per day for nonagricultural workers in the National Capital Region.
• A separate rate is set for the fishing and agriculture sectors. • Disabled workers may apply for an exemption from minimum wage provisions, and this would lead to the setting of the applicable wage rate.	PPP$0.47 per hour for the fishing and agricultural plantation sector. PPP$0.58 per hour for all other sectors.

(continued)

TABLE 3A.1. Characteristics of the Minimum Wage in Selected Countries (*Continued*)

Country	Minimum wage–setting procedure	Coverage: scope
Thailand	The National Wage Committee makes a recommendation concerning adjustments to the basic minimum wage rate. In addition, tripartite provincial committees can recommend a minimum wage higher than the basic rate for certain provinces. The National Wage Committee must report to the labor minister at least once a year.	The Labor Protection Act does not apply to central, provincial, and local administration and state enterprises governed by the Law on State Enterprises, or to agricultural workers, domestic workers, or employers who run private schools.
Vietnam	The Ministry of Labor, War Invalids, and Social Affairs may set minimum wage rates that vary across regions and for local or foreign firms. The legislation does not set specific time periods for adjustment.	The Labor Code applies to all workers.

Latin America and the Caribbean

Argentina	The National Council for Employment, Productivity, and the Adjustable Minimum Living Wage periodically determines the adjustable minimum wage. The government did not convene the council in setting the minimum wage for January 2004, since the economic crisis and the need for an urgent rise in wages constituted exceptional circumstances, but set the wage by presidential decree. The minimum wage can be adjusted at any time at the request of any social partner.	The minimum wage applies to both private and public sector workers.
Bahamas	Statutory minimum wage rates are set by the government. Separate rates are established for workers employed by the week, the day, or the hour. Prior to any increase in the minimum wage rates, consultation must take place with representatives of employers and an association of registered trade unions.	Minimum wages apply to all employees in the private and public sectors. The Minister of Labor may exclude certain persons or sectors. Children and young persons (no definition provided) are excluded from minimum wage protection.

Coverage: variations in minimum wage, by categories	Level(s)[a]
• Minimum wage rates have been established for certain provinces that are higher than the basic minimum wage rate.	From PPP$10.53 per day to PPP$13.38 per day.
• Two rates are set, for local and foreign-invested enterprises. • Apprentices and trainees must receive at least 70% of the applicable wage rate for an employee performing the same job. • Employees on a trial period must receive at least 70% of the applicable wage rate for the relevant rank of the job. • Piece-rate workers may be paid wages according to the number of items produced.	PPP$96.97 per month for workers in local enterprises. PPP$209.32 per month for workers in foreign-invested enterprises in Hanoi City and Ho Chi Minh City.
• The remuneration of home workers is determined by parity commission. • Minimum wages for domestic workers are set by the Ministry of Labor and Social Security Resolution. • A specific minimum wage rate, which may not be lower than the national minimum wage rate, may be set for agricultural workers by the executive. • Apprentices, minors, and disabled workers may receive a minimum wage lower than the national rate for adult workers.	PPP$531.81 per month.
	PPP$157.89 per week.

(continued)

TABLE 3A.1. Characteristics of the Minimum Wage in Selected Countries (*Continued*)

Country	Minimum wage–setting procedure	Coverage: scope
Belize	Minimum wage rates are set by the Minister of Labor for workers covered by a Wages Council. These councils were established in response to a lack of effective wage regulation by collective agreement for the workers concerned. Wages Councils submit wage proposals to the minister, who may make a wages regulation order for the workers concerned.	Only workers covered by a wages regulation order are covered. Casual workers are excluded.
Bolivia	The Ministry of Labor sets the minimum wage for different regions and categories of workers. In practice, the president, together with the Council of Ministers, sets the minimum wage by supreme decree.	The minimum wage applies to all workers in the public and private sectors. There is one general minimum wage rate for all employees except agricultural workers.
Brazil	The national minimum wage rate is set by law. Currently, the minimum wage is set by a provisional measure in accordance with the Federal Constitution and placed before Congress for conversion into law. The legislation establishes that minimum wage adjustments should take place every three years; however, in reality, the rate has been set annually.	
Chile	The government sets two minimum wage rates by law: one for workers between 18 and 65 years old, and one for workers under 18 and over 65. A rate for "nonremunerative" purposes is also set and used solely as a reference point for calculating fines, taxes, fees, and so on. It does not establish the actual minimum wage to be paid to workers.	Minimum wage legislation applies to workers in the private sector. Remuneration for apprentices and mentally disabled workers is freely agreed by parties and is not subject to minimum wage legislation.
Colombia	The minimum wage is set by the Permanent Commission on the Harmonization of Wage and Labor Policies through an executive decree. If the commission cannot reach consensus, the government sets the minimum wage. The commission is a tripartite institution made up of government, worker, and employer representatives. The minimum wage is adjusted once a year.	All workers in the private sector are covered by minimum wage legislation.

Coverage: variations in minimum wage, by categories	*Level(s)*[a]
• Minimum wages have been established for manual workers, shop assistants, and domestic helpers. • Workers that are infirm or incapacitated may apply for an exception from a wage regulation order. • Students employed as shop assistants are entitled to a lower minimum wage rate than regular workers.	PPP$2 per hour for students employed as shop assistants and manual workers engaged in agriculture, agroindustry, or export-oriented industries. PPP$2.25 per hour for other workers. PPP$163.71 (assumed to be per month).
• For piece-rate workers, the wage is set to ensure that it is no lower than the normal daily minimum wage.	PPP$235.41 per month.
• There is a specific minimum wage rate for workers under 18 or over 65. • The minimum remuneration for domestic workers cannot be less than 75% of the monthly minimum.	PPP$385.84 per month for workers aged 18 to 65.
• Part-time workers receive a pro rata minimum wage according to the hours effectively worked.	PPP$483.15 per month.

(continued)

TABLE 3A.1. Characteristics of the Minimum Wage in Selected Countries (*Continued*)

Country	Minimum wage–setting procedure	Coverage: scope
Costa Rica	The National Wage Council sets minimum wages by sector and occupation for workers in the private sector through executive decrees. The council's proposal for adjustments is sent every year to the Ministry of Labor for comment, and the final decision is made by the council. In addition, minimum wages can be revised at any time during the year at the request of 5 employers or 15 workers.	General rates tend to apply to workers in occupations requiring a professional qualification and vary according to qualification. Sectoral rates are set for nonqualified, partially qualified, and specialist workers. Occupational rates are defined by the National Wage Council in its "Occupational Profiles."
Cuba	Minimum wages are set by the Council of Ministers in consultation with the central union of workers.	All workers are covered by minimum wage legislation.
Dominican Republic	Minimum wages for private sector workers are set by occupation and sector by the National Salary Committee, which adjusts minimum wages at least every two years. In principle, the minimum wages cannot be changed within the first year of validity. However, if the employers or the workers prove that a certain minimum wage rate impairs one of the social partners and causes detriment to the national economy, the committee may adjust the rate. The minimum wage for public sector workers is set directly by executive decree.	Minimum wages are set by occupation and sector.
Ecuador	The government, through the National Wage Council, sets minimum wages for workers in the private sector and the general "vital" minimum wage rate, which is used as a reference point for calculating fines, taxes, fees, and so on. The National Wage Council is a tripartite institution made up of three representatives: one each from government, employers, and workers. In case the National Wage Council cannot reach a consensus, the Ministry of Labor sets the minimum wage rates. Minimum wages are updated yearly.	Minimum wage rates apply to all workers in the private sector and are set by sector and occupation.

Coverage: variations in minimum wage, by categories	Level(s)[a]
<ul><li>Rates vary by sector and occupation.</li><li>Minimum wage rates for youth are no less than 50% of the relevant minimum wage rate during the first year of employment and no less than 75% during the second year.</li><li>Workers carrying out dangerous or unhealthy work are entitled to an hourly minimum wage equivalent to one-sixth of the daily minimum wage for nonqualified workers set by sector.</li><li>Piece-rate workers cannot be paid less than what a worker would have received if working an ordinary working day.</li></ul>	PPP$345.35 per month for domestic workers. PPP$19.92 per day for nonqualified workers in the agricultural, fishing, forestry, and mining industries, or the electricity, commerce, tourism, services, transport, and warehousing sectors.
<ul><li>Minimum wage rates vary by sector and by occupation. They are set for laborers, administrative and service workers, technicians, and managers.</li><li>The minimum wage for part-time workers is proportional to the time worked.</li><li>A minimum wage rate is set for the agricultural sector.</li></ul>	
<ul><li>Minimum wages are set for workers operating heavy machinery, electricians, painters, carpenters, and plumbers.</li><li>Minimum wages are set for agriculture; hotels, restaurants, bars, cafes and other food service establishments; the construction industry; the sugar industry, and sectors that do not have a specific rate. In certain sectors, minimum wage rates depend on the size of a company and the nature of the business.</li><li>Minimum wage rates are set in accordance with production for the following occupations: carpenters, electricians, plumbers, painters, bricklayers, and heavy-machine operators in agriculture.</li><li>Minimum wages for part-time workers shall be calculated on a pro rata basis.</li><li>The remuneration for apprentices cannot be less than the minimum wage and should be calculated according to the hours of training.</li></ul>	PPP$7.40 per day for workers in the sugar industry. PPP$587.38 per month for workers in large industrial, commercial, or service companies.
<ul><li>Minimum wage rates are determined for the industry, agriculture, and textile sectors. The minimum wage rate for the industry and agriculture sectors is also applicable for other workers. The rate set for the textile sector is slightly lower.</li><li>Remuneration for apprentices cannot be less than 80% of the remuneration paid to an adult performing a similar work.</li><li>Part-time workers are paid the equivalent of the applicable minimum wage rate on a pro rata basis.</li></ul>	PPP$90.79 per month for domestic workers. PPP$256.11 per month for workers in the small-scale industry sector, agricultural sector, and other general workers.

(continued)

195

TABLE 3A.1. Characteristics of the Minimum Wage in Selected Countries (*Continued*)

Country	Minimum wage–setting procedure	Coverage: scope
El Salvador	Minimum wage rates are set by the government for certain sectors following proposals of the National Minimum Wage Council. The executive has the discretion to accept the proposals and set the rates by decree or direct the council to reconsider. The wages are adjusted at least every three years.	Minimum wage rates apply to selected sectors.
Guatemala	Minimum wage rates for private sector workers are set as follows. Joint minimum wage boards in each region and economic zone make recommendations to the National Wage Commission, a technical and advisory body attached to the Ministry of Labor and Social Welfare. The commission issues a report harmonizing all the proposed rates. Finally, the executive sets the rates (which apply nationwide with no regional variation) with the Ministry of Labor and Social Welfare. Rates are adjusted every year.	Minimum wage rates are set by sector and occupation, and rates apply to all workers except those employed by the state.
Haiti	The minimum wage is set by the government. In 1995, the Committee for Consultation and Arbitration was established to make recommendations concerning the minimum wage. The minimum wage is supposed to be adjusted for changes in the cost of living and must be increased when the annual inflation rate is more than 10%.	The national statutory minimum wage applies to all workers in commercial, industrial, and agricultural establishments. Domestic workers are not covered.
Honduras	The National Minimum Wage Commission sets minimum wages by sector. This tripartite institution comprises government, employer, and employee representatives. If it does not reach a consensus, the executive has the authority to increase the minimum wage. Minimum wages are adjusted each year. At the request of employers or workers, they can also be revised every six months if inflation is more than 12%.	All workers in the private sector are covered by minimum wage legislation except for apprentices. Minimum wages vary according to sector, the type of business concerned, and the number of employees.

Coverage: variations in minimum wage, by categories	Level(s)[a]
• Minimum wages are set for the commerce, services, industry, textile, clothing, agriculture, coffee, cotton, and sugar sectors. • Piece-rate workers must receive wages equal to at least the daily minimum wage. • Apprentices are entitled to at least 50% of the relevant minimum wage during the first year and 75% during the second year. • Employers must pay the full daily minimum wage to workers on the job five to eight hours a day. In any other case, the minimum wage must be proportional to the number of hours worked.	PPP$5.59 per day for workers in the agricultural sector. PPP$11.69 per day for workers in the industry sector.
• Minimum wage rates are set for the agricultural and nonagricultural sectors. In the nonagricultural sector, special minimum wage rates are set for bakers and pastry workers. • Minimum wage rates for all part-time workers in the nonagricultural sector and workers in the media who are not paid on a daily basis are 16% higher than the standard rates. • Remuneration for piece-rate workers cannot be lower than the applicable minimum wage rates. • Apprentices may be paid less than the minimum wage.	PPP$9.97 per day for agricultural workers. PPP$10.25 per day for nonagricultural workers.
	PPP$8.30 per day.
• Minimum wage rates are set for (1) agriculture, fishing, hunting, and forestry; (2) manufacturing, construction, commerce, hotels and restaurants, and social and personal services; (3) warehousing, transportation, communications, real estate, and other services; and (4) general services. Within certain sectors, rates also vary according to the number of workers employed. • A permit may be issued for a disabled worker stating the percentage of the minimum wage the worker is entitled to receive.	PPP$8.33 per day for workers in general services companies with 1–15 workers. PPP$13.70 per day for workers in companies in the temporary import regime.

(continued)

TABLE 3A.1. Characteristics of the Minimum Wage in Selected Countries (*Continued*)

Country	Minimum wage–setting procedure	Coverage: scope
Mexico	Minimum wage rates are set by the National Commission on Minimum Wages, a tripartite institution made up of representatives of the government, employers, and workers. Special boards may be appointed to provide advice to the commission. Minimum wages are adjusted each year and can be revised at any time if economic circumstances so warrant.	There are two types of minimum wage: the general minimum wages that apply to all workers and occupational minimum wages (higher than the general minimum wages). Both wages vary by geographic area. The legislation applies to private sector workers.
Nicaragua	Minimum wages are set by the National Minimum Wage Commission, which comprises representatives of the Ministries of Labor and of the Economy and Development, major national employer associations, and trade unions. The wages are supposed to be adjusted every six months.	Workers in both the private and public sector are covered by minimum wage legislation. There is no general minimum wage rate, but, rather, minimum wage rates that vary by sector.
Panama	Minimum wages are set by executive decree following recommendations of the National Minimum Wage Commission, a tripartite institution comprising worker, employer, and government representatives. Minimum wages are supposed to be adjusted at least every two years.	The legislation covers only workers in the private sector. There is no general minimum wage rate. Minimum wage rates vary according to regions, sectors, and company size. A worker providing services in more than one area receives the most favorable rate.
Paraguay	Minimum wages are set by the government according to proposals of the National Minimum Wage Council, a tripartite institution made up of government, employer, and worker representatives. The rates are supposed to be updated every two years. The government may change the rates earlier if there is a significant alteration in the conditions of a sector or industry or if there is a variation of at least 10% in the cost of living.	Minimum wage legislation applies to all workers in the private sector. Minimum wages are set by occupation and by sector. There is also a minimum wage rate applicable to those occupations and sectors that do not have a specific minimum wage rate.

Coverage: variations in minimum wage, by categories	Level(s)[a]
• There are 88 occupational minimum wages set for occupations such as bricklayers, archive workers, drugstore salespersons, cashiers, bartenders, carpenters, brush operators, chefs, mattress producers, accountants, shoemakers, tailors, car drivers, bus drivers, truck drivers, furniture restorers, electricians, supermarket workers, nurses, gas station workers, locksmiths, and jewelers.	PPP$5.83 per day for area C. PPP$6.27 per day for area A.
• Rates have been established for the following sectors: agriculture; fishing; mining; manufacturing; some industries; electricity, gas, and water; construction; commerce, the restaurant and hotel industry; transport, warehousing, communication; financial and insurance services; and central and local government. • Minimum wages for prison workers cannot be lower than the regular applicable minimum wage.	PPP$129.50 per month for agricultural workers. PPP$304.77 per month for construction workers.
• Rates are set for domestic workers, wood producers, furniture and mattress producers, food producers, personal services providers, and air and water transportation workers. • Rates are set for agriculture, forestry, hunting, fishing, the manufacturing sector, electricity, gas, water, construction, large- and small-scale commerce, hotels, restaurants, transport, warehousing, telecommunications, financial intermediaries, real estate, and social and personal services.	PPP$1.84 per hour for agricultural workers in small-scale companies.
• Apprentice remuneration may not be less than 60% of the minimum wage. • The remuneration of minors may not be less than 60% of the minimum wage and a progressive scale based on years effectively worked. A minor performing the same work as an adult must be paid the full minimum wage. • Remuneration for physically and mentally disabled persons can be lower than the minimum wage. • The daily minimum wage for piece-rate workers shall not be lower than the monthly minimum wage divided by 26.	The minimum wage rate applicable to those occupations and sectors that do not have specific minimum wage rates is PPP$694.03 per month.

(*continued*)

TABLE 3A.1. Characteristics of the Minimum Wage in Selected Countries (*Continued*)

Country	Minimum wage–setting procedure	Coverage: scope
Peru	The minimum wage is set by the National Labor and Employment Promotion Council, a tripartite institution made up of government, worker, and employer representatives. If there is no agreement on a minimum wage rate within the council, the president sets the minimum wage through emergency decree.	All workers in the private sector are covered by minimum wage legislation. There is one general minimum wage rate applicable to all workers in the private sector.
Trinidad and Tobago	The government sets the minimum wage in an order based on the recommendation of the Minimum Wages Board.	The order does not apply to trainees in government-approved training schools, registered apprentices, workers in certain government-approved schemes, students on vacation jobs, and volunteers in registered charities.
Uruguay	The government sets the national minimum wage by decree.	The national minimum wage applies to the public and private sectors. There are three minimum wage rates: general, for rural workers, and for domestic workers.
Venezuela	The Ministry of Labor sets minimum wages based on recommendations by the Tripartite Commission for the Revision of the Minimum Wage. In the absence of a recommendation, the executive may unilaterally set the rates. In case of large increases in the cost of living, the executive may set rates by decree, taking into account comments of worker and employer representatives, the National Economic Council, and the Central Bank. Rates are adjusted yearly.	Minimum wages apply to both private and public sector workers. There is no general minimum wage rate. There are different minimum wage rates for: urban workers, workers in companies with fewer than 20 workers, rural workers, and youth and apprentices.

Middle East and North Africa

Algeria	In accordance with the law on labor relations, the government sets a national minimum wage following consultation with social partners.	All workers, except national defense personnel, magistrates, state officials, and personnel of selected public establishments. Legislation may be enacted for managers, journalists, pilots, captains, seafarers, home workers, artists, commercial representatives, athletes, and domestic workers.

Coverage: variations in minimum wage, by categories	*Level(s)[a]*
• Remuneration for youth, trainees, and apprentices cannot be lower than the minimum wage. If they work less than a full working day, the remuneration should be set on a pro rata basis.	PPP$309.94 per month.
• Piece-rate workers and offsite workers must be paid an agreed piece-rate or an hourly rate based on a fair estimate of the equivalent number of hours and on the minimum wage.	PPP$282.62 per month.
• Minimum wage rates for domestic workers vary by region. • Minimum wage rates for agricultural laborers vary by occupation.	PPP$110.19 per month.
• The minimum wage rate applicable to workers in companies with fewer than 20 workers is also applicable to domestic workers. • If apprentices and youth render services under the same conditions as urban or rural workers, the regular minimum wage rates apply.	PPP$265.84 per month for rural workers. PPP$295.37 per month for urban workers.
• Apprentices receive a presalary equivalent to 15% of the national rate for six months (if the apprenticeship stays less than 24 months) or for 12 months (if the apprenticeship stays more than 24 months). • Wages for home workers may not be lower than the national minimum wage rate.	PPP$389.41 per month.

(*continued*)

TABLE 3A.1. Characteristics of the Minimum Wage in Selected Countries (*Continued*)

Country	Minimum wage–setting procedure	Coverage: scope
Lebanon	The national minimum wage rate is set by the government in accordance with a report of the tripartite Commission on the Cost of Living Index, comprising representatives of the government, employers, wage earners, and salaried earners.	The minimum wage applies to all workers over 20 years of age in the public and private sector except for domestic servants, workers in agricultural corporations not connected to trade and industry, workers in family businesses, and temporary workers in public administration.
Morocco	National minimum wage rates are set by the government following consultation with the most representative employee and employer organizations.	Rates are set for agricultural workers, industrial and commercial workers, and the liberal professions. Certain categories of employers may be excluded from the legislation following consultation with employee and employer organizations.
Tunisia	Minimum wage rates are set and revised by the government in a decree following consultations with worker and employer organizations. In practice, the National Committee on Social Dialogue is consulted. The legislation does not set forth how frequently rates should be adjusted, but, in practice, they are updated each year.	Rates are set for agricultural workers and other workers. The Labor Code applies to all public and private employers, including cottage industries, cooperatives, professionals, unions, and other organizations. It excludes domestic workers.
South Asia Bangladesh	The Minimum Wages Board may recommend the minimum wage rates for workers in industries. The Council of Minimum Wages and Prices for Agricultural Labor may recommend the minimum wage rate for agricultural laborers (the council has not yet been established). The Export Processing Zones Authority establishes separate minimum wage rate for companies within export processing zones. The Minimum Wages Board should review any recommendations at least once during any three-year period.	Minimum wage rates have been established for workers in the garment industry, export processing zones, and agriculture. Persons employed by federal or provincial governments are excluded from minimum wage rates set in wage board ordinances for workers in industries.

202

Coverage: variations in minimum wage, by categories	Level(s)[a]
	PPP$239.00 per month.
• Apprentices may be paid wages lower than the minimum rates. • Employees paid by the piece, output, or production must receive a salary equivalent to the minimum rate unless output is reduced as a result of factors within the control of the employee concerned. • Employees whose salaries are made up entirely of tips or tips and a base salary are entitled to receive at least the minimum wage rate. If the tips are not sufficient, the employer must pay the difference.	PPP$14.18 per day for agricultural workers.
• A minimum wage rate is set for workers under 18 years of age; this is currently at 85% of the relevant adult rate. • Wage rates for workers paid per piece produced must be set at the equivalent of the minimum wage rate.	PPP$14.58 per day for agricultural workers. PPP$411.97 per week for nonagricultural workers.
• Apprentices have a slightly lower minimum wage rate than regular workers in export processing zones. Separate wage rates are also set for trainees or apprentices in the garment industry.	PPP$49.23 per month for helpers in the garment industry. PPP$73.84 per month for machine operators in the garment industry. PPP$148.91 per month for helpers in export processing zones. PPP$248.18 per month for ordinary operators in electronics industries in export processing zones.

(continued)

TABLE 3A.1. Characteristics of the Minimum Wage in Selected Countries (*Continued*)

Country	Minimum wage–setting procedure	Coverage: scope
India	Minimum wage rates for occupations that are largely nonunionized or have little bargaining power may be set in accordance with the Minimum Wages Act, 1948. Both central and local governments may set minimum wage rates for nonunionized occupations. Reviews of the rates should take place at least every five years.	The law applies throughout India except in Sikkim. The central government sets rates for 45 different occupations, while states have set rates for 1,232 occupations in their jurisdictions. The law does not apply to organized occupations or to family members employing other members who live with and depend on them.
Nepal	The government sets minimum wage rates on the basis of recommendations by the Minimum Remuneration Fixation Committee (nonagriculture) and the High Level Monitoring Committee (agriculture). In the absence of recommendations, the government may prescribe the rates.	Minimum wage rates are set for all agricultural workers and for nonagricultural workers in enterprises with more than 10 workers (for unskilled, semiskilled, skilled, and highly skilled workers). Domestic workers are excluded from the provisions.
Pakistan	The government sets a minimum wage rate. Provincial minimum wage boards may recommend minimum wage rates that the provincial governments should adopt for unskilled and juvenile workers (not done in practice) and for skilled workers in industries without effective collective bargaining mechanisms (done in a few regions). The minimum wages boards should review recommendations not less than every three years.	The legislation applies to all unskilled workers in commercial and industrial establishments (all sectors). It does not apply to workers in agriculture, federal or provincial governments, coal mines, public utilities, defense, or public services.
Sri Lanka	Minimum wage rates are set by wage boards for 39 trades and by the Remuneration Tribunal for shop and office employees. The legislation does not provide specific dates when minimum wage rates should be adjusted.	Any person working in a trade for which no wages boards or remuneration committees have been established is excluded from the national system of minimum wage. The legislation makes no provision for domestic workers or for workers in the fishing sector.

Coverage: variations in minimum wage, by categories	Level(s)[a]
<ul><li>The regional minimum wage rates should not be less than the minimum floor wage set by the minister of labor.</li><li>Specific minimum wage rates may be established for apprentices, adolescents (14 to 18 years of age), and children under 14.</li><li>The appropriate government may exclude disabled employees from certain provisions of the legislation.</li></ul>	PPP$5.85 per day for unskilled construction workers in most rural areas. PPP$10.43 per day for unskilled agricultural workers in some areas.
<ul><li>A lower rate is set for workers between 14 and 16 years of age.</li></ul>	PPP$133.94 per month for unskilled workers on tea estates. PPP$197.3 per month for workers and employees not working on tea estates.
<ul><li>Apprentices are excluded from the legislation, but the apprenticeship rules provide that apprentices receive a guaranteed rate that starts at 50% of the regular rate in the first year and increases up to the regular rate after three years.</li></ul>	PPP$182.08 per month.
<ul><li>Minimum wage rates may vary in accordance with a worker's skill level.</li><li>Lower minimum wage rates than those set for adults have been established for apprentices, trainees, and learners in selected trades.</li><li>Many wage boards set lower minimum wage rates for children.</li><li>Disabled workers may be granted reduced minimum rates.</li><li>Wage boards may determine minimum wage rates for piece work.</li></ul>	PPP$3.85 per day for rubber workers. PPP$50.70 per month for preschool assistants. PPP$128.98 per month for textile workers.

Source: Conditions of Work and Employment Database. International Labor Organization. http://www.ilo.org/travaildatabase/servlet/minimumwages (accessed November 23, 2005).

[a] Most minimum wage rates are expressed here in terms of purchasing power using the purchasing power parity (PPP) factors elaborated by the World Bank for 2003. Where values in PPP dollars (PPP$) are not available, minimum wage rates have been converted to United States dollars (US$) using the average exchange rate for 2003 (*Source:* Economic Intelligence Unit). When there are multiple rates, the table typically presents the lowest and highest rates.

International Comparisons of Alternative Indicators of the Stringency of Employment Protection Legislation

TABLE 3A.2. International Comparisons of Alternative Indicators of the Stringency of Employment Protection Legislation

Region/ country	Difficulty of hiring index	Rigidity of hours index	Difficulty of firing index	Rigidity of employment index	Hiring cost (% of salary)	Firing costs (weeks of wages)
East Asia and the Pacific						
Cambodia	67	80	30	59	0	138.8
China	11	40	40	30	30	90
Fiji	22	40	0	21	8	27.8
Hong Kong, China	0	0	0	0	5	12.9
Indonesia	61	40	70	57	10.2	144.8
Kiribati	0	0	50	17	7.5	46.4
Lao PDR	11	60	80	50	5	35.9
Malaysia	0	20	10	10	13.3	65.2
Marshall Islands	33	0	0	11	10.5	0
Micronesia	33	0	0	11	6	0
Mongolia	11	80	10	34	19	16.9
Palau	0	0	0	0	6	0
Papua New Guinea	22	20	20	21	7.7	38.4
Philippines	56	40	40	45	9.3	90
Samoa	11	20	0	10	6	42.4
Singapore	0	0	0	0	13	4
Solomon Islands	11	20	20	17	7.5	51.7
Taiwan, China	78	60	30	56	9.5	90
Thailand	33	20	0	18	5	47
Timor-Leste	67	20	50	46	0	21.2
Tonga	0	40	0	13	0	0
Vanuatu	39	40	10	30	6	55
Vietnam	44	40	70	51	17	98
Europe and Central Asia						
Albania	44	80	20	48	30.7	63.6
Armenia	17	60	70	49	18.8	16.6
Azerbaijan	33	40	40	38	27	42.4
Belarus	0	40	40	27	39.1	20.9
Bosnia and Herzegovina	56	40	30	42	42	32.8
Bulgaria	61	60	10	44	32.2	29.8
Croatia	61	60	50	57	17.2	37.8
Czech Republic	33	20	20	24	37	21.6
Estonia	33	80	40	51	33	33.2

Region/ country	Difficulty of hiring index	Rigidity of hours index	Difficulty of firing index	Rigidity of employment index	Hiring cost (% of salary)	Firing costs (weeks of wages)
Georgia	0	60	70	43	31	4
Hungary	11	80	20	37	33.5	33.5
Kazakhstan	0	60	10	23	22	8.3
Kyrgyz	33	40	40	38	26.5	20.9
Latvia	67	40	70	59	22.4	17
Lithuania	33	60	40	44	28	33.8
Macedonia, FYR	61	60	40	54	32.5	40.7
Moldova	33	100	70	68	30	20.9
Poland	11	60	40	37	25.8	24.9
Romania	67	60	50	59	34	98
Russian Federation	0	60	30	30	35.8	16.6
Serbia and Montenegro	44	0	40	28	25	21.2
Slovak Republic	17	60	40	39	35.2	12.9
Slovenia	61	80	50	64	16.6	43
Turkey	44	80	40	55	22.1	112
Ukraine	44	60	80	61	36.4	16.6
Uzbekistan	33	40	30	34	36	30.5
Latin America and the Caribbean						
Argentina	44	60	40	48	30.4	94
Bolivia	61	60	0	40	14	98
Brazil	67	80	20	56	26.8	165.3
Chile	33	20	20	24	3.4	51.3
Colombia	72	60	40	57	28.4	43.9
Costa Rica	56	60	0	39	23.5	33.7
Dominican Republic	22	80	30	44	13.5	76.9
Ecuador	44	60	70	58	13	131
El Salvador	44	60	20	41	15.3	86
Guatemala	61	40	20	40	12.8	100
Guyana	. .	. .	. .	. .	7.2	0
Haiti	11	40	20	24	9	25.6
Honduras	22	40	40	34	9.5	46.4
Jamaica	11	0	20	10	11.5	60.2
Mexico	33	60	60	51	23.8	74.5
Nicaragua	11	80	50	47	17	23.5

(*continued*)

TABLE 3A.2. International Comparisons of Alternative Indicators of the Stringency of Employment Protection Legislation (*Continued*)

Region/ country	Difficulty of hiring index	Rigidity of hours index	Difficulty of firing index	Rigidity of employment index	Hiring cost (% of salary)	Firing costs (weeks of wages)
Panama	78	40	70	63	14	47.3
Paraguay	56	60	60	59	16.5	99
Peru	44	60	40	48	10	55.6
Puerto Rico	56	20	30	35	16.2	0
Uruguay	33	60	0	31	20	25.8
Venezuela	33	80	20	44	14.7	46.4
Middle East and North Africa						
Algeria	44	60	50	51	27.5	16.9
Egypt	0	80	80	53	26	162.3
Iran	78	60	10	49	23	90
Iraq	78	80	50	69	12	4
Israel	0	80	20	33	5.9	90
Jordan	11	40	50	34	11	90
Kuwait	0	60	0	20	11	42.4
Lebanon	33	0	40	24	21.5	17.3
Morocco	100	40	40	60	17.7	83.3
Oman	44	60	0	35	9	12.6
Saudi Arabia	0	40	0	13	11	79.3
Syria	11	60	50	40	17	79.3
Tunisia	61	0	100	54	18.5	28.9
United Arab Emirates	0	80	20	33	12.5	95.6
West Bank and Gaza	33	60	20	38	13	90
Yemen	0	80	30	37	17	16.9
South Asia						
Afghanistan	67	20	30	39	0	4
Bangladesh	11	40	20	24	0	47
Bhutan	78	60	0	46	0	94
India	56	40	90	62	12.3	79
Maldives	0	20	0	7	0	20
Nepal	22	20	90	44	0	90
Pakistan	67	40	30	46	12	90
Sri Lanka	0	40	80	40	16.3	175.7
Sub-Saharan Africa						
Angola	33	80	80	64	8	61.8
Benin	39	80	40	53	27.4	35.2
Botswana	11	40	40	30	0	18.9

Region/ country	Difficulty of hiring index	Rigidity of hours index	Difficulty of firing index	Rigidity of employment index	Hiring cost (% of salary)	Firing costs (weeks of wages)
Burkina Faso	83	100	70	84	22.5	57
Burundi	67	80	60	69	6.9	24.9
Cameroon	28	60	80	56	15.5	40
Central African Republic	89	80	60	76	18	37.2
Chad	67	80	70	72	21.2	20.6
Congo, Democratic Republic	100	100	70	90	9	30.8
Congo, Republic	89	80	70	80	16.1	41.5
Côte d'Ivoire	44	80	10	45	15.4	67.6
Eritrea	0	60	20	27	2	68.5
Ethiopia	33	60	30	41	0	40.2
Ghana	11	40	50	34	12.5	24.9
Guinea	33	80	30	48	27	25.5
Kenya	33	20	30	28	5	47
Lesotho	56	60	10	42	0	47
Madagascar	67	60	50	59	18	40.9
Malawi	22	20	20	21	1	90
Mali	78	60	60	66	23.9	80.8
Mauritania	100	60	60	73	17	30.9
Mauritius	0	60	50	37	7	15.2
Mozambique	83	80	20	61	4	141
Namibia	0	60	20	27	0.1	24.2
Niger	100	100	70	90	16.4	75.6
Nigeria	33	60	20	38	7.5	4
Rwanda	56	60	60	59	8	53.8
São Tomé and Principe	61	60	60	60	6	108
Senegal	61	60	70	64	23	38.3
Sierra Leone	89	80	70	80	10	188.3
South Africa	56	40	60	52	2.6	37.5
Sudan	0	60	70	43	19	36.9
Tanzania	67	80	60	69	16	38.4
Togo	78	80	80	79	25	66.3
Uganda	0	20	20	13	10	12
Zambia	0	20	10	10	9	176
Zimbabwe	11	40	20	24	6	29.2

Source: Doing Business Database. World Bank. http://www.doingbusiness.org/ (accessed November 30, 2005).

Public Sector Downsizing

Juan Jose Diaz

M any governments face the difficult task of reducing the size and improving the efficiency of an overstaffed public sector as part of a general endeavor to increase economic growth and cut fiscal deficits. These retrenchment efforts often face considerable political opposition. To overcome opposition and to treat public employees who lose their jobs fairly, governments often provide severance payments to workers who leave public employment. However, problems in the design and implementation of these compensation schemes frequently reduce their efficiency and may result in the failure of the retrenchment.

This chapter provides an economic analysis of downsizing operations, illustrated by examples of operations implemented during the 1980s and 1990s. It discusses the rationale for this sort of reform and addresses the problem of adverse selection in voluntary separation schemes and the difficulties in appraisals of financial and economic returns. The analysis also identifies key stakeholders in the reform, their likely responses, and the dissemination channels of reform impacts. The chapter examines the consequences for households and the economy at large, the ways downsizing may affect displaced public sector workers, and the distributional impacts of downsizing for different groups of these workers. In order to advise policymakers, the chapter presents a simple tool for designing compensation packages that can outperform typical rules of thumb on the grounds of both financial returns and fairness. Finally, some threats and risks to these reforms are discussed.

CONTEXT OF REFORM: TYPES OF DOWNSIZING OPERATIONS

During the 1980s and 1990s, public sector downsizing and retrenchment operations were implemented around the world, particularly in Africa, Latin America, and the transition economies.[1] These operations targeted government agencies, state-owned enterprises, and the military. Some of the options governments used to downsize overstaffed civil services and state-owned enterprises are as follows:

- *Voluntary departure schemes.* This mechanism uses an arbitrary rule typically based on seniority and current earnings so that the workers to be let go are offered higher compensation packages the longer their tenure in the firm. For instance, separated workers receive two years of salary, or one month of salary per year of service, or some other combination of these seniority and current earnings variables. This mechanism helps bypass the legal obstacles in countries where outright layoffs are not allowed. This "buying out" scheme greatly minimizes political costs. However, two common problems diminish the effectiveness of this mechanism: (1) targeting errors, because sometimes only the best public sector workers leave; and (2) overcompensation or undercompensation, because the compensation may bear little relation with the losses experienced by the workers as a result of separation.
- *Involuntary retrenchment schemes.* This option may entail involuntary "soft" separations involving the strict enforcement of mandatory retirement rules, as well as the removal of workers from the payroll who are not working (ghost workers), or "hard" separations, such as layoffs. Depending on the outcome of the voluntary program and on the political leverage of workers, redundant staff may still need to be laid off against their will. Similar to the voluntary case, a rule of thumb involving salary and perhaps seniority in the public sector is used to calculate the compensation package.
- *Contracting-out schemes.* One way to minimize labor redundancies is to contract out activities previously executed within the enterprise to private cooperatives established by former enterprise employees.
- *Employee ownership.* To build support for privatization, some governments have reserved shares for employees in the to-be-privatized enterprises. This mechanism has been used in several sectors in Argentina, Bangladesh, Bolivia, Chile, Ghana, Mexico, Morocco, Pakistan, Peru, Turkey, and other countries. In addition to the financial gains, employee ownership gives employees a direct stake in the performance of the companies.

■ *Privatization.* Privatization is also a way to achieve public sector downsizing. (This chapter covers cases in which state-owned enterprises are downsized and then privatized, but not cases in which the enterprises are first privatized and then downsized.)

Haltiwanger and Singh (1999) provide a review of 41 downsizing operations in 37 countries. Among these operations, the average program cost was $400 million, and the total financial cost of the operations was large, about $12 billion. In terms of retrenchment methods (see Table 4.1), involuntary hard separations (layoffs) dominated in the total reductions in employment; they accounted for 47 percent of total worker separations, partly because of the massive employment retrenchment experiences in Eastern Europe. In contrast, involuntary soft separations and voluntary separations were more common in Africa, Asia, and Latin America. However, even though most operations included components consisting of voluntary separation schemes (accounting for 77 percent of the operations studied), the employment reductions that resulted from these components accounted for only 23 percent of total worker separations.

In the majority of cases, some sort of compensation or safety net enhancement was provided to retrenched workers. Only 15 percent of all operations supplied no direct compensation. By contrast, compensations through severance payments were used in 68 percent of the cases, while pension enhancements were applied in 29 percent of the operations. Safety net enhancements that were intended to assist unemployed workers and workers attempting to relocate were utilized in 63 percent of the operations; a majority of these enhancements involved some form of training assistance (54 percent).

TABLE 4.1. Distribution of Employment Reduction Methods in Retrenchment Programs, 1990s
percent of total

Method	Programs	Worker separations
Involuntary hard (layoffs)	41.5	47.0
Involuntary soft (enforcement of rules, removal of ghost workers)	65.0	30.0
Voluntary	77.5	23.0
All three methods combined	17.5	13.4

Source: Haltiwanger and Singh 1999.
Note: Values are based on 41 retrenchment programs in 37 countries. Values in the middle column represent the percentage of operations where a particular method (or combination of methods) was applied. Since many operations applied a combination of methods, the values in the columns do not sum to 100 percent.

The extent of labor redundancies may be such that any serious downsizing is politically unfeasible, at least if it were to rely on involuntary dismissals. This explains the increasing popularity among developing-country governments, multilateral organizations, and donor countries of a voluntary approach to downsizing a public sector workforce. Specifically, this approach involves offering severance payments to encourage redundant workers to quit, thus overcoming their resistance to downsizing, restructuring, and privatization. In many developing countries, such buying out of redundant workers is, in fact, the only way to bypass the legal obstacles to the dismissal of public sector employees.

Voluntary separations, contracting-out schemes, and employee ownership alternatives help reduce political opposition to a downsizing operation. However, the risks of incurring errors in targeting and setting the wrong payment compensation need to be addressed. The evidence reported by Haltiwanger and Singh (1999) shows that the number of total separations is greater than the total reduction in employment, indicating that there is rehiring and new hires. Rehiring is a particularly acute problem in that it implies targeting errors in a retrenchment program. The need for rehiring makes evident that some workers essential to the running of the downsized agency or state-owned enterprise were incorrectly separated. Significant rehiring was found in about 20 percent of all operations studied by Haltiwanger and Singh. This is one among several risks in retrenchment programs, and it has implications for the economic returns to the operations. In addition, public sector retrenchment may entail fiscal, productive, and other forms of externalities that go beyond the pervasive effects of overstaffing. These externalities may also contribute to unexpected divergence in the financial and economic returns to a downsizing operation. In particular, externalities create additional economic costs that may not be taken into account in financial appraisals of downsizing, such as the diminished earnings and other economic loses experienced by private sector workers in activities linked to state-owned enterprises that are the focus of downsizing operations.

RATIONALE FOR UNDERTAKING PUBLIC SECTOR DOWNSIZING

The rationale for downsizing the public sector is to reduce the size (workforce) of public agencies and state-owned enterprises in an attempt to improve efficiency, while reallocating workers where they might be more productive. It may be part of an effort to move toward a more market-oriented economy. The operations are usually part of an overall effort to increase economic growth and cut financial deficits in the public sector. In most developing countries, the public sector is characterized by public agencies and state-owned enterprises that are overstaffed, bureaucracies that are bloated, and public services that are inefficient (Box 4.1):

- *Overstaffing.* High levels of public sector employment have been an important feature of African, Latin American, and transition economies for decades. In part, these high levels of employment reflect the belief that the public sector should be at the center of economic activity. Political patronage and cronyism may also be motives. Among other issues, overstaffing generates serious financial problems in terms of both payrolls and the funding of retirement pensions.
- *Burgeoning payrolls.* In many developing countries, public sector employees and employees of state-owned enterprises benefit from excessively high wages and fringe benefits relative to the opportunities they might face in the private sector. Coupled with overstaffing, this often leads to unsustainable fiscal deficits that limit the ability of governments to provide infrastructure and services such as education and health care.

BOX 4.1 **Labor Market Characteristics of State-Owned Enterprises**

In India and Turkey, state enterprises were estimated to be overstaffed by nearly 35 percent in the early 1990s. Of the approximately 120,000 people employed in Sri Lanka's state enterprises, 40–50 percent are estimated to be redundant. In Ghana and Uganda, overstaffing levels commonly run to 20–25 percent, according to estimates. Overstaffing usually occurs in administrative and clerical positions, not in the more technically skilled jobs for which there is high demand. Overstaffing is most pervasive in enterprises that have operated as monopolies and benefited from heavy government subsidies and other forms of protection. These typically include large industrial loss-making enterprises and enterprises responsible for infrastructure. Overstaffing in some Egyptian steel companies reached 80 percent in 1991, while Turkey's loss-making steel enterprises were overstaffed by as much as 30 percent. State-owned railway companies, burdened with excess capacity and declining demand as a result of competition from other transport sectors, are commonly overstaffed by 40–60 percent. In Brazil, about 20,000 of the railway enterprise's 42,000 employees were surplus and exhibited lower productivity levels than the corresponding employees in industrialized countries, as well as in neighboring countries such as Argentina and Chile. State telecommunications companies fare no better. By the end of 1988, employment in Mexico's Telmex had reached 50,000, and, by the end of 1990, labor productivity was about half the international standard (10.5 workers per 1,000 lines).

Source: Kikeri 1998.

■ *Inefficiency.* Attempts to reduce payrolls through wage compression and declining real wages frequently lead to absenteeism and the departure of more skilled staff, and this contributes to public sector inefficiency.

■ *Technological progress.* The pace of technological progress around the world is causing natural monopolies to disappear, thus obliging formerly somnolent state-owned enterprises to face competition.

The specific motives triggering downsizing decisions vary across countries and agencies, as Haltiwanger and Singh point out:

> The most prominent factors leading to retrenchment were fiscal crises and a general effort to reduce the size of government in the economy. However, in some cases, the compelling factors appeared to be structural problems with the type and mix of government workers. Wage compression among public sector workers leading to morale and staffing problems was a common complaint. Overstaffing, including the problem of ghost workers, was another common complaint. Finally, the downsizing of the military played a prominent role as well. (Haltiwanger and Singh 1999, 34)

The decision to downsize

Rama (1999) provides a decision tree intended to assist policymakers in analyzing the possibility of downsizing. This decision tree is organized around critical questions on downsizing. It is reproduced in Figure 4.1.

The first question in the decision tree refers to the appropriate private sector counterfactual: *is privatization advisable?* In some cases, the choice is not between downsizing or not downsizing, but rather between downsizing by the government or downsizing by the private sector. This choice involves efficiency considerations and public interest issues that need to be carefully evaluated in each case. But whether downsizing should precede privatization when the latter is advisable is an issue that needs to be addressed.

The second question in the decision tree refers to the overstaffing problem: *is overstaffing an obstacle to privatization?* One reason downsizing may be justified prior to privatization is the credibility of the reform process.[2] The ability to overcome labor resistance and trim employment may, indeed, be seen as a signal that the government is committed to privatization. This signal, in turn, would reduce the uncertainty faced by potential investors, thereby making privatization possible. If no action is taken to overcome the opposition of those who stand to lose from privatization, chances are there will be no bids for

FIGURE 4.1 **A Downsizing Decision Tree**

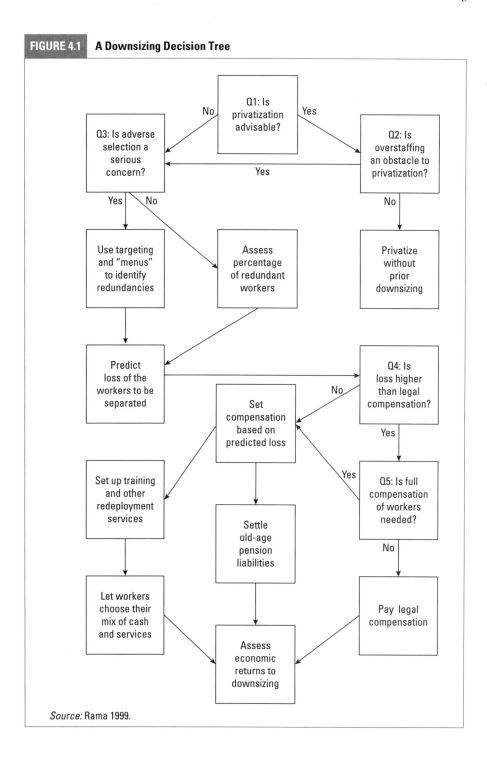

Source: Rama 1999.

the privatization of the enterprise. The irreversibility of investment decisions thus provides a rationale to buy out the workers as part of the preparation for privatization.

If downsizing has not been carried out by the government prior to privatization, the new private owners will have to deal with labor redundancies. The amount and composition of labor shedding would probably differ in both cases, and the average compensation per worker would be different, too. Moreover, the price the potential buyers would be willing to pay for a state-owned enterprise would vary depending on the extent to which the enterprise is overstaffed. Because of the ensuing differences in the extent of labor shedding, in the amount of the compensation offered, and in the price of the privatization of the enterprise, assessing the net gains from downsizing prior to privatization may be difficult. But a net loss is likely.

To begin with, if downsizing has been managed by the government before privatization rather than left to the new private owners, the total number of displaced workers is probably larger. There are examples in various countries in which the new owners have kept the labor force more or less intact, tending to confirm the claim that net reductions in employment have been generally small in privatized firms. Based on a systematic comparison of employment patterns across Polish firms during the transition to a market economy, Frydman et al. (1997) show that employment cuts were larger in state-owned enterprises than in otherwise similar privatized firms. It thus seems that the government may get rid of workers the new owners would prefer to keep. Furthermore, when the government is in charge of downsizing, the "wrong" workers may be separated from their jobs at an excessively high cost. A "wrong" composition of separations is possible because governments are usually not particularly good at managing human resources. If governments could make the right decisions regarding whom to retain and whom to lay off and were able to deliver on these decisions, the rationale for privatization would be seriously weakened. An excessively high cost of separation is likely because governments can shift part of the downsizing costs to the taxpayer, for instance, in the form of early retirement programs, while, in principle, the new owners cannot do this. The temptation to resort to golden handshakes is therefore likely to be stronger if downsizing takes place prior to privatization. Case studies suggest that this has happened in practice.[3]

Unnecessary downsizing costs cannot be recovered through a higher price for the state-owned enterprise during privatization. In theory, the privatization price would, of course, increase every time a redundant worker is separated from his or her job. But getting rid of workers who are not redundant would not increase the price. And, even for the genuinely redundant workers, the increase would be equal to the amount of resources the new owners would have spent to secure their separation, not to the amount of resources actually spent (directly and indirectly) by the government. Having studied 236 privatization experiences in Mexico during the 1980s and early 1990s, López (1997) concludes that employment reductions through downsizing prior to privatization have a marginal impact on privatization prices. Given the substantial cost of prior-restructuring policies, the key lesson from López is "do not do too much; simply sell."

The third important question concerns the adverse selection problem: *is adverse selection a serious concern?* Adverse selection arises when workers decide whether to accept or reject a severance payment offer based upon information only observable by them, such as the true productivity of the workers. Buying out the workers is a simple and convenient way to defuse the opposition to public sector reform. But severance payments create an incentive for the most productive workers to leave the public sector and for the least productive ones to stay. This is generally the case because workers who are more productive usually have better outside opportunities than do their less productive peers, and, so, when the compensation package is profitable, the workers who are more productive are the first to leave. This may not be socially desirable in the case of public sector units producing valuable services. In this case, it is better to target separations based on the observable characteristics of the workers and to use a more appropriate method to deal with the unobservable differences among workers.

The fourth and fifth questions concern the assistance to be provided to the separated workers: *Is the loss among separated workers greater than the legal compensation? And is full compensation among workers needed?* No matter the combination of cash, retraining, and redeployment services offered, there is no justification for spending more than would be needed to buy out the redundant workers. The expected losses from separation thus offer a benchmark against which to judge both the existing laws on compensation and the ad hoc packages that may be proposed in the context of downsizing. Labor market data can be used to predict these losses according to observable characteristics of the workers, such as education, seniority, or gender.

Retraining and other redeployment programs deserve special attention in assessing the cost of the assistance to be provided to separated workers. More resources may be spent on this component than on direct compensation. However, the evidence on the effectiveness of retraining and other redeployment programs is mixed at best. If these programs are to be part of the downsizing operation, a safeguard should be introduced so as to minimize resource waste. Basically, separated workers should be allowed to choose between enrolling in any of the programs offered and cashing in on the equivalent of the cost of these programs per individual. This demand-driven approach would make it more difficult for vocational training and (often ailing) government agencies to divert excessive resources from the downsizing operation.

The adverse selection problem

In a retrenchment program, the goal is to dismiss redundant workers, in particular to trim low effort and unproductive workers. However, in several cases, especially in government administration and state agencies, the effort levels or productivity of workers are not always observable or are difficult to measure. It is expected that workers will decide whether to accept or reject a severance payment offer using this private information strategically. This is the adverse selection problem.

Standard voluntary separation programs usually lead to the departure of workers who show high productivity because these workers have the best prospects outside the public sector. It follows from this that standard voluntary separation programs are not appropriate in all circumstances. For instance, these programs would lead to the wrong composition of layoffs if they were applied to public sector units that produce valuable services (such as health care) and operate in a tight labor market (where unemployment is low, and there are many vacancies). The fact that these programs have been used systematically in the past could be one of the reasons so many separated workers have been rehired in the aftermath of downsizing operations.

Several alternatives to standard voluntary separation programs have been proposed in cases where adverse selection is a serious concern. These include randomization, the menu approach to induce workers to reveal their productivity, and targeting mechanisms. These are now discussed in turn.

In the randomization of job separations (Diwan 1994), the probability that a public sector worker would be dismissed from his or her job would be equal to the estimated percentage of redundant workers. The advantage of this alternative is that the composition of separated workers resembles the composition of the workers who remain in the public sector (thus, "randomization"). For units producing socially valuable services in a tight labor market, the alternative therefore represents an unambiguous improvement compared with standard voluntary separation programs. However, Levy and McLean (1997) argue that, in general, randomization is not an efficient mechanism for downsizing the public sector. This is so because, in terms of profit maximization, closing down these units or leaving them untouched could be preferable to a randomized downsizing. Levy and McLean show that the same argument applies to standard voluntary separation programs as well.

In the presence of unobservable information, an efficient mechanism for downsizing must lead workers to reveal their productivity. Jeon and Laffont (1999) show how to implement such a mechanism by means of a menu of combinations of wages and severance payments. Each combination, called a pair, is associated with a different probability of separation. If the probability of separation is equal to 1, the pair can be interpreted as a standard severance payment offer. If it is equal to 0, it can be viewed as a typical open-ended public sector contract. All the workers choosing the first pair are retrenched, whereas all those choosing the second pair are retained. For pairs in between these two extremes, some of the workers are retrenched, whereas others keep their jobs. If the menu is appropriately designed, workers should choose the pairs associated with their socially optimal probability of separation. For instance, if the overstaffed public sector unit produces a valuable service and operates in a tight labor market, workers with low productivity should choose a pair associated with a strictly positive probability of separation.

However, setting up the right menu might be difficult in practice, so that other, simpler devices for identifying workers with low productivity in the public sector should be used as well. In their cross-country survey of downsizing operations, Haltiwanger and Singh (1999) find that the targeting of separations significantly reduces the probability of subsequent rehiring. The targeting mechanism can include such simple devices as chasing out ghost workers. The experience of the Central Bank of Ecuador, analyzed by Rama and MacIsaac (1999), is also interesting in this respect. After a first, disastrous attempt to downsize using voluntary separation programs, the bank decided to classify all its personnel in three categories: those who were essential for the bank's functioning, those who were clearly redundant, and those who were difficult to place in either of the first two categories. The classification was based on the nature of each worker's unit and on each worker's occupation and educational attainment. Essential workers did not have the option to leave; workers who were clearly redundant did not have the option to stay; and the rest of the workers were offered a voluntary separation program.

Financial and economic returns to downsizing

As in any investment project, it is useful to distinguish between the financial returns and the economic returns to a downsizing operation. The financial returns result from a reduction in public sector expenditures, particularly the public sector wage bill. When the present value of this reduction is higher than the upfront cost in terms of severance payments, safety nets, and the like, downsizing has positive financial returns. Economic returns, in contrast, result from a better allocation of labor across sectors. If the contribution of displaced workers to aggregate welfare is higher when the workers are outside rather than inside the public sector, downsizing is likely to yield positive economic returns. The failure to identify labor redundancies correctly in specific government agencies and state-owned enterprises explains the disappointing results of some downsizing operations.[4]

In the general case, however, assessing the returns to downsizing operations is a difficult task. The typical evaluation compares the savings in terms of public sector wages with the costs in terms of severance payment packages, retraining, and redeployment programs. But this comparison is misleading. Overstaffing is only one among several distortions characterizing the public sector. Another example of a distortion is the fact that public sector wages usually differ from private sector wages, and wages in the public sector are therefore not a good indicator of the opportunity cost of labor. Furthermore, the externalities from mass retrenchment should not be ignored. The most obvious externalities arise in the context of one-company towns, which may easily become ghost towns after downsizing has taken place. But public sector downsizing leads to fiscal externalities, too, because it reduces the equilibrium level of government expenditures and, hence, the burden of distortionary taxes. Because of all these distortions, the economic returns to public sector downsizing can be either higher or lower than might be suggested by the financial returns, and financial returns may thus be a poor indicator of economic returns.

The contrast between remarkably high financial returns and relatively low economic returns should be a warning for policymakers. The inability to distinguish between these two types of returns may give rise to an excessively upbeat assessment of the potential gains from downsizing. The problem is that economic returns are much harder to measure in downsizing projects than in standard investment projects. In the latter sort of projects, the difference between financial and economic returns arises from the different valuation of output prices and input costs in the presence of market distortions.[5] For instance, investing in an activity protected by import tariffs may yield high financial returns, but low or even negative economic returns. The gap between the two assessments stems from the use of different prices to value the output flow created by the investment project. The tariff-inclusive price is appropriate for the financial appraisal, while the international price needs to be used for the economic appraisal. But, apart from this difference in valuation, the items involved in the two appraisals are basically the same in standard investment projects. This is not true in the case of downsizing projects.

Haltiwanger and Singh (1999) evaluate the financial returns to selected operations based on the number of years it takes to recover the direct financial costs in the form of lower expenditures. This indicator is called the break-even period. In 15 downsizing operations for which the required information was available, the performance of downsizing operations was remarkably good. The average break-even period was two years and four months, and it exceeded four years in less than 10 percent of the cases. Few investment projects display such high financial returns. However, these results should come as no surprise. If, say, a couple of years of salary are offered to whoever is willing to leave the public sector, as is often the case in practice, the upfront spending is recovered in the form of a lower wage bill in a mere two years. However, this calculation does not indicate whether the workers who took the offer and left the public sector were redundant.

Haltiwanger and Singh provide an indirect measure of the economic returns to downsizing by examining the percentage of the displaced workers who were subsequently rehired by the restructuring agencies or state-owned enterprises. (Box 4.2 supplies the example of Peru.) Note that rehires are different from new hires. The latter are not necessarily an indication of failure because the new recruits may have skills that were missing among the displaced workers. Rehires, in contrast, indicate a poorly handled downsizing process. In the best case, they imply that workers who were essential to the operation of the restructured agencies or state-owned enterprises were mistakenly considered redundant. In the worst case, they suggest that workers who had no intention of leaving the public sector were able to cash in through golden handshakes. It is difficult to believe that downsizing projects characterized by incompetence (in the best case) or corruption (in the worst case) may have performed well at reallocating workers based on their productivity inside and outside the public sector. Other things being equal, a high percentage of displaced workers rehired can therefore be seen as an indication of low economic returns to downsizing.

Workers were subsequently rehired in 40 percent of the downsizing operations surveyed by Haltiwanger and Singh, and rehiring was

| BOX 4.2 | **Retrenchment and Rehiring in Peru** |

With the support of external donors, Peru initiated two labor adjustment programs in 1991, one for the civil service and one in the office of tax administration. The programs were completed in 1993 and 1992, respectively. The first used a wide variety of voluntary and involuntary reduction methods to dismiss 250,000 workers over three years. The induced departures involved both lump-sum severances and pension enhancements. Targeting by skill was not common. Targeting by age was implicit in the reliance on pension enhancements to induce voluntary separations. Poor targeting aggravated the shortage of human resources. This led to the significant rehiring of separated workers. In all, 163,000 of the originally retrenched workers were rehired. Severance packages equivalent to about $1,000 were provided to less than half (112,000) of the workers who were separated. This limited the direct financial losses associated with the significant rehiring. The break-even period was 2.6 years.

In contrast, the program in the office of tax administration appears to have been a model of good targeting. It also used a mix of voluntary and involuntary reduction methods. The incentive for voluntary separations was an enhanced pension. Workers targeted for involuntary separation were selected on the basis of a written test. Thus, targeting was worker specific and objectively determined. Two-thirds of the workforce (2,034 workers) were separated. Subsequently, the office of tax administration hired 1,309 workers who were new (not rehired), again based on a written test. Because the office established objective levels of productivity and competence, little basis remained for rehiring separated workers (skilled, but severance induced). Rehiring was barred for 10 years, and none was evident. Workers who remained in the office experienced a huge increase in their salaries. Tax collections more than doubled, and so did the office's revenues (2 percent of tax collections); however, these revenues were not sufficient to cover the salary increases, and the scheme incurred a net financial loss of $47 million in present-value terms. This highlights the importance of evaluating program performance along multiple dimensions; not only organization-level financial costs and benefits must be evaluated, but also the broader impact of the program.

Source: Haltiwanger and Singh 1999.

substantial in 20 percent of the operations. However, the fact that 60 percent of the operations display no rehiring does not imply that essential workers did not leave. Moreover, rehiring provides no information on a second type of error, which consists in retaining public sector workers who show low productivity. This second type of error is likely to occur even in programs that display no rehiring.

STAKEHOLDERS

Besides the financial costs of separation packages designed to compensate displaced workers, mass layoffs may create social and political costs. Downsizing operations directly affect stakeholders other than separated workers, such as entire communities in the case of one-company towns, caterers and providers of services to state-owned enterprises, and final consumers and taxpayers. The fiscal flows and political burdens of downsizing may affect central and local tiers of government differently. In some cases, this type of reform may also generate "signals" in the sense that multilateral organizations and donor countries supporting a structural reform process in progress might view the downsizing as a commitment to the overall process. A Poverty and Social Impact Analysis (PSIA) of downsizing operations must identify and take into account the interests and potential responses of these different and likely heterogeneous stakeholders.

Workers

Workers in state agencies or state-owned enterprises constitute the most visible stakeholders in this kind of reform. The welfare of separated workers is directly affected by a downsizing operation. Retrenched workers stand to lose in terms of earnings and benefits, but also in terms of forgone intangible benefits such as the lower levels of effort that may characterize jobs in the public sector, acquired job security, or maternity leave benefits for women. At the same time, even if public sector workers do not represent the poorest sector in a society, the families and other people who depend on the earnings of these workers may also experience welfare loses as a result of downsizing operations.

In preparation for a downsizing operation, the political power of public sector workers and the unions with which they are affiliated must be assessed. Public workers are usually the most vocal group in a society; they are usually affiliated with strong unions, and, as a group, have more education than the rest of society. In most countries, they represent a well-organized political force and form a contingent of hundreds of thousands of voters. Involuntary separation schemes that imply mass layoffs or voluntary departure schemes that cause workers to perceive that they are being coerced to volunteer would face strong political opposition since public sector workers can readily catch the attention of the media and mobilize large pools of citizens; this opposition can bring the operation to a halt and may even bring it to an end.

One-company towns and communities

Other directly affected groups may consist of entire towns or communities in which public companies have settled. Many developing countries and, especially, transition economies have numerous one-company towns, the distinctive feature of which is the presence of single, large employers within local labor markets. The term one-company towns applies to mining towns and to the communities growing up next to large manufacturing plants, such as steel mills or armament factories. In all cases, the company accounts for a substantial share of the jobs in the town, but a particular characteristic is that even those people who do not work for the company depend on it somehow to make a living. If the company were to cease operations, the one-company town could easily become a ghost town. Decisions affecting state-owned enterprises in one-company towns should therefore not be based solely on considerations of profitability, but, rather, they should incorporate the costs to the surrounding population in terms of employment and earnings. In some cases, it may be desirable from a social standpoint to keep a state-owned enterprise open instead of transforming the one-company town into a ghost town.[6]

Caterers and providers of services to state-owned enterprises

Another group of stakeholders directly affected by a downsizing operation is comprised of smaller businesses that cater for or provide services to public agencies or state-owned enterprises and their employees. As a result of retrenchment efforts, caterers and providers of services to state-owned enterprises may incur welfare losses or even abandon their means of livelihood. Thus, the reduction of public employment in overstaffed agencies may generate negative earnings and employment externalities for these people.

The state

Central government agencies such as a ministry of finance, a tax collection administration, or a social security administration will likely favor downsizing operations as long as these operations are perceived as helping to control fiscal imbalances by reducing the state wage bill, pension obligations, and other liabilities. Ministries of finance in developing countries are usually in charge of reform processes aimed at reducing the size of the public sector and making the public sector more efficient, and these will try to show off the advantages of the reforms for the sake of general opinion and potential private buyers of state-owned enterprises. In contrast, sector ministries will probably have more ambiguous responses. They stand to gain if a reform is seen to remove from the state the direct responsibility for the provision and the quality of the services provided by privatized state agencies and state-owned enterprises. By contrast, they may stand to lose if the reform is perceived to reduce their political power relative to other ministries or authorities.

Local government agencies will probably respond negatively to downsizing operations, particularly if the magnitude of the layoffs is considerable or if entire communities are affected, which is likely the case for one-company towns. Both scenarios represent extremely heavy political burdens at the local level. Local governments are generally on the frontline in facing increased unemployment rates and political protests and opposition to reform processes as a result of downsizing. Additionally, local bureaucracies will probably lose political power because they no longer have credible control over employment allocations in public companies or state agencies. Finally, local governments may also be concerned about the allocation of assets, asset ownership, and liabilities, especially if downsizing is an intermediate step toward privatization. Thus, as a result of downsizing operations, fiscal flows may not favor local governments at all; it is likely that the proceeds from privatizations will flow directly to the central government.

Multilateral organizations and donors

Multilateral organizations, such as the World Bank or the International Monetary Fund, and other donors are interested in the overall public sector reform processes undertaken by developing countries. Many of the loans made by these organizations and donors are conditioned by the progress of reforms. In the case of downsizing, these institutions may lend money to finance severance payments and compensation packages and may also be involved in advising governments on the processes.

Taxpayers

Consumers are the largest single class of stakeholders. However, consumers are usually less organized than are public sector workers. In part, this is because there are several distinct groups within this class, each with different, potentially conflicting interests (such as current versus potential consumers) and different relative levels of political power (such as urban versus rural consumers). As taxpayers, consumers may respond positively to downsizing operations if they perceive their taxes being used in more cost-effective ways and if inefficiencies are eliminated or at least reduced by the reforms. Supporting overstaffed state agencies and state-owned enterprises entails a double burden for society. A key direct cost is represented by the amount of resources that are transferred to public companies and that thus cannot be used for consumption or investment purposes. A more subtle burden results from the use of distortionary taxes to collect these resources because distortionary taxes may affect household decisions regarding labor force participation, the effort to be exerted on job productivity, savings, and so on. In other words, transferring one dollar to a public sector company may cost the rest of society more than one dollar because the distortionary taxes may reduce private sector productivity or the efficient allocation of resources.

IMPACT CHANNELS

This section explores the channels of the direct and indirect impacts of downsizing. These channels include employment and wages, fiscal flows, productive externalities, and the access to and quality and price of services.

Employment and wages

Changes in employment and wages both among affected workers and in society as a whole can be expected to occur because of downsizing. For some of the separated public workers and workers in state-owned enterprises, the immediate employment and wage effects may be negative. For most of these workers, the transition and relocation costs can be particularly burdensome. Some public sector employees will have spent a large portion if not all of their working lives in public agencies or state-owned enterprises. It is likely that their skills do not match those required by private companies. Moreover, some of these workers will be too old to find jobs in private companies at the wage levels commiserate with their experience. Some of them may never find other jobs, and, even if they do, they will probably spend time in unemployment. Meanwhile, some of the more productive workers who may choose to leave their public jobs will be able to perform well in the private sector. High-productivity workers with superior prospects in the private sector usually stay in the public sector only because they value intangible benefits that cannot be acquired in private companies. If they are offered compensation packages that offset the loss in such intangibles, these workers will likely leave. Likewise, when privatization occurs, employment conditions and wages may also change among the workers who remain at the state-owned enterprises, and they may obtain more flexible contracts and more favorable wage dispersion.

For society as a whole, however, downsizing operations may increase aggregate output in the medium run through the reallocation of workers to activities in which they can, presumably, be more productive and through a reduction in the equilibrium level of taxes. This scenario may occur if productivity in the public sector was very low before the reforms and if the potential earnings in the private sector are high.

Externalities

Public sector downsizing may affect the rest of an economy not only through its impact on the budget and the allocation of labor, but also through its direct impact on private sector output. An obvious illustration of this productive externality is provided by the one-company town. In such a case, many of the other jobs in the town depend on the employment and wage levels in the state-owned enterprise. The company's employees are probably the most important customers at the town's private shops. In the extreme case of a mining town, all the activities of the surrounding population may revolve around the mining company. A drastic employment reduction at the company is therefore likely to depress private sector activity in the town or even transform the town into a ghost town.

Productive externalities involved in downsizing may also occur at a nationwide level. Mass retrenchment programs that affect a substantial fraction of the urban labor force may increase unemployment rates over long periods of time. In some Sub-Saharan African countries where the public sector represents a large share of the modern economy, downsizing may depress economic activity in the short run. Productive externalities of this sort cannot be ruled out in more developed economies either, as suggested by the substantial increase in unemployment rates that followed the massive public sector downsizing program in Argentina.

Externalities like those arising in a one-company town may provide a justification for retaining some redundant workers. Limiting the extent of downsizing certainly entails a cost to the rest of society, which must pay for the redundancies in the form of higher taxes or lower social expenditures. Retrenching redundant workers also entails a cost to the population that surrounds the company and depends on it to sustain economic activity. The optimal extent of downsizing involves a trade-off between these two costs.

Fiscal flows

Downsizing operations generate financial gains and costs for the public sector. The first and most obvious financial gain is the cut in the wage bill.

For the government administration, this cut directly reduces budget expenditures. The budgetary impact may be smaller in state-owned enterprises if their wage bills are only partially subsidized by the central budget. A second financial gain results from the reduction in long-term liabilities because separated workers lose all or some of their entitlements to old-age pensions. A third potential gain is the increase in privatization prices when downsizing occurs in preparation for privatization and contributes to the success of privatization. The upfront cost is the amount of the resources spent in compensation, retraining, and other redeployment programs for separated workers.

In the assessment of financial returns, one should focus on the consolidated budget and not merely on the budget of the overstaffed unit (Box 4.3). Examples abound in which the fiscal burden of reform is simply shifted to another government body. For instance, the cost of the social services provided by state-owned enterprises in many transition economies is often paid by taxpayers in the form of explicit or implicit subsidies. Because downsizing reduces the number of the beneficiaries of these services, it also seems to reduce the burden on taxpayers. However, there is no such reduction if downsizing leads to a mere transfer of the services to central or local governments; the state-owned enterprise might be downsized, but overall public sector employment might not

---

BOX 4.3   **Unconsolidated Budgets and Downsizing in Brazil**

The fiscal illusion of downsizing may be particularly severe when downsizing affects entitlements to old-age pensions and other social security benefits. Downsizing in Brazilian states provides an interesting example. A federal government voluntary separation program was launched in 1996; it was the first such program to be implemented within the public administration at the federal level. The program was part of a broader modernization project aimed at increasing efficiency and reducing expenditures in the public sector. The redundancy program was designed and implemented by the Ministry of Federal Administration and Reform of the State, which had identified an excess of public civil servants in almost all areas of the federal administration. Of 327,000 workers in the eligible group, 30,000 were expected to join the redundancy program. In a preliminary assessment of this operation, Carneiro and Gill (1997) show that the savings deriving from the downsizing were substantially smaller for the consolidated government than for the individual states. This is because of the pension benefits granted to the 9,500 displaced workers, which increased the long-term liabilities of the federal government. As a result of the implicit transfer of obligations, budget savings were 15 to 25 percent lower than they appear at first glance.

Source: Carneiro and Gill 1997.

be, and the need for funds therefore does not disappear. Another example is provided by redeployment programs allowing redundant workers to take other public sector jobs. In this case, the payroll is cut in the restructured public sector unit, but wage bills are inflated elsewhere in the public sector.

DETERMINANTS AND DISTRIBUTIONAL IMPACTS OF WELFARE LOSSES

Downsizing may affect the welfare of other stakeholders in the reform process besides displaced public sector employees. Caterers and providers of services to state agencies and state-owned enterprises, as well as the communities surrounding the enterprises in one-company towns, will likely be affected by public sector retrenchment programs. Impacts among agents providing services to the enterprises are expected to be similar in direction (employment and wages losses) to those experienced by separated workers.

The following concentrates only on welfare impacts among separated workers. The welfare loss a separated public sector worker experiences may be disaggregated into three components. The first is the present value of the resulting change in earnings, including bonuses and other cash benefits. In general, the wage structure in the public sector is different from that in the private sector; wage differentials between public and private unskilled (blue-collar) workers is usually higher than that between public and private skilled (white-collar) workers. Moreover, it may take a long time for some of the separated workers to find new jobs, and earnings may be close to zero during that period. The second component is the present value of the loss in nonwage benefits. Public sector jobs usually provide health coverage and old-age pensions, among other benefits. In most developing countries, the jobs available to separated public sector workers do not carry such benefits. The third component is comprised by other, more intangible losses from separation. For instance, effort and productivity levels on the job tend to be lower in the public sector than in the private sector, whereas job security is almost invariably greater. In particular, intangible benefits such as flexible working hours and maternity leaves are highly valuable for women. The possibility of taking bribes or using government facilities also falls into this category. Formally, the total welfare loss is:

$$WL = EL + BL + OL \qquad (4.1)$$

where *WL* measures the welfare loss, *EL* is the present value of the earnings loss, *BL* is the present value of the loss in nonwage benefits such as old-age pensions, and *OL* is the loss in other, more intangible benefits.

In preparation for a downsizing operation, it is important to assess the welfare loss separated workers might experience. This assessment may help predict the cost of the downsizing operation in terms of severance payments, and it may also provide a cost benchmark. The welfare loss experienced by retrenched workers will depend on the observable characteristics the workers possess. These characteristics include salaries and seniority in the public sector, the two variables most commonly used when designing severance compensation (the most common rule of thumb). But they also include gender, age, education, job level, geographic location, and other characteristics.

Table 4.2, taken from Rama (1999), summarizes findings of several studies on the determinants of welfare losses and earnings losses from job displacements in developing countries and transition economies. It reports the signs of the impact of worker characteristics on the welfare and earnings losses among the workers. In the table, a "+" sign denotes a statistically significant positive association between the losses and specific worker characteristics; the opposite holds for the "−" sign, while "0" denotes nonsignificant relationships, and a "?" denotes changes in sign across specifications.

Several regularities emerge from the table. First, it appears that the wage level in the public sector is a poor predictor of welfare losses, at least as long as other observable characteristics of workers are taken into account. Second, with the exception of Egypt, where government hiring and compensation policies strongly distort the payoffs for schooling, the loss from displacement is usually smaller as the level of educational attainment of a worker rises. Third, while higher seniority in a public sector job may lead to larger losses from displacement, there is no clear link between total work experience and displacement losses. Fourth, women workers and workers with bigger families may suffer more from displacement. These distributional impacts are now discussed in more detail.

Education and specific skills

Traditional rules of thumb for compensation do not consider education in setting the amount of severance payments. However, education is an important predictor of earnings. In fact, it is an empirical regularity that, in most developing countries, the more educated the individual, the more he or she will be able to earn. If this is the case, the welfare losses of the

TABLE 4.2. Determinants of Losses from Job Separations

Worker characteristic	Welfare loss				Earnings loss			
	Argentina, white-collar employees	Ecuador, Central Bank employees	Egypt, public sector workers	Turkey, cement and oil workers	Ecuador, Central Bank employees	Ghana, civil servants	Slovenia, formal labor force	Turkey, cement and oil workers
Public sector wage	+[a]/	0	n.a.	0	0	0	n.a.	+
Seniority	n.a.	+	?	0	+	0	+[b]/	0
Education	0	–	+	–	–	0	0	–
Experience	?	+	–	+	0	0	+[b]/	–
Woman	n.a	0	+	0	+	+	–	0
Married	–	0	n.a.	0	+	0	n.a.	0
Number of dependents	?	+	n.a.	+	0	0	n.a.	0
Source	Robbins (1996)	Rama and MacIsaac (1999)	Assaad (1999)	Tansel (1997)	Rama and MacIsaac (1999)	Alderman, Canagarajah, and Younger (1996)	Orazem, Vodopivec, and Wu (1995)	Tansel (1997)

Source: Rama 1999.

Note: Statistically significant signs are indicated by + or –, while 0 indicates a nonsignificant coefficient, and ? indicates a change in sign across specifications or groups of workers. When the variable has not been included in the analysis, n.a. (not applicable) is reported.

a. The coefficient is positive as a result of an implicit restriction imposed in the selected specification.

b. Almost all work experience was under the self-management system that characterized Yugoslavia until the late 1980s.

more educated will typically be lower than the welfare losses of the less educated. Evidence provided by several studies suggests that, indeed, welfare losses are higher among less educated workers; this has been the case in Ecuador, Guinea-Bissau, and Turkey. Assessing the welfare impacts of downsizing in the cement and oil sectors in Turkey, Tansel (1997) reports that the probability of a similar or better current situation with respect to a predismissal status—a self-rated welfare measure—increased significantly with the level of education. Additionally, Tansel finds that earnings losses were smaller among the better educated; in particular, general high school graduates experienced the smallest losses, while the largest losses were experienced by middle school graduates. In the case of Ecuador, Rama and MacIsaac (1999) use an implicit welfare measure of the losses among workers after dismissal from the Central Bank. They find that more well educated employees fared better than did other retrenched bank employees; if their estimates are interpreted literally, the implicit welfare loss decreased by roughly 15 percent for each additional year of schooling. Chong and Rama (1998) also find that welfare losses are higher among less educated public sector workers in Guinea-Bissau. In the case of Egypt, in contrast, Assaad (1999) reports that welfare losses among dismissed workers at state-owned enterprises tend to be significantly higher among individuals with secondary and postsecondary education than among workers with lower levels of education.

Despite the specific relationship between education and welfare losses by country, it is clear that variations in welfare across education groups might be important, but that this is not considered in traditional rules of thumb. As Assaad points out:

> The significant difference in displacement losses among workers at different levels of education has important implications for the design of severance pay programs. If the same package of benefits is offered to all workers to achieve a certain rate of exit, the likely outcome is that all level-one workers, who tend to have lower losses, will exit first, leading to a highly distorted occupational structure. Some control can be achieved over the composition of the exiting workers by setting up separate programs for each level of education. (Assaad 1999, 133)

Besides education, other skills may be important, too. Public sector workers and workers in state-owned enterprises accumulate specific skills that may not be easily transferable to the private sector, where these skills may show low returns or are not rewarded at all. Workers may acquire and develop highly specific skills to perform tasks in the public sector that may not be standard elsewhere. Thus, after dismissal, workers with highly specific skills stand to lose more than do other workers. An example is production-line workers versus managers of state-owned enterprises. The technologies used in the private sector may not be the same as those used in state enterprises; thus, individuals who once worked on a state enterprise production line and acquired specific skills nontransferable to the private sector would likely experience longer unemployment spells after dismissal or may not be able even to find similar jobs in the private sector. In any of these situations, an earnings loss may be expected. On the other hand, managerial skills are general enough, and white-collar employees are likely to find similar jobs in the private sector even if the job level is lower or if the dismissed individuals are obliged to spend time among the unemployed before obtaining private sector jobs. Some evidence on these issues is reported by Tansel (1997) for workers in state-owned enterprises in the cement and oil sectors in Turkey. Tansel finds that, in postdismissal earnings regressions, years of experience at the enterprises are only marginally statistically significant or not statistically significant at all. This may suggest that the skills acquired in the public sector were not easily transferable to the private sector. More evidence on this issue is provided by Rama and MacIsaac (1999) on workers dismissed from the Central Bank in Ecuador, where the earnings losses after dismissal increased with years of tenure at the bank, but did not increase with work experience outside the bank. Rama and MacIsaac argue that longer careers at the Central Bank may be associated with higher investments in specific skills that have low returns in the private sector.

Geographic location

Geographic location and place of residence may also play an important role in terms of the differential distributional impacts of retrenchment programs. In particular, dismissed public sector workers and workers in state-owned enterprises in small towns or in rural areas are expected to lose more after separation than other workers. Local labor market conditions could be tighter—a situation involving low unemployment and many vacancies—in small towns than in capital cities or other medium-to-large cities, where more employment opportunities may be available for both blue- and white-collar workers. In several developing countries, private firms—good examples are manufacturing plants and seaport facilities—are concentrated in medium-to-large cities and especially in capital cities. Given that the typical rule of thumb would equally compensate dismissed workers from large cities and small or rural towns, retrenched workers in the latter group stand to lose more. However, this might not always be the case since, in smaller towns, the cost of living is probably much lower. In any case, both aspects, the prospects of getting a paid job and the costs of living, should be taken into consideration.

Analyzing the case of Guinea-Bissau, Chong and Rama (1998) find that potential earnings in the private sector are higher in Bissau than outside the city. They suggest that a well-tailored severance package should be more generous in remote areas, where job alternatives might be limited, than in the capital city. Similar differential distributional impacts in terms of geographic location are reported by Assaad (1999) in the case of Egypt. Assaad simulates severance packages that could be offered to workers in state-owned enterprises using alternative indexation schemes rather than the traditional rule of thumb. He finds that simulated acceptance rates would be higher in the Alexandria and Suez Canal regions and, to a lesser extent, rural Lower Egypt. In contrast, simulated acceptance rates would be disproportionately low in Upper Egypt, a region with poor private sector prospects.

Gender

Studies of public sector downsizing impacts summarized in Table 4.2 present direct evidence of the relative loss in incomes for women versus men. In both Ecuador and Ghana, women were shown to suffer greater earnings losses even after controlling for worker characteristics in a regression analysis. In Ecuador, a woman's loss in earnings was 30 percentage points higher than the loss of a comparable male colleague. In contrast, in Slovenia, women suffered a smaller loss than men, and, in Turkey, women's losses were the same as men's. As Table 4.2 illustrates, the total welfare loss, including loss of benefits, is greater among women than among men in Egypt (as the "+" sign in the third column in the "Woman" row indicates) and about the same in Ecuador and Turkey (as the "0" sign in the second and fourth columns in the "Woman" row shows). In Egypt, the total welfare loss among women was 85 percent higher than the loss among men.

There are at least three reasons one should care whether women are more negatively affected than men by public sector downsizing programs. First, the income of women workers is important to the welfare of households. Men workers tend to contribute more to total household incomes than do women workers, but the relevant issue is the incomes lost. As shown by Appleton, Hoddinott, and Krishnan (1999), Assaad (1999), and Rama (2001), laid-off women public sector employees will, on average, spend more time unemployed, and the gap between the wages they earned in their public sector jobs versus the wages in their private sector jobs will be greater. Additionally, studies from a wide set of countries indicate that women's and men's relative contributions to household incomes affect spending patterns. These studies show that increasing a woman's share of income in the household (controlling for total household income) significantly increases the share of the household budget allocated to children's education, health care, and nutrition-related expenditures.

Second, disproportionate layoffs of women, coupled with private sector discrimination, may result in an inefficient use of the labor force in the economy as a whole. In Egypt, economic reforms eliminating guaranteed civil service employment for graduates of secondary and higher education institutions have been found to have such an effect. While the educated men who were eligible for guaranteed public sector employment were generally able to find jobs in the private sector, their women counterparts were obliged to move into very low-productivity subsistence agriculture or otherwise leave the labor market.[7]

Third, disproportionate layoffs of women employees may exacerbate existing shortages of women in certain departments. In the case of agricultural extension agents or health care professionals, for example, it may be that women are needed to provide services to women farmers or women patients. Conversely, there may be few men in positions (for example, elementary school teachers) where it may be socially desirable to maintain a balance between men and women.

METHODS TO ASSESS DOWNSIZING IMPACTS ON WORKER WELFARE

As a result of downsizing, some displaced workers may face losses in earnings and welfare (losses in earnings, plus losses in nonwage and intangible benefits) following separation, while others may receive gains. This poses the problem of determining a severance payment to help compensate those who stand to lose, while avoiding overcompensation. This section discusses three approaches for assessing and measuring worker losses or gains, the data requirements for performing this sort of analysis, and a procedure for tailoring a separation compensation package.

Methods

In what follows, a list of three approaches is presented that may help in assessing the impacts of downsizing on worker welfare losses and in measuring these losses. For practical purposes, the first two approaches cannot be used in preparation for downsizing operations, but are nonetheless useful tools for analyzing ex post welfare impacts among dismissed workers and for generating insights on prospective operations.

- ■ *The "before and after" methodology.* The first strategy consists of interviewing former public sector workers one year after separation (for example) and asking them to evaluate any changes in their well-being. The interviews may be carried out according to subjective or objective criteria. In the subjective evaluation of well-being, the separated workers would be asked to assess their current well-being with respect to the predismissal situation. The change in well-being might be measured using a discrete variable indicating whether postdismissal well-being is much better, better, about the same, less, or much less than predismissal well-being. In the objective evaluation of well-being, the workers would be asked to report pre- and postdismissal earnings. The change in well-being could then be computed as the percent difference between pre- and postdismissal earnings. In both cases, these indicators are regressed against predismissal earnings and tenure in the public sector, as well as other observable worker characteristics, such as age, education, gender, marital status, and the like. This methodology has been used by Rama and MacIsaac (1999) to study welfare losses among dismissed civil servants at the Central Bank of Ecuador and by Tansel (1997) to assess welfare losses among dismissed workers in state-owned enterprises in Turkey.

- ■ *The "stayers and leavers" methodology.* A second empirical strategy relies on the welfare losses predicted by public sector workers before the downsizing. The idea is to compare the workers who accepted separation offers with those who rejected them. Those who accepted the offers expected that there would be a net welfare gain from separation, whereas those who rejected the offers expected that there would be a net welfare loss from separation. The probability of acceptance may therefore be estimated as a function of all the individual characteristics of the workers and the severance payments the workers were offered. This is then used to infer the amount of severance payments that would have made each worker indifferent about accepting or rejecting an offer. That amount is an indicator of the welfare loss or gain expected by each worker. The "stayers and leavers" methodology has been used by Robbins, Gonzales, and Menendez (1996) to assess the welfare change after dismissal among workers in seven state-owned enterprises in Argentina.

■ *The "in versus out" methodology.* This strategy compares the present value of earnings among workers inside and outside the public sector. Typically, the comparison shows that some public sector workers earn less over their working lives than similar workers in the private sector. If the public sector workers do not quit voluntarily, it is probably because they derive other benefits from their jobs. The gap in earnings observed for the most disadvantaged group of public sector workers may thus be used to infer the value of nonwage and other intangible benefits involved in public sector jobs, such as job security, health insurance coverage, in-kind payments, and other fringe benefits, or even low job-effort (productivity) requirements. For less disadvantaged workers, it is assumed that the loss of nonwage and intangible benefits is proportional to the public sector salary. Relying on the hypothesis that a stable relationship exists between the welfare losses and the earnings losses related to displacement, studies addressing the latter can be expected to provide information on the former. From the previous discussion, it may be inferred that, if a separated worker earns less in the private sector or the informal sector once nonwage and intangible benefits are accounted for, the resulting net present value of the difference between public sector and private sector ("in and out") earnings and benefits will be positive, and a welfare loss will have occurred. Similarly, if the separated worker earns more in the private or the informal sector, the resulting "in and out" net present value of the difference in earnings and benefits will be negative, and, in this case, a net welfare gain will have occurred. The "in versus out" method was initially proposed by Fiszbein (1994), who uses a forward-looking formula to assess the "just right" severance package to compensate dismissed workers for potential earnings losses. Assaad (1999) refined the forward-looking approach by taking into account both tangible and intangible losses. Many workers in public or state-owned enterprises might be able to earn more in the private sector, but, despite this, they prefer to stay at their public sector jobs; this means that these other, intangible benefits are highly valued. Chong and Rama (1998) build upon the work of Fiszbein and Assaad to propose additional methodological refinements, including the appropriate time spans that should be considered in computing present discounted values and the significance of measurement error problems in the calculation of intangible benefits. The "in versus out" methodology has been used by Assaad (1999) on Egypt, Chong and Rama (1998) on Guinea-Bissau, Fiszbein (1994) on Sri Lanka, and Rama (2001) on Vietnam.

Data sources

Before a downsizing operation is implemented, the "in versus out" methodology may be applied. After the operation, the "before and after" or the "stayers versus leavers" methodologies may be applied. Most of the information required is similar, and several sources of information may be used. The analysis will require data on earnings; it is important to use annual earnings instead of daily or weekly earnings, especially in developing countries, because many jobs in the private sector are casual or seasonal, such as in the case of self-employed or informal workers. Thus, total earnings during a year may be low despite occasionally high daily or weekly totals. In addition, annual earnings figures should include earnings from primary and secondary jobs where applicable because private sector workers frequently hold secondary occupations as additional sources of income. Other welfare measures could be useful as well, such as household consumption levels or the amount of the old-age pensions to which workers are entitled. Information on the individual characteristics of workers will also be required, such as age, education, gender, tenure or years of work experience, region of residence (urban versus rural, city versus town), and marital status, among others.

A first source of information useful for an assessment of the welfare implications of downsizing is administrative data on the public sector, such as public employment censuses or payrolls. Ad hoc household surveys may be particularly relevant as a supplement to these data given that the surveys may be specifically designed to assess the welfare impacts of downsizing on dismissed workers. Other individual or household surveys typically carried out in most countries, such as labor force surveys, household-expenditure surveys, or Living Standards Measurement Studies, might also serve as good sources of information.

Designing a separation package

Tailoring a separation compensation package may help minimize the welfare losses of dismissed workers and reduce the distributional impacts through education, gender, region of residence, or other worker characteristics and may also help reduce the total cost associated with a voluntary separation scheme. In a typical downsizing operation, the amount of compensation displaced workers receive is based on a rule of thumb involving their salaries and perhaps their seniority in the public sector. The implicit assumption is that their welfare losses from displacement can be accurately predicted based only on these two observable characteristics of the workers. However, such rules of thumb might generate two types of problems: (1) problems with the resulting composition of dismissed and retained workers; and (2) under- or overcompensation. A better rule might be obtained if other observable characteristics of workers, such as education and gender, for instance, were considered as well. Fewer workers would then be undercompensated or overcompensated. Moreover, tailoring a severance package to obtain the "just right" amount of compensation may help set the appropriate incentives and reduce the adverse selection problem. In sum, tailored compensation would not only contribute to the fairness of the downsizing process, but it would also reduce the total cost of downsizing in the context of voluntary separations, in which overcompensation is more likely to occur than undercompensation.

A five-step procedure developed through the World Bank Public Sector Retrenchment Project—see Chong and Rama (1998) and Rama (1999)—can be used to create compensation or severance payment packages in preparation for a downsizing operation. This procedure relies on the "in versus out" methodology used to estimate losses from displacement and may be applied before any retrenchment has taken place.

First step: earnings equations

The first step in the proposed five-step procedure is to estimate an annual earnings function for workers who are outside the public sector. The data should come from individual records in labor force surveys or living standards studies. A regression specification of an earnings function is given by:

$$W = \alpha_0 + \alpha_1 X_1 + K + \alpha_k X_k + \varepsilon \qquad (4.2)$$

The variables on the right-hand side include individual characteristics for private sector workers (X_j), which are also observable for workers who are in the public sector. Ideally, the list of variables should be exactly the same as a list gathered from the records the public sector maintains on its own employees. The left-hand variable (W) measures the labor earnings of all individuals who work outside the public sector, including the self-employed and workers in the informal sector. The goal of this first step is to predict the potential earnings of the public sector workers who are bound to be separated, using the coefficients estimated from the previous regression $(\hat{\alpha}_j)$ and the characteristics of public sector workers $(\tilde{X}_j)$:

$$E = \hat{\alpha}_0 + \hat{\alpha}_1 \tilde{X}_1 + K + \hat{\alpha}_k \tilde{X}_k \qquad (4.3)$$

These predicted earnings represent the potential earnings that dismissed workers would earn outside the public sector after separation if their earnings were calculated according to private sector valuation standards for the selected worker characteristics.

Second step: present value of earnings loss (EL)

The second step involves comparing each separated worker's public sector salary with the potential earnings estimated in Step 1. The difference between the two is discounted over the duration of the contract the worker would have in the public sector. In most cases, this duration is the number of years to retirement. Thus, the second step is to calculate the present value of the earnings loss, *EL*, that public sector workers will experience after they are separated. This may be formalized as:

$$EL = \sum_t \frac{S_t - E_t}{(1+r)^t} \qquad (4.4)$$

where *r* is a discount rate, and the sum refers to all the years until retirement age or to the expected length of the worker's contractual relationship. Data on the public sector salary *S* and on the number of years to retirement should be obtained from public sector records. Data on earnings after separation (*E*) are taken from Step 1.

Third step: loss in benefits (BL)

The third step is to assess the loss in benefits. In many developing countries, the most important component of this loss is old-age pensions. An actuarial calculation of the present value of forgone old-age benefits may be used to quantify this loss. As a simpler alternative, the calculation may rely on the present value of past contributions to the social security system, plus accrued interest, where applicable.

Whatever the chosen approach, experience with downsizing suggests that the loss in benefits needs to be dealt with separately. Explicitly canceling outstanding social security obligations is important to avoid misunderstandings (or opportunistic behavior) that can eventually lead to legal and political wrestling.

Fourth step: loss in intangibles (OL)

The fourth step is to evaluate the loss in other, more intangible benefits. Once estimates of the loss in earnings and the loss in benefits have been computed, it is possible to identify whether there are groups of public sector workers for whom the average sum of the earnings and benefits losses is substantial. If these workers stay in the public sector, it is because they derive some other benefits from their jobs. These other benefits may be estimated based on the absolute value of the earnings loss, plus the benefits loss. The monetary value of these other benefits is at least equal to the sum of the earnings and benefits losses. The ratio between this monetary value and the public sector salaries of the workers may be used to infer the intangible benefits enjoyed by other, less disadvantaged public sector workers.

Fifth step: a compensation formula

Step 5 involves the development of a simple formula to calculate compensation based on a few observable characteristics of public sector workers. It is assumed that losses related to old-age pensions will be settled separately. The problem thus becomes the identification of the minimum information necessary to allow one to predict the losses in earnings and intangible benefits in a convenient and noncontroversial way. This is important because making compensations contingent on individual characteristics such as gender or ethnicity would not be legally or socially admissible in some countries and because other characteristics, such as marital status or the number of dependents, may be subject to manipulation.

The compensation formula developed in Step 5 differs from the typical rules of thumb used to design severance payment packages in two important ways. First, the information required may or may not include data on salaries and seniority in the public sector, depending on how useful these two variables are in predicting the losses in earnings and intangible benefits. Second, the coefficients used to multiply these two variables, as well as the other variables in the relevant data set, are not arbitrary, but are the coefficients of a regression explaining the predicted losses in earnings and intangible benefits as a function of the observable characteristics of public sector workers.

The downsizing options simulation exercise

The Downsizing Options Simulation Exercise is an Excel application for assessing the consequences of various downsizing strategies.[8] It uses the five steps discussed above to estimate the value of a compensation package that would make some of the workers in state-owned enterprises accept a voluntary departure scheme. The tool has been used in preparation for downsizing operations in countries such as Guinea-Bissau, Guyana, and Vietnam, among others.

The tool relies on individual records from official databases and household surveys to construct a small-scale public sector, including all workers whose main jobs are in government administration or state-owned enterprises, depending on the focus of the operations. It estimates the value of the total loss from separations (earnings and intangible benefits) and uses this information to classify each public sector worker into one of two groups: those who would accept the offers (potential leavers) and those who would not accept the offers (potential stayers), depending on the combination of early retirement and voluntary separation offers made. This classification helps to identify the "right" voluntary separation package that could serve as a cost benchmark for downsizing options involving involuntary separations. The tool also calculates the financial and economic returns to the operations based on various assumptions.

Given that men and women employees may experience differentiated welfare impacts from job separations, a gender-sensitive version of the tool that has been designed for Vietnam is also publicly available.[9] The modified tool emphasizes the gender dimension. Specifically, it uses separate earnings functions for men and women in estimating the alternative earnings of separated public sector workers. Thus, the tool does not assume the same returns to skills and other observable characteristics for men and women workers. It also estimates the value of intangible benefits separately for men and women and produces summary statistics disaggregated by gender.

THREATS AND RISKS

There are several potential threats and risks that may prevent financial and economic returns to downsizing from materializing.

Overcompensation

Overcompensation is a potential bias of downsizing operations. To some extent, this bias is inevitable if the downsizing is based on voluntary separations. Workers who are offered compensations lower than the welfare losses they may experience will tend to prefer to stay in the public sector. Meanwhile, workers who are offered compensations that are greater than what they stand to lose will tend to accept the offers and leave. Thus, errors involving excessively low compensations have no serious practical implications for the public sector (though the compensations may be ineffective), whereas errors involving excessively high compensations may have serious financial and economic implications. Ill-designed compensation mechanisms exacerbate this second type of error. The most typical rule of thumb used to compensate workers is actually one such ill-designed mechanism.[10] Usually, severance payments are set as a multiple of the last public sector wages. Applying this rule of thumb to compensate displaced public sector workers frequently creates problems. Those at the top of the hierarchy (say, professionals) are offered much better deals than those at the bottom (say, janitors). But those at the top have less to lose in relative terms if they leave. Because of the egalitarian nature of the public sector, their wages are usually below the corresponding private sector wages, while the opposite is true for those at the bottom of the hierarchy. A severance payment offer based on public sector wages would therefore overcompensate those at the top of the hierarchy, but fail to encourage the departure of those at the bottom although redundancies tend to be more prevalent at the bottom. Studies show that a better tailoring of severance payment offers could reduce the total cost of downsizing by 20 percent or more.[11]

In addition, compensation offers may contradict the broader objectives of economic policy reform in developing countries. Many reform efforts supported by multilateral organizations and donor countries are aimed at reorienting public expenditures toward the neediest. Some would claim that there is a conflict between supporting such efforts to tilt the budgetary process in favor of the poor and lending generous amounts of money to finance severance payment packages for public sector workers, who usually are not poor.[12] Although the decision to offer severance payments should be made on a case-by-case basis, there is clearly no justification for overcompensating displaced workers.

Adverse selection and rehiring

Adverse selection can dramatically affect the economic returns to downsizing without modifying the financial returns very much. If the retrenched workers are genuinely redundant, their productivity in the public sector is probably low. However, if the retrenched workers are essential for the operation of a unit producing a socially valuable service, productivity in the public sector may actually be quite large. The contributions of good civil servants to society may be much greater than the cost in wages. If they leave, public sector downsizing may show negative economic returns in spite of any positive (and possibly high) financial returns. Poorly tailored downsizing operations may result in substantial rehiring of previously displaced civil servants and public workers, as reported by Haltiwanger and

Singh (1999). As a consequence the financial gains from the operation disappear; compensation packages become "golden handshakes," and overstaffing is not corrected.

Externalities

When confronted with productive externalities and other externalities such as those arising in the case of one-company towns, the optimal policy decision might involve a trade-off between two costs. First, there is the financial cost of keeping these companies in operation, which entails a cost for the rest of society because any company deficits translate into higher taxes or lower social expenditures. Second, shutting down or significantly downsizing the operations of such companies entails a cost for nearby populations that depend on the companies to sustain local economic activity. Unfortunately, relatively little is known about the magnitude of the costs to surrounding populations. As in other areas of public policy, externalities are more difficult to quantify than deficits. In the absence of information about the impact of the company's size on the town's earnings, decisions regarding labor retrenchment could be misguided.

Other distortions and imperfections

The initial situation of a public sector unit that is to be downsized is typically characterized by distortions and imperfections. Overstaffing is only one among these problems. Public sector agencies and state-owned enterprises are likely to use pay scales that are distorted relative to those in the private sector. They are also financed through taxes (at least partially in the case of enterprises), and this creates distortions and reduces aggregate output. Downsizing operations usually tackle only the overstaffing distortions. If other distortions remain after the downsizing, the downsizing operations may not succeed in improving economic efficiency.

CONCLUSIONS

Public sector downsizing operations are designed to reduce the size (workforce) of public agencies or state-owned enterprises in an attempt to improve the efficiency of the public sector. The operations are usually part of an overall effort to increase economic growth and cut financial deficits in the public sector. Overstaffing, burgeoning payrolls, and inefficiencies are still evident in the public sector and in state-owned enterprises in many developing countries. Downsizing operations therefore represent tangible policy alternatives. However, downsizing should be carefully assessed before implementation to avoid unexpected problems.

A PSIA assessment of downsizing operations must identify the stakeholders involved in the reform. Usually, these stakeholders have heterogeneous interests in and reactions to a reform process and, depending on their political power, may interfere with the process and compromise the outcome. The welfare of dismissed employees in the public sector and in state-owned enterprises is directly affected by retrenchment programs. These workers constitute the most visible and most well organized group of stakeholders in this kind of reform; they represent hundreds of thousands of votes and can easily attract the attention of the media and mobilize large numbers of citizens. The state is also an important stakeholder, with direct control over the operations. However, its stake in and responses to the reform will depend on the specific central or local tier of government involved. Other stakeholders whose welfare might be directly affected, but whose political power is likely weaker than that of the public sector employees include people in communities surrounding state-owned enterprises and caterers and providers of services to public agencies and state-owned enterprises. Taxpayers, taken as a group, multilateral organizations, and donor countries are also among the stakeholders in a downsizing operation.

This chapter concentrates on assessing the welfare losses among dismissed workers. These welfare losses consist of the present value of the resulting change in earnings (including bonuses and other cash benefits), the present value of the losses in nonwage benefits (such as health coverage and old-age pensions), and other intangible losses from separation (such as reduced job security or less effort or productivity on the job). Downsizing may generate differential distributional impacts. Traditional rules of thumb used to compute severance compensations take into account only current wages and years of tenure in the public sector. Changes in welfare after dismissal are related to other observable characteristics that may serve as the basis for the design of a "just right" compensation package. In particular, evidence suggests that a well-tailored downsizing operation may consider the education, geographic location, and gender of workers. Various studies also show that the "just right" severance compensation package outperforms more traditional rules of thumb on the grounds of both costs and fairness. To help assess the consequences of using various downsizing strategies to compute a severance package, the chapter refers the reader to the Downsizing Options Simulation Exercise, an Excel-based application that can be found on the "Shrinking Smartly" Web page of the

World Bank. This analytical tool has been used in preparation for downsizing operations in Guinea-Bissau, Guyana, and Vietnam, among other countries.

A PSIA assessment should also consider the differences between the financial and economic returns to downsizing operations. Financial returns are calculated according to the present value of the difference between the payroll savings and the direct costs of the operations, such as the total amount of severance payments, the administrative costs, and other costs associated with safety net services provided to retrenched workers. In most cases, financial returns should be positive; however, even if this is so, the economic returns may be negative. Economic returns are much harder to assess. An indirect measure is the percentage of rehired workers. Rehires indicate that downsizing operations have been poorly handled and may indicate that some employees essential to the public agencies or state-owned enterprises were incorrectly dismissed or, worse, that some workers who had no intention of leaving in the first place were able to cash in through golden handshakes. Other factors may also cause differences in financial and economic returns, such as distorted public sector pay scales, distortionary taxes, or the presence of externalities as in the case of one-company towns.

A last word on the risks and threats involved in this type of operation. Retrenchment programs usually face political opposition. For this reason, voluntary or similar separation schemes are often preferred to involuntary schemes. However, the risks of ill-designed operations may cause the reform process to derail. In a PSIA, these risks should also be addressed. Some important risk factors that should be taken into account in the design of downsizing operations are the problems of overcompensation and adverse selection and externalities and distortions other than overstaffing.

NOTES

1. See Haltiwanger and Singh (1999) and Rama (1997, 1999).
2. See, for example, Vickers and Yarrow (1991) and World Bank (1995).
3. See Galal et al. (1994).
4. Haltiwanger and Singh (1999).
5. See Squire (1989); see also Devarajan, Squire, and Suthiwart-Narueput (1995).
6. See the discussion in Rama and Scott (1999).
7. See Assaad and Arntz (2000), Mahdi (2000), Said (2000), Wahba (2000).
8. The tool can be downloaded from the "Shrinking Smartly" Web page of the World Bank. (At http://www.worldbank.org/, insert "Shrinking Smartly" into the search cell and click "GO.")

9. Gender-sensitive versions of the tool have also been designed for Peru and Yemen.
10. For surveys of typical rules of thumb, see Nunberg (1994) and Kikeri (1997).
11. Assaad (1999).
12. See London Economics (1996).

BIBLIOGRAPHY

Alderman, H., S. Canagarajah, and S. D. Younger. 1996. "A Comparison of Ghanaian Civil Servants' Earnings before and after Retrenchment." *Journal of African Economies* 4 (2): 259–88.

Appleton, S., J. Hoddinott, and P. Krishnan. 1999. "The Gender Wage Gap in Three African Countries." *Economic Development and Cultural Change* 47 (2): 289–312.

Assaad, R. 1999. "Matching Severance Payments with Worker Losses in the Egyptian Public Sector." *World Bank Economic Review* 13 (1): 117–54.

Assaad, R., and M. Arntz. 2000. "Does Structural Adjustment Contribute to a Growing Gender Gap in the Labor Market?: Evidence from Egypt." ERF Research Project ERF 99-US-1003, Economic Research Forum for the Arab Countries, Iran, and Turkey. Cairo.

Carneiro, F. G., and I. Gill. 1997. "Effectiveness and Financial Costs of Voluntary Separation Programs in Brazil: 1995–1997." Economic Notes 25, Country Department I, Latin America and the Caribbean Regional Office, World Bank, Washington, DC.

Chong, A., and M. Rama. 1998. "A Compensation Package for Separated Public Sector Workers in Guinea-Bissau." Unpublished manuscript, Development Economics Department, World Bank, Washington, DC.

Devarajan, S., L. Squire, and S. Suthiwart-Narueput. 1995. "Reviving Project Appraisal at the World Bank." Policy Research Working Paper 1496, Policy Research Department, World Bank, Washington, DC.

Diwan, I. 1994. "Public Sector Retrenchment and Severance Pay: Nine Propositions." In "Civil Service Reform in Latin America and the Caribbean: Proceedings of a Conference," ed. S. A. Chaudhry, G. J. Reid, and W. H. Malik, 97–108. World Bank Technical Paper 259, World Bank, Washington, DC.

Fiszbein, A. 1994. "An Opportunity Cost Approach to Redundancy Compensation: An Application to Sri Lanka." In "Labor Economics in Less Developed Countries," special issue, *Estudios de Economía* 21 (1): 115–26.

Frydman, R., C. W. Gray, M. Hessel, and A. Rapaczynski. 1997. "Private Ownership and Corporate Performance: Some Lessons from Transition Economies." Policy Research Working Paper 1830, Policy Research Department, World Bank, Washington, DC.

Galal, A., L. Jones, P. Tandoon, and I. Vogelsang. 1994. *Welfare Consequences of Selling Public Enterprises: An Empirical Analysis.* New York: Oxford University Press.

Haltiwanger, J., and M. Singh. 1999. "Cross-Country Evidence on Public Sector Retrenchment." *World Bank Economic Review* 13 (1): 23–66.

Jeon, D.-S., and J.-J. Laffont. 1999. "The Efficient Mechanism for Downsizing the Public Sector." *World Bank Economic Review* 13 (1): 67–88.

Kikeri, S. 1998. "Privatization and Labor: What Happens to Workers When Governments Divest?" World Bank Technical Paper 396, Washington, DC.

Levy, A., and R. McLean. 1997. "Optimal and Sub-Optimal Retrenchment Schemes: An Analytical Framework." Unpublished manuscript, Policy Research Department, Rutgers University, New Brunswick, NJ.

London Economics. 1996. "The Impact of Privatisation on Labour in Africa." Report prepared for the Africa Regional Office, World Bank, Washington, DC.

López, F. 1997. "Determinants of Privatization Prices." *Quarterly Journal of Economics* 112 (4): 965–1025.

Mahdi, A. 2000. "The Labor Absorption Capacity of the Informal Sector in Egypt." Report, Economic Research Forum for the Arab Countries, Iran, and Turkey. Cairo.

Nunberg, B. 1994. "Experience with Civil Service Pay and Employment Reform: An Overview." In *Rehabilitating Government: Pay and Employment Reform in Africa*. Regional and Sectoral Study, ed. D. L. Lindauer and B. Nunberg, 119–59. Washington, DC: World Bank.

Orazem, P. F., M. Vodopivec, and R. Wu. 1995. "Worker Displacement during the Transition: Experience from Slovenia." Policy Research Working Paper 1449, Policy Research Department, World Bank, Washington, DC.

Rama, M. 1997. "Efficient Public Sector Downsizing." Policy Research Working Paper 1840, Policy Research Department, World Bank, Washington, DC.

———. 1999. "Public Sector Downsizing: An Introduction." *World Bank Economic Review* 13 (1): 1–22.

———. 2001. "The Gender Implications of Public Sector Downsizing: The Reform Program of Vietnam." Policy Research Working Paper 2573, World Bank, Washington, DC.

Rama, M., and D. MacIsaac. 1999. "Earnings and Welfare after Retrenchment: Central Bank Employees in Ecuador." *World Bank Economic Review* 13 (1): 89–116.

Rama, M., and K. Scott. 1999. "Labor Earnings in One-Company Towns: Theory and Evidence from Kazakhstan." *World Bank Economic Review* 13 (1): 185–209.

Robbins, D. 1996. "Public Sector Retrenchment: A Case Study of Argentina." Paper presented at the World Bank conference, "Public Sector Retrenchment and Efficient Compensation Schemes," World Bank, Washington, DC, November 6–7.

Robbins, D., M. Gonzales, and A. Menendez. 1996. "Public Sector Retrenchment and Efficient Severance Pay Schemes: A Case Study of Argentina." Harvard Institute for International Development, Cambridge, MA.

Ruppert, E. 1999. "The Algerian Retrenchment System: A Financial and Economic Evaluation." *World Bank Economic Review* 13 (1): 155–83.

Said, M. 2000. "A Decade of Rising Inequality?: Gender, Occupation, and Public-Private Issues in the Egyptian Wage Structure, 1988–1998." Report, Economic Research Forum for the Arab Countries, Iran, and Turkey. Cairo.

Squire, L. 1989. "Project Evaluation in Theory and in Practice." In *Handbook of Development Economics,* ed. H. Chenery and T. N. Srinivasan, Vol. II, 1153–86. Amsterdam: Elsevier Science.

Tansel, A. 1997. "Public Sector Retrenchment and the Impact of Labor Shedding Programs on Workers in Turkey." Unpublished manuscript, Department of Economics, Middle East Technical University, Ankara.

Vickers, J., and G. Yarrow. 1991. "Economic Perspectives on Privatization." *Journal of Economic Perspectives* 5 (Spring): 111–32.

Wahba, J. 2000. "Labour Mobility in Egypt: Are the 90s Any Different from the 80s?" Report, Economic Research Forum for the Arab Countries, Iran, and Turkey. Cairo.

World Bank. 1995. *Bureaucrats in Business: The Economics and Politics of Government Ownership.* World Bank Policy Research Report. New York: Oxford University Press.

Indirect Tax and Public Pricing Reforms

David Coady

I t is common for governments in developing countries to manipulate the prices of goods and services using a range of policy instruments and institutional arrangements. The motivations behind these price manipulations reflect varying objectives, such as the need to raise revenue, the desire to redistribute income toward the poor or toward politically important groups, the desire to provide protection to domestic producers, or the desire to influence the levels of supply or demand in related markets in which prices cannot easily be influenced.[1] For example, the major source of revenue in most developing countries is commodity taxation such as domestic sales and excise taxes and taxes on international trade (Burgess and Stern 1993; Keen and Simone 2004); food prices are often kept artificially low for consumers in order to increase the real incomes of poor households (Pinstrup-Andersen 1988a; Gupta et al. 2000); and public sector prices (for example, for electricity, gas, petroleum, coal, other fuels, fertilizers) are also often controlled by governments, reflecting either the perceived strategic importance of these inputs for development or the need to provide these sectors with an independent source of revenue and thus greater financial autonomy (Julius and Alicbusan 1989).

Reform of these indirect tax systems and publicly controlled prices is often an important component of many structural adjustment programs.

The views expressed in this chapter are those of the author and do not necessarily represent the views of the International Monetary Fund (IMF), nor do they necessarily reflect IMF policy. The author is grateful for the comments of participants at World Bank seminars on Poverty and Social Impact Analysis (PSIA) and IMF seminars and for detailed discussion with staff at the IMF PSIA Group.

The reform of indirect tax systems can involve various approaches such as reducing high trade taxes and replacing lost revenue through other indirect taxes, replacing trade and sales taxes with a value-added tax, broadening the value-added tax base to include previously exempt goods and services, or simply raising existing tax rates (Barbone et al. 1999; Abed et al. 1998). The reform of publicly controlled prices typically involves raising subsidized prices so that they are closer to world or cost recovery prices, or, possibly, the replacement of government price controls by market-determined prices (Gupta et al. 2000).

Governments and other stakeholders commonly express concerns regarding the potential adverse impact of these reforms on poverty. The desirability of these reforms is usually motivated primarily by efficiency and fiscal considerations, that is, the desire to raise revenue, but limit the distortion of economic activity. However, the associated price changes can potentially decrease the real incomes of households and thus, possibly, increase poverty. This potential for adverse effects on poverty may underlie the reluctance on the part of governments and other stakeholders to support such reforms. A credible reform strategy therefore requires an analysis of the likely impacts of proposed reforms on household real incomes and the distribution of the impacts across households, with a particular emphasis on the impact on the poorest households. The insights from these analyses should influence program design (that is, the structure of tax reforms, as well as the speed and sequencing of the introduction of the reforms) and inform the choice of alternative approaches for mitigating the adverse effects.[2]

The objective in this chapter is to set out the various methodological approaches that can be used to analyze the impact of tax and price reforms on household real incomes, to explain how these are related and compare their resource requirements, and to identify general policy lessons from existing empirical studies. The next section describes the various methodological approaches used in the literature and identifies their time, data, and skill-resource requirements. This is followed by a review of the findings of the empirical literature using these various approaches and the identification of general lessons for policy reform. The final section concludes with a summary of the methodological and policy lessons suggested by the review.

Throughout the chapter, the alternative approaches to modeling the welfare implications of tax and price reforms are separated into three categories: general equilibrium, limited general equilibrium, and partial equilibrium approaches. This classification is motivated as follows. The total impact on household welfare can be separated into the *direct effect* on households arising from the price effects of the reforms and the *indirect effect* that results once households and firms respond by changing their demand for and supply of goods and services and factors of production (resulting in efficiency and revenue impacts). The net distributional effect will depend on the magnitude of these indirect effects and how these indirect effects are distributed across households, for example, how the extra revenue is spent. General equilibrium approaches allow for all commodity-demand and factor-supply responses and thus incorporate both the direct and the indirect welfare effects of the reforms. Limited general equilibrium approaches typically focus on a subset of price reforms (such as agricultural price reforms) or allow for only a subset of household responses (for instance, responses in closely related markets or demand responses alone), thus incorporating only a subset of the indirect effects. Partial equilibrium approaches focus only on the direct effect of reforms on prices and household real incomes.

A more comprehensive analysis of tax and price reforms would need to address other important determinants of successful reform strategies, in particular, the administrative and political constraints on reforms. The fact that such issues are not addressed in this chapter should not be interpreted as an implicit assessment as to their relative importance for policy advice, but rather as a desire to keep the review manageable and focused. Such issues are only addressed indirectly in so far as they influence the set of tax and price reforms under consideration. Note also that the equity and efficiency implications of reforms can be expected to influence both the need for administrative reforms and the likely political economy of reforms.

ALTERNATIVE METHODOLOGICAL APPROACHES

As indicated in the introduction, one can distinguish three methodological approaches to the analysis of tax and price reforms: general equilibrium, limited general equilibrium, and partial equilibrium approaches. The total impact of a reform can be separated into the *direct effect* and the *indirect effect* on household welfare.[3] The direct effect captures the impact arising from the change in consumer prices that is due to the reform and that affects household real incomes. The indirect effect captures the welfare impacts that result from demand- and supply-side responses to the reforms with associated implications for efficiency and revenue. The net distributional effect of a reform will therefore depend on the magnitude of these indirect effects and how they are distributed across households, for example, how the extra revenue is spent. The three methodological alternatives differ according to the extent to which the indirect welfare effects are incorporated into the analysis. In addition, the data, time, and modeling-resource requirements differ substantially across these methodological alternatives (see Table 5.1 below).[4]

Partial equilibrium approach

The partial equilibrium approaches focus solely on the direct effect of reforms on consumer prices and household real incomes. These studies therefore ignore all household and producer responses and focus on the first-order effect on the real incomes of households (or, equivalently, the effect on household cost of living). It is common to interpret these effects as the short-run impact of reforms prior to household and producer responses. Household responses such as switching consumption away from taxed goods or toward subsidized goods tend to decrease adverse welfare impacts and increase beneficial welfare impacts. First-order effects are thus often interpreted as an upper bound on longer-term adverse impacts and a lower bound on beneficial impacts. Producer responses can affect the degree to which the incidence of taxes is pushed onto final-goods prices or factor prices and thus also the overall distribution of the welfare impact.

Estimation of these first-order impacts requires household-survey information on the consumption of the relevant goods and services. Such surveys, which are now available for many developing countries, can be used to calculate the budget shares for goods and services. By multiplying budget shares by the proportional increase in the corresponding prices attributable to the reforms, one obtains an estimate of the proportional change in household real incomes. For example, if a household allocates 10 percent of its total expenditures to food and the price of food increases by 10 percent, this results in a 1 percent decrease in household real income. If the prices of many goods are affected, this procedure can be carried out for each good and summed to get the total real-income effect. One can then analyze the pattern of these real-income changes across households at different levels of income, for example, by income deciles.[5] If the percentage decrease in income that is due to taxes is higher (lower) for higher-income deciles, then the incidence of the tax burden is said to be progressive (regressive).

If reforms involve a change in the prices of intermediate goods (such as energy products), one needs to model the pass-through of these price changes to final-goods prices. This requires information on the input-output structure of the economy, as well as information regarding the sectors that are internationally traded or nontraded or for which the prices are

TABLE 5.1. Alternative Approaches for Evaluating the Welfare Impacts of Tax and Price Reforms

	Characteristics	Resource requirements	Modeling requirements
Partial equilibrium	Incorporates only the direct effect of reforms, focusing only on welfare impacts arising through changes in consumer prices. Ignores the efficiency effects of demand and supply responses. Can also incorporate revenue effects and alternative mitigating measures.	*Data:* Requires information on the tax and price system and reforms, as well as household-survey data on the consumption of relevant commodities. Input-output tables are required in evaluating changes in the prices of intermediate goods. *Time:* The basic analysis can be completed in about two person-weeks once the relevant data have been collected and processed.	Simple models capturing the key features of the tax and public price system are relatively easy to construct and implement using household-survey and tax data. Typically, only welfare effects through consumer-price changes are captured.
Limited general equilibrium (multimarket models; demand-side models)	Incorporates direct effects and a subset of indirect effects such as demand and supply responses in a subset of (typically, agricultural) markets or only demand effects in all final-product markets. Ignores factor-market responses. Can also address alternative mitigating measures.	*Data:* As above, but now require detailed information on the sectors being analyzed and the demand and supply elasticities. *Time:* The basic analysis can be completed in about eight weeks once the relevant data have been collected and processed.	One needs to model sector supply and demand responses explicitly, as well as the interaction among sectors. The relevant modeling skills take longer to acquire.
General equilibrium (shadow-pricing approach; CGE models)	Incorporates direct effects and indirect effects through product and factor markets. Can address the equity and efficiency implications of a wide range of policy scenarios, including mitigating measures.	*Data:* A very data-intensive approach, requiring detailed information on the consumption and income patterns of households, factor intensities in all relevant sectors, and trade statistics. Typically, one has to make assumptions about a wide range of consumption- and production-response parameters. *Time:* Can take up to six person-months to organize data and complete the basic analysis.	The approach is very modeling intensive and therefore requires substantial modeling skills.

Source: Compiled by the author.

directly controlled by the government. One typically assumes that such price increases are pushed forward onto the output prices for nontraded goods, but backward onto factor prices or quasi-fiscal deficits for traded or price-controlled sectors. Since the modeling of price shifting is relatively straightforward (subject to data availability), so too is the simulation of price-shifting outcomes.[6]

Partial equilibrium analyses can provide a valuable input into policy dialogue and reform, especially when combined with a qualitative discussion of the likely efficiency effects of reforms. For example, switching taxes to products with inelastic demands or negative social externalities (such as petroleum products, tobacco, and alcohol) when these are initially small can be expected to increase the overall efficiency of the tax system. Similarly, broadening the tax base to include previously exempt final-consumption goods and services is also generally expected to improve the overall efficiency of the tax system. Such gains can then be juxtaposed against the distributional implications of these reforms in order to identify possible welfare gains from reforms or any trade-offs between efficiency and distributional considerations.

The policy relevance of such analyses can be strengthened even further by using household-survey data to simulate the likely effectiveness of existing or potential safety net expenditures in mitigating any adverse effects of reforms on poor households. Household-survey data, combined with knowledge of the design of any existing safety net programs, can be used to simulate the potential for such programs to protect the poorest households during the reform process and the implications for the net revenue effects of the reforms. If information on existing safety net programs is weak, one can construct the likely impact of (well-implemented) hypothetical programs as a way of focusing attention on the need for cost-effective programs. The aggregate first-order income effects also provide an estimate of the first-order revenue impacts of the reforms. Similarly, using household data, one can simulate the likely incidence of alternative social expenditures (such as increased education and health expenditures) that may be financed by the revenue gains from reforms. Such analyses help highlight the motivation behind and potential benefits from reforms.[7]

Limited general equilibrium approach

Limited general equilibrium approaches can be separated into two categories: multimarket models and demand-side models. *Multimarket models* typically focus on a limited set of price reforms (usually agricultural price reforms) and allow for only a subset of demand and supply responses (for example, in closely related agricultural output markets). *Demand-side models* focus on demand-side responses only and implicitly assume fixed producer prices so that all tax and price reforms are shifted fully forward onto final-goods prices. Both these approaches thus incorporate only a subset of the indirect welfare effects.

Multimarket models are useful when one is interested in price reforms in what are perceived as important markets, for example, the rice market. These markets are often directly controlled by governments through a range of policy instruments (such as trade taxes or direct price controls) and institutional arrangements (such as marketing boards). These models attempt to identify important demand and supply responses in a subset of closely related markets, for instance, in rice and maize markets, that can have important implications for the efficiency and distributional implications of reforms. This, in turn, requires the estimation of a system of demand and supply elasticities for well-defined sectors using a combination of household-survey information on the pattern of consumption, production, and prices across households and, possibly, time-series data on production and prices for important crops.

Demand-side models usually cover a broader range of goods and explicitly incorporate the efficiency implications of reforms by allowing for demand-side responses. The basic approach is to calculate the welfare (that is, combined efficiency and distributional) impact of raising one unit of revenue via different indirect taxes. These welfare impacts can then be compared across commodities to identify revenue-neutral and welfare-improving reforms of the current system, that is, by switching revenue-raising from commodities with relatively high welfare costs per unit of revenue to those with relatively low welfare costs. Alternatively, such an analysis can be used to determine how to raise extra revenue at the lowest welfare cost.

Incorporating the efficiency implications of taxation into the model essentially allows for the fact that the magnitude of the aggregate welfare loss will increase when households respond by reducing consumption, for example, by switching away from a taxed good.[8] Partial equilibrium models assume away efficiency effects. They do this by assuming that demand is fixed, so that a household's share of the tax burden resulting from taxing any commodity is given by the household's share in the total consumption of that commodity. If, to take an extreme example, one only cares about the impact on poor households, then one should increase taxes on goods for which the poor have a relatively low share of total consumption such as luxuries. However, the fact that households respond to a tax increase by decreasing their consumption of the taxed commodity means that taxes have to be higher to raise a given amount of revenue, thus increasing the total tax burden on households.[9] The tax burden on poor households is calculated as the share of these households in the tax burden (that is, the share of these households in total consumption), times the total tax burden. For example, if luxuries have high price elasticities, then raising revenue by taxing luxuries as opposed to taxing necessities may actually result in a higher tax burden for the poor even though the *share* of the poor in the total burden is lower. Therefore, when elasticities differ sufficiently across commodities, partial equilibrium analyses can give a misleading picture regarding the best way to raise revenue.

Introducing efficiency implications into the analysis requires the additional estimation of a system of price elasticities. The data requirements for calculating the distributional effects are the same as they are under partial equilibrium approaches, that is, the availability of household-level data, with consumption matched to tax categories and rates, as well as an input-output table when tax cascading is an issue. On the efficiency side, one needs to estimate the price elasticities of demand or supply, which can be done using information in the household survey. Typically, there is a trade-off between simplifying assumptions regarding the structure of household demand or supply and the ease of the calculation of the elasticities.[10] But a useful approach in practice is to start off with a simple model, run through the analysis, and then increase the sophistication of the analysis over time. The calculation of elasticities within the standard utility and profit-maximizing framework also facilitates the estimation of so-called exact (as opposed to first-order) measures of the welfare impact of tax reforms, for example, through the use of "equivalent variation" measures of the real-income impact on households. These measures allow for the fact that households can avoid some of the tax burden by substituting away from highly taxed goods.

General equilibrium approach

General equilibrium approaches incorporate indirect effects arising from demand and supply responses in all commodity and factor markets. Implicit in the demand-side general equilibrium models discussed above is the assumption that producer prices and, thus, production-technology coefficients are fixed. This is then consistent with the incidence of all taxes being fully pushed forward onto consumers.[11] However, in general, producer and factor prices cannot be assumed to be fixed, so that some of the burden of taxation is pushed backward onto factor prices.

In the literature, one can find two approaches to capturing these wider general equilibrium effects of taxes. One approach is to use a *computable general equilibrium* (CGE) model, which involves setting out a fully articulated system of demand and supply functions for each of the various sectors of the economy. An alternative approach uses *shadow prices* (which are interpreted as summary statistics from a model that is not fully articulated) in place of producer prices, and the standard welfare analysis goes through as above, except that "shadow taxes" (that is, consumer prices, minus shadow prices) are used in place of actual taxes.

Building CGE models is time, data, and modeling intensive.[12] However, once constructed, a model can be used to simulate a wide variety of reforms and market structures. One first sets out a system of equations on the supply and demand of commodities and factors for each sector in the economy and specifies market-clearing and macroeconomic closure rules. The various model parameters are either specified exogenously or calibrated with existing data on consumption, production, and trade flows, leading to a set of equilibrium-relative prices. Most of these models tend to be Walrasian in that all commodity and factor markets clear through adjustments in prices, although straightforward extensions are possible to allow for simple factor-market distortions.[13] Demand functions are typically some modified version of the linear expenditure system, while production functions are typically of the constant elasticity of substitution variety. The domestic production of traded goods can also be differentiated according to the degree of substitutability in consumption between imported and domestically produced goods so that domestic prices for traded goods do not necessarily move together with world prices one for one. Factor markets are often separated into skilled and unskilled labor, irrigated and nonirrigated land, and capital. Total factor supplies are usually fixed, but can be reallocated among sectors and even segmented by regions within a country. Note that, although the model uses country-specific data on consumption, production, and international trade (such as from household surveys, manufacturing surveys, and input-output tables), the production parameters are often "guesstimates" based on parameters available in the literature. In this sense, the models are part empirical and part analytical, and sensitivity analyses using different parameters are important.[14]

Once in place, the model is "shocked" by a tax reform, and a new set of equilibrium commodity and factor prices is calculated. These are used to calculate either "first-order" or "exact" welfare changes as above by applying the price changes to household-level data. One can then decompose the total welfare impacts across households into the impact caused by changes in consumer prices and in factor prices. One can also separately identify both the efficiency and the distributional implications of the tax reform. Welfare-improving tax-reform packages can be constructed by first examining the welfare cost of raising a fixed amount of extra revenue through the manipulation of individual tax rates and using the insights provided by such an analysis to construct "reform packages." Given the sophistication and complexity of the models, with many commodity and factor markets interacting simultaneously in the presence of numerous distortions, it is important to decompose the source of the welfare changes for an initial set of "narrow" reforms to develop a clear understanding of the channels through which the welfare effects are operating.

The use of shadow prices provides a less resource-intensive approach for incorporating the general equilibrium welfare effects of tax reforms. The parameters of the models underlying the calculation of shadow prices are smaller in number than are those for a typical CGE model. However, this is traded off against a greater level of sectoral detail than is typical in a CGE model and the greater flexibility in incorporating the sensitivity of the results to alternative market structures and government policies. For example, the most widely used approach for specifying shadow prices is that of Little and Mirrlees (1974), which uses world prices as the basis for shadow prices for traded goods and the marginal social cost of production as the shadow price for nontraded goods. These shadow prices depend on underlying government policies, as well as underlying market structure. For example, binding trade quotas are captured by treating the relevant goods as nontraded. Shadow wages are calculated based on a simple model of the labor market that adjusts for the fact that producer prices are not equated with shadow prices, that labor markets may not clear through wage adjustments, but through some form of (often poorly understood) rationing process across sectors, and that the underlying distribution of income is not socially optimal. Other factor markets can similarly be adjusted to allow for price distortions (for example, in agricultural output and input prices for land, or import prices, or the interest rate for capital). These simple shadow pricing rules are consistent with a wide class of second-best analytical models. The calculation of shadow prices is relatively straightforward, using data available in input-output tables and household surveys.

A limitation of the shadow-pricing approach from the perspective of distributional analysis is the fact that the distribution of the indirect welfare effects is not typically analyzed in detail. This reflects, in part, the fact that the main channel through which indirect distributional effects are incorporated is the shadow wage rate. This compares with the CGE approach, wherein the change in factor prices is modeled explicitly, and these changes can be imposed on household-survey data to analyze the distribution of factor-income changes across households in different parts of the income distribution.

LESSONS FROM THE EMPIRICAL LITERATURE

The discussion below of the empirical tax-reform literature distinguishes the literature in terms of both the modeling approach used and the type of tax or price reform considered. The first distinction is drawn, as above, in terms of the modeling approach used in the analysis, that is, among partial equilibrium, limited general equilibrium, and full general equilibrium models. Within each of these categories, a distinction is made among three categories of reforms: tax reform, trade liberalization, and the reform of public sector prices.[15]

Indirect tax reforms include reforms such as the introduction of a value-added tax (VAT) system in place of existing sales or excise taxes. VAT is often seen as superior to sales taxes since intermediate inputs are not taxed (thus avoiding the distortion of production techniques) and is often applied to a broader consumption base. Sales taxes are typically levied on both final and intermediate goods, resulting in "tax cascading," as tax rates are levied on output prices that have already been adjusted upward in response to higher production costs, reflecting taxes on intermediate inputs. Other issues that arise include the inability to tax the "informal sector" (including household agriculture), the existence of tax-exempt and zero-rated goods and services, and the choice of differential or uniform VAT rates.

Trade liberalization refers to reforms that replace taxes on international trade with taxes levied on domestic consumption (including the consumption of imported goods). Such reforms are often motivated by a desire to reduce the distortion in the domestic production and consumption of traded goods. Any revenue losses can be recouped by replacing such taxes by taxes levied on a broader base that does not differentiate between traded and nontraded goods.[16] Since these reforms can be anticipated to result in relatively large changes in relative producer prices (such as between tradables and nontradables), one expects that modeling factor-price changes is especially important for this set of reforms.

Public sector pricing reform includes reforms that adjust prices controlled by the government. Developing-country governments often control the prices of a range of goods. This might involve the use of marketing boards, combined with domestic trade and government procurement restrictions, to control the price of agricultural food production. These reforms may be motivated by revenue concerns (such as in the case of important agricultural exports) and distributional concerns (such as in the case of subsidized agriculture). In some instances, governments also sell processed foods at subsidized prices, subject to quantity rationing. Governments also often control energy prices, for example, petroleum products or electricity, especially in the face of rapidly increasing world oil prices.

Before one reviews the literature, it is useful to distinguish between two distributional concepts: *relative progressivity* and *absolute progressivity*.[17] The concept of relative progressivity is commonly used in studies evaluating tax incidence, whereas the concept of absolute progressivity is more commonly used in studies evaluating the incidence of public expenditures. A tax system is relatively progressive if the percentage decrease in income is lower for low-income households. This will be the case if the share of low-income households in the tax burden is less than the share of these households in total income. In this case, then, a neutral (or reference) tax system is one in which the percentage decrease in income attributable to the tax burden is equal for all households. A tax system is absolutely progressive if the share of low-income households in the aggregate tax burden is less than the population share of these households, for example, if the bottom 20 percent of the population pays less than 20 percent of the tax burden. The reference for neutrality here is thus a uniform absolute tax burden across all groups. It should be fairly obvious that, in the context of taxes, relative progressivity is a stricter definition of progressivity compared with absolute progressivity, since the former implies the latter, but not vice versa. In the context of price subsidies or direct transfers, the opposite holds, that is, absolute progressivity implies relative progressivity, but not vice versa. Below, unless specifically stated, the terms *regressive* and *progressive* will be used to refer to the relative concept.

Partial equilibrium studies

Distributional studies based on the consumption patterns in household-level data suggest that reforms emphasizing VAT and excise taxes are progressive. For example, Sahn and Younger (1999) examine the likely incidence of various taxes in six African countries: Côte d'Ivoire, Ghana, Madagascar, South Africa, Tanzania, and Uganda. Their analysis of consumption patterns suggests that gasoline and diesel excise taxes are relatively progressive, followed by the VAT system. Kerosene excise taxes are found to be the most regressive, and export taxes also often appear to be regressive. Since excise taxes are typically levied on products that are thought to have relatively low price elasticities and are associated with negative consumption externalities (such as petroleum products, tobacco, and alcohol) and since VAT is intended to be levied on a broader tax base, tax reforms that shift revenue raising to these tax instruments are typically assumed to improve both the equity and the efficiency impacts of the tax system. Reforms that switch tax revenue from trade taxes (which distort both production and consumption) to VAT (which, in principle, taxes only consumption) are similarly attractive.

The perception that excise taxes on petroleum products are attractive from a distributional perspective is not altered in studies that allow for the cascading effect of these taxes and the indirect effect on households through changes in other prices.[18] The progressiveness of petroleum excise taxes indicated above is based on the fact that low-income households directly consume relatively small amounts of petroleum products. However, a substantial proportion (sometimes over 50 percent) of petroleum-product consumption is typically used as an intermediate input into transport and other production activities. Therefore, the net effect on households will depend on how these higher costs are passed on in consumer prices. Studies that use input-output techniques to model these indirect impacts find that, although these taxes appear less progressive (because of the indirect consumption by lower-income groups of petroleum products), they are still more progressive than other taxes.[19] Import taxes are similarly found to be more progressive (or less regressive), which is consistent with the more intensive consumption of imported intermediate inputs by higher-income groups.

VAT often appears to be an even more progressive tax once one adjusts for the fact that agriculture and small-scale economic activities are typically VAT exempt. For example, low-income households often consume food directly from their own production or from small outlets that fall outside the VAT system. This feature tends to make VAT more progressive. In principle, these households may still pay some tax since the VAT on the inputs in these sectors is not rebated and is thus pushed onto consumer prices. However, the level of this taxation tends to be relatively low, and, in any case, many agricultural inputs are often zero rated.

A number of studies have found that replacing a sales tax with VAT has made the tax system more regressive (or less progressive). Although VAT is typically progressive, it is often less progressive than the sales taxes it has replaced, mainly because sales taxes have not been imposed on basic foods.

■ Muñoz and Cho (2004) evaluate the impact of replacing a system of sales taxes with a VAT in Ethiopia.[20] Although the VAT was progressive, partly reflecting the importance of own-consumption among the poorest households (and in spite of the disproportionate consumption of exempt goods by the non-poor), it was less progressive than the sales taxes it replaced.

■ Hossain (1995, 2003) undertakes a similar analysis for Bangladesh, which introduced a VAT in 1991 to replace a system of excise taxes on domestic producers, import duties, and sales taxes levied on both imports and domestically produced goods. The analysis shows that a uniform, revenue-neutral VAT would be substantially more regressive; the reform would result in a more than 2–3.5 percent decrease in the real incomes of the lowest-income households compared with a 4.5–8.1 percent increase for the highest-income households.[21] This reflected the inclusion of basic cereals and other food within the VAT system.

■ More recently, Tareq et al. (2005) analyze the distributional impact of introducing a VAT in Bosnia and Herzegovina. The existing sales tax had a standard rate of 20 percent, a preferential rate of 10 percent, and a zero rate for exports and a number of basic food items and certain services. The sales tax was collected at the retail stage, except for excisable products (alcohol and alcoholic beverages, soft drinks, coffee, oil and derivatives, and tobacco and tobacco products), for which it was collected at the importer or manufacturer stages. The proposed VAT was expected to involve a single rate of 17 percent, and the inclusion of previously exempt goods at this higher rate gave rise to concerns within the government regarding the impact of the reform on low-income households. The analysis found that the VAT was slightly less progressive than sales taxes. It was estimated that the tax reform would result in an increase in the average tax burden in the range of 1.9 to 2.6 percent across deciles and would be highest for the lower-income deciles.

The progressiveness of VAT can be improved by zero-rating basic foods. For example, Hossain (1995, 2003) examined how the zero-rating of food in Bangladesh would affect the distribution of the tax burden. The existing system (which taxed food) was compared with a system that zero-rated foodgrains and vegetables, applied a uniform rate on other goods and services, and levied excise taxes on tobacco, energy goods, and sugar. The latter system was found to be less regressive; it was estimated that a switch to the latter system would result in gains for lower-income households in the range of 1.2 to 2.7 percent and losses for higher-income households in the range of 0.8 to 6.6 percent.[22] Note, however, that, although VAT can be restructured to enhance its progressivity, the substantial leakage of benefits to higher-income households makes such an approach much less attractive than, say, a well-designed and well-targeted direct transfer program.

In many cases, the direct effect of agricultural trade liberalization that increases prices appears to be to decrease overall poverty, but increase extreme poverty.[23] For example, Ravallion and Lokshin (2004) examine the likely distributional consequences of agricultural trade reform in Morocco. The authors take the output price changes generated by a CGE analysis of the removal of cereal-import tariffs and apply them to a household survey to identify the first-order welfare effects, taking into account that some households are net producers, and others are net consumers of cereals.[24] They find that the consequent price decreases in cereals result in an increase in the rural poverty headcount index and that this reflects the fact that the rural poor are, on average, net producers of cereals. Note, however, that this could also be consistent with the extremely poor benefiting if they were net consumers. For example, in their analysis of an increase in rice prices in Indonesia, Ravallion and van de Walle (1991) found that the rural extreme poor, who tend to be landless and net consumers of rice, suffered decreases in income, whereas the moderately poor tended to be net producers and to gain from the reform. In addition, as shown below, the impact of the reforms on factor markets tends to reverse these effects so that the output-price effects may be interpreted as short-run impacts prior to adjustments on factor markets (for example, adjustments in unskilled wages).[25]

Limited general equilibrium models

One of the central findings of early empirical work on tax reform was the strong trade-off between efficiency and distributional concerns (Ahmad and Stern 1984, 1987, 1991). Commodities that were very attractive sources of revenue from the perspective of efficiency (such as food, which typically has a low price elasticity and thus a low "deadweight loss" associated with the relevant taxation) were very unattractive from the perspective of distributional impact (for example, food is relatively more important in the budgets of the poor). In other words, taxing commodities for which low-income households have a relatively small *share* of the commodity-tax burden will not necessarily lead to a smaller welfare loss for these households. This finding has two important implications for tax-reform policy. First, ignoring the efficiency implications of taxes can give a misleading indication of the commodities on which taxes should be increased if one wants to minimize the welfare impact on poor households. Second, improved distributional outcomes via commodity taxation are typically bought at the expense of substantial inefficiency. Therefore, using the indirect tax system should generally be viewed as a short-term measure until more cost-effective redistributional policy instruments are developed, for instance, a well-designed and well-implemented social protection program.[26]

However, it may be possible to identify commodities that are relatively attractive sources of tax revenue even when both equity and efficiency considerations are taken into account. For example, in the Ahmad and Stern (1991) studies of tax reform in Pakistan, the marginal social costs of raising revenue via taxes on rice; edible oils; housing, fuel, and light; and clothing were always below the median cost. The attraction of taxation on cereals, on the other hand, depended sensitively on how concerned one was about distribution when setting tax levels. If effective direct redistribution instruments do not exist, then the taxation of cereals is not desirable, even though the distributional gains come at a high efficiency cost.

The ranking of commodities may, however, be sensitive to the initial structure of taxes in a country. The marginal social cost of raising revenue through increasing a tax on a specific commodity depends on the existing level of taxes on commodities, as well as on the patterns of own- and cross-price elasticities and consumption across income groups. Therefore, even if one expects that the latter patterns are similar across "similar" countries, the former may differ greatly. One should thus be cautious when transporting policy lessons across countries.

Studies of agricultural price reforms (for example, as part of trade liberalization) using multimarket models reinforce the partial equilibrium finding that the rural extreme poor and the urban poor lose from price increases, while the rural moderate poor gain. Minot and Goletti (2000) evaluate the distributional impact of the removal of rice export-quota controls in Vietnam using a multimarket model. Their model simulates the demand and supply responses in the markets for four staple foods in seven regions of the country (that is, rice, maize, sweet potatoes, and cassava). The resulting welfare impacts thus take account of important demand and supply responses of households. The model also allows for the impact of higher rice production in terms of lower world prices. The results of the analysis of the welfare impact of rice price changes indicate that the poorest rural farmers lose from the higher domestic rice prices, as do the urban poor, reflecting the fact that both groups are net consumers. Non-poor rural households gain, which reflects the net producer status of these households. A similar, but less pronounced pattern was observed through a simple first-order partial equilibrium analysis, reflecting the fact that the higher rice production reduces world prices so that domestic rice prices do not increase by as much.[27]

General equilibrium models

The results produced by tax-reform analysis can differ substantially if one uses shadow taxes in place of effective taxes. For example, Ahmad and Stern (1990, 1991) look at the implications of this in the context of tax reform in Pakistan.[28] As one would expect given the implicit assumption in the calculation of effective taxes that all goods are nontraded, both sets of taxes differ substantially when goods are traded and are subject to trade taxes or price controls. For example, when wheat and rice were treated as nontraded, their revenue collections were applied to the total consumption base, implying tax rates of −1.8 percent and 1.7 percent, respectively. When treated as traded, these revenues were applied to the smaller trade base to give substantially higher rates of −30.3 percent (reflecting import subsidies) and −10.8 percent (reflecting export taxes). But note that effective and shadow taxes can also differ for nontraded goods when factor markets are distorted or the prices of important traded inputs are distorted.

Not surprisingly, since existing tax rates enter into the efficiency side of the analysis, the differences that arise do so with regard to the efficiency implications of tax reform. For example, the large initial subsidy on wheat when shadow prices are used now makes wheat a much more attractive source of revenue (that is, by reducing the subsidy) from an efficiency perspective. But such an increase remains as unattractive as before from a distributional perspective. The result is that the trade-off between efficiency and distributional concerns is increased, indicating a potential efficiency gain deriving from access to an effective transfer system that would enable efficiency considerations to be more prominent in the setting of tax rates.

The empirical shadow-pricing literature also highlight the fact that, when one evaluates reforms that liberalize agricultural prices, it is extremely important to capture the nature of and the constraints on the policy instruments used, as well as the precise consumption and production relationship among alternative agricultural commodities. Coady (1997a) extends the above results for Pakistan to allow for a more realistic and broader set of policy instruments, including the fact that households are both producers and consumers of agricultural commodities, so that only net market trades (or marketed surplus) can be taxed. In this context, what matters for efficiency is the net trade (as opposed to total-consumption) elasticities. When one allows for the fact that net trade is only a small proportion of total consumption and that some commodities may be substitutes in consumption, but complements in production, not only are the own- and cross-price net trade elasticities substantially higher than the consumption elasticities, but their sign may also be different.

For example, in Pakistan in the early 1980s, about 60 percent of wheat and 20 percent of rice were consumed on farms. Reflecting this and the fact that wheat and rice are sown in rotation on the same land and are thus production complements, the own- and cross-price net trade elasticities were very high and positive.

The constraint of being able to tax only net trades can therefore have substantial implications for both the distributional and the efficiency implications of taxes. For example, in Coady (1997a), although rural households were, in aggregate, net producers of wheat, poor households in rural areas tended to be net consumers, while non-poor households were net producers. As a result, low wheat prices (reflecting low procurement prices) acted as a subsidy for low-income households that was financed by a tax on high-income households, so that low prices were an extremely powerful redistributive instrument. However, net trade elasticities were also very high, so that the efficiency costs of low prices were very large. Therefore, the constraint of being able only to tax net trade magnifies the trade-off between efficiency and distribution when setting taxes.

The corollary of this is that the efficiency gains obtained by reforming the existing system of tax and price controls were also very substantial; in fact, the direct revenue-reducing effect of higher procurement prices for wheat were swamped by the positive indirect revenue effects through higher government procurement, which replaced more expensive wheat imports, as well as the increased production and export of rice, which resulted in higher export-tax revenue. In other words, existing taxes were on the wrong side of the Laffer curve.[29] This finding also reinforces the argument implicit in multimarket modeling, whereby focusing on the price reform for one agricultural commodity in isolation may give misleading results. For example, the welfare impacts of lowering wheat prices were strongly influenced by the indirect revenue effects through rice markets. Note also that the presence of this indirect revenue effect through rice suggests that low wheat prices may be less inefficient if rice prices are higher. In other words, higher rice prices enable the distributional gains from low wheat prices to be achieved at a lower efficiency cost. This sequential approach to price reform could help mitigate the adverse distributional effects of a move to a more efficient price and tax system until an effective social protection system can be developed.

Analyses of tax systems using CGE models have supported the partial equilibrium findings that energy taxes are progressive and that the distributional effect of VAT depends on how basic foods are treated.[30] For example, Go et al. (2005) test the partial equilibrium findings of Fourie and Owen (1993) that VAT in South Africa was mildly regressive. Applying the same partial equilibrium method for 2001, they found similar results, with low-income households paying over 5 percent of their incomes in VAT compared with only 3.5 percent among high-income groups. This occurred in spite of the fact that certain food items (such as brown bread, maize meal, milk and milk powder, rice, and unprocessed vegetables and fruits) were zero rated, and small-scale firms were not required to register for VAT.

To evaluate the welfare impact of the current VAT, the models remove VAT completely and replace it with a proportional income tax to balance the government budget and not influence the overall incidence of indirect taxes. Whereas the overall tax system (including direct taxes, fuel and excise taxes, tariffs, and VAT) is progressive, VAT is found to be mildly regressive. Overall, the high-income groups pay over 20 percent of their income in taxes, while low-income groups pay less than 10 percent. With VAT, high-income groups pay less than 4 percent, while low-income groups pay over 5 percent. When VAT is removed and revenue is replaced by scaling up sales taxes (which are levied on petroleum, beverages, and transport equipment) by 262 percent, the overall tax burden becomes slightly more progressive, indicating that VAT is more regressive than sales taxes. This partly reflects the fact that there was a relatively high VAT rate on food, which is particularly important for poor households, and sales taxes are higher on goods disproportionately consumed by high-income households. Removing the VAT on food and increasing the base rate on other goods to 16.4 percent to keep VAT revenue constant transforms VAT from a regressive to a progressive tax; low-income households pay less than 2 percent in VAT, whereas high-income households pay more than 3 percent (compared with more than 5 percent and less than 4 percent, respectively, under the previous VAT structure).[31]

Analyses of the distributional impacts of trade liberalization using CGE models completely overturn the findings of studies using partial equilibrium and limited general equilibrium models. The distributional impacts through factor markets are likely to be particularly important in the context of trade liberalization, which results in substantial changes in relative producer prices, that is, the relative prices of traded and nontraded commodities. Hertel and Reimer (2004) and Reimer (2002) provide surveys of the empirical findings from analyses of the distributional impact of trade liberalization. They find that a key channel for these impacts is the effect of reforms on factor markets, particularly labor markets. This is to be expected in so far as: (1) classical trade theory shows that changes in output prices brought about by trade reforms lead to magnified changes in factor prices for intensively used factors; the degree of magnification is higher in the short run when some sector-specific factors exist; and (2) households are typically more specialized in terms of sources of income rather than consumption patterns. For example, the removal of an export subsidy on rice will lead to an increase in domestic prices. If rice is relatively intensive in unskilled labor compared with other sectors, then the unskilled wage rate can be expected to increase proportionally more than do rice prices. If the poor are net consumers of rice and receive most of their income from their unskilled labor, then the positive wage effect can be expected to dominate the negative effect of higher rice prices. Therefore, evaluations of the distributional effects of trade liberalization need to incorporate these factor-price effects through general equilibrium analysis.[32]

There is also evidence from CGE analysis that the use of optimal export taxes on agricultural exports can have adverse effects on poverty, besides any adverse effects on market share in the long run. Warr (2001) provides a very interesting and rigorous example of the use of CGE modeling to evaluate the distributional implications of controlling the domestic price of rice in Thailand using export taxes. Thailand is perceived to have some monopoly power in international rice markets, so that, based on first-best efficiency arguments, a positive export tax is optimal. Based on an export-demand elasticity for rice of 0.25, the optimal tax from this perspective turns out to be about 42 percent, and the net welfare gain is 0.63 of a percentage point of gross domestic product relative to a situation with a zero export tax. However, the tax decreases the domestic price of rice, so that this aggregate gain comes at the expense of both the rural and the urban poor, reflecting lower prices for poor producers and lower unskilled wages for poor consumers. Incorporating even relatively modest distributional concerns into the analysis substantially changes this outcome; the optimal situation quickly switches to a subsidy of 20 percent. The results highlight that: (1) the main distributional effects come through factor-market prices, (2) higher rice prices are distributionally powerful in the long run even if poor net consumers lose in the short run before unskilled wages increase, and (3) any short-term efficiency gains from export taxes may come at the cost of higher poverty.

The results from CGE analysis also reinforce the finding that there may be substantial welfare gains from using more direct policy instruments to protect the incomes of low-income households instead of adjusting tax rates. For example, Coady and Harris (2004) look at the welfare impacts of using the revenue generated by efficiency-improving tax reforms to finance a (perfectly targeted) direct transfer program in Mexico. The initial indirect tax system was characterized by large agricultural food subsidies and a differentiated VAT structure with a low rate (zero) applied to raw and processed food. The tax reforms considered are aimed essentially at (1) removing agricultural subsidies; (2) keeping the current VAT structure, but scaling up the rates; and (3) increasing the VAT rate on food. When the revenue is raised by removing food subsidies, the cost to households is only 62 percent of the revenue raised (that is, the cost of a unit of public funds is 0.62). Similarly, when revenue is raised through a single VAT applied to all sectors, the cost of public funds is only 0.95, so that the gains from reforming the VAT structure outweigh the losses from the higher average rate required to finance the introduction of the transfer program. The other tax reforms considered all showed the costs of public funds in the range of 1.05 to 1.07. Although low-income and high-income households bore a disproportionate amount of this higher tax burden, the existence of a well-targeted transfer program more than offset this negative effect on the poorest households. The gains from introducing such a program are thus twofold. First, the transfers are targeted better than the subsidies implicit in the differentiated tax structure. Second, the presence of the program enables one to focus on efficiency considerations when setting VAT rates. These findings were found to be very robust to alternative parameter values for the underlying consumption, production, and trade functions.

When using CGE models to evaluate tax reforms, it is important to present the sources of the welfare impacts in a transparent manner both to have a clear understanding of the channels at work and to enhance the credibility of the findings. For example, in Go et al. (2005), the nominal wages of semiskilled and unskilled labor are fixed, reflecting unemployment among these types of labor. Therefore, tax reforms that increase demand in domestic sectors that are intensive in relatively unskilled labor will tend to increase welfare. For example, reducing taxes on a nontraded sector that is intensive in unskilled labor can be expected to result in a substantial efficiency gain arising from the conventional decrease in deadweight loss, but also the reduction in unemployment. In the language of the shadow-pricing model discussed earlier, the shadow tax (for example, the consumer price, minus the social marginal cost of production) is high for these sectors; decreasing them can thus lead to large welfare gains because of the elimination of this "shadow deadweight loss." It would therefore be useful to identify the various sources of the overall welfare impact, for example, changes in output prices, changes in factor prices, and changes in unemployment. In the Walrasian model, with markets clearing through price adjustment, welfare impacts can be expressed solely in terms of price changes, but, in models in which commodities or factors are rationed (such as with unemployment), welfare impacts depend on both price and quantity changes. Note also that results may, in general, be very sensitive to the mechanisms used to allocate rationed quantities across households with different socioeconomic characteristics, and the relatively simple allocation process used in a CGE model may give results that are very different form those produced by a more sophisticated allocation process, say, similar to those being used in recent CGE-cum-microsimulation models.

CONCLUSIONS

In this section, the main issues and findings discussed in the chapter are summarized. Lessons regarding the use of the alternative methodologies are dealt with first. Findings from the empirical literature are then summarized.

Methodological lessons

1. Simple partial equilibrium analyses can provide valuable information on the likely magnitude of the impacts of tax and price reforms on household real incomes, as well as the distribution across households. These studies have relatively low resource costs in terms of data, time, and modeling requirements and can therefore be undertaken on a routine basis. When combined with a qualitative discussion of the likely efficiency and fiscal implications of reforms and a quantitative analysis of the potential uses of revenue (for example, mitigating measures or the financing of other social expenditures), these studies can be a very effective input into policy dialogue and the development of credible and acceptable reform strategies. As with all studies of tax reforms in developing countries, it is important that one incorporate the constraints on tax instruments into the analysis (for example, the inability to tax the consumption of own-production in rural areas or informal sector transactions) since these can greatly affect the distributional impacts of reforms.

2. General equilibrium models are necessary when one wishes to evaluate and highlight the magnitude of the efficiency implications of reforms and the trade-off with distributional impacts. These studies can help emphasize the fact that using indirect taxes to mitigate the adverse effects of taxation on the real incomes of poor households can be a very inefficient approach relative to more a direct approach to social protection through well-designed and well-implemented social safety net programs. While the "shadow-pricing" approach can provide a flexible and relatively low resource-cost approach to explicitly incorporating the magnitude of the efficiency impacts, it is less useful when one wishes to

disaggregate the distribution of these indirect effects. For this, a CGE model is required. Building such a model from scratch is a resource-intensive activity. However, if a model is available, the cost of adapting it for the analysis at hand is much lower.

3. The use of a CGE model is particularly valuable in analyzing the distributional impact of reforms that involve significant changes in producer prices, for instance, trade liberalization. This reflects the fact that the distributional impacts of such reforms arise mainly through changes in factor prices as opposed to changes in consumer prices, and the relative distributional impacts can differ substantially across these two channels. The consumer-price effects are often interpreted as short-run impacts until factor prices can adjust.

Empirical lessons

1. Typically, the introduction of a relatively broadbased VAT in place of sales taxes has reduced the progressivity of the tax system by enlarging the tax base to include previously exempt goods and services that are usually relatively more important in the budgets of the poor or by reducing taxes on goods that are relatively more important in the budgets of higher-income households. Therefore, revenue-neutral reforms will generally lead to gains by upper-income groups at the expense of lower-income groups.

2. Excise taxes on petroleum products (except kerosene), tobacco, and alcohol are highly progressive, even after allowing for their indirect effects, which tend to be less progressively distributed compared with the direct effects.

3. Since both these tax instruments are often associated with a more efficient collection of tax revenue (reflecting their broader base, lower price elasticities, and negative consumption externalities), opportunities exist for improving both the efficiency and the equity effects of tax reform. The introduction of VAT and the use of excise taxes on petroleum products and tobacco play an important role in realizing these welfare gains. For example, the use of excise taxes can help generate sufficiently large revenues, thereby enabling VAT to be introduced at a lower rate. The introduction of differential rates, with lower rates on goods consumed disproportionately by the poor, would improve the progressivity of VAT.

4. In practice, distributional gains from tax reform often come at the expense of efficiency, and this efficiency cost may be particularly large in the context of agricultural commodities if households are both

consumers and producers and the tax base is limited to the net market trades of these commodities. It is therefore useful to have some indication of the relative magnitude of these trade-offs across commodities.

5. Similarly, although differentiating excise taxes within aggregate commodity groups—for example, low taxes on kerosene, combined with higher taxes on gasoline and diesel—may help mitigate the impact on the real incomes of the poor, this is likely to come at a high efficiency and revenue cost given the relatively high degree of substitutability among these different commodities, especially over the long term.

6. In general, manipulating commodity taxes to mitigate the impact on poor households is a very blunt second-best approach to protecting the real incomes of the poor given the substantial leakage of benefits to higher-income households and the potentially large efficiency costs. In cases in which price manipulations provide a very effective approach to distribution (for example, low prices for agricultural goods both produced and consumed by rural households), this usually comes at a very high efficiency cost. The introduction of a well-designed and well-implemented social safety net offers a more effective way of protecting the poor and can generate substantial gains by allowing taxes to be raised more efficiently. In this regard, the paucity of the information often available on the design, implementation, and performance of targeted social programs is a major constraint on policy advice in this area. If an effective safety net system is not in place, then knowledge of the magnitude and pattern of the equity-efficiency trade-off can guide the choice of the tax mitigating mechanism that should be used as a short-term social protection measure.

NOTES

1. On the structure of taxation and tax reform in developing countries, see Bevan et al. (2000), Bird (1992), Burgess and Stern (1993), Coady (1997b), Gemmell (1987), Gemmell and Morrissey (2003, 2005), Gillis (1989), Heady (2001), Keen and Simone (2004), Tanzi (1987, 2000), and Thirsk (1997).

2. Indeed, there is a clear expectation that the design of IMF programs in low-income developing countries under the so-called Poverty Reduction and Growth Facility should explicitly recognize these distributional issues (Gupta et al. 2002).

3. A more formal discussion of the welfare impact of tax and price reforms is presented in Annex 1. A similar categorization is used by Hertel and Reimer (2004) in the context of trade liberalization. Some of the issues discussed in the text are discussed in more detail in Ahmad and Stern (1984, 1991); Coady and Drèze (2002); Coady and Harris (2004); Deaton (1997); Drèze and Stern

(1987); Dervis, de Melo, and Robinson (1982); Gunning and Keyser (1995); Newbery and Stern (1987); and Sadoulet and de Janvry (1992). An alternative approach to the "simulation approaches" discussed in this chapter would involve using the price data available in household surveys to estimate a reduced-form impact of price changes on household real incomes. However, because no such empirical studies have been found, this approach is not discussed here. The lack of empirical studies in this area may reflect econometric problems related to identifying price effects and separating these from, say, location-fixed effects.

4. Note that, with all these methodologies, one can also distinguish between first-order welfare measures (in which household net demand is assumed to be fixed) and "exact" welfare measures (those that incorporate demand changes). For example, in the case of increases in the consumer prices of final goods, first-order measures will, in general, overestimate the adverse welfare impact since they ignore the potential for households to switch demand away from goods for which prices increase (Banks, Blundell, and Lewbel 1996). Similarly, they will underestimate the benefits from consumer price decreases. The analysis of "marginal reforms" essentially assumes that price changes are sufficiently small and that second- and higher-order welfare effects are also relatively small, so that first-order measures are accurate approximations. Note that, although one focuses here on welfare impacts for "marginal reforms," one simply needs to replace first-order welfare effects with "exact" welfare measures (for example, equivalent variations) for large changes, and then the discussion goes through more or less as in the text.

5. Typically, total household consumption (for instance, in per capita or per capita adult equivalent form) is used to categorize households by welfare level since this is perceived to be a more accurate reflection of household "permanent income" (Deaton 1997).

6. Annex 2 presents two examples of the types of price-shifting models that can be used for reforms of indirect taxes and price subsidies.

7. Note that such simulations of alternative expenditures can also be motivated by a desire to identify the relative distributional implications of alternative ways of, say, reducing a budget deficit.

8. In practice, the aggregate welfare loss can either increase or decrease depending on the existing structure of taxes. For example, it could decrease if a higher tax leads to a switch in demand to other, relatively highly taxed goods.

9. Note that this example implicitly assumes that the efficiency losses are "returned" to households via changes in the tax under consideration.

10. See Deaton (1995, 1997) for a discussion of alternative approaches to estimating elasticities and the inherent trade-offs among different approaches in terms of data and the restrictiveness of the underlying assumptions.

11. To the extent that producer prices (including commodity and factor prices) are truly fixed, for instance, because of the existence of perfectly competitive imports or government price controls, this assumption is obviously valid.

More generally, this assumption would be valid if production technology were characterized by constant returns to scale with a single nonproduced factor of production and no joint products; under these assumptions, the so-called nonsubstitution theorem holds, and producer prices are unaffected by the pattern of demand. See, for example, Mas-Colell, Whinston, and Green (1995, 157–60) for further details on this issue.

12. For a discussion of the various resource costs for developing empirical CGE models, see Dahl and Mitra (1991). For examples of the importance of modeling assumptions, see Clarete (1991) and Shah and Whalley (1991).

13. For example, rationing in the labor market (through unemployment, for instance) can be relatively easily incorporated by allowing increased production to draw on unemployed labor at a fixed wage, or imperfect competition can be captured through simple price-markup rules. How appealing these extensions are will depend on the policy context. Note also that the presence of rationing means that welfare effects occur not only through price changes, but also through changes in quantity allocations (for example, the reallocation of labor between segmented markets with differential labor returns and wage rates for otherwise identical labor types). This possibility has generated a related "microsimulation" literature, which projects the new equilibrium (that is, prices and quantities) from the CGE to household data and supplements the standard CGE analysis with an empirical reduced-form rationing model that allocates household labor to different sectors and generates a new distribution of income. For more detailed discussion on these issues, see Bourguignon and Pereira da Silva (2005) and Kehoe, Srinivasan, and Whalley (2005).

14. See Warr (2001), which evaluates a reform of Thailand's rice-export taxes, for an example of a CGE model that incorporates substantial country-specific estimates of the various parameters.

15. Annex 2 provides basic models that can be used to represent the partial equilibrium effects of tax and price reforms. Annex 3 provides a brief summary of the theoretical tax literature, the insights from which are often the motivating factors behind these reforms.

16. See Ebrill, Stotsky, and Gropp (1999) for empirical evidence on the revenue implications of trade tax reforms.

17. See Besley and Preston (1988), Coady and Skoufias (2004), Pfahler (1987), and Pfingsten (1986) for more detailed discussion.

18. Many developing-country governments directly control the price of petroleum and other energy products. For example, the determination of petroleum prices is fully liberalized (that is, the private sector determines prices without having to seek government permission) in only a few countries in Sub-Saharan Africa (Chad, Kenya, Lesotho, South Africa, and Tanzania). In the majority of countries, prices are either fully controlled by the government without a functioning formula (11 countries) or are government determined through a functioning price formula (17 countries). In a smaller group of countries, governments negotiate prices with the private sector based on a

formula (7 countries) or the private sector determines prices using a formula (4 countries). For a discussion of the welfare and fiscal implications of alternative price-smoothing rules, see Federico, Daniel, and Bingham (2001).

19. See, for example, Chen, Matovu, and Reinikka (2001), on Uganda; Coady and Newhouse (2005), on Ghana; Gillingham and El-Said (2005), on Jordan; Gillingham and Medas (2005), on Bolivia; Hughes (1986, 1987), on Indonesia, Thailand, and Tunisia; and Rajemison, Haggblade, and Younger (2003), on Madagascar.

20. Their analysis adjusts for the fact that many households consume from their home production, especially food, and are not normally covered by the VAT system, so that they only pay VAT on their purchases from the market. In common with much of the earlier literature, the analysis also allows for the existence of tax evasion through the use of "implicit tax rates," that is, actual tax revenue divided by the tax base, as opposed to statutory rates, which assume perfect implementation. Because of data constraints, an input-output table for Tanzania for 1992 was used as a substitute. Note that there are two dimensions in which this is unsatisfactory: using Tanzania data for Ethiopia and using 1992 data when the reforms took place in 2003. Still, what matters here is not really that the economic structure of these countries may differ (for example, greater reliance on agriculture or industry), but that the input-output coefficients, which capture technologies and relative prices, may differ. However, given the importance of taxation on intermediate goods, the alternative would be to focus only on the impact arising from direct consumption by households, which would be even more unsatisfactory given that the impact through the indirect consumption by households can dominate. (For example, over 50 percent of petroleum products are often consumed in the production and distribution of goods and services.) Although results based on imperfect data need to be qualified, they can still provide a valuable input into the policy debate.

21. Real-income effects were calculated using estimates of equivalent variation based on estimated demand elasticities. Note also that the analysis focused on total consumption and did not distinguish between households that were net producers and households that were net consumers of foodgrains. Refaqat (2003) uses household-survey data for 2001 to evaluate the distributional impact of the VAT in Pakistan and finds that it is very slightly progressive. Chen, Matovu, and Reinikka (2001) find that the VAT introduced in Uganda in 1996 was no less progressive than the sales taxes it replaced.

22. For other examples of the distributional gains resulting from introducing differential VAT rates, see Ahmad and Ludlow (1989) and Ahmad and Stern (1991, ch. 7), in the context of Pakistan, and Gibson (1998), in the context of Papua New Guinea. The first two papers also find that the general distributional picture is unchanged when one uses equivalent variation measures of welfare impacts to adjust for the fact that tax changes are not marginal.

23. There are many partial equilibrium studies evaluating such impacts; see, for example, Barrett and Dorosh (1996), on Madagascar; Budd (1993), on Côte

d'Ivoire; Case (2000), on South Africa; Chen and Ravallion (2003), on China; Deaton (1989), on Thailand; Fletcher (2005); Chia, Wahba, and Whalley (2000); Krueger, Schiff, and Valdès (1988); and Trairatvorakul (1984), on Thailand. Hertel and Reimer (2004) and Reimer (2002) provide very good surveys of different trade-reform studies and should be consulted for a more detailed and exhaustive summary of this literature. See Cornia, Jolly, and Stewart (1987) and Pinstrup-Andersen (1988a) for a discussion of the motivation behind these policies. For an overview of alternative approaches to accessing the welfare impacts of trade policies, see McCulloch, Winters, and Cirera (2001).

24. Note that, although a CGE model generated the price changes, factor-price changes are not incorporated into the analysis. The likely implications of this are discussed in later sections. But note that Löfgren (2000) found that, in the short run, although domestic trade liberalization produced aggregate gains for the country, the rural poor lost out.

25. Ravallion (1990) discusses the importance of wage effects when evaluating reforms in rice pricing in Bangladesh and indicates that wage effects are likely to dominate commodity-price effects over the long term, as would be expected from the well-known Stolper-Samuelson theorem. See also Porto (2003a, 2003b) and Nicita (2004a) on trade liberalization in Argentina and Mexico, respectively. In the former case, trade liberalization was found to benefit the poor more than it did the rich. In the latter, although trade liberalization was found to decrease poverty, inequality increased.

26. A recent paper by Nicita (2004b) is indicative of the detail that can be introduced on the efficiency side of the analysis. The paper evaluates the potential for welfare-improving marginal price reforms across different food groups in Mexico—the paper abstracts from the issue of effective versus nominal taxation—and makes three interesting innovations. First, using a model developed by Deaton (1987, 1988, 1990) and Deaton and Grimard (1992), it estimates demand elasticities with a model that allows for quality differences in commodities. Second, it estimates separate sets of elasticities for income quintiles and rural and urban areas. Third, it estimates these elasticities using a series of six household surveys covering a period of 12 years, from 1989 to 2000. The results show that income and price elasticities vary substantially across households and that lower-income households tend to have significantly larger income and price elasticities. The results also indicate that, even within this smaller subgroup of consumption, there is potential for welfare-improving price reforms and that there is a trade-off between efficiency and distributional concerns. An interesting extension of this work would be to evaluate separately the importance of calculating "exact" welfare impacts, as opposed to "first-order" impacts, for the distributional and efficiency implications of tax reforms.

27. See also Sadoulet and de Janvry (1992) for an analysis of the likely short- and long-run effects on the poor in different African and Asian economies. These

authors also examine the potential for social protection programs to offset the short-run adverse welfare effects on the poor.

28. See also various chapters in Newbery and Stern (1987) for further discussion of the theory and application of the shadow-pricing approach.

29. For a similar result in the context of factor-market distortions, see Devarajan, Thierfelder, and Suthiwart-Narueput (2001). Using CGE analysis for Bangladesh, Cameroon, and Indonesia, these authors find that some tax increases have a "negative deadweight loss," reflecting reallocation of factors across sectors with differential factor productivities. Their analysis shows that the results can be very sensitive to the underlying assumptions about factor-market functioning and that the potential for efficiency-improving tax reforms are great.

30. Using a CGE model for Mexico, Sobarzo (2000) found that increasing VAT rates did not lead to substantial changes in producer prices. This is not surprising given the openness of the economy since, for traded sectors, producer prices are determined by world prices. The incidence of VAT increases was found to be progressive, while the pattern of the incidence of higher energy prices was found to have an inverted "J" shape, with welfare decreases higher among the middle-income group, followed by the "poor" and the "rich" ordered by magnitude. Reducing VAT, combined with higher energy prices, had a progressive incidence. The poor gained least from the removal of tariffs.

31. Similar results are produced by the Devarajan and Hossain (1995) analysis of taxes in the Philippines, which finds that indirect taxes as a whole are near neutral. Energy taxes are found to be progressive, reflecting the relatively high energy-intensity of goods consumed by higher-income households, while import and VAT were found to be neutral in incidence. When combined with the substantial progressive incidence of expenditures, the overall tax-cum-expenditure incidence is strongly progressive. The effect of taxes is virtually identical across income deciles, leading to a 20 percent decrease in real incomes. But there are substantial differences among the incidences of expenditures; the bottom decile experienced a 47 percent increase in income, this falling to about 11 percent for the middle two deciles and to less than 7 percent for the top three deciles. The net effect of the tax-expenditure system led to a 26 percent increase in income for the lowest decile, a decrease of about 8 percent in income for the middle two deciles, and close to a 20 percent decrease in income for the top decile.

32. See Clarete (1991), on the Philippines; Harrison, Rutherford, and Tarr (1993), on Turkey; and Shah and Whalley (1991), on Pakistan, for analyses of the impacts of trade liberalization in specific countries.

33. The model discussed in this section draws heavily on the works of Drèze and Stern (1987) and Guesnerie (1979).

34. Note also that, subject to regularity conditions, the constrained demand functions $\bar{x}^h(.)$ also have the standard properties with respect to $\mathbf{q}$ and m^h. For

instance, Roy's identity and the Slutsky equations continue to apply. Similarly, the Slutsky matrix $\mathbf{S}$ is symmetric and negative semi-definite, and $\mathbf{q \cdot S} = \mathbf{0}$. The main difference is that the matrix $\mathbf{S}$ has columns of zero entries for commodities such that the quantity constraint is binding (because a small change in the price of such a commodity works like a change in lump-sum income).

35. Strictly speaking, one only needs convexity in the space of commodities for which the quantity constraints are not binding.

36. Note also that the quantity constraints enable us to treat the net supply vectors of firms operating under constant returns to scale as functions rather than as correspondences.

37. This does not require the assumption that producer prices are *actually* constant. If producer prices are among the "control variables," then the derivation remains valid by the envelope theorem. Furthermore, it should be remembered that the "control variables" formally *include* the market-clearing variables, that is, the variables that implicitly adjust to clear the scarcity constraints. Seen in this light, the device of holding producer prices constant is much more general than appears at first sight. More precisely, the derivation is valid if any of the following hold: (1) producer prices are actually fixed (as in Diamond and Mirrlees 1975), (2) producer prices adjust endogenously to clear the scarcity constraints, or (3) producer prices are directly controlled by the planner.

38. See, also, Newbery and Stern (1987) and Sadoulet and de Janvry (1992) for further details on these approaches.

39. Note the slight difference regarding the definition of partial equilibrium compared with definitions in standard introductory text books, which often include responses in the market under analysis.

40. See Coady (1997a) and Newbery and Stern (1987) for further discussion and applications.

41. Ignoring income-distribution issues and assuming that government revenue is optimal (that is, $\lambda = \beta = 1$), if the gain in revenue is less than the aggregate direct income effect (so that $\eta < 1$), then the difference captures the welfare loss from the price increase. This is analogous to the partial equilibrium Harberger welfare-loss triangle from taxes. See Coady and Drèze (2002) for more detailed discussion.

42. For a discussion of price-shifting within a broader class of models (for example, incorporating different degrees of competition), see Stern (1987).

43. Throughout the chapter, lowercase in equations refers to row vectors, and uppercase to matrices.

44. This would not be the case in vatable sectors for the VAT component in taxes on traded sectors.

45. The solution vector of prices is a $(1 \times n)$ vector in which the elements are interpreted, in general, as the "weighted average prices" for aggregate sectors. Alternatively, one could treat each component of p as a separate $(1 \times n)$ vector and solve out for each vector simultaneously.

46. Note also that, if taxes are imposed at the wholesale stage, then these rates will need to be adjusted to reflect the (lower) tax proportion of retail prices.
47. In this case, for t>0, then dq<0.
48. See Coady and Drèze (2002) for a recent survey of the literature in the context of these three roles.
49. Note that a proportional reduction in tariffs "financed" by a proportional increase in any existing consumption taxes will not be unambiguously welfare improving; see Anderson (1999).
50. Note that the "radial" and "concertina" reforms are now only unambiguously welfare improving in the space of "shadow taxes."

BIBLIOGRAPHY

Abed, G., L. Ebrill, S. Gupta, B. Clements, R. McMorran, A. Pellechio, J. Schiff, and M. Verhoeven. 1998. "Fiscal Reforms in Low-Income Countries: Experience under IMF-Supported Programs." IMF Occasional Paper 160, International Monetary Fund, Washington, DC.

Ahmad, E., and S. Ludlow. 1989. "The Distributional Consequences of Tax Reform: On a VAT for Pakistan." PPR Working Paper 238, World Bank, Washington, DC.

Ahmad, E., and N. Stern. 1984. "Theory of Reform and Indian Indirect Taxes." *Journal of Public Economics* 25 (3): 259–98.

———. 1987. "Alternative Sources of Government Revenue: Illustrations from India, 1979–80." In *The Theory of Taxation for Developing Countries,* ed. D. Newbery and N. Stern, 281–332. Oxford: Oxford University Press.

———. 1990. "Tax Reform and Shadow Prices for Pakistan." *Oxford Economic Papers* 42: 135–59.

———. 1991. *The Theory and Practice of Tax Reform in Developing Countries.* Cambridge: Cambridge University Press.

Anderson, J. 1999. "Trade Reform with a Government Budget Constraint." In *International Trade Policy and the Pacific Rim,* ed. J. Piggott and A. Woodland. London: Macmillan.

Banks, J., R. Blundell, and A. Lewbel. 1996. "Tax Reform and Welfare Measurement: Do We Need Demand System Estimation?" *Economic Journal* 106 (438): 1227–41.

Barbone, L., A. Das-Gupta, L. De Wulf, and A. Hannson. 1999. "Reforming Tax Systems: The World Bank Record in the 1990s." Tax Policy and Administration Thematic Group, World Bank Institute, World Bank, Washington, DC.

Barrett, S., and P. Dorosh. 1996. "Farmers' Welfare and Changing Food Prices: Nonparametric Evidence from Rice in Madagascar." *American Journal of Agricultural Economics* 78 (3): 656–69.

Besley, T., and I. Preston. 1988. "Invariance and the Axiomatics of Income Tax Progression: A Comment." *Bulletin of Economic Research* 40 (1): 159–63.

Bevan, D., P. Collier, N. Gemmell, and D. Greenway, eds. 2000. *Trade and Fiscal Adjustment in Africa.* London: Macmillan.

Bird, R. 1992. *Tax Policy and Economic Development.* Baltimore: Johns Hopkins University Press.

Bourguignon, F., and L. Pereira da Silva, eds. 2005. *The Impact of Economic Policies on Poverty and Income Distribution: Evaluation Techniques and Tools.* New York: Oxford University Press.

Budd, J. 1993. "Changing Food Prices and Rural Welfare: A Non-Parametric Examination of the Côte d'Ivoire." *Economic Development and Cultural Change* 41 (3): 587–603.

Burgess, R., and N. Stern. 1993. "Taxation and Development." *Journal of Economic Literature* 31 (June): 762–830.

Case, A. 2000. "Implications of Policy Reform Given Income Distribution and Expenditure Patterns in South Africa." Paper presented at "Conference on Poverty and the International Economy," Stockholm, October 20–21.

Chen, D., J. Matovu, and R. Reinikka. 2001. "A Quest for Revenue and Tax Incidence in Uganda." IMF Working Paper 01/24, International Monetary Fund, Washington, DC.

Chen, S., and M. Ravallion. 2003. "Household Welfare Impacts of China's Accession to the World Trade Organization." Policy Research Working Paper 3040, World Bank, Washington, DC.

Chia, N.-C., S. Wahba, and J. Whalley. 2000. "Analyzing the Incidence of Taxes in the Côte d'Ivoire." In *Trade and Fiscal Adjustment in Africa,* ed. D. Bevan, P. Collier, N. Gemmell, and D. Greenway, 149–75. London: Macmillan.

Clarete, R. L. 1991. "A General Equilibrium Analysis of the Tax Burden and Institutional Distortions in the Philippines." In *Tax Policy in Developing Countries,* ed. J. Khalilzadeh-Shirazi and A. Shah, 188–200. Washington, DC: World Bank.

Coady, D. 1997a. "Agricultural Pricing Policies in Developing Countries: An Application to Pakistan." *International Tax and Public Finance* 4 (1): 39–57.

———. 1997b. "Fiscal Reform in Developing Countries." In *Fiscal Reforms in the Least Developed Countries,* ed. C. Patel, 18–46. Cheltenham, United Kingdom: Edward Elgar.

Coady, D., and J. Drèze. 2002. "Commodity Taxation and Social Welfare: The Generalized Ramsey Rule." *International Tax and Public Finance* 9 (3): 295–316.

Coady, D., and R. Harris. 2004. "Evaluating Transfer Programs within a General Equilibrium Framework." *Economic Journal* 114 (October): 778–99.

Coady, D., and D. Newhouse. 2005. "Ghana: Evaluation of the Distributional Impacts of Petroleum Price Reforms." Technical Assistance Report, Fiscal Affairs Department, International Monetary Fund, Washington, DC.

Coady, D., and E. Skoufias. 2004. "On the Targeting and Redistributive Efficiencies of Alternative Transfer Programs." *Review of Income and Wealth* 50 (1): 11–27.

Cornia, G. A., R. Jolly, and F. Stewart, eds. 1987. *Adjustment with a Human Face: Protecting the Vulnerable and Promoting Growth.* Vol. 1. Oxford: Clarendon Press.

Dahl, H., and P. Mitra. 1991. "Applying Tax Policy Models in Country Economic Work: Bangladesh, China, and India." In *Tax Policy in Developing Countries,* ed. J. Khalilzadeh-Shirazi and A. Shah, Washington, DC: World Bank.

Deaton, A. 1987. "Econometric Issues for Tax Design in Developing Countries." In *The Theory of Taxation for Developing Countries,* ed. D. Newbery and N. Stern, 92–113. New York: Oxford University Press.

———. 1988. "Quality, Quantity, and Spatial Variation in Price." *American Economic Review* 78 (3): 418–30.

———. 1989. "Rice Prices and Income Distribution in Thailand: A Non-Parametric Analysis." *Economic Journal* 99 (395), Conference Supplement, 1–37.

———. 1990. "Price Elasticities from Survey Data: Extensions and Indonesian Results." *Journal of Econometrics* 44 (3): 281–309.

———. 1995. "Data and Econometric Tools for Development Analysis." In *Handbook of Development Economics.* Vol. IIIa, ed. J. Behrman and T. Srinivasan, 1785–1882. Amsterdam: Elsevier.

———. 1997. *The Analysis of Household Surveys: A Microeconomic Approach to Development Policy.* Baltimore: Johns Hopkins University Press.

Deaton, A., and F. Grimard. 1992. "Demand Analysis for Tax Reform in Pakistan." LSMS Working Paper 85, World Bank, Washington, DC.

Deaton, A., and N. Stern. 1986. "Optimally Uniform Commodity Taxes, Taste Differences, and Lump-Sum Grants." *Economic Letters* 20: 263–66.

Dervis, K., J. de Melo, and S. Robinson. 1982. *General Equilibrium Models for Development Policy.* New York: Cambridge University Press.

Devarajan, S., and S. Hossain. 1995. "The Combined Incidence of Taxes and Public Expenditures in the Philippines." Policy Research Working Paper 1543, World Bank, Washington, DC.

Devarajan, S., K. Thierfelder, and S. Suthiwart-Narueput. 2001. "The Marginal Cost of Public Funds in Developing Countries." In *Policy Evaluations with Computable General Equilibrium Models,* ed. A. Fossati and W. Weigard, 39–55. London: Routledge.

Diamond, P. 1975. "A Many-Person Ramsey Rule." *Journal of Public Economics* 4: 335–42.

Diamond, P., and J. Mirrlees. 1971a. "Optimal Taxation and Public Production I: Production Efficiency." *American Economic Review* 61 (1): 8–27.

———. 1971b. "Optimal Taxation and Public Production II: Tax Rules." *American Economic Review* 61 (3): 261–78.

———. 1975. "Private Constant Returns and Public Shadow Prices." *Review of Economic Studies* 43 (1): 41–47.

Dixit, A. K. 1975. "Welfare Effects of Tax and Price Changes." *Journal of Public Economics* 4 (2): 103–23.

———. 1985. "Tax Policy in Open Economies." In *Handbook of Public Economics,* ed. A. Auerbach and M. Feldstein, Vol. 1, Chap. 6, 313–74. Amsterdam: North-Holland.

Drèze, J., and N. Stern. 1987. "The Theory of Cost-Benefit Analysis." In *Handbook of Public Economics,* ed. A. Auerbach and M. Feldstein, Vol. 2, Chap. 14, 909–89. Amsterdam: North-Holland.

Ebrill, L., J. Stotsky, and R. Gropp. 1999. "Revenue Implications of Trade Liberalization." IMF Occasional Paper 180, International Monetary Fund, Washington, DC.

Emran, M. S., and J. E. Stiglitz. 2005. "On Selective Indirect Tax Reform in Developing Countries." *Journal of Public Economics* 89 (4): 599–623.

Federico, G., J. Daniel, and B. Bingham. 2001. "Domestic Petroleum Price Smoothing in Developing and Transition Countries." IMF Working Paper 75, International Monetary Fund, Washington, DC.

Fletcher, K. 2005. "Increasing Public Sector Revenue in the Philippines: Equity and Efficiency Considerations." IMF Working Paper 22, International Monetary Fund, Washington, DC.

Fourie, F., and A. Owen. 1993. "Value-Added Tax and Regressivity in South Africa." *South African Journal of Economics* 61 (4): 281.

Gemmell, N. 1987. "Taxation and Development: A Survey." In *Surveys in Development Economics,* ed. N. Gemmell, 269–306. Oxford: Basil Blackwell.

Gemmell, N., and O. Morrissey. 2003. "Tax Structure and the Incidence on the Poor in Developing Countries." CREDIT Research Paper 03/18, University of Nottingham, Nottingham, United Kingdom.

———. 2005. "Distributional and Poverty Impacts of Tax Structure Reform in Developing Countries: How Little We Know." *Development Policy Review* 23 (2): 131–44.

Gibson, J. 1998. "Indirect Tax Reform and the Poor in Papua New Guinea." *Pacific Economic Bulletin* 13 (20): 29–39.

Gillingham, R., and M. El-Said. 2005. "Jordan: Distributional Effects of Eliminating Subsidies for Petroleum Products." Technical Assistance Report, Fiscal Affairs Department, International Monetary Fund, Washington, DC.

Gillingham, R., and P. Medas. 2005. "Bolivia: Distributional Effects of Reducing Subsidies to Hydrocarbon Products." Report, Fiscal Affairs Department, International Monetary Fund, Washington, DC.

Gillis, M., ed. 1989. *Tax Reform in Developing Countries.* Durham, NC: Duke University Press.

Go, D., M. Kearney, S. Robinson, and K. Thierfelder. 2005. "An Analysis of South Africa's Value-Added Tax." Unpublished manuscript, World Bank, Washington, DC.

Guesnerie, R. 1979. "General Statements of Second-Best Pareto Optimality." *Journal of Mathematical Economics* 6: 169–94.

Gunning, J. W., and M. Keyser. 1995. "Applied General Equilibrium Models for Policy Analysis." In *Handbook of Development Economics,* ed. J. Behrman and T. Srinivasan, Vol. III, Chap. 35, 2025–2107. Amsterdam: Elsevier.

Gupta, S., M. Verhoeven, R. Gillingham, C. Schiller, A. Mansoor, and J. P. Cordoba. 2000. "Equity and Efficiency in the Reform of Price Subsidies." Report, International Monetary Fund, Washington, DC.

Gupta, S., M. Plant, B. Clements, T. Dorsey, E. Baldacci, G. Inchauste, S. Tareq, and N. Thacker. 2002. "Is the PRGF Living Up to Expectations?: An Assessment of Program Design." IMF Occasional Paper 216, International Monetary Fund, Washington, DC.

Harrison, G. W., T. F. Rutherford, and D. G. Tarr. 1993. "Piecemeal Trade Reform in the Partially Liberalized Economy of Turkey." *World Bank Economic Review*, 7 (May): 191–217.

Heady, C. 2001. "Taxation Policy in Low-Income Countries." WIDER Discussion Paper 2001/81, United Nations University–World Institute for Development Economics Research, Helsinki.

Heady, C., and P. Mitra. 1982. "Restricted Redistributive Taxation, Shadow Prices, and Trade Policy." *Journal of Public Economics* 17 (1): 1–22.

———. 1987. "Optimal Taxation and Shadow Prices in a Developing Economy." In *The Theory of Taxation for Developing Countries,* ed. D. Newbery and N. Stern, 407–25. New York: Oxford University Press.

Hertel, T., and J. Reimer. 2004. "Predicting the Poverty Impacts of Trade Liberalization: A Survey." Unpublished manuscript, World Bank, Washington, DC.

Hossain, S. 1995. "The Equity Impact of the Value-Added Tax in Bangladesh." IMF Staff Papers 42 (June): 411–32.

———. 2003. "Poverty and Social Impact Analysis: A Suggested Framework." IMF Working Paper 03/195, International Monetary Fund, Washington, DC.

Hughes, G. 1986. "A New Method for Estimating the Effects of Fuel Taxes: An Application to Thailand." *World Bank Economic Review* 1 (1): 65–101.

———. 1987. "The Incidence of Fuel Taxes: A Comparative Study of Three Countries." In *The Theory of Taxation for Developing Countries,* ed. D. Newbery and N. Stern, 533–59. New York: Oxford University Press.

Julius, D., and A. Alicbusan. 1989. "Public Sector Pricing Policies: A Review of Bank Policy and Practice." Policy Planning and Research Working Paper 49, World Bank, Washington, DC.

Keen, M., and J. Ligthart. 2002. "Coordinating Tariff Reduction and Domestic Tax Reform." *Journal of International Economics* 56 (2): 489–507.

Keen, M., and A. Simone. 2004. "Tax Policy in Developing Countries: Some Lessons from the 1990s and Some Challenges Ahead." In *Helping Countries Develop: The Role of Fiscal Policy,* ed. S. Gupta, B. Clements, and G. Inchauste, 302–52. Washington, DC: International Monetary Fund.

Kehoe, T., T. Srinivasan, and J. Whalley, eds. 2005. *Frontiers in Applied General Equilibrium Models.* Cambridge: Cambridge University Press.

Khalilzadeh-Shirazi, J., and A. Shah, eds. 1991. *Tax Policy in Developing Countries.* Washington, DC: World Bank.

Krueger, A. O., M. Schiff, and A. Valdès. 1988. "Agricultural Incentives in Developing Countries: Measuring the Effect of Sectoral and Economy-Wide Policies." *World Bank Economic Review* 2 (3): 255–71.

———. 1991. *The Political Economy of Agricultural Pricing Policy.* 5 vols. Baltimore: Johns Hopkins University Press.

Little, I., and J. Mirrlees. 1974. *Project Appraisal and Planning in Developing Countries.* London: Heinemann.

Löfgren, H. 2000. "Trade Reform and the Poor in Morocco: A Rural-Urban General Equilibrium Analysis of Reduced Protection." In *Earnings Inequality, Unemployment, and Poverty in the Middle East and North Africa,* ed. W. Shahin and G. Dibeh, Chap. 4. Westport, CT: Greenwood Press.

Mas-Colell, A., M. Whinston, and J. Green. 1995. *Microeconomic Theory.* New York: Oxford University Press.

McCulloch, N., A. Winters, and X. Cirera. 2001. *Trade Liberalization and Poverty: A Handbook.* London: Centre for Economic Policy Research and Department for International Development.

Minot, N., and F. Goletti. 2000. "Rice Market Liberalization and Poverty in Vietnam." Research Report 114, International Food Policy Research Institute, Washington, DC.

Muñoz, S., and S. Cho. 2004. "Social Impact of a Tax Reform: The Case of Ethiopia." In *Helping Countries Develop: The Role of Fiscal Policy,* ed. S. Gupta, B. Clements, and G. Inchauste. Washington, DC: International Monetary Fund.

Newbery, D. 1986. "On the Desirability of Input Taxes." *Economic Letters* 20: 267–70.

Newbery, D., and N. Stern, eds. 1987. *The Theory of Taxation for Developing Countries.* New York: Oxford University Press.

Nicita, A. 2004a. "Who Benefited from Trade Liberalization in Mexico: Measuring the Effects on Household Welfare." Policy Research Working Paper 3265, World Bank, Washington, DC.

———. 2004b. "Efficiency and Equity of a Marginal Tax Reform: Income, Quality, and Price Elasticities for Mexico." Policy Research Working Paper 3266, World Bank, Washington, DC.

Patel, C., ed. 1997. *Fiscal Reforms in the Least Developed Countries.* Cheltenham, United Kingdom: Edward Elgar.

Perry, G., J. Whalley, and G. McMahon, eds. 2000. *Fiscal Reform and Structural Change in Developing Countries.* 2 vols. London: Macmillan.

Pfahler, W. 1987. "Redistributive Effects of Tax Progressivity: Evaluating a General Class of Aggregate Measures." *Public Finance* 42 (3): 1–31.

Pfingsten, A. 1986. "The Measurement of Tax Progression." Studies in Contemporary Economics, 20. Berlin: Springer Verlag.

Pinstrup-Andersen, P., ed. 1988a. *Food Subsidies in Developing Countries: Costs, Benefits, and Policy Options.* Baltimore: Johns Hopkins University Press.

———. 1988b. "Macroeconomic Adjustment and Human Nutrition." *Food Policy* 13 (1): 37–46.

Porto, G. 2003a. "Trade Reforms, Market Access, and Poverty in Argentina." Policy Research Working Paper 3135, World Bank, Washington, DC.

———. 2003b. "Using Survey Data to Access the Distributional Effects of Trade Policy." Unpublished manuscript, Development Research Group, World Bank, Washington, DC.

Rajemison, H., S. Haggblade, and S. Younger. 2003. "Indirect Tax Incidence in Madagascar: Updated Estimates Using the Input-Output Table." Working Paper 147, Cornell Food and Nutrition Policy Program, Cornell University, Ithaca, NY.

Ramsey, F. 1927. "A Contribution to the Theory of Taxation." *Economic Journal* 37 (March): 47–61.

Ravallion, M. 1990. "Rural Welfare Effects of Food Price Changes under Induced Wage Responses: Theory and Evidence for Bangladesh." *Oxford Economic Papers* 42: 574–85.

Ravallion, M., and M. Lokshin. 2004. "Gainers and Losers from Trade Reform in Morocco." Policy Research Working Paper 3368, World Bank, Washington, DC.

Ravallion, M., and D. van de Walle. 1991. "The Impact on Poverty of Food Price Reforms: A Welfare Analysis for Indonesia." *Journal of Policy Modeling* 13 (2): 281–99.

Refaqat, S. 2003. "Social Incidence of the General Sales Tax in Pakistan." IMF Working Paper 216, International Monetary Fund, Washington, DC.

Reimer, J. 2002. "Estimating the Poverty Impacts of Trade Liberalization." Policy Research Working Paper 2790, World Bank, Washington, DC.

Sadoulet, E., and A. de Janvry. 1992. "Agricultural Trade Liberalization and the Low-Income Countries: A General Equilibrium-Multimarket Approach." *American Journal of Agricultural Economics* 74 (2): 268–80.

Sahn, D., and S. Younger. 1999. "Fiscal Incidence in Africa: Microeconomic Evidence." Working Paper 91, Cornell Food and Nutrition Policy Program, Cornell University, Ithaca, NY.

Shah, A., and J. Whalley. 1991. "The Redistributive Impact of Taxation in Developing Countries." In *Tax Policy in Developing Countries*, ed. J. Khalilzadeh-Shirazi and A. Shah, 166–87. Washington, DC: World Bank.

Sobarzo, H. 2000. "Interactions between Trade and Tax Reform in Mexico: Some General Equilibrium Results." In *Fiscal Reform and Structural Change in Developing Countries*, ed. G. Perry, J. Whalley, and G. McMahon, Vol. 1. London: Macmillan.

Stern, N. 1987. "The Effects of Taxation, Price Control, and Government Contracts in Oligopoly and Monopolistic Competition." *Journal of Public Economics* 32: 133–58.

Stiglitz, J. E., and P. S. Dasgupta. 1971. "Differential Taxation, Public Goods, and Economic Efficiency." *Review of Economic Studies* 38 (114): 151–74.

Tanzi, V. 1987. "Quantitative Characteristics of the Tax Systems of Developing Countries." In *The Theory of Taxation for Developing Countries*, ed. D. Newbery and N. Stern, Vol. 2, 205–41. New York: Oxford University Press.

———. 2000. "Taxation and Economic Structure." In *Fiscal Reform and Structural Change in Developing Countries*, ed. G. Perry, J. Whalley, and G. McMahon, Vol. 2, Chap. 8. London: Macmillan.

Tareq, S., J. Ligthart, A. Segura-Ubiergo, N. Wandwasi, and I. Izvorski. 2005. "Bosnia and Herzegovina: Assessing the Distributional Impact of a VAT."

Technical Assistance Report, Fiscal Affairs Department, International Monetary Fund, Washington, DC.

Thirsk, W., ed. 1997. *Tax Reform in Developing Countries.* Washington, DC: World Bank.

Trairatvorakul, P. 1984. "The Effects on Income Distribution and Nutrition of Alternative Rice Price Policies in Thailand." Research Report 46, International Food Policy Research Institute, Washington, DC.

Triest, R. 1990. "The Relationship between the Marginal Cost of Public Funds and Marginal Excess Burden." *American Economic Review* 80 (3): 557–66.

Warr, P. 2001. "Welfare and Distributional Effects of an Export Tax: Thailand's Rice Premium." *American Journal of Agricultural Economics* 83 (4): 903–20.

Theoretical Approach to Evaluating the Social Welfare Impact of Price Reforms

The empirical literature evaluating the welfare impact of changes (or "reforms") in commodity taxes or prices covers a broad range of methodological approaches, which can be usefully classified according to whether they are general equilibrium, partial equilibrium, or somewhere in between (often referred to as limited general equilibrium or multimarket models). In this annex, a general equilibrium model is set out that captures the key ingredients of any analysis of the welfare impacts of reforms in commodity taxes or prices. The model helps to clarify the three different roles played by commodity taxation and price controls, namely, resource mobilization (that is, government revenue), resource reallocation (or efficiency), and resource redistribution (or equity). Although the primary concern will be the distributional consequences of price changes, a comprehensive evaluation of such reforms must recognize the other dimensions of these reforms since these may be the main factors motivating the reforms in the first place and can be expected to have important implications for household welfare. For example, price changes may reflect the desire to reform the structure of commodity taxes to raise either the same or greater revenue more efficiently. Or the price changes may reflect a desire to make public sector prices better reflect the true cost of meeting demand. If revenues increase, these may be used to enhance the coverage of social safety nets among the poorest households or to expand access to valuable publicly supplied services such as education, health-nutrition, or various types of physical infrastructure. A comprehensive evaluation of price effects therefore needs to take all these implications into account.

The next section describes the model and derives the analytical equations used to identify the main ingredients in a general equilibrium analysis of the welfare impacts of *marginal* reforms. This analysis is then used to interpret partial equilibrium analyses as a special case, making explicit the assumptions behind these analyses. How an analysis needs to be adapted for the evaluation of nonmarginal tax and price reforms is also briefly discussed. The final section examines the various data and modeling requirements of each approach and the trade-offs inherent in these choices.

THE MODEL

Consider an economy made up of households (denoted by superscript $h=1,H$), producers (denoted by superscript $g=1,G$), and the government.[33] Households choose consumption bundles (x^h) based on the following constrained maximization problem:

$$\text{Max } U^h(x^h) \quad \text{s.t.} \quad q.x^h = m^h$$

$$x_i^h \leq \tilde{x}_i^h \qquad \text{for each } i,$$

where $x(q, \tilde{x}^h, m^h)$ is an n-dimensional vector of net demands of household h, x_i^h is the consumption of commodity i by household h (with $i=1,N$), $\tilde{x}_i^h$ is a vector of rationing constraints faced by the household, q is a vector of consumer prices (with factor prices entering as negative numbers), and m^h is the lump-sum income of household h. The vector x of net consumer demands has the standard properties with respect to q and m^h.[34] The lump-sum income of household h consists of the sum of the household's share in private profits and a lump-sum transfer (r^h) from the government:

$$m^h \equiv r^h + \sum_g \theta^{hg} \Pi^g \qquad (5.1)$$

where $\Pi^g \equiv p \cdot y^g$ is the profit of firm g, θ^{hg} is the share of household h in firm g's profit, p is a vector of producer prices, and y^g is the net supply vector (or "production plan") of firm g.

Producers choose net supply vectors y^g (with positive entries for outputs and negative entries for inputs) to maximize the following profit maximization problem:

$$\text{Max } p \cdot y^g \quad \text{s.t.} \quad y^g \Leftrightarrow Y^g$$

$$y_i^g \leq \tilde{y}_i^g \qquad \text{for each } i,$$

where $\tilde{y}_i^g$ is an n-dimensional vector of quantity constraints, and Y^g is the production set of firm g, which is assumed to be convex.[35] The solution is denoted by $y^g(p, \tilde{y}^g)$ and has the standard properties with respect to p, the vector of producer prices.[36]

Let $(\mathbf{p}, \mathbf{t}, \{\bar{\mathbf{x}}^h\}, \{\bar{\mathbf{y}}^g\}, \{r^h\}, \{\theta^{hg}\})$ be the vector of "signals" to which households and firms respond. These signals can be partitioned into two types: exogenous signals (or "parameters") and control variables. The social planner chooses among the set of variables under his or her control (the control variables), taking other variables (that is, exogenous variables) as given, to maximize social welfare, subject to a set of scarcity constraints (that is, the constraint that demands equal supplies) and its own budget or revenue constraint (discussed below). If the set of control variables is denoted by $\mathbf{s}$, and the set of exogenous variables is denoted by $\boldsymbol{\omega}$, then the planner's problem can be written as choosing the former to:

$$\text{Max } W\left(\ldots, V^h\left(\mathbf{s}; \boldsymbol{\omega}\right), \ldots\right) \text{s.t.} \quad \sum_h \mathbf{x}^h\left(\mathbf{s}; \boldsymbol{\omega}\right) - \sum_g \mathbf{y}^g\left(\mathbf{s}; \boldsymbol{\omega}\right) = 0,$$

where $V^h(.)$ is the household's indirect utility function, and $W(.)$ is a Bergson-Samuelson social welfare function. If $V^*(\mathbf{s}; \boldsymbol{\omega})$ denotes the maximum value function of this problem, then, from the envelope theorem, the gradient of V^* is the same as the gradient of the following Lagrangian:

$$L = W\left(\ldots, V^h\left(\mathbf{s}, \boldsymbol{\omega}\right), \ldots\right) - \boldsymbol{v}\left[\mathbf{x}(\mathbf{s}, \boldsymbol{\omega}) - \mathbf{y}(\mathbf{s}, \boldsymbol{\omega})\right],$$

where $\mathbf{x} \equiv \sum_h \mathbf{x}^h$ and $\mathbf{y} \equiv \sum_g \mathbf{y}^g$ denote the aggregate (net) consumer demands and aggregate (net) producer supplies, respectively, and $\boldsymbol{v}$ is a vector of Lagrangian multipliers or *shadow prices*. If ω_k is a particular component of the vector $\boldsymbol{\omega}$ of parameters (such as a tax or lump-sum transfer), then the social value of a marginal change in ω_k (or the "marginal social value of ω_k," the "reform" MSV_k) is:

$$MSV_k \equiv \frac{\partial V^*}{\partial \omega_k} \equiv \frac{\partial L}{\partial \omega_k} = \sum_h \frac{\partial W}{\partial V^h} \frac{\partial V^h}{\partial \omega_k} - \boldsymbol{v} \cdot \frac{\partial(x - y)}{\partial \omega_k}.$$

The first term on the r.h.s. is the *direct* effect on social welfare, and the second term is the *indirect* effect capturing the social value of the additional excess demands generated by the proposed reform. Note that the shadow prices will also depend on the specification of "choice variables."

So far, the government's budget constraint has not been explicitly introduced. However, by Walras' law, if commodity markets balance, then so, too, does the remaining government budget constraint. Then, as shown by Drèze and Stern (1987), using Walras' law, the above Lagrangian can be equivalently rewritten as:

$$L\left(\mathbf{s}; \boldsymbol{\omega}\right) = W\left(\ldots, V^h\left(\mathbf{s}; \boldsymbol{\omega}\right), \ldots\right) + \lambda R,$$

where R is the "shadow revenue" of the government defined as:

$$R \equiv \tau \cdot x + \tau^p \cdot y + \sum_g \theta^{0g} \prod^g - \sum_h r^h \qquad (5.2)$$

where $\tau \equiv (\mathbf{q}-\mathbf{v}^*)$ and $\tau^p \equiv (\mathbf{v}^*-\mathbf{p})$ can be interpreted as "shadow consumer taxes" and "shadow producer taxes," respectively, and $\mathbf{v}^* \equiv \mathbf{v}/\lambda$ is a vector of normalized shadow prices. Note that λ, the shadow value of government revenue, is basically a normalization parameter: a different cardinalization of the social welfare function $W(.)$ leads to a different λ, but leaves $\mathbf{v}^* \equiv \mathbf{v}/\lambda$ unchanged. This reformulation is very useful in that it converts this complex general equilibrium model into a more standard format of a trade-off between consumer welfare and (shadow) government revenue.

The relationship between shadow prices and market prices will depend on both the structure of markets and government policy. For example, for a small open economy, the shadow price of traded goods is the world price, and a tariff will drive a wedge between market prices and shadow prices with $\mathbf{q}=\mathbf{p}>\mathbf{v}^*$. For nontraded goods, the shadow price is the marginal social cost of production so that, for example, if the government keeps the price of such a publicly supplied good below this level, this gives $\mathbf{q}=\mathbf{p}<\mathbf{v}^*$. Imported commodities subject to binding import quotas can be treated as nontraded goods since extra demand must be met through increased domestic production.

PRICE REFORMS

The above model is now used to derive analytical equations for evaluating the welfare impact of a marginal change in the consumer price of commodity i (that is, dq_i), for example, because of a change in the tax rate or a change in public sector pricing. Differentiating the Lagrangian w.r.t. q_i (and assuming that producer prices are fixed[37]) gives:

$$dW \equiv \frac{\partial L}{\partial q_i} dq_i \equiv -\sum_h \beta^h x_i^j dq_i + \lambda \left(x_i + \tau \cdot \frac{\partial x}{\partial q_i} \right) \cdot dq_i \qquad (5.3)$$

where $\beta^h \equiv \dfrac{\partial W}{\partial V^h} \dfrac{\partial V^h}{\partial m^h}$ is the social valuation of the marginal utility of extra income to household h, more commonly referred to as the "social marginal utility of income" or the "welfare weight." This weight is higher for lower-income households, which reflects a concern for income inequality.

The first term in (5.3) gives the *direct effect* on household welfare of the price change and simply says that, for marginal price changes, the level of household consumption gives a money measure of the welfare loss from a price increase; this is valued using the social welfare weight of each household. The second term in brackets gives the *indirect effect* on social welfare arising from the change in consumer demands brought about by the price change, which leads, in turn, to a change in revenue that reflects a more or less efficient pattern of consumption and production.

To illustrate, consider the case in which the price reform involves an increase in the price of a publicly supplied nontraded commodity that was previously priced below the marginal cost of production; so $\tau<0$ for this commodity, leading to a excessively high level of consumption. The price increase will lead to an efficiency gain when it results in a decrease in the demand for this commodity, and this will show up in higher government revenue. If the price increase leads to a shift in the demand toward other commodities that have consumer prices above (below) the shadow value, then this will also lead, ceteris paribus, to a more (less) efficient pattern of consumption and production, and this will again show up as an increase (decrease) in revenue. So increases (decreases) in revenue are associated with more (less) efficient consumption and production patterns. Note that the indirect effect is likely to be relatively large when demand responses are large or existing price distortions (that is, shadow taxes) are large.

The above equation provides a useful focus for classifying the various methodologies used in the empirical literature evaluating the welfare impact of price reforms. These can be categorized into three different types of approaches: (1) general equilibrium, (2) limited general equilibrium, and (3) partial equilibrium.[38] Equation (5.3) gives the full *general equilibrium* welfare impact of a price change and requires one to allow for responses in all commodity and factor markets. *Limited general equilibrium* approaches focus on a few key markets or only on the demand side of the economy. For example, "multimarket models" typically focus only on key agricultural sectors in the analysis of agricultural price reforms. "Demand-side models" implicitly assume producer prices are fixed, focus on household demand responses, and ignore producer responses. Both approaches ignore factor market responses. *Partial equilibrium* approaches ignore responses completely.[39] In the text, the empirical literature is reviewed in detail using the above three classifications.

The above discussion has also focused on *marginal* price reforms, although, in practice, price reforms are often sizable, so that second-order (and higher-order) welfare effects are likely to be important. However, it is straightforward to incorporate this aspect into the above analysis. For the direct welfare effect on households (that is, partial equilibrium approaches), the first expression is simply replaced by an estimate of the compensating or equivalent variation of a price change (Triest 1990). This, of course, involves estimating demand responses, at least in the relevant market. The size of the price response determines how much the direct welfare impact of the price reform differs between "marginal" and "nonmarginal" reforms, with the former tending to be an overestimate (underestimate) of the latter, reflecting the abilities of households to switch away from (toward) a commodity whose price has increased (decreased). Note also that these responses may, in principle, differ substantially across income groups and that this could have important implications for the distribution of welfare changes.

For nonmarginal reforms, one should, in principle, also replace "local" estimates of responses by estimates of responses over the related price change. In addition, the assumption of constant producer prices is less likely to be valid; one may therefore want to model the supply side of the economy more explicitly. One also needs to consider the implications for what constitutes the appropriate shadow price and whether this changes with the reform, for example, the extreme case in which the price increase results in the commodity being exported rather than imported.

The obvious advantage of analyzing marginal reforms is that the data requirements are less demanding since one only needs information on the pattern of consumption across households (for the direct effect) and estimates of aggregate price elasticities (for the indirect effect). Cross-sectional household surveys, which are now widely available, typically provide sufficient data for these purposes.

Note, however, that the above model implicitly assumes all consumption could be taxed. In many developing countries, especially for agricultural commodities, households consume some or all of what they produce (own-consumption), so that this proportion of consumption cannot be taxed. In this case, it is useful to treat these "producers" as if they were part of the household sector, and replace total consumption by "net trades" and consumption elasticities by net trade elasticities in (5.3).[40] Note that the pattern of net trades across households—for example, if poor and landless households are net consumers of food and large-landholder households are net producers—may increase the distributional power of price controls since low prices are effectively a subsidy to the poor that is financed by a tax on the rich. However, since net trade elasticities are likely to be relatively large, such price controls are likely to be extremely distortionary, so that more efficient transfer instruments probably exist.

It is also common for studies to focus explicitly on the distribution of direct and indirect welfare impacts across households in different parts of the income distribution. To focus on income distribution, it is useful to rewrite (5.3) above as:

$$dW = -\sum_h \beta^h x_i^h dq_i + \lambda \eta x_i dq_i \qquad (5.4)$$

where $\eta \equiv \dfrac{x_i + \tau \dfrac{\partial x}{\partial q_i}}{x_i}$ captures the size of the indirect welfare effect relative to the aggregate direct income effect.[41] Fully differentiating the social welfare function and assuming that lump-sum incomes and government revenue are constant and that the price of commodity i is controlled by the government gives:

$$dW \equiv -\sum_h \beta^h x_i^h dq_i - \sum_h \sum_{j \neq i} \beta^h x_j^h dq_j \qquad (5.5)$$

Equating the last term on r.h.s. of (5.4) to that in (5.5) gives:

$$dW = \left[-\sum_h \beta^h \frac{x_i^h}{x_i} - \frac{\sum_h \sum_{j \neq i} \beta^h x_j^h dq_j}{\sum_h \sum_j x_j^h dq_j} \frac{\sum_h \sum_j x_j^j dq_j}{x_i dq_i} \right]$$

$$\cdot x_i \cdot dq_i \equiv -(\lambda_D - \lambda_1 \mu) x_i dq_i \qquad (5.6)$$

where λ_D and λ_1 capture the distributional impact of the direct and indirect income effects, respectively (arising solely from changes in commodity and factor prices), and μ captures the efficiency impacts of the price reform. The distributional parameters are essentially a weighted average of welfare weights, whereby the weights are the share of each household in the total direct and indirect income effects, respectively. For example, in the absence of any efficiency effects, welfare will only increase if the direct income effect is distributed more (less) progressively (regressively) than the indirect income effects, that is, if $\lambda_D > \lambda_1$. The efficiency parameter μ is greater than 1 if there are additional efficiency gains from the reforms.

Analyses of the distributional impacts of reforms typically capture these effects through indexes similar to λ_D above (Coady and Skoufias 2004). For example, if welfare weights are {1,0} for {poor, non-poor}, then this distributional index is equivalent to the share of the aggregate income effect accruing to the poor. One could also use the concentration coefficient, which aggregates income shares based on household rankings in the income distribution (regardless of the size of income differences). One may likewise look at the posttransfer distribution of income and compare it to the pretransfer distribution using inequality indexes such as the Gini coefficient, the Atkinson index, and the General Entropy Family of inequality indexes. Since these indexes either explicitly or implicitly assume some underlying welfare weights, it is therefore important to undertake sensitivity analyses. Alternatively, one could simply present numbers on the shares accruing to households in the various income deciles or plot the related concentration curves.

One may wish to focus on the size of the income effects (and not merely the distribution) to understand the proportionate change in household incomes and the resulting effects on income poverty and to inform a policy discussion on the design of appropriate compensating policy measures. One may also wish to understand the distributional effects across socioeconomic groupings (for example, by region or ethnic group) to understand the implications for horizontal (as opposed to vertical) equity or for political economy.

Alternative Price-Shifting Models

In general, tax and price reforms will involve changes in the prices of intermediate goods. The extent to which these price changes are passed forward onto output prices or backward onto factor prices will depend on, for example, the structure of the economy (how substitutable different commodities are with internationally traded goods) and the degree of control the government has over prices in general. To the extent that taxes are pushed forward onto output prices, the actual tax content of the final equilibrium price, that is, the "effective tax" (t^e), will exceed the nominal or statutory tax on the sector (t). Obviously, subsidies on intermediate goods may mean that $t^e < t$.

In addition, in practice, existing tax systems in developing countries include a range of different tax components (such as excise taxes, trade taxes, and VAT), and some sectors fall outside the tax sector (for instance, agriculture, the informal sector, and sectors "exempt" from VAT). It is therefore important, in modeling the price effects of tax reforms, to capture these important features of the tax system, which can be expected to have significant implications for the equity and efficiency effects of tax reforms.

In this annex, a simple price-shifting model is set out that can be used to capture these different features of a tax system and that simply requires the use of the available data on the input-output structure of the economy. The model allows for different degrees of tradedness within each aggregate sector of the input-output table. Note that, to the extent that price changes are not pushed forward onto output prices, the changes must be pushed backward onto factor prices. The model presented does not follow through the implications of these factor-price changes or the changes in output prices. The model is very similar in spirit to that presented in Hughes (1986) and also has much in common with the effective tax model of Ahmad and Stern (1984, 1991).[42] Once price changes have been calculated, one can apply these to household-level consumption data (as discussed in the main chapter) to evaluate the household real-income effect of the equilibrium output-price changes.

A PRICE-SHIFTING MODEL FOR ENERGY TAXATION

The implications of the higher costs for output or factor prices will, of course, depend on the structure of the economy (for example, whether commodities are traded internationally or nontraded), the nature of commodity taxes, and the extent to which prices are controlled by the government. Commodities are therefore first grouped into three broad classifications, reflecting the assumed relationships between higher production costs and output prices:

- *Cost-push sectors:* These are sectors in which higher input costs are pushed fully onto output prices. One can therefore (loosely) think of these as nontraded commodities.
- *Traded sectors:* These are sectors that compete with internationally traded goods and for which the output prices are determined by world prices and the import or export tax regime. Therefore, higher input costs are not pushed forward onto output prices; the brunt of these higher costs is thus borne through lower factor prices or lower profits.
- *Controlled sectors:* These are sectors in which output prices are controlled by the government. Therefore, the relationship between output prices and production costs depends on whether and how the government adjusts the controlled prices. If the controlled prices are not adjusted, then the burden of the higher costs will be borne by factor prices, profits, or government revenue.

In modeling *price changes,* it is useful to think of "aggregate" commodity categories (for example, the aggregate categories available from an input-output table) as made up of a certain proportion of cost-push, traded, and controlled commodities; these proportions can be given by α, β, and γ, respectively. These proportions should obviously sum to unity and never be negative, that is:

$$0 \leq (\alpha, \beta, \gamma) \leq 1$$

$$\alpha + \beta + \gamma = 1$$

Alternatively, one could interpret these proportions as capturing the degree of tradedness of a single commodity.

The technology of domestic firms is captured by a standard input-output coefficient matrix, A, with the typical a_{ij} denoting the cost of input i in producing one unit of output j; one might think of units of output defined such that they have a user price of unity, so that price changes can be interpreted as percentage changes. Consistent with the interpretation that A captures an underlying Leontief (that is, fixed-coefficient) production technology, one can interpret a_{ij}'s as the change in the cost of producing a unit of j caused by a unit change in the price of input i.

For *traded* sectors, user prices, q^*, are determined by world prices, p^w, and by trade taxes (including tariffs and sales taxes), t^*:

$$q^* = p^w + t^* \tag{5.7}$$

and $q^* = p^* - t^*$, since taxes on domestic production alone (as opposed to international trade) do not affect user prices, but are, instead, pushed backward onto lower producer prices and, in turn, lower factor payments and profits. In this sense, foreign goods are deemed to be perfectly competitive with domestically produced traded goods. Changes in the user prices for traded sectors are then given by:

$$\Delta q^* = \Delta p^w + \Delta t^* \tag{5.7'}$$

and both terms on the r.h.s. will be specified exogenously by the reform package under consideration.

For *controlled* sectors, producer prices are determined by pricing controls (say, $\tilde{p}$), and one can think of domestic taxes as zero for convenience, so that:

$$\tilde{q} = \tilde{p} \tag{5.8}$$

Alternatively, one could think of the difference between user prices and average unit production costs as an implicit tax, with the revenue accruing to the public sector enterprise and thus entering government revenue through the quasi-fiscal side of the budget. The formula for price changes is then given simply as:

$$\Delta \tilde{q} = \Delta \tilde{p} \tag{5.8'}$$

where the r.h.s. is specified exogenously in the reform package.

For *cost-push* sectors, the relationship between user and producer prices is given by:

$$q^c = p^c + t^c \tag{5.9}$$

where q^c is the price paid by users of a commodity, and p^c the price received by producers; the difference between these is any sales or excise taxes, t^c, imposed by the government. Producer prices are, in turn, determined as follows:

$$p^c = p^c(q, w) \tag{5.10}$$

where q is the user costs of intermediate inputs, and w is factor prices. For these sectors, cost increases are assumed to be fully pushed forward onto user prices, so that factor payments are fixed. From (5.9), one gets:

$$\Delta q^c = \Delta p^c + \Delta t^c \tag{5.10'}$$

Using (5.10) and the input-output coefficient matrix and assuming that factor prices are fixed, the change in producer prices is derived as:

$$\Delta p^c = \Delta q^c.\alpha.A + \Delta q^{*}.\beta.A + \Delta \tilde{p}.\gamma.A \tag{5.11}$$

where Δ signifies a price change; all price changes are interpreted as $n \times 1$ row vectors, where n is the number of commodity groups; (α, β, γ) are now $n \times n$ diagonal matrices, and A is a $n \times n$ input-output coefficient matrix. Substituting in from (5.10)' for Δq^c and using (5.7)' for Δq^*, one gets:

$$\Delta p^c = \Delta p^c.\alpha.A + \Delta t^c.\alpha.A + \Delta p^w.\beta.A + \Delta t^{*}.\beta.A + \Delta \tilde{p}.\gamma.A,$$

so that:

$$\Delta p^c = \Delta t^c.\alpha.A.K + \Delta p^w.\beta.A, K + \Delta t^{*}.\beta.A.K + \Delta \tilde{p}.\gamma.A.K \tag{5.12}$$

where $K=(I-\alpha.A)^{-1}$, I being a $n \times n$ identity matrix. The typical element of the inverse matrix K, k_{ij}, captures the combined direct and indirect use of cost-push sector i used to produce one unit of cost-push sector j. Notice that, if the only price changes are changes in controlled prices, then one has $\Delta t^c = \Delta p^w = \Delta t^* = 0$, so that the final term of (5.12) gives the effect on cost-push sectors of a change in these controlled prices and also $\Delta q^c = \Delta p^c$.

The change in sector aggregate prices is then given by:

$$\Delta q = \alpha.\Delta q^c + \beta.\Delta q^{*} + \gamma.\Delta \tilde{q} \tag{5.13}$$

This price change is analogous to the effective tax calculations by Ahmad and Stern (1984, 1991), except the model of these authors assumes that imported goods are perfect complements to domestically traded goods, whereas the current model assumes different degrees of substitutability with imported goods.

A PRICE-SHIFTING MODEL FOR VAT REFORMS

For the purpose of deriving the price effects of tax reforms, the study categorizes goods and services (or sectors) into five groups, as follows:

- *Vatable sectors* (V): These are sectors falling within the VAT system; they include sectors that are subject to positive VAT rates, as well as sectors that are zero rated. These sectors receive rebates on the VAT paid on any inputs, but not on other indirect taxes.
- *Exempt sectors* (E): These are sectors that are exempt from VAT and therefore do not receive rebates on VAT or other indirect taxes paid on the inputs.
- *Excisable sectors* (X): These are sectors on which an excise tax is imposed on the output, and they are also exempt from VAT, so that they do not receive rebates on any indirect taxes paid on the inputs.
- *Vatable and excisable sectors* (Z): These are sectors on which both an excise tax and a VAT are imposed. They therefore receive rebates on VAT paid on inputs. In addition, VAT may be levied on the excise tax, inclusive of the price.
- *Traded sectors* (T): These are sectors that have to compete with imported goods. They may be subject to VAT or other sales taxes.

For each of these sectors, one can define two sets of prices: the prices received by producers (p) and the prices paid by users (q); the two sets differ in the presence of indirect taxes.[43] For each sector, one will have:

Vatable sectors (V): $\qquad q^V = p^V + t^V$ $\qquad\qquad$ (5.14)

Exempt sectors (E): $\qquad q^E = p^E$ $\qquad\qquad$ (5.15)

Excisable sectors (X): $\qquad q^X = p^X + t^X$ $\qquad\qquad$ (5.16)

Vatable and excisable sectors (Z): $\quad q^Z = p^Z + t^X + t^V$ $\qquad$ (5.17)

Traded sectors (T): $\qquad q^T = p^T + t^T$ $\qquad\qquad$ (5.18)

where superscripts are used to denote sectors, and t denotes the relevant indirect taxes. Taxes are set exogenously through government policy decisions. User and producers prices are determined endogenously, except for the traded sector, in which they are exogenously determined by world prices and taxes. User prices are determined by producer prices and exogenously fixed taxes. Producer prices are determined endogenously through the following system of equations:

$$p^V = p^V.A^{VV} + p^E.A^{EV} + (p^X + t^X).A^{XV} + (p^Z + t^X).A^{ZV} + (p^T + t^T).A^{TV} \quad (5.19)$$

$$p^E = q^V.A^{VE} + p^E.A^{EE} + (p^X + t^X).A^{XE} + q^Z.A^{ZE} + (p^T + t^T).A^{TE} \quad (5.20)$$

$$p^X = q^V.A^{VX} + p^E.A^{EX} + (p^X + t^X).A^{XX} + q^Z.A^{ZX} + (p^T + t^T).A^{TX} \quad (5.21)$$

$$p^Z = p^V.A^{VZ} + p^E.A^{EZ} + (p^X + t^X).A^{XZ} + (p^Z + t^X).A^{ZZ} + (p^T + t^T).A^{TZ} \quad (5.22)$$

where A^{ij} is an input-output matrix, in which the typical element a^{ij} denotes the amount of sector i used in producing one unit of sector j. The main difference between the equations (5.19)–(5.22) is that, whereas V and Z pay producer prices on V inputs (since VAT on inputs is rebated), other sectors pay user prices (that is, VAT inclusive). In other words, for E and X, VAT operates like sales or excise taxes. Note also that all sectors pay tax-inclusive prices for E, X, and T inputs,[44] and, to the extent that ad valorem taxes are levied on producer prices that already include these taxes, the tax system is subject to cascading. This system of equations essentially treats sectors V, E, X, and Z as nontraded sectors in which all costs (including taxes) are pushed fully forward onto user prices. This is not the case for traded goods the prices of which are determined by border world prices and any taxes levied on imports (including VAT). Therefore, the greater the importance of traded goods, the less the overall tax system is subject to tax cascading.

In solving out for producer prices, it is useful to think of sectors as "aggregate sectors" made up of different components of vatable, exempt, excisable, vatable and excisable, and traded goods and services. Then, substituting in for consumer prices, one can rewrite (5.19)–(5.22) as follows:

$$p = p.\alpha.A + p.\beta.A + p.\gamma.A + p.\eta.A + t^X.(\gamma + \eta).A$$
$$+ p^T.\delta.A + t^T.\delta.A + t^V.(\alpha + \eta).A.(\beta + \gamma) \quad (5.23)$$

where $p \equiv [p^V \; p^E \; p^X \; p^Z]$ is a row vector of all producer prices; $(\alpha \; \beta \; \gamma \; \eta \; \delta)$ are diagonal square matrices, with diagonal elements indicating the share of each sector that is vatable, exempt, excisable, vatable and excisable, and traded, respectively; and the typical element of square matrix A is a_{ij}, which is the total input of sector i into sector j. If there are n aggregate sectors, then p is a $1 \times n$ row vector, A is an $n \times n$ matrix of input-output coefficients, and (α β γ η δ) are $n \times n$ diagonal matrices. For each sector, ($\alpha + \beta + \gamma + \eta + \delta$) = 1.

Taking all terms with p to the left-hand side of (5.23) and solving out for p gives:[45]

$$p = t^X.(\gamma + \eta).A.K + p^T.\delta.A.K + t^T.\delta.A.K + t^V.(\alpha + \eta).A.(\beta + \gamma).K \qquad (5.24)$$

where $K \equiv [I - (\alpha + \beta + \gamma + \eta).A]^{-1}$. Once one solves out for p, one can then calculate q using (5.14)–(5.18). By choosing commodity and services units so that user prices, q, are unity, one can interpret taxes as ad valorem, and A is then the input-output coefficient matrix. This is very useful empirically since, typically, one does not have information on unit prices, especially when sectors are aggregations over a number of goods and services. Note that, if tax rates, t, are expressed as a proportion of producer prices, these need to be renormalized and expressed as a proportion of user prices through the transformation t/(1+t).[46] One also needs to allow for the fact that, for the vatable and excisable sectors, VAT is levied on the excise tax, inclusive of price. This can be done by using ($t^V + t^V . t^E$), instead of t^V.

Equation (5.24) solves out for the level of producer prices as a function of world prices and indirect taxes. One can rewrite (5.24) in terms of percentage price changes (dp) by simply replacing t by dt and then use (5.14)–(5.19) to calculate dq. Note that, by interpreting existing taxes as changes (that is, dt = −t), one can derive "basic prices," defined as the prices that would exist in the absence of taxes, as:[47]

$$q^0 = p^0 = (1 + dq) \qquad (5.25)$$

Effective taxes, defined as the difference between current tax-inclusive prices and basic prices, can then be derived as:

$$t^e = (q - q^0) = -dq \qquad (5.26)$$

As written, t^e is a percentage of current tax-inclusive prices, that is, the proportion of taxes in the final-user price. If one prefers to set them as a percentage of basic prices, then one can simply derive these as $t^{e0} = t^e/(1+dq)$.

The main objective of such an analysis is to evaluate the effect of the tax reforms on household real incomes. The effect on a household real income can be calculated by multiplying proportional price increases, dq or dq*, for each good or service by the corresponding budget share for the household and aggregating this product across goods and services. One can then evaluate the magnitude and distribution of this real-income effect for different tax reforms, including a reform that involves a change in a tax regime.

3

ANNEX

General Lessons from Tax Theory

This annex briefly identifies key insights provided by the theoretical literature addressing the issue of how to design or reform a structure of commodity taxes. One can find three potential roles for commodity taxation in the literature:[48] (1) raising revenue to finance government activities when lump-sum taxation is not available to the government; (2) reallocating resources to bring about more efficient allocation, for example, Pigouvian taxes; and (3) redistributing income when lump-sum taxes and transfers are not available to the government. The evolution of the theoretical literature will be very briefly discussed below in terms of the extension of tax rules to incorporate each of these roles. One will also distinguish between the "theory of optimum taxation" and the "theory of tax reform," where the former focuses on what a system of optimum taxes would look like, while the latter focuses on the identification of welfare-improving reforms. There is obviously an intimate link between these two strands of the literature since an optimum tax system is one in which no welfare-improving reforms are possible.

OPTIMUM COMMODITY TAXATION

One of the earliest contributions to the formal literature on the structure of optimum commodity taxes was Ramsey (1927). The paper examined the optimum structure of commodity taxes when the government had a fixed *revenue requirement* that could not be financed through lump-sum taxation. The main insight from the paper is captured by the so-called Ramsey Inverse-Elasticity Rule, which indicates that taxes should be higher on commodities with low price elasticities of demand. The basic intuition behind this result is straightforward: optimum taxes require that the reduction in (compensated) demand be the same for all commodities, and this means that tax rates must be relatively high on commodities with relatively low price elasticities.

The seminal papers in the area of optimum commodity taxation are Diamond and Mirrlees (1971a, 1971b), which also focused on the revenue-raising role of commodity taxes. These papers developed the basic analytical framework used in the modern optimum commodity-tax literature. A key contribution of this work was the identification of the conditions under which "production efficiency" was desirable, implying that the taxation of intermediate goods was undesirable. In particular, intermediate-goods taxation is only potentially desirable when some final-consumption goods cannot be optimally taxed (for example, because of the presence of consumption from own-production in rural areas or the existence of an untaxable informal sector), but can be taxed indirectly via taxes on inputs. Similarly, input taxes may be desirable as a way of taxing economic profits if these cannot be taxed directly via an optimum profits tax. If all consumption by households can be taxed, and an optimal profits tax exists, then all revenue should be raised via taxes on final consumption (such as a VAT) without distinguishing among commodities according to whether they are traded or nontraded. This also implies that trade taxes are not desirable.

Diamond (1975) extended the above model to allow for the *redistributive role* of commodity taxes. The paper showed that, relative to the efficient tax structure identified above, taxes should be lower on commodities that are relatively more important in the budgets of low-income households. Since these commodities (necessities, for instance) are often those with relatively low price elasticities, this suggests the existence of a trade-off between equity and efficiency when setting taxes, that is, reducing the burden of taxation on lower-income households is likely to come at the cost of a higher aggregate burden.

Drèze and Stern (1987), building on an earlier model by Guesnerie (1979), developed a fairly general model that captures a wide range of second-best worlds and incorporates a resource *reallocation role* for commodity taxes, in addition to the revenue-raising and redistributional roles. They derived a "Generalized Ramsey Rule," which showed that the previous rules go through as before, but now actual taxes are replaced by "shadow taxes," defined as the difference between consumer prices and shadow prices. This rule incorporates, for example, the standard Pigouvian argument for commodity taxation, as well as other second-best departures from the standard Ramsey Rule.

REFORM OF COMMODITY TAXES

The earliest work in the area of tax reform was undertaken in the context of trade taxation, whereby revenue requirements were not considered, and optimal lump-sum taxes and transfers were implicitly assumed to be available to the government to raise and redistribute revenue. Therefore, this literature was primarily concerned with efficient resource reallocation. Dixit (1975, 1985), which played an important role in integrating a separate body of theory on trade taxation into the standard analytical approach used in public finance theory, examined the conditions under which "radial reforms" (an equi-proportionate reduction of commodity taxes) and "concertina reforms" (reducing only the highest taxes) are welfare improving. Such reforms are obviously less interesting in the context of a government-revenue requirement.

Ahmad and Stern (1984) introduced the general theory of tax reform in the context of a government-revenue requirement and a redistributive role for commodity taxes. This was extended by Drèze and Stern (1987) to incorporate a resource-allocation role. Their approach involved identifying the marginal social cost of raising a unit of revenue using alternative commodity taxes, while keeping all other taxes fixed. Revenue-neutral and welfare-improving tax reforms can then be identified by decreasing the tax rates on commodities with high marginal social cost and replacing the lost revenue by raising taxes on commodities with low marginal social cost. While this approach helps to identify potentially welfare-improving and revenue-neutral reform strategies, the focus on single tax rates and keeping all other rates fixed introduces limitations on this approach from a policy perspective.

Another, related strand of the tax-reform literature identifies the conditions under which specific (and commonly discussed) tax-reform "packages" are welfare improving. A corollary of the Diamond-Mirrlees production efficiency theorem is simply that replacing trade taxes with optimal commodity taxes and keeping revenue constant will always be welfare improving under the conditions discussed above (that is, that all consumption can be taxed, and production exhibits constant returns to scale or, if not, that optimal profit taxes are available to the government).[49] Keen and Ligthart (2002) examine the conditions under which replacing *any* trade taxes with consumption-tax reforms that keep consumer prices constant and increase production efficiency are unambiguously welfare improving (that is, improve production efficiency, increase revenue, and keep household welfare unchanged). A corollary of this is that eliminating all tariffs and adjusting domestic consumption taxes to keep consumer prices unchanged will unambiguously increase both household welfare and government revenue. Note that the Diamond-Mirrlees result keeps revenue unchanged and requires optimal commodity taxes.

A key assumption in the above literature is that all the consumption base can be taxed. However, this is an implausible assumption for developing countries where many agricultural households consume out of their own food production and the informal sector (including small-scale rural and urban enterprises) is a substantial proportion of the economy. An important finding in Diamond and Mirrlees (1971a, 1971b) is that, if the total consumption of a given commodity cannot be taxed, then production efficiency is only desirable among the fully taxed sectors. The informal sector can then be incorporated as part of the household sector, with production inputs treated the same as any household purchases. In addition, the efficiency implications of taxation will then depend on net trade elasticities (Newbery and Stern 1987). Note that, under these conditions, there is no presumption that the taxation of inputs is undesirable, and such taxes may be a desirable way of taxing the informal sector indirectly (Heady and Mitra 1982; Newbery 1986; Stiglitz and Dasgupta 1971). This is essentially the issue addressed in Emran and Stiglitz (2005), who show that, in the presence of an informal sector not subject to VAT, replacing trade taxes with revenue-neutral VAT reforms is not necessarily welfare improving.

TAX REFORM AND REDISTRIBUTION

A key assumption in all of the above literature is that the government has access to optimal lump-sum transfers. Once one introduces a distributional role for indirect taxes, for example, because direct transfer systems are unavailable or ineffective, then one can say very little regarding the welfare impacts of the tax-reform packages conventionally discussed in the literature (Coady and Drèze 2002).[50] These welfare impacts will depend on the specific patterns of production and consumption found in a country, particularly the patterns across income groups, as well as the range of policy instruments available for redistributing income (for example, see Deaton and Stern 1986). However, a common finding in the empirical literature is that using indirect taxes (including price controls) is a very ineffective instrument for protecting poor households from the adverse effects of taxation (for example, reflecting the fact that these households account for a small proportion of the consumption base of most commodities), or, when they are distributionally attractive, they come at very high efficiency costs

(Coady 1997a). One therefore expects substantial gains from developing effective direct transfer programs, that is, the gains from having more well-targeted transfers, plus those from not having them incur the standard trade-off between equity and efficiency when using taxes to redistribute income (Coady and Harris 2004).

Decentralization Reforms

Kai Kaiser

hree levels of analysis are outlined in this chapter that offer a potentially tractable means of mapping out Poverty and Social Impact Analysis (PSIA) for decentralization given the institutional characteristics of decentralization, the probable mechanisms of impact, and the likely available sources of information. In the first instance, the level and distribution of public resources across places is a focus. At the second stage, the analysis concerns the distribution of public resources across people, such as the poor and non-poor, given the prevailing institutional and governance arrangements within places. Finally, the chapter highlights attempts to investigate impacts on local governance and public service delivery, that is, how effectively public resources are translated into public services.

OVERVIEW

The distributional impact of decentralization, notably on the poor, ultimately depends on the specific design and implementation in a given country context. The decentralization of public resources, officials, political power, and accountability affects both places and people. In theory and practice, the changes in the benefit incidence of public expenditures, services, and local governance that are associated with decentralization can make a specific group or even the majority better or worse off in aggregate. Given the ambiguity in the potential impacts, the application of PSIA

Special thanks to Emanuela Galasso, Markus Goldstein, and Jennie Litvack for comments. All errors are due to the author.

is especially pertinent for the variety of forms of decentralization likely to be encountered at the country level. Those pursuing distributional analyses of decentralization reforms will therefore have to determine an assessment methodology that identifies probable impact channels and tackles the typical data constraints confronted in quantitatively capturing effects on places and people at the subnational level.

There is an extensive theoretical literature on the potential advantages and disadvantages of decentralization. Decentralized decisionmaking can bring governments closer to the people; overcome information asymmetries; enhance transparency and accountability; allow for a better matching of local preferences, especially when these are heterogeneous across places; make for more responsive government through interjurisdictional competition for investment and the hearts and minds of inhabitants and taxpayers by, for example, allowing for "voting with your feet"; take into account local innovation; and increase the legitimacy of the state, while incorporating previously marginalized stakeholders such as the poor, women, ethnic groups, or castes.

Decentralization may also be associated with significant risks. Local entities may underprovide particular services, immunizations, for example, because of the presence of externalities. Disparities in local revenue capacity may constrain public services, especially in poorer areas. Local capacity constraints may deteriorate the provision of public goods in needy areas; a lack of clarity concerning the roles and responsibilities of central and subnational entities may do likewise. Weak bottom-up accountability and political economy factors such as elite capture may marginalize particular stakeholders and make local expenditure decisions less pro-poor (see, for instance, Bardhan 2000, Bardhan and Mookherjee 2002).

The impact of decentralization on poverty may be direct by flowing from the targeting of fiscal transfers and expenditure disparities, for instance, or indirect, such as the impacts that decentralization may have on the quality of public services or economic growth (von Braun and Grote 2000). Despite the expanding literature assessing the general links between decentralization and poverty reduction (Bossuyt and Gould 2000), the overall results are mixed and inconclusive (Jütting, Corsi, and Stockmayer 2005; Jütting et al. 2004).[1]

Table 6.1 speculates on a number of benefits and risks of decentralization, grouping these by potential time horizons, for example, within three to five years or beyond. The actual importance and direction of these considerations will depend on the country context, design, motivations, and phasing in of the decentralization. Given the significant lags with which some of these potential developments are associated, this

TABLE 6.1. Potential Links between Decentralization and the Poor

	Benefits	Risks
Short term	Brings choices closer to the preferences of the people, including the poor and previously marginalized groups. Potentially allows for greater transparency in the interregional and local allocation of public resources. Allows for local innovation in responding to the needs of the poor.	The possibility of local elite capture. Greater disparities emerge in interregional transfers and fiscal capacity in the absence of fiscal equalization. Lack of clarity and awareness concerning roles and responsibilities may weaken top-down and bottom-up accountability mechanisms.
Long term	Promotes tax and policy competition across jurisdictions for mobile capital and people. Underpins long-term political reform.	Fragments economies of scale. Fails to address or exacerbates disparities between lagging and advanced localities.

Source: Compiled by the author.

chapter focuses, in the first instance, on short-term impacts, especially as these are associated with the distribution and use of public resources.

In practice, countries pursue broader decentralization reforms for a number of reasons. In reality rather than rhetoric, poverty reduction is rarely the primary driving force. Political factors such as democratization, state legitimacy, and center versus subnational power relations often predominate.

Given the diversity of these experiences and stated objectives, this chapter attempts to provide a framework for mapping out the distributional impacts of decentralization experiences and examines several applied assessments. The next section reviews operational examples of decentralization reform and sets out the main types and dimensions of decentralization. The subsequent section proposes a simple framework to distinguish among different stages of the "distributional chain" of decentralization. The following section discusses a number of key instruments applied mainly by the World Bank in conducting this type of analysis. The final section concludes.

DIVERSITY IN DECENTRALIZATION

It is useful to highlight the diversity in decentralization that occurs in and across countries and at the operational level. While the operational cases presented in this chapter focus on World Bank experiences, they reflect examples of projects and polices adopted by governments and donors across the world equally well. Clarifying the types, dimensions, and extent of decentralization evident in a given country and operational context serves as a starting point for mapping the potential distributional channels of proposed or ongoing reforms.

Decentralization: operational perspectives

Within World Bank operational experience, decentralization reforms are widespread, but diverse. Over one-quarter of development policy operations—135 of 511 approved in fiscal years 1995–2005—listed at least one condition with a decentralization theme. During that decade, task managers explicitly chose decentralization as a theme in almost 5 percent of cases of development policy lending and 9 percent of cases of investment lending (or 249 of 2,927 projects in the latter case).[2]

Closer inspection of World Bank development policy conditionality highlights the range of reforms embraced under decentralization. In fiscal year 2005, development policy conditionality was utilized in 18 countries.[3] For the cases of Ghana and Mozambique, these focused on the adoption of a *general legal framework* for decentralization. In Pakistan, conditions called for passing on additional *fiscal space to provinces and local governments.* Conditionality in Mozambique argues for the implementation of *participatory planning programs* in a specific number of districts. Measures in Peru were designed to promote a more *participatory, transparent, and results oriented* decentralized monitoring and evaluation process. The first Senegal Poverty Reduction Support Credit called more specifically for *resource allocation mechanisms to decentralized units* based on poverty, health needs, and performance. A sectoral focus in Timor-Leste saw decentralization reforms centered on decentralized management at the school level. In contrast, proposed reforms in Burkina Faso and Mali focused on deconcentrated entities, that is, decentralized offices of the central government.

Investment lending relies on a variety of decentralized mechanisms to meet project objectives focused on different institutional levels and sectors. In fiscal year 2005, these included large-scale examples of *community-driven development* such as Indonesia's Subdistricts (*Kecamatan*) Development Program and an operation in Benin; district-level capacity-building and good governance promotion, for example, Tanzania and Indonesia's Governance Reform Initiative Programs; education projects such as those in Afghanistan, Bangladesh, and Democratic Republic of Congo; or health, for instance, in India, Lesotho, Malawi, and Vietnam.

Decentralization projects frequently only intervene in a subset of localities. For example, Rwanda's Decentralization and Community

Development Program is directly engaged in about one-third of the country's 106 districts with assistance for strengthened planning and implementation.[4] As is common in many countries, Rwanda's decentralization framework was nonetheless implemented on a nationwide basis. Project impact analysis would clearly not only be concerned with the extent to which additional financial resources benefit the covered districts, for example, relative to the existing fiscal resources or relative poverty rate of the localities in a national context. Another important issue would be whether improved outcomes such as the greater incidence of priority services for the poor are more evident over time in these localities relative to other, *initially comparable* districts.

The foregoing examples underscore the range of approaches required to assess this diverse set of reforms falling under the rubric of decentralization. In the first instance, the analysis must seek to specify the mechanisms through which decentralization might have distributional implications. Common examples include new interregional allocation criteria for resources, greater decentralized autonomy over front-line resource allocation and public investment or service delivery decisions, or changes in the institutions or groups participating in decisions made at the local level, such as the mandated representation of women and previously marginalized groups, newly selected or elected bodies, or facility-level decisionmaking bodies such as parent-teacher associations.

Types of decentralization

At the heart of all decentralization reforms lies the extension of some degree of autonomy for decisionmaking over public resources, staff, and regulations that was previously centralized. Table 6.2 presents three principal types of decentralization: deconcentration, delegation, and devolution (Litvack, Ahmad, and Bird 1998).[5] *Deconcentration* entails granting increased responsibilities to decentralized agencies. These may be decentralized agencies within a ministry, such as regional education offices, or territorial entities, such as provinces and provincial heads. *Delegation* entails the assignment of a particular function or program to a decentralized entity, for example, a poverty targeting program. *Devolution* is often considered the most far-reaching form of decentralization in that it assigns a degree of political autonomy and taxing powers to subnational governments.

These types of decentralization also differ along fiscal, administrative, and political dimensions. The fiscal dimension encompasses the degree to which revenue-raising and spending authority is decentralized. Administrative decentralization pertains to civil servants and may influ-

TABLE 6.2. Types of Decentralization

Deconcentration	The dispersion of the responsibility for certain services to regional branch offices.	Accountability remains largely top-down within administration; many theoretical benefits of decentralization may be more limited, but risks may be lower.
Delegation	The transfer of responsibility for decisionmaking and the administration of public functions to local governments or semiautonomous organizations not wholly controlled by the central government, but ultimately accountable to it.	Assignment of a specific task or function may make use of greater local information and downward accountability, but decentralized entities are restricted in prioritizing across functions or across sectors.
Devolution	The authority for decisionmaking, finance, and management is transferred to quasi-autonomous units of local government.	There is greater emphasis on bottom-up institutions of political autonomy.

Source: Compiled by the author.

ence their distribution across space and their accountability. Political decentralization relates to the extent actual power and political accountability are passed along from the center. These three dimensions are clearly integrally related. For example, in the absence of fiscal and administrative decentralization, political decentralization is likely to have limited traction in practice.

On the revenue side, fiscal decentralization entails granting subnationals their own tax and nontax revenue sources or intergovernmental transfers. Own-source revenues require that subnational governments have some *autonomy* over rate-setting and the determination of tax effort (Ebel and Yilmaz 2001). Differences in effort may explain some of the differences in own-revenue collection; localities will invariably be subject to significant variations in fiscal capacity, for example, the obviously different potential for property tax collection in a large metropolitan area versus a rural hinterland. Typically, the expenditure assignments of a subnational government will exceed the revenues from that government's own-source revenue base. The resulting *vertical imbalances* will confirm the need for fiscal transfers from higher or central levels of government.

Major distributional issues in this context relate to the amount of fiscal resources higher levels of government transfer (vertical sharing) and the modalities through which the higher levels of government distribute these resources across localities (horizontal sharing). Transfers may be based on the origin of the resource collection, for example, shared natural-resource revenues; they may be formula based; or they may be discretionary and ad hoc. Impact analysis in this context needs to assess whether needy areas receive more or fewer resources in absolute and relative terms. While needy might be defined based on criteria such as poverty as measured by a poverty headcount ratio, need would ideally incorporate some concept of the difference between expenditure needs and fiscal capacity, or the capacity to raise revenues at similar effort levels given a particular revenue base such as property. Subnational expenditure needs will, in turn, depend on prevailing expenditure assignments. For example, primary education is typically a prominent expenditure assignment in many countries. The literature provides substantial guidance on the optimal design of intergovernmental transfers (Bahl 1999; Bird and Smart 2002), including the design of allocation formulas. At the operational level, the challenge typically lies in providing workable measures of fiscal capacity and expenditure needs.

Administrative decentralization refers to arrangements concerning civil servants (Evans 2004). Along with fiscal resources, this may impact the spatial distribution of staff such as teachers and doctors and, hence, the access to staff by various groups, for example, urban or rural, remote or nonremote groups. In practice, attracting good civil servants and teachers to poor and remote regions is often a challenge in developing countries in any case (World Bank 2005b). The incentives provided may be affected by decentralization. The accountability relationship involved in the management of civil servants, for instance, the right by local governments to hire and fire or the right of central agencies to reassign across localities, may also be important not only in determining the ultimate distribution of civil servants, but also the effectiveness of the provision of services by civil servants.

Political decentralization involves the granting of decisionmaking autonomy to lower levels of government such as for resource allocations across sectoral priorities. This autonomy implies some form of local accountability mechanism. Electoral institutions and local representation are typically at the heart of the relevant decisionmaking processes. Beyond periodic voting, a range of other processes may be embraced, such as efforts to enhance citizen participation, including that of the poor, in the local budgeting process (Blair 2000). Often, important questions about the impact of decentralization will focus on how changes in political decentralization have affected local accountability given the fiscal and administrative decentralization arrangements, for example, by allowing a voice for a previously marginalized constituency.

While these various forms of decentralization often coexist in a single country or even in a single sector, the distinctions entail important differences in the nature of decentralized decisionmaking and, by extension, the distributional impacts. Devolution is often understood as the most pronounced form of decentralization. It entails some sort of locally accountable entity, generally an elected one; the emphasis is on a greater degree of autonomy and accountability at a more local level. Such entities will be able to set priorities across a greater range of alternatives, for example, sectoral preferences between infrastructure and social expenditures, while, at the margin, depending on taxes from their own constituencies. In contrast, deconcentration and delegation imply a greater predominance of top-down accountability and, potentially, a more limited set of decentralized choices, such as delegation over a very narrow function. Devolution may guarantee (but not necessarily) greater scope for realizing some of the broader gains from more full-fledged decentralization. At the same time, devolution may be subject to greater risks from factors such as local capture owing to less stringent forms of top-down accountability.

The nature of decentralization may also be subject to important differences within a country, including urban and rural differences. Federal countries such as India manifest important differences in the degree of decentralization to local governments and communities across states. Asymmetric decentralization arrangements are important features in some countries, for example, Indonesia's special autonomy provisions for the provinces of Aceh and Papua. Ladder approaches, whereby increased resourcing and autonomy are granted over time depending on the demonstrated development of capacity, may also generate differences in decentralization across localities. Examples include Cambodia's early implementation of the *Seila* Commune Decentralization Program. While these types of asymmetrically phased decentralization approaches may have attractive features from the perspective of dealing with capacity differences across what are often very heterogeneous subnational entities, they may be difficult to sustain politically. Thus, in the context of political decentralization, it would be very difficult for a national government to withhold elections from some localities, but not others.

Extent of decentralization

International comparisons of decentralization have typically focused on the extent to which fiscal resources are managed by subnational entities. The International Monetary Fund's Government Finance Statistics provide the widest international coverage on revenue and expenditure decentralization measures (World Bank 2004a). These data refer to funds that are devolved or delegated to state, provincial, and local governments, but do not distinguish deconcentrated resources. Figure 6.1 presents regional averages for subnational shares of expenditures and own-revenues. Expenditure shares are, on average, almost 30 percent in observations on countries of the Organisation for Economic Co-operation and Development. South Asia is represented only by India, with subnational expenditure shares over 40 percent. Shares are significantly lower in all other regions, notably Africa. Regrettably, data coverage is especially limited for developing countries, but nonetheless provides a useful benchmark against which to assess other countries using supplementary data. At an aggregate level, impact analysis of decentralization reforms might assess the extent to which more or fewer resources are available to subnational entities over time, for example, as part of an overall national fiscal space.

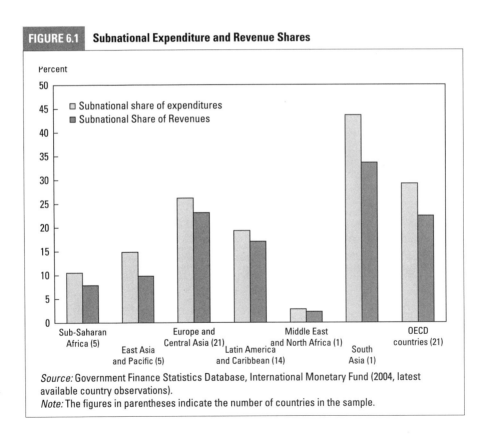

FIGURE 6.1 **Subnational Expenditure and Revenue Shares**

Percent

☐ Subnational share of expenditures
■ Subnational Share of Revenues

Sub-Saharan Africa (5)
East Asia and Pacific (5)
Europe and Central Asia (21)
Latin America and Caribbean (14)
Middle East and North Africa (1)
South Asia (1)
OECD countries (21)

Source: Government Finance Statistics Database, International Monetary Fund (2004, latest available country observations).
Note: The figures in parentheses indicate the number of countries in the sample.

In all regions, subnational expenditures are greater than revenues. These vertical imbalances—defined as the difference between own-revenue capacity and prevailing expenditures—give rise to intergovernmental transfers. Within countries, vertical imbalances may be especially large for poorer or rural localities, highlighting the need to assess the degree of horizontal difference across localities within a country.

Critically, the data of the International Monetary Fund do not reveal the degree of *autonomy* subnational governments have over revenues or expenditures. Even if state, provincial, or local governments are assigned a tax base such as property, the governments may be restricted in the degree to which they can exploit this revenue source (Ebel and Yilmaz 2001). Higher levels of government may significantly restrict the allocations of subnational governments, for instance, by earmarking or other administrative measures, thus narrowing the extent of decentralization (and comparability) across countries.

A scoring exercise by Ndegwa (2002) suggests that, in most African countries, the actual amount of fiscal and administrative decentralization is low. While political decentralization expanded rapidly through a wave of democracy movements in the 1980s and 1990s, denoted by the existence of elected local governments, this has not been matched by corresponding increases in fiscal and administrative decentralization. Very rarely do subnational governments control more than 5 percent of total expenditures, let alone their revenues.

The international evidence suggests that central government control over public resources remains predominant in most developing countries. Given this centralized control over public resources, care must be taken not to attach excessive weight to the ability of decentralized expenditures to contribute to aggregate poverty reduction. Nonetheless, decentralized decisionmaking may be growing in significance for those public expenditures that are especially important for the poor, such as social sector spending, equalization transfers, and social funds. Thus, a clear understanding of the scope of a particular decentralization reform should set the stage for assessing the potential distributional impacts.

ASSESSING DISTRIBUTIONAL IMPACTS OF DECENTRALIZATION

Figure 6.2 presents a simple framework to help map distributional impacts. In the first instance, the framework is concerned with capturing the *distribution* of public resources across decentralized places and people. This distribution can be interpreted as the targeting of decentralized resources, particularly if these are derived from central transfers. In addition to mea-

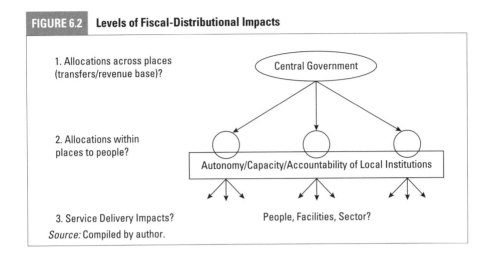

FIGURE 6.2   Levels of Fiscal-Distributional Impacts

1. Allocations across places (transfers/revenue base)?

Central Government

2. Allocations within places to people?

Autonomy/Capacity/Accountability of Local Institutions

3. Service Delivery Impacts?   People, Facilities, Sector?

Source: Compiled by author.

suring the ultimate distributional patterns quantitatively at these levels, such an analysis typically seeks to understand the factors that appear to be driving progressive or regressive distributions, for example, the identification of the characteristics of individual localities, including the use of proxies to gauge factors that would increase the likelihood of capture.

The fiscal analysis of people and places is primarily concerned with public resources as an input that may or may not translate into better service delivery. Another level of analysis involves trying to assess changes in the quality of public services owing to decentralization. Do poor people get more of the services they want or need at a higher standard because of the decentralization reform such as in basic health or education service delivery? Better local governance can be seen as an intermediate input for service delivery outcomes. Within given fiscal resources, are accountability arrangements so established that services are properly provided? However, improvements in local governance may also themselves be a focus of analysis. Thus, decentralization may increase or decrease the sorts of corruption that have a disproportionate impact on poor households or small firms. The empowerment effects of decentralization, such as those resulting from the existence of reformed or new political institutions, may be especially promising for the poor.

Distributional impacts across places

Decentralization reforms may alter the level and distribution of transfers from central or other higher levels of government. In the case of devolution, changes in the local own-source revenue base may also be important, especially if the fiscal capacity to raise resources differs significantly across localities. For example, the assignment of a property tax will have different implications for urban and for rural areas.[6] In many developing countries, donor flows to subnational governments may be quite substantial. These flows are often not captured by central transfers and may even be off budget. The distributional analysis of decentralized resources may therefore be faced with serious obstacles to comprehensiveness. In the case of Rwanda, for instance, differences in direct donor allocations across districts can dwarf the corresponding differences in formal channels of allocation.

An important element in fiscal analysis across places is the focus on actual allocations to localities versus budgeted or notional allocations. The introduction of more transparent, formula-based criteria may reduce the use of fiscal transfers for political patronage (see, for example, Diaz-Cayeros, Magaloni, and Weingast 2003 on the historical case of Mexico). Indonesia's 2001 "big bang" decentralization affected the criteria by which intragovernmental fiscal transfers were allocated. While the reforms introduced a new formula, legacy allocations and existing civil service salaries remained important driving forces behind the actual fiscal distributions, leading to significant errors in targeting, depending on which benchmark formula one believes to be "ideal" (see Box 6.1).

BOX 6.1 **Assessing Fiscal Equalization: The Case of Indonesia**

Starting in 2001, Indonesia devolved almost a third of public expenditure to subnational governments, notably its 434 districts (*kabupaten, kota*) and, to a lesser degree, 32 provinces. Regions depend heavily on central government transfers to finance the gap between their limited own-source revenue base and prevailing expenditure levels. Transfers consist of a general-purpose transfer or general block grant (*dana alokasi umum*, DAU); natural-resource revenue sharing (*sumber daya alam*), for example, from oil and gas; property taxes; income; a special autonomy grant for the easternmost province of Papua; and a minor special-grant facility. Disparities in own-source revenues and revenue sharing mean that Indonesia's districts enjoy significantly different levels of fiscal resources on a per capita basis (Hofman et al. 2005; World Bank 2003a).

At the start of devolution in 2001, DAU allocations were made based largely on existing establishment costs. These were estimated using the sum of the previous transfers for the deconcentrated structures and staff that had been handed over to local governments, as well as the prevailing capital transfers to local governments. Over time, policymakers envisioned moving more steadily toward a transparent, formula-based allocation system through the decentralization reforms. A new formula sought to distribute a national pool of DAU resources (now 26.5 percent of national resources) based on a fiscal-gap formula. This formula incorporates indicators of fiscal capacity and expenditure needs as measured by population, area, poverty, cost, Human Development Index, and so on. The fiscal-capacity measures rely on own-source revenues that are predicted based on a regression analysis of the relationship between district gross domestic product and taxes. Opting for actual collections would have penalized local revenue-collection efforts since higher results for the fiscal-capacity measures would have led to less in transfers.

In any case, the actual allocations deviate in practice from the "ideal," formula-based allocations. Figure 6.3 highlights this mistargeting in allocations across places that was found in practice for the 2006 DAU, which totals about $14.6 billion.

FIGURE 6.3   DAU 2006: Actual versus Formula-Based Distribution

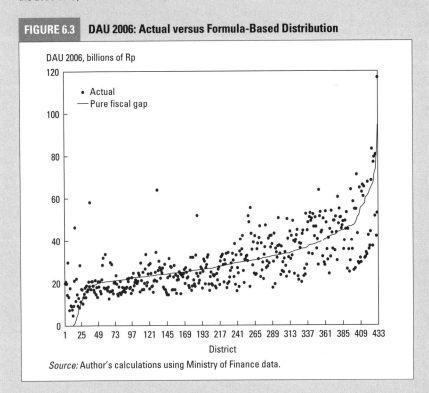

DAU 2006, billions of Rp

Source: Author's calculations using Ministry of Finance data.

Figure 6.4 recasts this deviation by ranking the ratios of actual to formula-based DAU allocations for Indonesia's 434 districts. The left part of the distribution is underresourced because of the formula, whereas the right side is overresourced by up to 34 times. This method is more revealing than simply assessing correlations with local poverty indicators or after-transfer variations in per capita total revenues, that is, per capita own-source revenue, natural-resource revenue sharing, DAU, and the minor special-grant facility. It provides an explicit statement of a benchmark distribution of the actual and formula-based allocations, thereby supplying direct insights on the winners and losers created by the deviation (Hofman et al. 2005). In this example, about 12 percent (or $1.8 billion) was misallocated.

The misallocation can also be summarized through a poverty-gap-type measure that weighs the degree to which localities are underresourced.[7] The greater the resulting figure (for example, the changes in actual allocations against formula allocations over time), the more regressive the impact.

Clearly, the design of this formula benchmark distribution may be open to criticism. Some experts may see poverty as the preferred proxy for expenditure needs. For any country context, the appropriate specification of the transfer should be guided by the assignment of roles and responsibilities, for example, social sector or infrastructure needs, and the available data. Hence, an important exercise in assessing the importance of a design is to simulate the sensitivity of the measure of the fiscal-resource gap to the choice of different horizontal allocation benchmarks.

FIGURE 6.4 Ratio of Actual to Formula-Based DAU, 2006

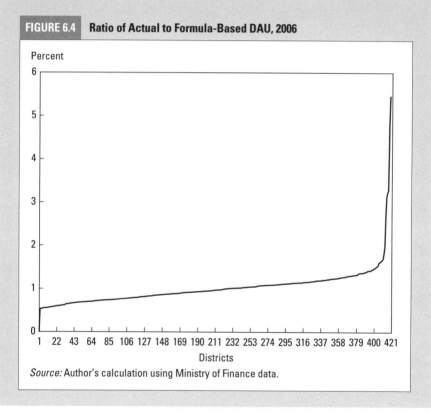

Source: Author's calculation using Ministry of Finance data.

Before-and-after comparisons of fiscal allocations across places are often complicated by the lack of comparable data, especially in transitions from central to more decentralized arrangements. For example, a large part of Indonesia's deconcentrated expenditures in the case highlighted above were transferred to devolved structures in 2001. However, data on the spatial incidence of deconcentrated expenditures and the remaining central government expenditures before and after decentralization are only partially available. The fiscal recording systems of the central government simply did not produce geographically disaggregated data in line with the new subnational jurisdictions. From this perspective, one of the benefits of a decentralized system may be that it increases transparency concerning the spatial incidence of fiscal resources (assuming all subnational governments provide reports for national-level comparisons).

A review of the evolution of intragovernmental fiscal systems for eight countries in the process of accession to the European Union finds that most have moved to more transparent formula-based allocations. This represents an advance over the predominance of nontransparent and discretionary allocations during the communist era. Beyond the apparent redistributional aspects of intergovernmental transfers, it is important to bear in mind the potential incentive effects for economic growth and revenue mobilization. While the European Union–8's new allocations significantly reduce disparities across localities relative to the extent to which revenues are collected in an area, the equalization may actually be excessive from the perspective of economic efficiency (Dillinger 2005). Poor design in intragovernmental fiscal transfers may also have very detrimental effects on own-source revenue mobilization. Thus, Russia's system of ad hoc grants penalized regions that raised more own-resources (Zhuravskaya 2000).

Understanding the amount of resources that actually arrives at the local level is an often neglected element of distributional analysis. Rwanda's common development fund provides, in principle, each of the country's 106 districts with an equal allocation for infrastructure projects such as in markets. The disbursement of these funds, however, relies on the preparation of an adequate proposal and on progress in project implementation, including processes such as procurement. Data for 2004 suggest that actual disbursements ranged from no disbursement to full disbursement against the basic allocation. This has raised concerns that poorer, lower-capacity districts may be experiencing regressive allocations.

There may be any number of reasons why allocated fiscal resources may not actually arrive at the decentralized level. Reinikka and Svensson (2004) examined variations in the degree of leakage in fiscal transfers to schools in Uganda. Leakages were defined as the difference between the amounts schools were supposed to receive, that is, capitation grants, and the amounts they actually received. The authors found that poorer schools suffered from greater leakages, potentially because of their more limited bargaining power vis-à-vis districts.

Distributional impacts across places and people

The distributional incidence of public resources within places depends on the way lower-level institutions such as local governments allocate these resources in terms of types of programs and services, for example, and what this implies for the ultimate distributional incidence across different beneficiaries such as poor and non-poor households or persons by gender, by ethnicity, by caste, and so on.

Distributional outcomes based on the way fiscal resources are allocated at the local level in a decentralized context will depend on the degree of autonomy and accountability and the associated capacity at the various institutional tiers. The amount of *autonomy* will determine the amount of discretion a given level of the state will have in targeting public resources. Are local decisionmakers only able to select from a limited menu of projects? Can they make broad choices concerning activities and implicit or explicit beneficiaries given available resources? The *capacity* and *accountability* to allocate effectively decentralized resources may differ not only vertically across levels of government, for example, between central and local governments, but also horizontally (urban or rural, small or large, and so on);[8] that is, are agents at any given tier both willing and able to make choices that benefit the poor? Do local governments have the capacity, including sufficient information, to identify poor beneficiaries effectively and implement activities to help them?

The theoretical literature suggests that the degree and impact of central versus local capture are ambiguous (Bardhan and Mookherjee 2000, 2005). A key challenge facing distributional analysis therefore is to assess whether prevailing institutional arrangements tend to favor or threaten desirable distribution outcomes such as pro-poor allocations across localities. For any given context, it will be important to provide a more stylized assessment of the local governance mechanisms and characteristics that might affect distributional outcomes. Are decisionmaking processes sufficiently inclusive of stakeholders at the local level such as the rich or poor, landed or landless, literate or illiterate, women or men, minorities, particular ethnic and caste groups? Are the incentives such that decisionmakers would act in accordance with broadbased or narrow distributional outcomes (for example, elite capture)?

An increasing number of quantitative analyses of decentralized decisionmaking seek to link observed outcomes with local characteristics in terms of poverty targeting or the choice of certain projects. To varying degrees, these characteristics serve as either indirect or direct proxies for local arrangements mediating distributional decisions. Thus, high degrees of inequality or ethnic polarization could undermine more broadbased or pro-poor distributional outcomes at the decentralized level. Consequently, distributional analysis should, ideally, provide an inventory of the risks of capture in a given context. The analysis should also seek to encapsulate the salient differences across places in a given context such as the composition of the population and its characteristics, resource endowments, and social traditions vis-à-vis stakeholders such as women. These differences are not static, and decentralization will not simply affect fiscal allocations; at one and the same time, decentralization may transform underlying decision-making processes, institutions, and the behavior of key stakeholders. Any decentralization analysis will therefore confront a number of simultaneous, overlapping processes. Nonetheless, an important dimension of the assessment of first-order effects would be the focus on how given decentralized mechanisms or reforms impact the targeting of fiscal resources.

Galasso and Ravallion (2005) provide a good example of two-stage targeting analysis in the context of Bangladesh's Food for Education Program. The central government delegated to communities the responsibility for allocating program transfers across people. It was assumed that these levels would have better information for identifying the poor. Whether actual allocations might be undermined by inadequate accountability, for example, program capture by local elites, is an open question. The central program office allocates across the communities. Its information partly relies on national statistical sources for aggregate poverty indicators on given localities, but the accountability is also open to doubt because of, for instance, the political pressure to favor particular constituencies in allocations.

The study finds that decentralized targeting within villages is pro-poor, but that targeting can be more or less effective given particular community characteristics such as inequalities in land holdings. In comparison, the central level performs comparatively badly in its allocations across communities when its contributions targeting the poor are decomposed. This suggests that, at least in this case, the accountability for pro-poor targeting appears to be more effective at the local level rather than the central level.

Findings from Bolivia indicate not only that previously marginalized localities have received more resources under decentralization, but that the structure of expenditures has tended to be more reflective of local priorities. The approach has relied on linking the sectoral structure of expenditures to the performance of proxies for expenditure needs based on a number of socioeconomic indicators across localities (Faguet 2004).

Evidence from decentralized social investment funds in Ecuador suggests that inequality—a proxy for local capture—both reduces the likelihood that places will receive funds, but also affects the types of investment priorities of localities (Arauja et al. 2005). A simple choice seems to influence more general distinctions in the types of projects selected by localities, notably, private goods benefiting primarily the poor, such as latrines, versus public goods benefiting also the more well off, such as schools and community infrastructure. Higher inequality tends to reduce the likelihood that communities will chose the pro-poor latrines. Whereas the evidence does not offer a fuller account of the way inequality may act as a proxy for less progressive forms of local governance, such analytical distinctions among types of goods according to their distributional incidence and the local conditions may be useful for analyses in other contexts.

Studies of fiscal equalization are typically concerned with the allocation of transfers across places. Since own-source revenue assignments are typically insufficient to meet all assigned expenditure needs even among the wealthiest, such as in urban localities, central transfers will usually be required. Fiscal equalization is often analyzed on the basis of whether more central government resources are destined for poorer localities. A common question is: do transfers reduce the per capita disparities in the combined revenues available to local governments? However, per capita equalization is often not the best benchmark for equalization (see Box 6.1, Hofman et al. 2005).

The nature of center-subnational relations can be highly instructive regarding the potential outcomes of decentralization. Evidence that a national government is strongly disposed toward encouraging better outcomes at the subnational level is often an important sign of potential success (for instance, as revealed by a proactive commitment to monitoring and evaluation). The choice of types of intragovernmental transfers and poverty targeting designs, whether based on poverty or political patronage, for instance, is also often indicative. Institutionally, the incentives set by particular sorts of decentralization act to discipline subnational and central governments in very different ways (Blanchard and Shleifer 2000; Quian and Weingast 1995). Such comparative conclusions are naturally subject to debate, but do hint at the value of mapping out the apparent motivations of central government and the principal incentives a decentralized system offers to subnational entities.

A better understanding of the political economy of decentralized decisionmaking can help map out the likely dynamics for ensuring distributional outcomes. Efforts to arrive at a stylized model of decisionmaking can bring more focus on those interest groups that would be key in driving local decisionmaking and those that may be marginalized. For example, in Indian villages, relevant groups might emerge around landed and landless constituencies (Foster and Rosenzweig 2002). Even in the absence of more detailed expenditure benefit-incidence data, these types of analyses can yield hypotheses about the distributional dynamics behind certain expenditure patterns, for instance, irrigation versus other public goods such as road construction.

Decentralized governance and service delivery

A final level of distributional analysis focuses on the impact of decentralization on local governance and public service delivery. Prevailing conditions of governance at the local level may have significant implications in terms of whether public resources are used regressively at the local level. Consequently, if local governance appears to be ineffective, this may signal that public resources are subject to poor decentralized distribution through local capture, theft, and so on. This section attempts to unbundle potentially relevant local governance issues, including the potential impacts on decentralized service delivery.

The accountability triangle described in *World Development Report 2004* (World Bank 2003b) provides a useful framework for mapping out the potential weaknesses and strengths in local governance that may, in turn, have an impact on distributional outcomes and service delivery (Figure 6.5). Key links in the accountability triangle include *voice* (how citizens relate to politicians and policymakers at the national, state, and local levels), *client power* (how citizens as clients of service delivery relate to providers within a given sector), and *compact* (how politicians and policymakers relate to public and private providers).

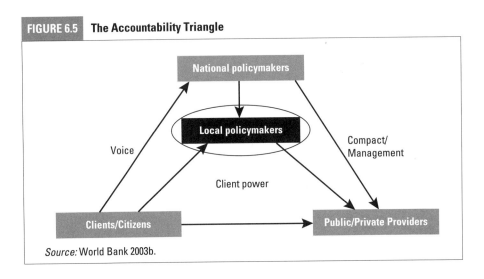

FIGURE 6.5   **The Accountability Triangle**

Source: World Bank 2003b.

These drive the effectiveness of public service delivery (see Ahmad et al. 2005; World Bank 2003b).

Decentralization is likely to shift the onus of accountability in terms of voice between citizens and local policymakers and change the compact between central and subnational governments (such as through greater fiscal decentralization in the case of devolution and delegation) and decentralized providers (in the case of deconcentration, for instance). Compacts will be strongly affected by the nature of fiscal and administrative decentralization, for example, how localities are financed and staffed. Decentralization, including greater autonomy for front-line providers, will also have the potential of strengthening client power if citizens hold local providers more directly accountable, such as by targeting their feedback at specific providers or choosing alternative providers. While a range of accountability mechanisms may be formally established, different constellations of these mechanisms may actually exist in a given context (Blair 2000). Hence, attention also needs to be paid to the functioning of informal institutions.

A variety of voice mechanisms may influence the actions of local policymakers, including taxing and spending priorities, and the extent to which these policymakers are compelled to transform public resources into outcomes that benefit local households. Key questions concerning the quality of voice mechanisms might include the following: Can the selection of local policymakers be made to hinge on the responsiveness of the policymakers to broadbased political demands? Are decisionmaking bodies representative of all local groups? Are more direct forms of oversight, such as participatory budgeting, established and effective?

Distributional impacts depend on the scope of decentralized decisionmaking. Following wide-ranging devolutions, local policymakers may be able to sway the preferences of stakeholders across a broad set of priorities, including education versus infrastructure, hiring more staff versus spending more on buildings, fewer versus more taxes, and so on. In the context of delegated programs, the choices may be more limited, for example, the identification of the individual beneficiaries of a cash-transfer poverty program. Decisionmaking about local facilities will be limited to a specific sector or function, such as the rates or opening hours for particular services. The nature of the compacts between central and local officials and between officials and providers, public or private, at various levels will determine the spectrum of the choices.

The inability of voters to hold local leaders to account through the ballot box undermines the effectiveness of electoral voice mechanisms in ensuring the delivery of goods to meet broadbased needs. If politicians cannot or do not fulfill promises and if they cannot be made to do so, if, for instance, they will not pursue measures that strengthen local education to benefit all residents, then elections may merely breed patronage and clientelism, and politicians may secure control over the public sector by providing narrow spoils to limited constituencies, such as their own tribes (Keefer and Khemani 2003). The contrasts in the Indian states of Kerala and Uttar Pradesh highlight the importance of differences in public action. While they share similar income levels, Kerala achieves significantly better results in health and education indicators because public choices support spending substantially larger amounts of public resources to attain this outcome.

A comparative study of decentralization in the Philippines and in Uganda suggests that apparent bottom-up accountability may be quite weak in practice (Azfar, Kähkönen, and Meagher 2001). Survey evidence indicates that citizens in both countries relied heavily on community leaders rather than on the media for information on local politics and on corruption, potentially heightening the risk of local capture. A series of governance and decentralization surveys in Indonesia combined surveys and studies on households, facilities, and governance with the specific objective of revealing community- and district-level disparities in autonomy, accountability, and service delivery. The surveys found significant differences in how well informed citizens were about leaders at various levels of government, as well as in the perceptions of citizens concerning local corruption and capture (Hofman and Kaiser 2005; World Bank 2005c).

Informal accountability arrangements may act as a substitute for formal mechanisms of electoral voice. Tsai (2005) examines the conditions that might make local governments in China more responsive to local community needs. She finds some support for the notion that the presence of encompassing social groups, temple groups, for example, combined with the participation of embedded local officials, is associated with better outcomes on such issues as the quality of local infrastructure. She finds that, under current circumstances, these informal arrangements in particular localities are a passable substitute for the sort of accountability that might be expected from elections. Her paper cautions, however, that these informal arrangements may not represent a sustainable, broad-based institutional foundation for local accountability in China. Moreover, she found such arrangements effective in less than a fifth of the villages she surveyed.

Recent contributions have focused on designing decentralized institutions to enhance policy responsiveness to marginalized groups. The designs include the mandated representation of women and the castes often found in South Asia. Evidence from India suggests that mandated representation does increase spending on goods and initiatives likely to benefit the targeted groups, such as special programs or reserved employment. Besley et al. (2004) find some evidence that the mandated representation of a *pradhan* (village head) in India impacts the types of expenditures that are prioritized in local decisionmaking.

The greater participation engendered by decentralization through the empowerment of local institutions or the specifically mandated representation of previously uninvolved or marginalized groups may not always translate into more equitable resource allocations and more responsive service delivery. The opportunity of increased participation may initially raise expectations, but prove difficult to sustain over time especially because the opportunity costs are high and the apparent returns low. Consequently, greater participation may give a boost to voice and client-power mechanisms, but, for these to be sustainable and produce tangible outcomes, the corresponding compact arrangements, including sufficient financing and staffing at the local and front-line levels, must be established.

No matter what the nature of the prevailing relationships are between key actors in a decentralization process, it is important to bear in mind that these are likely to evolve over time. Decentralization may initially be largely a top-down affair, with the central government determining the new fiscal targeting mechanisms. Gradually, however, subnational governments may strengthen their bargaining positions vis-à-vis the central government, for example, through subnational government organizations. Subnational governments may thus begin to play a far greater role in the way national fiscal resources are distributed.

Local revenue collection can contribute to the generation of public resources, but, potentially more importantly, it can help enhance local accountability (Raich 2005). While a greater reliance on the local tax base may increase interregional disparities in fiscal capacity, linking the spending choices of local officials more directly to the local tax effort through rate setting, for instance, may strengthen the voice relationships. Citizens who are taxed or charged fees for general or specific services may be more attentive to how and how well resources are used. A fundamental problem in many developing countries, however, is that the local revenue base is often quite limited, and higher levels of government are reluctant to yield a larger revenue base to subnational governments.

The effectiveness of different local accountability mechanisms in reducing corruption is often doubtful. An investigation of community projects in Indonesia sought to assess the impact on corruption of a threat of stricter auditing and compare this to the impact of measures designed to stimulate greater community participation (Olken 2004). Audits can be interpreted in this context as a form of top-down compact accountability, whereas participation puts the emphasis on bottom-up voice accountability. The study sought to generate a hard measure of corruption based on engineering assessments of community road projects. The analysis suggested that audits were more effective at reducing corruption, while greater participation merely shifted the expenditure composition to areas where leakages could be more readily masked. This type of analysis does not assess decentralization per se, but it is indicative of the type of institutional mechanisms that may influence outcomes in a decentralized context.

A study in Cambodia showed that changes in the compact with respect to health facilities improve performance. The study found that districts that had contracted out to nongovernmental organizations performed better than those retaining traditional compacts relying on government facilities (Bhushan, Keller, and Schwartz 2002).

Citizen score cards provide one mechanism for enhancing client feedback on schools and clinics (World Bank 2004b). Randomized experiments gauging the impact of this feedback on facility-level performance can be used to assess this accountability mechanism.

An outcome-focused distributional analysis of decentralization needs to be clear about the dimensions of service delivery that are of interest and relevant. Public service delivery is, by its very nature, multidimensional in terms of quantity, quality, structure, cost, and so on. Does decentralization enhance access by improving, for example, proximity to a school or providing clean water? Does it enhance dimensions such as responsiveness? Are the "right" services being provided? Is service delivery conditioned on informal payments? Has decentralization affected the standard of service delivery? How well are teachers now teaching? Distributional analysis will also need to be concerned with the benefit incidence of these various dimensions. Does decentralization mean the poor are receiving more goods that are important for their welfare, such as basic infrastructure or vaccines, and at a lower price? Does it mean the poor are getting more of the goods that are important to them such as latrines versus sports facilities?

Given that trends in service delivery are subject to a number of concurrent developments, including changes in fiscal allocations and institutional reforms that alter the prevailing accountability constellation for service delivery, it is difficult to establish the causal relationships that are due to decentralization. Formal impact evaluation typically requires the identification of a treatment group and a control group (Minkel 2005). Decentralization is generally national in scope. Politically, it is very difficult to devolve voting rights and resources to one set of localities, but not others. Projects often face substantial hurdles in randomizing intervention districts. In practice, formal impact evaluation within decentralization projects is complicated by the fact that the selection criteria for intervention locations are typically not random or clear cut. Regional clustering to economize coordination costs, a history of previous interventions, or an individual locality's proven success or willingness to participate in reform tend to predominate. Moreover, the impacts of such projects may only emerge over time.

Using test scores as an outcome variable in a study on education in Argentina, Galiani, Gertler, and Schargrodsky (2005) find that richer and better administered schools benefit from decentralization, while the impact on poorer schools with less administrative capacity is negative. The fact that not all schools were decentralized at the same time provided an identification strategy in the study that was unique in many ways.[9] While decentralization may increase the overall performance of service delivery in terms of access and quality, it may also exacerbate geographic inequalities. The Argentina education study suggests that, in the absence of countervailing policy measures, decentralization may widen disparities between more advanced and less advanced regions. Granting greater autonomy over own-source fiscal resources will likely increase fiscal disparities in the absence of equalization measures. Increased autonomy may allow high-capacity, well-governed localities to forge ahead, while low-capacity and poorly governed districts risk falling behind. Consequently, decentralization may initially trigger some divergence in outcomes relative to initial conditions across key socioeconomic indicators (Kaiser, Pattinasarany, and Schulze 2006).

Decentralization may also have effects on interregional growth and investment patterns and on firms. Granting greater policy leverage to subnational governments may induce them to pursue policies aimed at attracting mobile investment, including in the area of taxation. Alternatively, because of local conditions, subnational governments may initially veer toward predatory behavior against incumbent firms. If bureaucrats at the central and decentralized levels are engaged in corruption in, for example, the issuance of licenses, then, if no effective disciplining mechanisms are instituted, this may significantly raise the costs of doing business for firms and negatively impact investment, such as during Russia's post-communist transition and decentralization (Shleifer and Vishny 1993).

If it is well designed, decentralization can generate incentives for innovation and better subnational performance. Policy design needs to foster these developments, while mitigating some of the risks, including through equalizing measures. Local outcomes are likely to be subject to significant lags. Hence, applied distributional analysis of decentralization will need to focus equally on ex post assessments. Providing an appraisal of distributional mechanisms and priority indicators is critical to setting out a forward-looking monitoring and evaluation strategy that can then feed back into policy design.

Finally, ongoing power or bureaucratic struggles between central and decentralized actors may compromise the quality of the compact and erode the efficacy of potential voice and client power. In situations where the roles and responsibilities of local officials and politicians are poorly defined, accountability may be blurred, and officials may be unwilling or unable to respond effectively. Overcoming these institutional constraints may therefore also represent an important ingredient in improving the distributional impact of decentralization.[10]

APPLIED METHODS AND INSTRUMENTS

Practitioners of the distributional analysis of decentralization will typically be confronted with significant information, data, time, and resource constraints. Box 6.2 presents a checklist of key sets of questions and types of evidence that are critical in setting out such analysis. Obviously, the more well defined a decentralization reform and the more focused the associated analysis, the more likely it is that the analysis will yield the direction and magnitude of the distributional impacts.

A number of instruments and methodologies offer valuable entry points for applied analysis (Table 6.3). Existing analytical reports often yield a significant stock of information to inform a prospective distributional analysis of decentralization. However, targeted primary qualitative and quantitative information collection and analysis will still frequently be necessary. Given that the impacts of decentralization are frequently subject to significant lags or are indirect, an important facet of the analysis should also be the identification of prospective baseline data for future rounds of impact assessment.

Public expenditure reviews have helped analyze the aggregate level, composition, and operational efficiency of public expenditures (Pradhan 1996). Country public expenditure reviews can help set the context for decentralized expenditures, including those derived from local own-source revenues, which are typically not covered in central government

BOX 6.2	Checklist for Distributional Impact Analysis of Decentralization

- What is the nature of the decentralization reform being assessed: devolution, delegation, deconcentration? What are the fiscal, administrative, and political dimensions, or combinations thereof? Are subnational governments given the ability to raise their own revenues and prioritize across services? Has decisionmaking over the local allocation of a specific program, such as transfers to the poor, been delegated to local entities?
- Through which mechanisms will the reform have the most immediate or pronounced distributional impacts? The introduction of new fiscal allocation criteria? Are new institutions and processes of decisionmaking changing distributional outcomes through local elections, mandated representation, participation, and accountability mechanisms in budget planning, implementation, or evaluation, and so on?
- What is the main level of decentralized analysis: state governments, local governments, communities, special-purpose districts in health care or education, committees?
- What are the primary subnational institutions and jurisdictions affected by the decentralization: counties, communes, *waredas* (districts), facilities, or committees?
- Which impacts of decentralization are likely to be observable in the short term? Changes in fiscal allocations that may be observed on a year-to-year basis? Which impacts will be subject to significant lags? Changes in service delivery and institutions such as capture in local governments?
- Which data are available to determine changes in the incidence of fiscal flows across people and places? Are revenue and expenditure data available only for devolved expenditures or specific programs? Are spatially disaggregated, deconcentrated expenditure data also available?
- Are data on the characteristics of relevant places and people available, such as poverty mapping data and local administrative data?
- Are assessments available of the prevailing accountability relationships such as are mapped in the *World Development Report 2004* accountability triangle (World Bank 2003b)? Does accountability condition the distribution of decentralized public resources or service delivery? Do decisionmaking arrangements at the subnational level appear to favor progressive or regressive distributional outcomes?
- How sensitive is the central government concerning the distributional implications of decentralization? Does the government care strongly about assuring positive distributional outcomes through targeting decisions or other measures?
- Are there winners and losers from the decentralization process in the central bureaucracy that may impact how decentralization is implemented? Will central agencies that are perceived to be losing power, prestige, and resources attempt to derail the decentralization reforms?
- Which key decentralized service delivery outcome indicators should be the focus of the distributional analysis? Local access to basic education or health care among the poor? Satisfaction with services?
- Is there evidence that the voice and client power of citizens have been enhanced? Broadly, is decentralization leading to an increase in empowerment? Do local elections seem to be providing politicians and officials with incentives for providing more public goods and better services, especially to the poor?
- Are baseline and other monitoring and evaluation indicators in place for future analysis?

TABLE 6.3. Core World Bank Instruments for Impact Analysis on Decentralization

Instrument	Issues addressed	Key data and data issues
Public expenditure review	Degree to which revenues and expenditures are decentralized. Incidence of revenue sources and expenditures across places and people.	Sufficient availability of disaggregated fiscal data across places and people; timely data on both budgeted and realized figures.
Public expenditure tracking survey	Extent to which resources such as higher-level transfers actually reach the front line. Identification of links in this expenditure chain that appear to be prone to leakage.	Mapping all relevant institutional levels and allocation processes in the expenditure chain; significant range of "leakage" phenomena.
Poverty mapping	Provide more disaggregated measures of poverty across places.	Data-intensive effort that requires a combination of census and household-survey data, often with significant delays in availability.
Quantitative service delivery survey	Measures of service delivery outcomes, including user perspectives, and delivery processes, for instance, provider accountability.	Survey design needs to cater for the local context and sector-specific issues such as the modes of provision and establish direct causality between outcomes and decentralization reforms.
Institutional and governance review	Assessment of key driving forces behind and constraints on decentralization, including political constraints. Institutional design issues.	Qualitative and quantitative assessments of key stakeholders and prevailing accountability relationships, as well as a better understanding of reform bottlenecks (for example, stalled decentralization) and operational responses.

Source: Compiled by the author.

budgets. These reviews can provide a good starting point for benchmarking the extent of aggregate decentralized public resource allocations, as well as changes brought on by decentralization policies. Relevant information might be collected on the level of and changes in devolved and delegated expenditures, such as the share of gross domestic product and the share of total public expenditures, and on the levels of and changes in the composition of devolved and delegated revenues, such as the share of own-source revenues, shared revenues, and general and earmarked transfers, as well on the composition of decentralized expenditures, for example, on the social sectors versus infrastructure. Ideally, this aggregate perspective would also lead to an assessment of the levels of and trends in interregional disparities. Similar information on the level and structure of and interregional variations and changes in deconcentrated expenditures may supply important distributional insights into decentralization. In many cases, however, these figures may be subsumed in the central government fiscal accounts and may therefore be difficult to disaggregate.

A number of public expenditure reviews have focused on decentralization and related subnational issues. The analysis of fiscal disparities across subnational jurisdictions, including local governments, will require nationally representative data on local own-source revenues and transfers from the central level. During Indonesia's 2001 big bang decentralization, transfers and an expanded revenue base, including shares in natural-resource revenue, were granted to district governments (*kabupaten, kota*). There were significant fiscal disparities in these 336 places in the wake of the decentralization (World Bank 2003a).[11] It was not possible to assess changes in the incidence of public expenditures or the impacts of these changes in terms of service delivery at the local level following decentralization owing to the absence of predecentralization data on deconcentrated and central government expenditures across places. However, a selection of provincial case studies has provided insights into interregional differences in capacity and the prevailing disparities arising in practice during the implementation of decentralization.

The impact of special autonomy status and the fiscal windfalls deriving from special autonomy status and natural-resource revenues in Indonesia's remote Papua province were the focus of a subsequent provincial public expenditure review (World Bank 2005d). The analysis found that, while the province was generally well treated and well endowed in fiscal terms, there were substantial differences across districts. Moreover, a relative abundance of fiscal resources did not appear to translate into better outcomes everywhere. Especially in remote districts, the effectiveness of service delivery was undermined because localities could not attract and retain key personnel such as doctors and trained teachers. This highlights the fact that decentralized distributional impacts depend on the level of resources available to localities, but also on the accountability and capacity constraints affecting resource use.

Public expenditure tracking surveys strive to produce detailed analyses of the extent to which public resources actually reach localities and front-line service delivery points. The methodology consists of mapping fiscal flows all the way to the front line, for example, to schools, and comparing actual receipts to planned receipts. By measuring flows across all levels of government, such analyses help identify key breaks in the public expenditure chain (Dehn, Reinikka, and Svensson 2003). An important component of these surveys is often the simple measures of horizontal differences in the resources reaching front-line facilities across major areas of public finance, including wages, nonwage recurrent expenditure, and capital investment.

The first-ever public expenditure tracking survey conducted in Uganda (Reinikka and Svensson 2004) remains the most successful example of diagnosis and subsequent improvements in the expenditure chain for capitation grants aimed at schools. Surveys in more than two dozen countries following decentralization have typically confronted more complex and ambiguous fiscal flows in the health and education sectors (Kaiser and Kushnarova 2005). In a decentralized context, this method can be especially useful in clarifying the de facto institutional and structural origins, methods, and impacts of expenditure decisions at the intermediate levels and the extent to which these detract from benefit incidence at other levels.

The distribution of centrally allocated resources is administered via two mechanisms: deconcentrated branch offices of the central government, such as education sector offices, or local municipalities through transfers and other delegated financing pathways. An example of the latter is the Glass of Milk program in Peru. In that case, an expenditure tracking exercise found that funds were quickly being dissipated by lower-level decisionmaking about onward disbursement and procurement. Using household-level survey data, the exercise was also able to estimate the extent of leakage attributable to beneficiary dilution (World Bank 2002a). Each expenditure channel manifested particular challenges in terms of fiscal leakage. The case highlights an issue running through the vast majority of public expenditure tracking surveys: decentralized leakage cannot always be attributed simply to theft. In many instances, resources may actually be reallocated at the local level for other purposes of unknown merit. Such reallocations may often be a symptom of chronic underfunding among local governments.

Data on the characteristics of poverty and the needs in expenditure both in places and among people are a key ingredient of the distributional analysis of decentralization. However, even if decentralized fiscal data across places are available, detailed socioeconomic data on localities are often not available. The sampling design of national surveys is typically such that they are not representative at the decentralized level. This makes it difficult to assess whether the poorest or richest places are benefiting from decentralization. Periodic census data provide one means of generating indicators for low levels of geographic disaggregation. Thus, poverty map approaches are being applied to leverage household-welfare surveys and census data so that indicators can be generated at very low levels of spatial disaggregation, for example, communes in Madagascar (Demombynes et al. 2002). Such approaches are being used for geographic targeting in poverty programs or the ex post assessment of decentralized revenues.

Subnational fiscal data, poverty mapping data, and other socioeconomic data can be usefully combined to assess incidence across places. A distributional analysis might begin with poverty indicators and simple correlation analysis, including, for instance, per capita transfers and total revenues. More systematic analysis might specify an ideal benchmark allocation based on multiple criteria such as projected fiscal capacity and poverty and compare this to actual allocation (see Box 6.1). Special care should be taken to ensure that data reflect actual allocation and are not subject to leakages relative to notional allocation assessed, for instance, by public expenditure tracking surveys.

Front-line service delivery surveys can provide important insights into decentralized outcomes. These have typically focused on basic health and education facilities, that is, schools and clinics. Absenteeism surveys, which usually consist of surprise visits to schools and clinics, may shed light on interregional differences in teacher and health worker attendance and the extent to which poor places and people are prone to this source of erosion in public service delivery. Facility surveys have found that, on average, 19 percent of teachers and 35 percent of health workers are absent at any given time in developing countries (Chaudhury et al. 2006). Evidence from India suggests that poorer states are more prone to absenteeism. Empirical studies have relied on a variety of methodologies, including specialized surveys. Ideally, the analysis would cover a sufficiently large sample of localities to provide some sense of the diversity of outcomes across localities.

Specialized surveys, including household and facility surveys, may also target dimensions of service delivery not usually found in standard household socioeconomic surveys, which normally provide evidence on basic service use and access, but not service quality. Such surveys might provide an indicative or even representative assessment of the strength of the various forms of accountability (voice, client power, and compact). Given the diversity in the dimensions of decentralized service delivery, distributional analysis that focuses on service delivery should strive to articulate the key variables of interest. These might include intermediate variables such as teacher absenteeism, local rates of access and enrollment, or outcome indicators on, for example, household-level incidence or satisfaction with service delivery.

A key decision in any distributional analysis of decentralization will revolve around whether to initiate a bespoke survey (an ad hoc survey tailored to specific needs) or whether data from, for instance, existing household surveys are sufficient. Given that subnational diversity is an important lens through which decentralized impacts might be assessed, surveys often face a small-area estimation problem. To cover a sufficient number of regions, the actual sample size of surveys within localities may be quite constrained to avoid prohibitive costs and long survey schedules. Thus, a sufficient number of poor people and poor households must be sampled within each locality if the differences in impacts across places (as defined in the checklist in Box 6.2) are to be adequately measured. Trade-offs stemming from this problem can typically be managed in a number of ways, must notably by trying to make national inferences based on a more limited subset of localities. Other methods may involve selecting localities based on some ex ante hypothesis about distributional impacts according to types of localities, such as by degree of ethnic diversity, rural-urban composition, and so on.

Institutional and governance reviews can serve as venues for describing the political economy of decentralization reforms (World Bank 2002b). An assessment of Pakistan's 2000 devolution was focused on ascertaining the scope for action and incentives among *nazims,* or district leaders (ADB, DfID, and World Bank 2004). The assessment highlighted a number of areas for improvement, including the excesses of clientelism and the provision of narrow private goods by local councilors because of the prevailing political economy of the devolution. It relied on detailed case studies in six of more than 100 districts across Pakistan's four provinces, as well as the collection of a national fiscal database on districts. A variant of the accountability triangle served as a useful foundation for structuring the discussion (see Figure 6.5). However, the primary objective of the assessment was not to pursue a distributional analysis, but rather to provide a broader analysis for the early implementation of a newly instituted decentralization framework.

A range of quantitative and qualitative methods may be used to fathom local institutions and the way they function both formally and informally (DfID and World Bank 2005). Focus groups and more structured surveys are helpful in identifying key actors and groups and their respective accountability and power relationships. Thus, stakeholder analysis of a certain aspect of decentralized decisionmaking can inform the way distributional decisions are made in a given context or, more broadly, the forces shaping an evolving decentralization project.

At one level, these methods may shed light on the relations among various central and subnational actors and determine how they are positioned vis-à-vis the decentralization reform. While certain agencies may act as champions for the reform, others, especially those central bureaucracies that may lose prestige or resources owing to the decentralization, may see few benefits. At the subnational level, this type of stakeholder analysis can provide a more nuanced assessment of the conditions under which local capture might endanger distributional outcomes, and it can suggest potential approaches for mitigating these risks by, for example, strengthening the transparency of particular decisionmaking processes.

The accountability triangle presented in Figure 6.5 is a useful guide on the types of indicators collected for distributional analysis. One class of indicators aims at assessing the *actual degree of autonomy and responsibility of subnational entities* within a particular area. While the functions of these entities may be formally decentralized in terms of, for instance, control over staffing decisions or local-level targeting, this may not always be the case in practice. Thus, a survey of health providers and local officials in Nigeria found that local governments rather than states were perceived to be responsible for basic health service delivery (Das Gupta, Gauri, and Khemani 2004; Khemani 2005). These sorts of measures can be especially valuable in contexts in which decentralized autonomy may vary both formally and informally within a country, as in the case of local government autonomy across states in India and Nigeria. The Indonesian governance and decentralization surveys asked about the primary responsibility across a set of functions, including hiring and firing, disciplinary actions, budgetary allocations, and drug purchases, to construct measures of decentralized responsibility and autonomy (World Bank 2005c). Measurement of these types of issues from multiple perspectives provides a useful cross-check on the validity of the statements of officials. Inconsistencies in the responses of various actors, such as central versus local government officials, can also supply useful insights into problems, including the lack of clarity in roles and responsibilities, that may be undermining accountability. Additional questions might focus on the apparent quality of *compact and management.* Thus, public expenditure tracking surveys can offer an indication of the extent to which financial allocations to decentralized entities are transparent and predictable.

Similarly, household surveys, citizen report cards, and user-group surveys between parent-teacher associations and other community groups can provide measures of the *degree to which client power and voice mechanisms function* at the local level. Questions might focus on the degree to which local constituents are informed about the identity and actions of local decisionmakers and how local budgets are allocated and implemented. Additional questions might probe the degree to which citizens, including the poor, feel they actually influence decentralized decisionmaking processes.

While administrative data can supply useful information on such matters as local budget allocations, care must be taken that these are not subject to misreporting or bias. Thus, if local governments are compensated for enrollment numbers under a new decentralization reform, there may be clear incentives to overreport outcomes. Measures focused on the education or training of local staff may also provide proxies for local capacity, although such formal input measures may not necessarily be gauging actual capacity, especially if local absenteeism among the most skilled is a significant problem.

The geographic variation in distributional outcomes and the various potential constellations in the accountability and capacities underlying any given decentralization mean that a special effort should be made to leverage many sources of data for analysis. The combination of fiscal and poverty mapping data provides one promising avenue. The critical role played by differences in local accountability and capacity in shaping distributional outcomes suggests that pertinent information on both dimensions may prove especially fruitful. For example, the analysis on Uganda was able to link local-level information on leakages with the characteristics of poverty to show that, while the formal distribution of capitation grants was quite egalitarian, outcomes in practice were more regressive (Reinikka and Svensson 2004).

Since decentralization processes typically encompass a number of simultaneous changes, it is often quite difficult to make strong claims concerning causality. However, some proximate indicators of the factors associated with poor distributional outcomes can help identify potential areas for policy reform within a given context by, for instance, increasing the amount of transparency and information associated with the process. In the context of more overarching decentralization reforms through, say, devolution, understanding which agencies stand to win or lose in terms of power, prestige, resources, and so on may also help clarify the likely proponents or opponents of the proposed measures.

This chapter has highlighted that a growing number of analyses have attempted to gain a better empirical understanding of the distributional impacts of decentralization and the underlying driving forces as they emerged, for example, from the formal and informal functioning of local institutions and governance processes.

In fact, an assessment of 10 local governments in Ghana (ClayDord Consultancy Services 2004) appears to be the only formal PSIA of decentralization. The assessment finds that local governments were generally underresourced and characterized by low capacity. As is typical of many decentralization projects, the relationship between absorptive capacity and the additional fiscal resources actually granted by the central level was entangled in a chicken-and-egg type debate. The assessment also finds that the reliance on and knowledge about district-level governments by the public were often quite limited, though this conclusion was based on a limited number of respondents (250). The PSIA on Ghana represents a useful perspective on the state of devolution there. However, the assessment does not spell out the scope of Ghana's decentralization, noting only that, in a major reform, the common fund of the district assemblies will receive or has already received 7.5 percent of national revenues. Ultimately, it is a more general assessment of the country's decentralization reform, rather than an explicit distributional analysis.

Examples like this demonstrate that the distributional impacts of decentralization tend to be quite context specific. Greater clarity about the main dimensions and mechanisms being assessed under a PSIA as part of a decentralization reform might help strengthen international insights into comparable decentralization experiences and potential policy responses.

CONCLUSIONS

Decentralization can refer to a wide range of reforms. Examples span major changes in a country's intragovernmental fiscal, administrative, and political arrangements, or they may be focused more simply on the introduction or reform of a cash-transfer program. In any case, it is important to determine the principal mechanisms through which the distributional impacts of the reforms occur. Building on such an applied framework, the analysis would ideally muster a realistic base of information to enable an empirical assessment. Inherent in decentralization is the expectation that the outcomes are diverse across subnational jurisdictions. Hence, studies should attempt to gather evidence from a sufficiently large number of localities to be representative and at least indicative of national patterns.

The limited record on PSIAs on decentralization suggests that future efforts need to provide a more explicit statement of the type of decentralization being assessed, the general magnitude of the public resources involved relative to overall public resources, and the effect of institutions in mediating distributional impacts. A range of complementary quantitative and qualitative methodologies is available to address these issues. The accountability triangle presented in Figure 6.5 can provide a useful organizing framework. Such an approach should help sharpen the understanding of the ways local governance arrangements across countries and localities shape distributional outcomes.

The objective of this chapter is to examine approaches that focus on identifying and assessing the short-term distributional impacts of decentralization reforms, primarily through the channel of public expenditures. A growing literature has been concentrating on the medium- to long-term, direct, and indirect impacts of decentralization, including the broader effects on democratic decentralization and empowerment. Some of the work has speculated on the impacts of decentralization on subnational growth, although the evidence is largely inconclusive (Martinez and McNab 2003). This chapter suggests that even the short-run evidence on decentralization is quite fragmented. One explanatory factor may be that decentralization projects are, by design and manner of implementation, quite diverse and difficult to compare. Another issue is that the methodologies for establishing the direction and magnitude of distributional impacts have been idiosyncratic. One research agenda might therefore involve promoting a more coherent understanding of the nature of decentralization and the application of consistent methodologies. At a minimum, this would contribute to more systematic insights into the impact of decentralization and a more compelling body of evidence on the first-order direction of the distributional implications.

Whereas changes in the allocation of fiscal inputs across peoples and places may be fairly rapid, the impacts in terms of local governance and public service delivery are likely to be subject to more significant lags and may even be negative. Consequently, it may be necessary to determine the proper timing for the assessment of particular impacts. In the case of many reforms, it may be simply "too early to tell." Especially with a process as wide-ranging and complex as decentralization, special care must be taken not to arrive at hasty or incomplete judgments. Nonetheless, assessments should attempt to identify early trends (and warnings) and develop indicators on emerging benefits and risks. The systematic cataloging of best and worst practices—say, across a representative sample of districts, councils, or *waredas*—would provide a very useful complement to a distributional analysis focused on short-term factors.

Assessing the distributional impacts of decentralization will typically require a threshold level of subnational data. Even if these data are available at the start of the decentralization, reporting systems often run the risk of deteriorating or even collapsing in the wake of decentralization. This may be aggravated by the fact that many central governments (and donors) are wont to demand more reporting by local entities. Such information is rarely used and, moreover, can overwhelm the capacity if not the willingness of localities to report. Agreement on a set of core decentralization monitoring and evaluation indicators, including, for example, a poverty reduction strategy that brings together government, donors, and other key stakeholders, will be an important step in moving from short-run assessments to sustainable, ongoing assessments. Consequently, the analysis of trends over time should be accompanied by critical investments in the collection of key baseline data and the tracking of indicators. Information does not flow only from the local level to the center, but useful information is also conveyed back to local governments, allowing for benchmarking across localities. This would enhance the incentives for quality reporting.

NOTES

1. For example, Bird et al. (1995) suggest that decentralization was associated with a deterioration of public services during the initial stages of transition in Eastern and Central Europe. In China, decentralization was associated with increased regional disparities in the provision of health and education services (Wong and West 1995). In contrast, Faguet (2004) finds that decentralization in Bolivia benefited marginalized regions and made service delivery more responsive.
2. Data on World Bank operations have been compiled from the Business Warehouse, and complementary data on conditionality for development policy have been drawn from the Adjustment Lending Conditionality Implementation Database (World Bank 2005a).
3. Albania, Brazil, Burkina Faso, Cape Verde, Chad, Ethiopia, Ghana, India, Mali, Mozambique, Pakistan, Peru, Romania, Rwanda, Senegal, Sierra Leone, Timor-Leste, and Vietnam.
4. Rwanda embarked on a territorial reform in late 2005, consolidating existing districts to one-third the original number.
5. Privatization, not discussed here, could also be considered a form of market-based decentralization.
6. Another example would be in the case of greater facility autonomy, such as through the retention of user fees.
7. The measure is akin to a Foster-Greer-Thorbecke poverty-gap index in summarizing the deviations from ideal allocations (the Figure 6.3 ratio is 1) by those below 1 (Deaton 1997):

$$\text{fiscal resource gap}^* = 1/N \Sigma (1 - Xi)^2 \tag{6.1}$$

where $X_i \leq 1$, (i) is the district, X the ratio, and N the total number of localities. The square implies a greater weight for outliers, but can be suitably increased or decreased.

8. The concepts of accountability and capacity are often overlapping in the sense that effective accountability (World Bank 2003b) implies capacity, for instance, the ability effectively to muster and utilize information. In practice, it is important to highlight the points where key capacity bottlenecks may be constraining more favorable distributional allocations and the transformation of resources into public services.

9. The study was able to leverage a unique set of circumstances. Any examination of the short-run distributional impacts of decentralization in a project or more general reform should exploit such fortuitous or intended variations across localities, for example, as part of a baseline with a two- to five-year forward-looking time horizon. When there are clear-cut rules that qualify one set of localities rather than another for a decentralization initiative, such as a poverty threshold or the receipt of a grant, one approach might be to identify comparable intervention and control localities along this demarcation.

10. At the operational level, the challenge is not simply to avoid creating unnecessary structures, but to leverage decentralized decisionmaking into strengthened, more general voice, client power, and compact-management accountability in public sector institutions (Bhatia 2003).

11. The number of local governments was subsequently increased to 434.

BIBLIOGRAPHY

ADB (Asian Development Bank), DfID (U.K. Department for International Development), and World Bank. 2004. "Devolution in Pakistan: An Assessment and Recommendations for Action." Report, Islamabad, Asian Development Bank, U.K. Department for International Development, and World Bank.

Ahmad, J., S. Devarajan, S. Khemani, and S. Shah. 2005. "Decentralization and Service Delivery." Policy Research Working Paper 3603, World Bank, Washington, DC.

Arauja, M. C., F. H. G. Ferreira, P. Lanjouw, and B. Özler. 2005. "Local Inequality and Project Choice in a Social Investment Fund." First draft of a work in progress, World Bank, Washington, DC.

Azfar, O., S. Kähkönen, and P. Meagher. 2001. "Conditions for Effective Decentralized Governance." IRIS Center, University of Maryland, College Park, MD.

Bahl, R. 1999. "Implementation Rules for Fiscal Decentralization." International Studies Program Working Paper 30, Georgia State University, Atlanta.

Bardhan, P. 2002. "Decentralization of Governance and Development." *Journal of Economic Perspectives* 16 (4): 185–205.

Bardhan, P., and D. Mookherjee. 2000. "Capture and Governance at Local and National Level." *American Economic Review* 90 (2): 135–39.

———. 2005. "Decentralizing Anti-Poverty Program Delivery in Developing Countries." *Journal of Public Economics* 89 (4): 675–704.

Besley, T., L. Rahman, R. Pande, and V. Rao. 2004. "The Politics of Public Good Provision: Evidence from Indian Local Governments." *Journal of the European Economic Association* 2 (2): 416–26.

Bhatia, M. 2003. "Public Sector Management and Institutional Issues in Social Funds." Draft report, Social Protection Unit, Human Development Network, World Bank, Washington, DC.

Bhushan, I., S. Keller, and B. Schwartz. 2002. "Achieving the Twin Objectives of Efficiency and Equity: Contracting Out Health Services in Cambodia." Brief 6, Economics and Research Department, Asian Development Bank, Manila.

Bird, R. M., R. Ebel, and C. Wallich, eds. 1995. *Decentralization of the Socialist State.* Washington, DC: World Bank.

Bird, R. M., and M. Smart. 2002. "Intergovernmental Fiscal Transfers: Some Lessons from International Experience." *World Development* 30 (6): 899–912.

Blair, H. 2000. "Participation and Accountability at the Periphery: Democratic and Local Governance in Six Countries." *World Development* 28 (1): 21–39.

Blanchard, O., and A. Shleifer. 2000. "Federalism With and Without Political Decentralization: China Versus Russia." Paper 1889, Harvard Institute of Economics Research, Harvard University, Cambridge, MA.

Bossuyt, J., and J. Gould. 2000. "Decentralisation and Poverty Reduction: Elaborating the Linkages." Policy Management Brief, European Centre for Development Policy Management, Maastricht, the Netherlands.

Chaudhury, N., J. Hammer, M. Kremer, K. Mularidharan, and H. Rogers. 2006. "Missing in Action: Teacher and Health Worker Absence in Developing Countries." *Journal of Economic Perspectives* (forthcoming).

ClayDord Consultancy Services. 2004. "Poverty and Social Impact Analysis (PSIA) on Resource Allocation, Mobilization, Management, and Capacity Building at District Level in Ghana." Report, ClayDord Enterprises Limited, Accra, Ghana.

Das Gupta, M., V. Gauri, and S. Khemani. 2004. "Decentralized Delivery of Primary Health Services in Nigeria: Survey Evidence from the States of Lagos and Kogi." Africa Region Human Development Working Paper 32815, World Bank, Washington, DC.

Deaton, A. 1997. *The Analysis of Household Surveys: A Microeconometric Approach to Development Policy.* Baltimore: Johns Hopkins University Press.

Dehn, J., R. Reinikka, and J. Svensson. 2003. "Survey Tools for Assessing Performance in Service Delivery." In *The Impact of Economic Policies on Poverty and Income Distribution: Evaluation Techniques and Tools,* ed. François Bourguignon and Luiz A. Pereira da Silva, Chapter 9. New York: Oxford University Press.

Demombynes, G., C. Elbers, J. Lanjouw, P. Lanjouw, J. Mistiaen, and B. Özler. 2002. "Producing an Improved Geographic Profile of Poverty." Discussion Paper 39, United Nations University–World Institute for Development Economics Research, Helsinki.

DfID (U.K. Department for International Development) and World Bank. 2005. *Tools for Institutional, Social and Political Analysis (TIPS): Sourcebook for PSIA.* London: Poverty Analysis and Monitoring Team, Department for International Development.

Diaz-Cayeros, A., B. Magaloni, and B. R. Weingast. 2003. "Tragic Brilliance: Equilibrium Hegemony and Democratization in Mexico." Unpublished manuscript, Hoover Institution, Stanford University, Stanford, CA.

Dillinger, W. 2005. "Intergovernmental Fiscal Relations (in the EU 8 Countries)." Report, Poverty Reduction, and Economic Management Unit, Europe and Central Asia Region, World Bank, Washington, DC.

Ebel, R. D., and S. Yilmaz. 2001. "Fiscal Decentralization: Is It Happening?, How Do We Know?" Paper presented to "Public Finance in Developing and Transition Countries: A Conference in Honor of Richard Bird," Georgia State University, Atlanta, April 5–6.

Evans, A. 2004. "Administrative Decentralization: A Review of Staffing Practices during Decentralization in Eight Countries." Report, World Bank, Washington, DC.

Faguet, J.-P. 2004. "Does Decentralization Increase Responsiveness to Local Needs?: Evidence from Bolivia." *Journal of Public Economics* 88 (3–4): 867–94.

Foster, A. D., and M. R. Rosenzweig. 2002. "Democratization, Decentralization, and the Distribution of Public Goods in a Poor Rural Economy." Working Paper 010, Bureau for Research and Economic Analysis of Development, Berkeley, CA.

Galasso, E., and M. Ravallion. 2005. "Decentralized Targeting of an Anti-Poverty Program." *Journal of Public Economics* 89 (4): 705–22.

Galiani, S., P. Gertler, and E. Schargrodsky. 2005. "School Decentralization: Helping the Good Get Better, but Leaving the Poor Behind." Unpublished working paper, Universidad de San Andres, Buenos Aires.

Hofman, B., Kadjatmiko, K. Kaiser, and B. Suharnoko. 2005. "Evaluating Indonesia's Fiscal Equalization." Unpublished working paper, World Bank, Washington, DC.

Hofman, B., and K. Kaiser. 2005. "Decentralization, Democratic Transition, and Local Governance in Indonesia." In *Decentralization and Local Governance in Developing Countries: A Comparative Perspective*, ed. P. Bardhan and D. Mookherjee, 81–124. Cambridge, MA: The MIT Press.

Jütting, J., E. Corsi, and A. Stockmayer. 2005. "Decentralization and Poverty Reduction." Development Centre Policy Insights 56, Organisation for Economic Co-operation and Development, Paris.

Jütting, J., C. Kaufman, I. McDonnel, H. Osterrieder, N. Pinaud, and L. Wegner. 2004. "Decentralization and Poverty in Developing Countries: Exploring the Impact." Development Centre Working Paper 236, Organisation for Economic Co-operation and Development, Paris.

Kaiser, K., and I. Kushnarova. 2005. "Public Expenditure Tracking Surveys (PETS): International Stocktaking." Presentation to the Public Sector Governance Board, World Bank, Washington, DC, July 14.

Kaiser, K., D. Pattinasarany, and G. G. Schulze. 2006. "Decentralization, Governance, and Public Services in Indonesia." In *Decentralization in Latin America and Asia: An Inter-Disciplinary Perspective*, ed. G. Peterson, P. Smoke, and E. J. Gómez. Cheltenham, United Kingdom: Edward Elgar.

Keefer, P., and S. Khemani. 2003. "Democracy, Public Expenditures, and the Poor." Policy Research Working Paper 3164, World Bank, Washington, DC.

Khemani, S. 2005. "Local Government Accountability for Service Delivery in Nigeria." *Journal of African Economies* 14 (October).

Litvack, J., J. Ahmad, and R. Bird. 1998. "Rethinking Decentralization in Developing Countries." PREM Network Sector Studies, Poverty Reduction and Economic Management Network, World Bank, Washington, DC.

Martinez, J., and R. M. McNab. 2003. "Fiscal Decentralization and Economic Growth." *World Development* 31 (9): 1597–1616.

Minkel, J. R. 2005. "Trials for the Poor: Rise of Randomized Trials to Study Antipoverty Programs." *Scientific American* December.

Ndegwa, S. N. 2002. "Decentralization in Africa: A Stocktaking Survey." Africa Region Working Paper Series 40, World Bank, Washington, DC.

Olken, B. 2004. "Corruption and the Costs of Redistribution: Micro-evidence from Indonesia." Paper prepared for National Bureau of Economic Research, Cambridge, MA.

Pradhan, S. 1996. "Evaluating Public Spending: A Framework for Public Expenditure Reviews." Discussion Paper 323, World Bank, Washington, DC.

Quian, Y., and B. R. Weingast. 1995. "China's Transition to Markets: Market-Preserving Federalism, Chinese Style." Unpublished report, Hoover Institution, Stanford, CA.

Raich, U. 2005. "Fiscal Determinants of Empowerment." Policy Research Working Paper 3705, World Bank, Washington, DC.

Reinikka, R., and J. Svensson. 2004. "Local Capture: Evidence from a Central Government Transfer Program in Uganda." *Quarterly Journal of Economics* 119 (2): 679–705.

Shleifer, A., and R. W. Vishny. 1993. "Corruption." *Quarterly Journal of Economics* 108 (3): 599–617.

Tsai, L. 2005. "Accountability without Democracy: How Solidarity Groups Provide Public Goods Provision in Rural China." Paper presented at the Public Sector and Anticorruption Brown Bag Series, Poverty Reduction and Economic Management Network, World Bank, Washington, DC, November.

von Braun, J., and U. Grote. 2000. "Does Decentralization Serve the Poor?" Paper presented at the Conference, "Fiscal Decentralization," International Monetary Fund, Washington, DC, November.

Wong, C., and L. West. 1995. "Fiscal Decentralization and Growing Regional Disparities in Rural China: Some Evidence in the Provision of Social Services." *Oxford Review of Economic Policy* 2 (4): 70–84.

World Bank. 2002a. "Peru: Restoring Fiscal Discipline for Poverty Reduction, Public Expenditure Review." Economic Report, Latin America and the Caribbean Region, World Bank, Washington, DC.

———. 2002b. "Institutional and Governance Reviews: A New Type of Economic and Sector Work." PREMnotes 75, Poverty Reduction and Economic Management Network, World Bank, Washington, DC.

———. 2003a. "Decentralizing Indonesia: A Regional Public Expenditure Overview Report." East Asia Poverty Reduction and Economic Management Unit, World Bank, Washington, DC.

———. 2003b. *World Development Report 2004: Making Services Work for Poor People.* New York: Oxford University Press.

———. 2004a. "Measuring Fiscal Decentralization." Data Note, Decentralization and Subnational Regional Economics Thematic Group, World Bank, Washington, DC.

———. 2004b. "Citizen Report Card Surveys: A Note on the Concept and Methodology." Social Development Notes: Participation and Civic Engagement 91, World Bank, Washington, DC.

———. 2005a. "Public Sector Governance (PSG) in Operations." Internal background document, Public Sector Group, World Bank, Washington, DC.

———. 2005b. "Examples of Effective Incentives and Mechanisms to Attract and Retain Personnel in Disadvantaged Areas." Public Sector Group, World Bank, Washington, DC.

———. 2005c. "Decentralization, Service Delivery, and Governance in Indonesia: Findings from the Governance and Decentralization Survey." World Bank, Jakarta.

———. 2005d. "Papua Public Expenditure Analysis: Regional Finance and Service Delivery in Indonesia's Most Remote Region." Report, Provincial Government of Papua, Support Office for Eastern Indonesia, World Bank, Makassar, Jakarta.

Zhuravskaya, E. V. 2000. "Incentives to Provide Local Public Goods: Fiscal Federalism, Russian Style." *Journal of Public Economics* 76 (3): 337–68.

Macroeconomic Shocks and Policies

B. Essama-Nssah

The importance of distributional issues in policymaking creates *a need for empirical tools* that can help assess the impact of economic shocks and policies on the living standards of relevant individuals. The purpose of this chapter is therefore to review some of the modeling approaches that are currently in use at the World Bank and other international financial institutions in the evaluation of the impact of macroeconomic shocks and policies on poverty and income distribution. The hope is that the interested reader might then be able to make an informed choice among the reviewed approaches.[1]

Developing countries face a host of macroeconomic challenges in the design and implementation of development strategies and policies. Some of the recurrent issues include (1) fiscal adjustment, (2) monetary policy reforms, (3) trade liberalization, and (4) the impact of terms-of-trade shocks. *Fiscal adjustment* involves a modification of government tax, spending, and borrowing policies to achieve a sustainable macroeconomic framework consistent with the objectives of economic growth and poverty reduction. *Monetary policy* reforms entail control of foreign capital flows and adjustments in the money supply and in the exchange rate. *Trade liberalization* implies a reduction or removal of trade barriers such as quantitative restrictions and tariffs. In fact, trade liberalization has

The author is grateful to Stefano Paternostro, Aline Coudouel, Vijdan Korman, Moataz Mostafa Kamel El Said, Hans Löfgren, Delfin S. Go, Oleksiy Ivaschenko, David P. Coady, Limin Wang, and Philippe H. Le Houerou for useful suggestions and insightful comments on an earlier draft. Vijdan Korman also provided excellent support during the preparation of this chapter.

become a prerequisite for participation in the World Trade Organization. Finally, *terms-of-trade* shocks are important determinants of the performance of open economies. Many developing countries are, indeed, primary commodity exporters or net oil importers and hence vulnerable to volatility in the world prices of these commodities.

The need to consider the distributional implications of such macroeconomic events stems from at least two basic considerations related to the *goal of development* and the *heterogeneity of the stakeholders.* In the context of the Millennium Declaration (United Nations 2000), the international community has included poverty and hunger eradication among the *basic objectives of development* and has thus made poverty reduction a benchmark measure of the performance of socioeconomic systems. This vision is consistent with the notion of development as empowerment, meaning a process that entails the expansion of the ability of participants to achieve their freely chosen life plans. In this perspective, poverty is seen as the deprivation of basic capabilities to live the kind of life that one has reason to value (Sen 1999).

Furthermore, political factors are essential determinants of economic outcomes, and distributional issues underpin the political dimension of policymaking (understood to include implementation) because of the heterogeneity of interests. Heterogeneity may stem from differences in tastes, in resource endowments, or in views of the world. There could be conflicts of interest even in situations where the socioeconomic agents are identical ex ante. They may value a good equally, yet be in conflict over the distribution of the good (Drazen 2000). Approaches to policymaking may be characterized according to whether they account for *political constraints* arising from a heterogeneity of interests. With no conflict of interest, optimal policies could be found by maximizing the utility of a representative agent. This is essentially the *normative approach to policymaking* (Dixit 1996). In the positive approach, policymaking is considered a political process involving strategic interactions among various socioeconomic agents subject to potential conflict over distribution.

Two basic dimensions define the desirable properties of a policy model: *relevance* and *reliability* (Quade 1982). A relevant model focuses on issues of concern and on politically significant socioeconomic groups and the interactions among them. A reliable model is based on sound analytical linkages between available policy instruments (part of the exogenous variables) and relevant outcomes such as poverty or inequality (part of the endogenous variables) to ensure a high degree of confidence in the model's predictions. Modeling the poverty and distributional impacts of macroeconomic shocks and policies therefore requires *a clear understanding of the transmis-*

sion channels. This relates to the specification of the linkages among macroeconomic shocks and policies, as well as the fundamental determinants of the distribution of economic welfare. In the terminology of Bourguignon, Ferreira, and Lustig (2005), macroeconomic events may have three types of effects on income distribution: (1) *endowment effects* represent changes in the amounts of the resources available to individuals or households; (2) *price effects* translate changes in the remuneration of these resources; (3) finally, *occupational effects* represent changes in resource allocation.

The outline of the chapter is as follows. The following section focuses on simulation models of the size distribution of an indicator of economic welfare. In the section, two types of approaches to modeling the size distribution of economic welfare across a population are reviewed. The first includes purely statistical models such as *POVCAL* (Chen, Datt, and Ravallion 1991) and *SimSIP Poverty* (Wodon, Ramadas, and Van der Mensbrugghe 2003). These two tools rely on a parameterization of the *Lorenz curve* and, arguably, offer the simplest way of simulating the poverty effect of macroeconomic shocks and policies. The second approach relies on *unit record data* and includes (1) *PovStat* (Datt and Walker 2002), (2) the *maximum value or envelope* model[2] (Chen and Ravallion 2004; Ravallion and Lokshin 2004), and (3) the *household income and occupational choice model* (Bourguignon and Ferreira 2005).

The subsequent section discusses poverty and distributional analysis within a general equilibrium framework (Dervis, de Melo, and Robinson 1982; Decaluwé et al. 1999).

The penultimate section examines *modular* approaches to linking macroeconomic models to models of income distribution. The section focuses on the 123PRSP model—the name stands for one country, two sectors, and three commodities, and the model is built to feed into the macroeconomic framework for Poverty Reduction Strategy Papers—(Devarajan and Go 2003); the Poverty Analysis Macroeconomic Simulator I (PAMS I) (Pereira da Silva, Essama-Nssah, and Samaké 2003); PAMS II (Essama-Nssah 2004, 2005); a macro-micro simulation model for Brazil that uses the investment savings–liquidity money (IS-LM) framework for macroeconomic analysis (Ferreira et al. 2004); and the integrated macroeconomic model for poverty analysis (IMMPA) framework, which links a dynamic computable general equilibrium (CGE) model to unit record data (Agénor, Izquierdo, and Jensen 2006).

Concluding remarks are presented in the last section. Table A7.1 in the annex provides a summary description of the tools reviewed in this chapter.

Table 7.1 presents a synoptic view of the modeling approaches described in this chapter, with a focus on three elements: the treatment

TABLE 7.1. Modeling the Poverty and Distributional Impacts of Macroeconomic Shocks and Policies

Models/approaches	Macroeconomic model	Linkage variables	Specification of distribution (micromodel)
A. Distributional focus (no explicit macromodel)			
Lorenz curve approach			
1. POVCAL	• Implicit	• Mean consumption/ income of the distribution	• Parameterized Lorenz function
2. SimSIP Poverty	• Implicit	• Mean consumption/ income of the distribution	• Parameterized Lorenz function
Unit record approach			
1. PovStat	• Implicit	• Per capita household consumption • Sector of employment of the household head • Growth rate of per capita output in the sector of employment	• Unit record data
2. The envelope model (microsimulation-1)	• Implicit	• Changes in supply prices for household production activities • Changes in demand prices • Changes in incomes	• Unit record data
3. Household income and occupational choice models (microsimulation-2)	• Implicit	• Changes in commodity prices • Changes in incomes (wages and self-employment income) • Changes in employment by type of occupation	• Unit record data

B. Standard general equilibrium analysis

1. CGE–representative household	• Static CGE	• Changes in factor and commodity prices • Changes in employment	• A few representative households
2. CGE–extended representative household	• Static CGE	• Changes in factor and commodity prices • Changes in employment	• A few representative households • A model of size distribution

C. Sequential macro-micro linkages

1. PAMS I	• Revised minimum standard model extended (RMSM-X)	• Growth rate of output • Changes in sectoral wages • Changes in disposable income by group	• Unit record data
2. PAMS II	• Static CGE model	• Changes in factor and commodity prices • Changes in employment • Household-level real consumption	• Unit record data • Parameterized Lorenz function
3. 123PRSP	• Financial programming model • Growth models • 123CGE model	• Changes in commodity prices • Changes in incomes	• Unit record data • Envelope model
4. CGE-microsimulation-1	• Static CGE model	• Changes in factor and commodity prices • Changes in incomes	• Unit record data • Envelope model

(continued)

TABLE 7.1. Modeling the Poverty and Distributional Impacts of Macroeconomic Shocks and Policies (*Continued*)

Models/approaches	Macroeconomic model	Linkage variables	Specification of distribution (micromodel)
5. CGE-microsimulation-2	• Static CGE model	• Changes in commodity prices • Changes in incomes (wages and self-employment income) • Changes in employment by type of occupation	• Unit record data • Household income and occupational choice models
6. IS-LM microsimulation-2	• IS-LM model	• Changes in commodity prices • Changes in incomes (wages and self-employment income) • Changes in employment by type of occupation	• Unit record data • Household income and occupational choice models
7. IMMPA	• Dynamic CGE model with a financial sector	• Real growth rates in per capita consumption and disposable income for six representative households	• Unit record data

Source: Compiled by the author.

of the macroeconomic framework, the modeling of the size distribution, and the variables linking the macroeconomic framework to the model of distribution. The first category has no explicit macromodel. The second embeds distributional mechanisms in a general equilibrium model.

The last approach links a macroeconomic model to a distribution model in a top-down fashion. All the models reviewed fall within the class of policy models. The specification of such models is dictated by the issues at stake, the knowledge about the nature of the process involved, and the availability and reliability of relevant data. It is impossible to provide, in the context of an overview like this one, enough implementation details for each model under consideration. However, an effort has been made to include a long list of relevant references, as well as boxes describing examples of the approaches. In addition, the annex to this chapter supplies a description of many of the tools considered. It also includes an estimation of the cost of implementation and information on appropriate software for some of the tools.

SIMULATION MODELS OF THE SIZE DISTRIBUTION OF INCOME

The idea of simulating the distribution of income among individuals or households originated in the field of public finance because of the need to have reliable models for the detailed analysis of the incidence of a tax-benefit system. The basic idea is to model the distribution of household income and consumption *taking household behavior as exogenous,* but fully accounting for applicable taxes and transfers (Davies 2004). To reflect the diversity of the characteristics in a population adequately, these simulation models require a nationally representative microdata set. The fact that household behavior is exogenous means that these accounting models can predict only the first-round effects of a tax-benefit policy on inequality and poverty.

All the approaches reviewed in this section are various interpretations of the basic idea underlying tax-benefit simulation models. *POVCAL* and *SimSIP Poverty* illustrate the use of the Lorenz curve for poverty and distributional impact analysis. These two tools are particularly useful when only aggregate or grouped data are available. The second class of simulation tools considered under this heading relies on unit record data on the distribution of some money-metric measure of economic welfare at the individual or household level. Three approaches are examined. *PovStat* uses per capita consumption as a measure of welfare. The second approach relies on *the envelope theorem* and employs the *maximum value function* to model the determinants of individual welfare (Chen and

Ravallion 2004; Ravallion and Lokshin 2004). The last approach is based on a *reduced-form model of household income generation* (Bourguignon and Ferreira 2005). Even though the envelope model and the income-generation models include some aspects of household behavior, these microsimulation models must be viewed as *statistical* devices to the extent that they fail to account fully for market adjustment through endogenous prices or the adjustment of the behavior of agents from one equilibrium state to another (Ferreira and Leite 2003).

The Lorenz curve approach

Given that poverty indexes are computed on the basis of a distribution of living standards that is entirely characterized by the mean and by the degree of inequality, it is reasonable to think of a poverty indicator as a function of these two factors. In fact, procedures have been developed for the decomposition of poverty changes into growth and inequality components (Datt and Ravallion 1992; Kakwani 1993, 1997; Shorrocks 1999). The growth component is associated with a variation in the mean of the distribution, while the inequality component is linked to a change in an inequality indicator. The Lorenz-based approach to simulating poverty and inequality relies on this basic idea and the fact that most common poverty and inequality measures can be recovered from the mean of the distribution and a fully specified Lorenz function. Indeed, given these two pieces of information about an income distribution, the level of income at a given percentile can be recovered from the mean and the first-order derivative, while the corresponding density can be calculated from the mean and the second-order derivative.

Generally speaking, at the most aggregate level, the poverty implications of any policy affecting aggregate output (or consumption) can be analyzed within this framework. The conclusions from such an analysis hinge on the assumption maintained about the behavior of inequality. One frequently used assumption is distributional neutrality, whereby inequality is assumed to be constant. Another possibility is to specify a pattern of change in inequality. For instance, one can assume a *Lorenz-convex transformation* that entails a distribution-neutral change in everyone's income level, coupled with a redistribution process that taxes every income at a given percentage and redistributes the proceeds equally over the entire population (Ferreira and Leite 2003).

Two basic tools are reviewed that are grounded on this framework: *POVCAL* and *SimSIP Poverty*. These simulation tools are most convenient if distributional data are available only in aggregate form.

POVCAL

The following types of simulations can be performed using POVCAL (Datt 1992, 1998): (1) sensitivity analysis with respect to the poverty line, (2) analysis of the poverty implications of distributionally neutral growth, (3) decomposition of poverty changes into growth and redistribution components, plus a residual, and (4) the contribution to overall poverty of regional or sectoral disparities in mean consumption. As far as policy analysis is concerned, POVCAL can be used to trace the poverty and distributional implications of any policy that affects the overall mean or the sectoral means.

This tool presents two major limitations for the analysis of the distributional impact of macroeconomic shocks and policies: the modeling of the macroeconomic framework remains implicit, and the level of aggregation of the household level limits the ability of the tool to account for heterogeneity.

For POVCAL, data are expected to be structured in "records" and "subgroups."[3] The number of records is determined by the number of class intervals or quantiles in the data. A data set presented in deciles contains 10 records. The number of subgroups corresponds to the number of exhaustive and mutually exclusive socioeconomic groups, for example, rural and urban households.[4]

Eight data configurations are possible: (1) the cumulative proportion of individuals and the corresponding cumulative proportion of income; (2) the proportion of the population and the associated proportion of income; (3) the cumulative proportion of the population and the proportion of income; (4) the proportion of the population and the cumulative proportion of income; (5) the percentage of people in a given class interval and the class mean income; (6) the upper bound of the class interval, the percentage of the population in the class, and the class mean income; (7) the upper bound of the class interval, the cumulative proportion of the population in the class, and the class mean income; and (8) the upper bound of the class interval and the percentage of the population in the class.

When the class mean income is unknown, the following rule of thumb is recommended (Chen, Datt, and Ravallion 1991): (1) set the mean for the poorest class at 80 percent of the upper bound of that class interval; (2) set the mean of the highest class at 30 percent above the lower bound of that class; and (3) use the midpoint for all other classes.

POVCAL will prompt the user for five key inputs: (1) the name of the ASCII input data file, (2) the number of subgroups, (3) the number of records, (4) the type of data configuration (codes 1 through 8), and

(5) the DOS name for the output file. Once this input has been received for each of the two specifications of the Lorenz curve underlying the simulation tool, the program provides an estimate of the Lorenz curve, along with relevant statistical summary measures. It prompts the user to supply a poverty line and a different estimate of the mean of the distribution (if he/she does not want to use the estimate based on the data).

An application of POVCAL is illustrated in Box 7.1.

It is important to make sure that the poverty line is expressed in the same units as the mean of the distribution. The program then computes the Gini index of inequality, poverty measures of the Foster-Greer-Thorbecke (1984) family, and the associated elasticities with respect to the mean and the Gini index. The computation of the elasticities with respect to the Gini index assumes a Lorenz-convex transformation whereby the Lorenz curve shifts proportionately up or down at all points. Finally, the program plots the fitted Lorenz curves and the corresponding first and second derivatives and provides an assessment of the Lorenz curve that seems to fit the data most closely.

SimSIP Poverty

SimSIP Poverty is a member of the SimSIP family of simulation tools, a collection of Excel-based modules designed to simulate social indicators and poverty. The following inputs are expected for the tool: (1) income or consumption distribution by groups (deciles or quintiles), (2) the mean income or consumption for each group, (3) the population shares for each group, and (4) the relevant poverty lines. Depending on data availability, the analysis can be performed at the national level and for socioeconomic groups classified by place of residence (urban or rural) or by sector of employment (agriculture, manufacturing, and services).

The key limitation on SimSIP Poverty arises because changes in per capita income (or expenditure) and the linkages between macroeconomic shocks and policies are exogenous. The tool thus imposes a minimal structure upon the complex relationship between policy instruments and poverty outcomes. No behavioral or market adjustment is modeled explicitly. The reliability of the predictions of the simulator thus depends on the modeling of the process that engendered the changes in the means and the accuracy of the population shares that are fed into the simulator. Another limitation is due to the requirement that the input data be aggregated. This implies a loss of information with respect to the heterogeneity of households. In fact, SimSIP Poverty shares these limitations with POVCAL.

The use of SimSIP Poverty is illustrated in Box 7.2.

BOX 7.1 **Lorenz Curve Approach, POVCAL: Assessing Poverty Dynamics in Madagascar**

Essama-Nssah (1997) uses POVCAL to analyze the dynamics of poverty in Madagascar between 1962 and 1980. Over this period, different governments showed various levels of concern over poverty issues. Some of the policy choices targeted either the rural or the urban sector. From the early 1960s to the mid-1970s, public policy favored the rural sector by lifting the poll and cattle tax applicable to the sector and by providing farmers free access to agricultural inputs. In 1977, an urban bias was introduced in public policy when the government increased the minimum wage and decided to subsidize basic items such as rice, edible oils, and condensed milk.

The study is based on two published aggregated data sets on income distribution in the rural and urban sectors. These data are in the form of class intervals with the associated frequency and mean incomes. The analysis through POVCAL revealed that, while poverty in Madagascar remained a predominantly rural phenomenon, poverty generally increased between 1962 and 1980 in both rural and urban areas. A decomposition of the poverty outcomes into growth and inequality components showed that increased income inequality in the rural sector was the major cause of the observed increase in rural poverty (see Table 7.2). In the urban sector, however, increased poverty was most likely due to the lack of economic growth.

The study concluded that the urban bias introduced into government social policies in the mid-1970s was not justifiable strictly on grounds of poverty reduction. A simulation of what the level of poverty would have been had rural and urban mean incomes been set to the national average showed that a significant reduction in aggregate poverty could have been achieved had the government pursued effective policies to lessen the regional disparities.

TABLE 7.2. Poverty Measures and the Decomposition of Poverty Outcomes, Madagascar, 1962–80

Measure	Value (1962)	Value (1980)	Change	Growth	Inequality	Residual
Rural						
Headcount	46.65	42.25	−4.40	−17.72	6.24	7.08
Poverty gap	10.50	15.24	4.74	−5.67	10.29	0.12
Squared poverty gap	3.15	7.51	4.36	−2.06	7.68	−1.26
Urban						
Headcount	13.35	18.47	5.12	9.74	−1.34	−3.28
Poverty gap	2.72	6.73	4.01	3.88	1.20	1.07
Squared poverty gap	0.73	3.31	2.58	1.73	1.00	−0.15

Source: Essama-Nssah 1997.

BOX 7.2 **Lorenz Curve Approach, SimSIP Poverty: Predicting the Effect of Aggregate Growth on Poverty in Paraguay**

Datt et al. (2003) have applied SimSIP Poverty to data for Paraguay in order to study the impact of growth patterns on poverty for a period of five years (from 1997 to 2001). Six cases are considered: (1) each sector (agriculture, industry, services) of the economy grows at 3 percent, (2) a 2 percent growth rate in each sector, (3) a 1 percent growth rate per sector, (4) a 2 per percent growth rate in agriculture and a 3 percent rate elsewhere, (5) a 1 percent growth in agriculture and a 3 percent rate elsewhere, and, finally, (6) a 3 percent growth in agriculture and a 1 percent rate in other sectors. The underlying data include (1) population shares by sectors (rural/urban) and three economic activities (agriculture, industry, and services), as well as the total national-level population, and (2) the mean income per capita corresponding to the population shares.

The impact of different sectoral growth patterns on the poverty headcount is reported in Table 7.3. Holding inequality constant, a 3 percent annual growth in per capita income in every sector for five years would reduce poverty by 3 percentage points, to 28.95 percent. Using the table, one can compare the contribution of different growth patterns to poverty reduction. Moreover, given that poverty rates are higher in rural areas and in agriculture, any migration out of those sectors is likely to decrease poverty.

The reported results for each scenario vary slightly depending on whether aggregate poverty is computed from the rural/urban perspective or as a weighted average of outcomes in each sector of employment. The exercise illustrates the fact that the analyst may use SimSIP Poverty to assess different patterns of growth.

TABLE 7.3. Simulations of the Impact of Growth Patterns on Poverty in Paraguay: Some Examples

National poverty headcount, %	Period 1	Period 2: national simulation	Period 2: national as weighted average of urban/rural sectors	Period 2: national as weighted average of employment sectors
3% per sector for five years	32.13	27.46	27.48	27.42
2% per sector for five years	32.13	28.95	28.97	28.92
1% per sector for five years	32.13	50.51	30.53	30.49
2% in agriculture, rural sector, 3% elsewhere for five years	32.13	–	28.15	27.94
1% in agriculture, rural sector, 3% elsewhere for five years	32.13	–	28.82	28.46
3% in agriculture, rural sector, 1% elsewhere for five years	32.13	–	29.06	29.34

Source: Datt et al. 2003.

Computations are based on a parameterization of the Lorenz curve. Two parameterizations are provided by the general quadratic and the Beta models. For robust poverty comparisons over time and among sectors, the simulator produces poverty dominance and Lorenz curves. It also computes the Gini coefficient, poverty measures of the Foster-Greer-Thorbecke family, and the associated elasticities with respect to growth and inequality. Any member of this family for a given group can be written as a weighted sum of poverty within all the subgroups. The weights are equal to the population shares. Based on this fact, SimSIP Poverty provides decompositions of poverty outcomes in three components. The first component represents change in within-group poverty. The second term measures the effects of population shifts among groups. The last component captures the interaction between inter- and within-group effects (see Ravallion and Huppi 1991 for details). It is also possible to decompose changes in poverty over time into the following contributing factors: growth, inequality, and a residual. These decompositions require two sets of observations on the distribution of income or expenditure. This is the same approach discussed above in the case of POVCAL.

Unit-record-based approaches

PovStat

PovStat is an Excel-based tool primarily designed to simulate the poverty implications of alternative growth paths. This simulation tool arose out of the basic idea that the rate and pattern of economic growth determine the evolution of poverty over time. In particular, *it is assumed that per capita consumption for a household grows at the same rate as per capita output in the sector of employment of the head of the household.* Households are classified into four sectors on the basis of the employment status of the head: (1) agriculture, (2) industry, (3) services, and (4) residual. The residual sector amalgamates households with unemployed or inactive heads and those with unknown occupational status.

A major advantage of PovStat over SimSIP Poverty stems from the use of unit-level data. This has the potential to improve the precision of the estimates of the poverty and inequality measures. Otherwise, the tool shares in the major limitations that have been flagged for POVCAL and SimSIP Poverty: (1) there is no explicit modeling of the macroeconomic framework, and (2) there is a loss of information about the heterogeneity of households because the sectoral classification of households is based on the status of the heads of household.

Finally, the flexibility provided in setting assumptions about changes in inequality comes at the price of an increased uncertainty in the results.

The two key inputs are country-specific unit record household-level data representing the distribution of living standards for a base year and a set of user-supplied projection parameters characterizing the paths of growth. Household-level data involve six variables that must be submitted to the simulator in the following order: (1) a household identifier, (2) monthly per capita consumption in local currency units for the base year, (3) household weight (or a population expansion factor), (4) an urban dummy, (5) household size, and (6) sector of employment of the household head.

For each year within the projection horizon, the per capita consumption for each household is computed recursively using a growth rate that is equal to the rate of per capita output. The latter is calculated as the real growth in gross domestic product (GDP) in the sector of employment of the head of household, minus the rate of population growth in that sector. For the first three sectors, the sectoral population growth rate is computed from the overall population growth rate and an adjustment factor that depends on the share of each sector in total employment and sector-specific growth rates of employment. The population in the residual sector is assumed to grow at the same rate as the overall population. Household weights are also adjusted recursively using sectoral rates of population growth.

Assuming that inequality within sectors remains constant, PovStat computes the following indicators for the forecast horizon: (1) poverty measures of the Foster-Greer-Thorbecke family, (2) the number of people below the poverty line, (3) mean monthly per capita consumption, (4) Gini coefficients, (5) two inequality measures of the generalized entropy family, and (6) the variance of log consumption per person.

In general, the simulation framework offers the user the opportunity to control the simulation process by setting the following parameters: (1) the forecast horizon, (2) the poverty line, (3) the base and survey years, (4) the survey-year population, (5) the country's purchasing power parity exchange rate, (6) the base and survey-year consumer price indexes (CPIs), (7) the sectoral output growth rates for each projection year, (8) the population growth rates and employment growth rates for each projection year, (9) the survey-year sectoral GDP and employment shares, (10) the GDP deflator and the CPI for each projection year, (11) changes in the relative price of food by year, (12) the share of food in the bundle defining the poverty line, (13) the share of food in the CPI, (14) the change in the Gini within each sector for each projection year, (15) changes in the average propensity to consume, and (16) the drift between surveys and national accounts.

PovStat is illustrated in Box 7.3.

The envelope model

One approach in studying the impact of economic shocks and policies on an economic agent consists in analyzing the impact of those shocks and policies on the determinants of the agent's optimizing behavior. This behavior may be characterized in terms of the actions the economic unit can take and the objective function used to evaluate such actions. The *maximum value function* indicates the maximum attainable value of the objective function in terms of various parameters that enter both the objective function

---

BOX 7.3   **Unit Record Approach, PovStat: Growth, Inequality, and Simulated Poverty Paths for Tanzania**

Tanzania achieved rapid growth in per capita GDP in the 1995–2001 period, but household-budget survey data suggest that the decline in poverty between 1992 and 2001 was relatively small. Demombynes and Hoogeveen (2004) argue that a possible explanation for this outcome is that poverty increased during the period of economic stagnation in the early 1990s, while economic growth in the second half of the 1990s was able to offset only part of the early rise in poverty.

To test this hypothesis, the authors use PovStat to simulate the likely trajectory of poverty rates over the 1992–2002 period. They employ data from two household-budget surveys (1991/92 and 2000/1), along with growth rates derived from national account data. These growth rates are then applied to unit record data to estimate the full evolution of poverty over the course of the nine-year period.

The simulated poverty trajectories show that poverty rates followed a hump-shaped path during the period. Under a variety of scenarios, poverty incidence first increased to above 40 percent in the early 1990s and then declined below 36 percent by 2000/1. The sectoral simulations suggest that the poverty reduction impact of economic growth in Tanzania was more significant in urban areas than in rural areas. For example, in Dar es Salaam, economic growth reduced poverty by about 16 percentage points, assuming no change in inequality. In reality, the growth-induced reduction in poverty was partially offset by increased income inequality, which caused poverty to rise by 9.8 percentage points. The sectoral decomposition of the poverty outcomes also indicates that only a small part (11.6 percent) of the decline in head-count poverty at the national level could be explained by a shift in the population from poorer rural areas to wealthier urban areas such as Dar es Salaam (see Table 7.4). The study concludes that achieving the poverty-related Millennium Development Goal by 2015 will require changing patterns of growth to include the rural areas where most Tanzanians live.

(continued)

BOX 7.3 Unit Record Approach, PovStat: Growth, Inequality, and Simulated Poverty Paths for Tanzania (Continued)

TABLE 7.4. Sectoral Decomposition of the Change in Poverty

	Population share, 1991/92	Contribution to change in the national headcount rate	
		Absolute change	% of Total change
Dar es Salaam	5.50	−0.56	17.08
Other urban areas	12.60	−0.34	10.49
Rural areas	82.06	−1.82	55.41
Total intrasector change		−2.72	82.98
Population-shift effect		−0.38	11.60
Interaction effect		−0.18	5.41
Total change in poverty		−3.28	100

Source: Demombynes and Hoogeveen 2004.

On the methodological side, the authors propose an extension of the basic projection method underlying PovStat. This extension involves the use of estimates of growth rates of consumption and population for the quantile and the sector to which the household belongs. Applying this method to the initial year survey would produce a final year distribution that is very close to the final year survey data.

and the constraints (Dixit 1990). In modeling welfare at the household level, one can use either the indirect utility function or the cost function.

One can thus model a consumer's optimal choice through either of these functions. Under the simple assumption that the household has an exogenous budget to spend on a set of commodities at fixed prices within a period of time,[5] indirect utility is the maximum attainable utility given the *outlay* and the prevailing *prices*. The corresponding cost function is the minimum expenditure required to achieve a given level of utility at given prices.

Marshallian demand functions can be derived from the indirect utility function through the application of *Roy's identity*, while Hicksian demand curves are linked to the cost function via Shephard's lemma (Deaton and Muellbauer 1980). Roy's identity and Shephard's lemma are both manifestations of the envelope theorem; hence, the name "*envelope model*" for this approach. In the context of a parameterized optimization problem, the envelope theorem shows how to compute the impact of a parametric change on the objective function at the optimum. According to the theorem, the change in the objective function induced by a change in a parameter while the choice variable adjusts optimally is equal to the partial derivative of the optimal value of the objective function with respect to the parameter (Varian 1984). Thus, the first-order welfare impacts of changes in prices can be evaluated on the basis of the indirect utility function by treating quantity choices as given.

According to Roy's identity, the Marshallian demand function of a commodity is equal to the negative of the first-order derivative of the indirect utility function with respect to the commodity price, divided by the marginal utility of income. The marginal utility of income is the first-order derivative of the indirect utility function with respect to income. By Shephard's lemma, the Hicksian demand function is equal to the first-order derivative of the cost function with respect to the relevant commodity price.

These are the key results that allow one to trace the welfare implications of any policy that affects commodity prices and household budgets in a way that also accounts for heterogeneity among households by using household-survey data. Within this simple framework, heterogeneity stems from differences in demand patterns, other sociodemographic characteristics of households, and the fact that households may face different prices for the same commodity.

The *envelope approach* to policy impact analysis has some limitations because one can only capture the static effects of the policy reform. Furthermore, the fact that the envelope theorem is valid only in the neighborhood of the initial optimum makes the method inappropriate for the study of large price changes or in situations in which the household is out of equilibrium due to restrictions such as rationing. As noted by Chen and Ravallion (2004), these cases require an estimation of complete demand and supply systems. Chen and Ravallion also note that such an estimation is hampered by the general lack of household-level data on prices and wages.

In the context of the envelope approach, a household is assumed to have preferences among consumption goods and work effort. Thus, the arguments of the utility function include both the quantities of the commodities consumed and the labor supply by activity (including the household's own productive activities). The budget to be spent on consumption goods is equal to the wage income, plus the profits from household enterprises. One can see that, on the assumption that a household will optimize behavior in both production and consumption, the indirect utility of the household is a function of the supply prices of the goods the household is selling on the market, the demand prices of the consumption and intermediate goods, and the wage rates in various activities.

An example of the envelope model is provided in Box 7.4.

In a background paper for a poverty assessment on the Kingdom of Morocco, Ravallion and Lokshin (2004) use the envelope approach to identify the gainers and losers in agricultural trade reforms. The government imposed high tariffs (100 percent) on cereal imports to create incentives for domestic cereal production. The elimination of the high tariffs would reduce domestic cereal prices and therefore hurt net cereal producers at least in the short run. On the other hand, consumers would benefit from lower cereal prices.

The identification of winners and losers based on a representative sample of 5,000 households focuses along two dimensions: (1) the position on the distribution of consumption and (2) non-income characteristics (for example, geographic residence, sector of employment). Based on these dimensions, the authors decompose changes in inequality into a vertical component and a horizontal component. The impact of the reforms is considered "vertical" (that is, between income levels) if the initial income level predicts perfectly the winners and losers in the reforms. In the case of no systematic link between reform impacts and income, there is a "horizontal" element reflecting the fact that impacts vary among people at the same level of initial income. This variation is likely due to non-income characteristics (observable and nonobservable).

Four policy options are considered: (1) a 10 percent cut in the tariff rate, (2) a 30 percent cut, (3) a 50 percent cut, and (4) a complete elimination of tariffs. (Summary results are presented in Table 7.5.) Ravallion and Lokshin (2004) find that the overall impact of the complete liberalization of the cereal trade on household mean consumption and inequality is very small. However, the impacts vary greatly by household type and region, with different income sources and patterns of consumptions. A decomposition of the overall change in inequality as measured by the mean logarithmic deviation (identified as the "impact on inequality" in the table) shows that all the impact on inequality is horizontal rather than vertical.

TABLE 7.5. Winners and Losers in Four Trade Reform Scenarios

National	Baseline	Policy 1 (10%)	Policy 2 (30%)	Policy 3 (50%)	Policy 4 (100%)
Poverty rate (%)	19.61	20.01	20.33	21.04	22.13
Mean log deviation	0.2850	0.2892	0.290	0.2914	0.2917
Gini index	0.385	0.387	0.389	0.391	0.395
Per capita gain	0	6.519	−23.967	−54.816	−133.81
Production gain	0	−32.078	−69.012	−106.308	−201.017
Consumption gain	0	38.598	45.046	51.492	67.207

	Policy 2: Partial de-protection (30%)	Policy 4: Full de-protection (100%)
Impact on inequality: baseline (0.2850)	0.289	0.292
Vertical component	58%	−20%
Horizontal component	42%	120%

Source: Ravallion and Lokshin 2004.

Policy reforms will generally have implications for the domestic structure of prices and wages and thus for household welfare. To analyze the *first-order welfare impacts* associated with changes in commodity and factor prices, one can apply the *envelope theorem* to the extended indirect utility function. This leads to an expression of each household's welfare *gain or loss* as a weighted sum of proportionate changes in prices and wages. The weights are relevant income or expenditure levels. For instance, the proportionate change in the selling price of a commodity is weighted by the corresponding initial revenue. The change in the demand price is weighted by the initial expenditure. The change in a wage is weighted by earnings from external (to the household) labor supply.

To explain the heterogeneity of estimated welfare impacts in more detail, one can assume that the indirect utility profit functions vary with the observed household characteristics (Chen and Ravallion 2004). It is important to distinguish characteristics that affect preferences in consumption (for example, the number of children, the stage in the life cycle, or education) from those affecting outputs from household production activities (for example, land ownership).

In this extended interpretation of the maximum value model, the net gain from the price induced by trade reform depends on a household's consumption, labor supply, and production activities. In turn, these variables depend on prices and household characteristics such as: (1) the age of the household head, (2) educational and demographic characteristics, and (3) land as a fixed factor of production. One may then use regression analysis to attempt to isolate covariates that might help in the design of a social-protection policy response to changes in household welfare induced by shocks or policy reforms. One obvious advantage of linking policy impacts to household characteristics is the possibility of identifying types of households that are particularly vulnerable on the basis of their consumption or production behavior. This information is useful in designing targeted compensatory programs.

The household income and occupational choice model

What are the basic determinants of economic welfare distribution at the household level? Bourguignon and Ferreira (2005) note three groups of factors and propose a simulation framework wherein the process of household income generation is described in terms of these factors. The configuration of the distribution of income at a given time thus depends on (1) the distribution of factor endowments and sociodemographic characteristics among the population, (2) the returns to these assets and characteristics, and (3) the behavior of socioeconomic agents with respect to resource allocation, subject to prevailing institutional constraints. This behavior is reflected in labor market participation and occupational choice, consumption patterns, or fertility choices.

Based on this view, the household-income-generation process can be described parametrically through a set of four equations: (1) an occupation equation, (2) a wage equation, (3) a self-employment income equation, and (4) an equation for the computation of household per capita income. The occupational equation, which is based on a multinomial logit model, describes how household members of working age allocate their time among wage work, self-employment, and nonmarket activities. The allocation of the workforce across activities depends on observed characteristics specific to the individual and the household to which he or she belongs. The allocation also depends on a set of unobserved variables represented by random variables that are assumed to follow the law of extreme values and to be identically and independently distributed across individuals and activities. Given the discrete choice model underlying the allocation of the labor force, the occupation equation determines the likelihood that a working-age member of a household will be a wage earner, self-employed, or a non-earner. This likelihood depends on individual characteristics such as education, age, and experience. It is also a function of household characteristics such as education of the household head, household size, the dependency ratio, and the place of residence.

The wage equation follows the Mincerian specification, whereby the logarithm of earnings in a given occupation is a linear function of individual characteristics and random variables that are assumed to follow the standard normal distribution and to be distributed identically and independently across individuals and occupations. Self-employment income is similarly modeled. The wage and self-employment equations are estimated on the basis only of individuals and households with nonzero earnings or self-employment income. There is thus a need to correct for selection bias.

One approach is to use Heckman's two-stage estimator. Given the previous three equations of the model, the last equation of the model computes the per capita household income in two steps. First, total household income is obtained from the aggregation, across individuals and activities, of earnings and self-employment income with unearned income. Second, total household income is divided by household size.

To avoid the difficulties associated with the joint estimation of the participation and earnings equations for each household member, the model is estimated in reduced form. Thus, results should never be regarded as corresponding to a structural model, and no causal inference is implied. Bourguignon and Ferreira (2005) explain that the parameters generated by these equations are merely descriptions of conditional distributions based on the chosen functional forms.

The model can be used to analyze changes in household income distribution in a manner analogous to the *Oaxaca-Blinder decomposition* of changes in mean income (Bourguignon and Ferreira 2005). Within the Oaxaca-Blinder framework, the income of an individual is viewed as a linear function of his or her observed characteristics, say, endowments, and some unobserved characteristics represented by a random variable. The linear coefficients are interpreted as rates of return to individual endowments or the prices of the services from these endowments. If the unobserved characteristics are distributed independently of the endowments, then one can use ordinary least squares to estimate the rates of return. If one also assumes that the expected value of the residual term is equal to zero, then the *change in mean earnings* can be expressed as the sum of two effects: (1) the *endowment effect* (associated with a change in the mean endowment at constant prices) and (2) the *price effect* (associated with a change in prices at constant mean endowments).

The interpretation of the above decomposition within the household-income-generation model generalizes the counterfactual simulation techniques from the single earnings equation model to a system of multiple nonlinear equations that is meant to represent mechanisms of household income generation; hence, the name "*generalized Oaxaca-Blinder decomposition*." The approach entails simulating counterfactual distributions, changing market and household behavior one aspect at a time (ceteris paribus), and noting the effect of each change on the distribution of economic welfare. Three major effects may thus be identified: (1) endowment effects, (2) price effects, and (3) occupational effects.

The household income and occupational choice model is demonstrated in Box 7.5.

EMBEDDING DISTRIBUTIONAL MECHANISMS IN A GENERAL EQUILIBRIUM MODEL

The distributional models reviewed in the section above have only a limited application to the analysis of the impacts of macroeconomic shocks and policies on poverty and income distribution. *This limitation stems mainly from the fact that these approaches fail to account fully for various market and household behavioral adjustments induced by the shocks or policies.* This is the basic reason why these frameworks are interpreted as reduced-form models. The reliability of their predictions depends on the reliability of the assumptions made about the impact of macroeconomic

BOX 7.5 **Unit Record Approach, Household Income and Occupational Choice Model: A Microsimulation Study on Côte d'Ivoire**

Between 1978 and 1993, Côte d'Ivoire experienced a sharp deterioration in the terms of trade and a significant increase in external debt. The average annual per capita growth of GDP became negative. Following the 1994 devaluation of the CFA franc and a series of structural reforms supported by both the World Bank and the International Monetary Fund, growth recovered, mainly in the export sector, agroindustry, manufacturing, and energy.

Grimm (2004) has studied the inequality and poverty implications of macroeconomic adjustment in Côte d'Ivoire. The study focuses on the effects of three phenomena on income distribution: changes in returns to labor, changes in occupational choice, and sociodemographic changes. The analysis is based on the 1993 and 1998 household surveys. Monthly wage and profit functions are estimated in terms of these changes and unobservable effects (reflecting unobservable individual and household characteristics). Income for different sources is aggregated at the household level for 1993 and 1998.

The study concludes that income-inequality patterns were different across regions, but poverty trends were similar. In the case of Abidjan, the observed reduction in inequality and poverty is linked to a boost in employment in the formal wage sector and an increase in returns to observable determinants of wage earnings. Rural areas also experienced a strong growth in household income and a significant reduction in poverty. However, these developments were accompanied by a rise in inequality. The negative income growth in Abidjan and the positive income growth in the rural sector were both connected with increasing inequality. Moreover, while within-region inequality increased, between-region inequality declined. For example, while within-inequality had increased from 44 percent to 54 percent by 1998, between-region inequality had decreased from 7 percent to 3 percent at the national level by 1998 (see Table 7.6).

TABLE 7.6. Decomposition by Microsimulation of the Change in the Distribution

National	1992/93			1998		
	Gini	dGini	E(0)	Gini	dGini	E(0)
Initial values	0.494		0.512	0.508		0.563
Within-group inequality			0.441			0.537
Between-group inequality			0.071			0.026
Observed change		0.014			0.014	
Price observables	0.483	−0.011	0.497	0.540	−0.032	0.630
Returns to schooling	0.471	−0.023	0.473	0.547	−0.039	0.640
Returns to experience	0.476	−0.017	0.486	0.512	−0.004	0.573
Ivorian/non-Ivorian wage differential	0.495	0.001	0.515	0.508	0.000	0.562
Regional differential	0.484	−0.010	0.496	0.511	−0.003	0.574
Returns to land	0.489	−0.005	0.506	0.500	0.008	0.550
Residual variance	0.498	0.004	0.525	0.482	0.026	0.515
Total price effects	—	−0.007	—	—	−0.006	—
Occupational choice	0.496	0.003	0.505	0.515	−0.007	0.557
Price and occupational choice		−0.005			−0.014	
Population structure effect		0.019			0.028	

Source: Grimm 2004.
Note: E(0) is the mean logarithmic deviation.

shocks and policies on the key exogenous variables. General equilibrium models can be used to introduce more structure in the analysis.

In this section, the logic of general equilibrium modeling is first reviewed. Two ways of modeling distributional mechanisms are then examined based on two key sources: Dervis, de Melo, and Robinson (1982) and Decaluwé et al. (1999).

The logic of general equilibrium modeling

What is a general equilibrium model?

A general equilibrium model is a logical representation of a socioeconomic system wherein the behavior of all participants is compatible. The key modeling issues thus entail the following: (1) the identification of the participants, (2) the specification of individual behavior, (3) the mode of interaction among socioeconomic agents, and (4) the characterization of compatibility.

The basic Walrasian framework serves as a template for most applied general equilibrium models. There are two basic categories of agents: consumers and producers, which are also referred to as households and firms. The behavior of each economic agent is supposed to conform to the optimization principle, which holds that the agent attempts to implement the best feasible action. Thus, modeling optimizing behavior entails the specification of (1) actions that an economic unit can undertake, (2) the constraints it faces, and (3) the objective function used to evaluate such actions (Varian 1984). Within this framework, each household buys the best bundle of commodities it can afford. The objective that guides household choice is therefore utility maximization, and the constraints are expressed in terms of budget constraints. Choices by a firm are characterized by profit maximization, subject to technological and market constraints.

Households and firms are supposed to interact through a network of perfectly competitive markets. Market interaction is a mode of *social coordination* through a mutual adjustment among participants based on quid pro quo (Lindblom 2001).[6] Market participants are buyers and sellers whose supply and demand behavior is an observable consequence of the optimization assumption. In this setting, behavioral compatibility is described in terms of market equilibrium. General equilibrium is achieved by an incentive configuration (as represented through relative prices) such that, for each market, the amount demanded is equal to the amount supplied. Alternatively, we can say that, when the economic system is in a state of general equilibrium, no feasible change in individual behavior is worthwhile, and no desirable change is feasible.

Comparative statics entail a comparison of the equilibrium states associated with changes in the socioeconomic environment. Such changes may be induced by shocks or policy reforms. The comparison of equilibrium states can be framed within a social evaluation. The evaluation has two perspectives: individual and social. If one focuses on individual objectives, then *Pareto efficiency* implies that no participant can be made better off without making some other participant worse off. A *poverty-focused criterion* would say that less poverty is preferable to more.

Empirical implementation

For policy analysis, one needs to move from a conceptual framework to a computable model. Applied general equilibrium models are commonly represented by systems of equations. These equations fall into the following basic categories: (1) demand equations from the optimizing behavior of consumers, (2) supply equations from the optimizing behavior of firms, (3) income equations describing the income of each agent based on prevailing prices and the quantities exchanged on goods and factors markets, and (4) equilibrium conditions for all markets. All supply and demand equations are homogeneous of degree zero. If one multiplies all commodity and factor prices by a constant factor k, the equilibrium supply and demand will not change. Thus, the model is money neutral and can determine only relative prices. This creates the need to normalize the price system by fixing a *numéraire* price. The model also satisfies Walras' Law. Accordingly, if all economic agents satisfy their budget constraints and all but one of the markets are in equilibrium, then the last market must automatically be in equilibrium (Dinwiddy and Teal 1988).

The choice of the functional forms determines the set of structural parameters that must be estimated to make the model computable. The necessary data usually come in the form of a social accounting matrix (SAM). The matrix reflects *the circular flow of economic activity* for the chosen year. It provides an analytically integrated data set that reflects various aspects of the economy, such as production, consumption, trade, accumulation, and income distribution. A SAM is a square matrix, the dimension of which is determined by the institutional setting underlying the economy under consideration. Each account is represented by a combination of one row and one column with the same label. *Each entry represents a payment to a row account by a column account.* Thus, all receipts into an account are read along the corresponding row, while payments by the same account are recorded in the corresponding column. In accordance with the principles of double-entry bookkeeping, the whole construct is subject to a consistency restriction that makes the column sums equal to the corresponding row sums. This restriction also means that the SAM obeys Walras' Law in the sense that, for an *n-dimensional* matrix, if the (n–1) accounts balance, so must the last one. Table 7.7 shows the structure of a SAM for a model of an open economy.

For the purpose of analyzing the impact of macroeconomic shocks and policies on poverty and income distribution, *it is important to understand how shocks and policies affect key macroeconomic balances before considering how the repercussions are transmitted to households.* In general, the macroeconomic properties of a static general equilibrium model of a real economy such as the one described here depend on the *closure rule* chosen. Such a rule refers to the equilibrating mechanisms governing product and factor markets, as well as the following three basic macrobalances: the *balance of trade,* the *government budget* balance, and the *savings-investment* balance. The inevitable inclusion of these macrobalances in the basic Walrasian framework requires the specification of a corresponding flow equilibrium condition for which a closure rule has to be stated (Robinson and Löfgren 2005).

Robinson (2003) discusses four possible closures for this class of models. Two of these assume the full employment of factors of production, while the other two do not. Assuming that output is a function of two factors of production (capital and labor), there are 10 potential closure variables: the GDP deflator, the wage rate, the exchange rate, investment demand, the trade balance, labor supply, the government consumption of goods and services, capital, the savings rate, and the income tax rate. Closure rules differ on the basis of which three (the number of macrobalances in the model) of these 10 variables are made endogenous, while all the rest are exogenous.

The first full-employment closure, also known as *neoclassical,* considers the wage rate, the exchange rate, and investment demand as endogenous variables. The second full-employment closure considers the wage rate, the exchange rate, and the balance of trade as endogenous. Closure rules that assume unemployment are known as Keynesian. The first rule makes the GDP deflator, the exchange rate, and labor supply endogenous. For the second rule, the endogenous variables are the GDP deflator, the trade balance, and labor supply. It is worth noting that the GDP deflator is a numéraire price in the full employment case, while the wage rate plays that role in the Keynesian case.

TABLE 7.7. Structure of a SAM for an Open Economy

	Activity	Commodity	Factor	Household	Government	Investment	World	Total
Activity		domestic sales			export subsidies		exports	total sales
Commodity	intermediate consumption			household consumption	government consumption	investment		total demand
Factor	GDP at factor cost							GDP at factor cost
Household			GDP at factor cost		transfers		foreign remittances	household income
Government	indirect taxes	tariffs		income tax				government revenue
Savings				household savings	government savings		foreign savings	total savings
World		imports						total imports
Total	production cost	total supply	GDP at factor cost	total household expenditure	government expenditure	total investment	total foreign exchange	

Source: Adapted from Robinson 1989.

A further examination of the neoclassical rule illustrates the types of analytical restrictions that such rules place on a general equilibrium model for the purpose of macroeconomic analysis. This rule makes the current account balance[7] exogenous, along with savings rates and government expenditure. Given that the current account balance is related to the functioning of the asset market, making it exogenous means that the corresponding flow of funds must be added to or subtracted from the savings-investment account (in the SAM). Equivalently, the budget constraint of at least one agent includes an exogenous net asset change (Robinson and Löfgren 2005). This closure rule leaves unexplained the decision of households to save at fixed rates and the allocation by households of savings across different assets.

With respect to the government account, it is commonly assumed that government expenditure (both consumption and transfers) is fixed in real terms and that government revenue depends on fixed tax rates. The government deficit or surplus is computed residually and added to the savings-investment account without any consideration of the specific financial mechanisms involved.

The above discussion clearly shows that a general equilibrium model based on this closure will certainly be useful in tackling the medium- to long-term structural implications of a shock or a policy that works through individual markets, provided it is sufficiently disaggregated to account for policy-relevant sectors. The model, however, would have a limited ability to deal with flow-of-funds issues related to the determination of aggregate savings, the savings-investment balance, and the allocation of investment across the production sector. This requires the addition of financial mechanisms to the general equilibrium model.

Robinson and Tyson (1984) offer an illustration through an example of a terms-of-trade shock and the interdependence between structural issues that are essentially microeconomic in nature and aggregate flow-of-funds issues that are basically macroeconomic. They also suggest a framework for analyzing this interdependence and the implications for policy trade-offs and effectiveness. *The basic idea is to link a proper macroeconomic model to a Walrasian general equilibrium model through variables that are endogenous in one, but exogenous in the other.* For instance, a macromodel may treat the price level and various macroeconomic aggregates, such as employment, investment, and consumption, as endogenous. These variables may then be specified as exogenous in the general equilibrium model. However, the closure rules for macrobalances and factor markets must be designed in such a way that the general equilibrium model behaves in a manner that is consistent with the outcome of the macromodel.

Modeling distributional mechanisms

Dervis, de Melo, and Robinson (1982) note that policymakers might be interested in how income is distributed among the following: (1) factors of production, (2) institutions, (3) socioeconomic groups, (4) households, and (5) individuals. Distribution to factors of production is known as *functional distribution,* while distribution to individuals is called *size distribution.* The choice of the Walrasian framework with a neoclassical closure focuses analysis on the microeconomic determinants of income distribution based on relative factor intensities in production and the interaction among supply, demand, and employment.

A sufficiently disaggregated SAM provides a data framework for mappings among various types of distributions of income. Referring back to Table 7.7, we note that the functional distribution of income is given by the intersection of the factor-row and the activity-column. Depending on data availability, this functional distribution can be disaggregated by sector of production (agriculture, industry, and services) and by labor categories if the labor market is segmented. When, in addition, factors of production are disaggregated so that labor is differentiated by skill, education, or sector of employment and capital is differentiated by type, sector, or region, we get what Löfgren, Robinson, and El-Said (2003) call the *extended functional distribution* of income.

GDP at market prices that includes indirect taxes is distributed among various institutions such as households, enterprises, and government.[8] Government revenue from all taxes is spent on export subsidies, government consumption, and transfers to households. The residual is put in the capital account. This framework does not explain various flows of funds related to the activities of the central bank, such as money creation or credit and interest rate policies. Therefore, it would be difficult to analyze the distributional implications of these macroeconomic policies within this model. Both the functional and institutional distributions classify flows of funds according to the functional (factor employment) and institutional structure of the economy.

The household account in the SAM actually stands for all the people in the economy and may in fact cover all nongovernmental institutions, including enterprises. Thus, the distributions by socioeconomic groups, households, and individuals are various representations of the distribution of income within this account (Dervis, de Melo, and Robinson 1982). *The classification of individuals or households by socioeconomic group is dictated by policy issues and data availability.* One simple scheme differentiates groups by type and source of income. Given an exhaustive and mutually exclusive partition of the entire population into socioeconomic groups, it is possible to derive the overall size distribution of income as a weighted sum of within-group density functions. Using the log variance as an indicator of relative inequality, overall inequality can be decomposed into within-group and between-group components. Thus, ceteris paribus, an increase in inequality in any one group or an increase in the distance between one group's average income and the overall mean income will boost overall inequality. Given that the overall size distribution is derived empirically, one can compute any desired measure of inequality or poverty (given a poverty line). *In the simulation of the inequality implications of shocks and policies, only between-group inequality can be generated endogenously by this framework through changes in group means. This is because within-group distributions are exogenous.*

The fact that the overall distribution of income is derived numerically as a weighted sum of individual group distributions makes it possible to allow the functional form to vary from group to group. The lognormal distribution that has often been used in this context is known to provide a poor approximation of the distribution at the upper extreme. One could use the Pareto distribution for high-income groups. Employing a different function for every within-group distribution increases the ability of the model to capture the heterogeneity of socioeconomic groups. Decaluwé et al. (1999) use the Beta distribution to this effect. This function is fully characterized by the minimum income, the maximum income, and two shape parameters defining the skewness of the distribution. In a model of an archetypical developing country, these authors allow the four characteristic parameters of the Beta distribution to vary across six socioeconomic groups: (1) landless rural households, (2) rural smallholders, (3) big landlords, (4) urban households with poorly educated heads, (5) urban households with highly educated heads, and (6) capitalists.[9] Instead of aggregating group distributions into an overall distribution, the authors compute, for each group, poverty measures of the Foster-Greer-Thorbecke family. Overall poverty can then be inferred as a weighted sum of within-group poverty whereby the weights are given by population shares. Decaluwé et al. (1999) allow the nominal poverty line to be determined within the model. *The value of the reference basket of goods is adjusted on the basis of equilibrium prices computed by the model.*

An application of the CGE model is shown in Box 7.6.

The basic idea underlying the approach discussed here involves linking an extended functional distribution to a size distribution of income. Various socioeconomic groups are considered as representative households. This approach is thus called the *extended representative household* (ERH) approach to distinguish it from the standard *representative house-*

CGE Model: The Impact of Trade Policies on Income Distribution in a Planning Model for Colombia

De Melo and Robinson (1980) use a multisector static CGE model to simulate the effect of trade on the functional and the size distributions of income in Colombia. The model focuses on the real economy and tries to capture the economic dualism and structural rigidities characteristic of Colombia. Seven broad socioeconomic groups are considered: small farmers, marginal laborers, industrial laborers, service-sector laborers, agricultural capitalists, industrial capitalists, and service-sector capitalists. These groups are assumed to have different consumption patterns, and the size distribution within each group is represented by a lognormal distribution. The CGE model endogenously determines various incomes, consumption and investment, and trade flows. Based on these results, the distribution of income to socioeconomic groups and the overall size distribution by individuals are estimated.

The study investigates the impact of three alternative trade regimes on the distribution of income in Colombia and compares them with the free trade alternative (FT): an inward-looking strategy with a 50 percent tariff on manufacturing sectors (ILS), an outward-looking strategy with a 50 percent subsidy on agricultural and manufacturing exports (OLS), and a direct-subsidy strategy that provides a 50 percent value-added subsidy to manufacturing sectors (DDS). The simulation results are presented in Table 7.8.

The study finds that the domestic price system in Colombia is insulated from changes in world market prices. Furthermore, outward-looking trade policies with increased primary exports are likely to have an adverse impact on the distribution of income in the medium term compared to inward-looking policies. This conclusion depends on the structure of exports and imports. Colombian exports are concentrated in primary goods; imports are mostly manufactured goods, and the country is self-sufficient in food production. In such a case, an open trade strategy is likely to decrease the purchasing power and real incomes of most socioeconomic groups.

TABLE 7.8. Income Distribution Measures for a Model of Colombia

	FT	ILS	OLS	DSS
Net mean income				
Rural income	5.55	5.60	5.53	4.88
Unskilled urban	11.82	11.89	11.79	12
Skilled labor	25.72	26.44	25.46	30.39
Rural capitalist	37.47	36.75	38.62	33.55
Manufacturing capitalist	160.85	166.50	159.02	204.82
Service capitalist	67.68	66.30	66.14	63.12
Economy-wide mean income	19.00	19.09	19.00	19.47
Aggregate measures				
Mean income (top 10%)	98.09	98.36	98.44	104.86
Mean income (bottom 10%)	2.90	2.93	2.88	2.69
Rural poverty	58.51	58.05	59.53	62.92
Urban poverty	41.48	41.95	40.47	37.08
Total poverty	29.90	29.40	30.30	32.10
Gini coefficient	0.581	0.580	0.583	0.601

Source: de Melo and Robinson 1980.

hold (RH) approach, which limits the analysis of the distributional impact of shocks and policies to their effects on representative socioeconomic groups. There is one other way of implementing the ERH approach (discussed in Agénor, Chen, and Grimm 2004). The treatment of the size distribution in this case is analogous to the approach underlying PovStat. Indeed, it is assumed that, following a shock or the implementation of a policy, per capita consumption and disposable income for a household change at the same rate as the rate predicted by the general equilibrium model for the socioeconomic group to which the household belongs.[10] Thus, the size distribution is represented directly by relevant unit records from a household survey. Following a shock or the implementation of a policy, a new distribution of income and consumption is generated by applying the predicted rates of change to the initial data. New measures of poverty and inequality can therefore be computed and compared to baseline values.

This approach can only predict changes in between-group inequality because the income and consumption of all the households belonging to a single socioeconomic group are scaled (up or down) by the same factor. Another limitation noted by the authors is the fact that the approach does not account for changes in the structure of employment. Therefore, they propose an extension of the approach based on a reweighing procedure that reassigns population weights to households in a manner that is consistent with predicted changes in the structure of employment.

LINKING A MACROECONOMIC FRAMEWORK TO A MODEL OF INCOME DISTRIBUTION

To be sure, both the standard RH and the ERH approaches reveal the basic principles involved in linking a macroeconomic model to a representation of the distribution of economic welfare across individuals or households. This section focuses on some specific models (tools) that have been built more or less around these principles. The first one described is the 123PRSP model, a three-layer and parsimonious framework designed to link macroeconomic policies to poverty outcomes via a two-sector general equilibrium model of an open economy.

Two implementations of the PAMS framework are then considered. The first interpretation of this framework uses the ERH approach based on unit records to simulate the poverty impact of macroeconomic shocks and policies analyzed within a macroconsistency model such as the Revised Minimum Standard Model Extended (RMSM-X). The second interpretation is a reduced form of the first, whereby a CGE model is linked recursively (in a top-down fashion) to a poverty module built upon a parameterization of the Lorenz curve *à la* POVCAL.

A different macro-micro simulation model is then reviewed, wherein the macroeconomy is represented by an IS-LM model.

Finally, the IMMPA framework is described briefly. The framework links a dynamic CGE model including a financial sector to a distributional module that is analogous to PovStat.

Given the distributional concerns, these models must ultimately be judged on the basis of how well they use the wealth of available information (from national accounts and household surveys) to explain the interdependence among sectors and institutions and the heterogeneity of actors. Naturally, in a particular environment, additional criteria come into play, such as the skills required of the analyst in implementing a given approach.

The 123PRSP model

The 123PRSP model is based on the idea that the impact on poverty of macroeconomic shocks and policies is transmitted through two basic channels. The first channel involves distributional-neutral *changes in the average income,* while the second is the change in the sectoral pattern of growth induced by *changes in relative prices* (for example, shifts in the real exchange rate). The overall impact is thus equal to the pure growth impact, plus the distributional impact.

This idea is implemented within a three-layer model. The *macro*layer has three components: (1) a financial programming model, (2) a trivariate vector autoregressive (VAR) model, and (3) a medium-term growth model based on cross-country regression analysis. The *meso-* (or intermediate) layer is represented by a two-sector general equilibrium model of an open economy. Finally, the *micro*layer relies on the envelope theorem to model the distribution of welfare across households.

The financial programming module

Generally speaking, financial programming is the process of designing a consistent set of macroeconomic policies, whereby instruments (for example, domestic credit) are set in such a way that a target variable (official reserves, for instance) follows a desired trajectory. In the context of policy reform programs supported by the International Monetary Fund, *this approach is used to set monetary and fiscal policies aimed at restraining aggregate demand and adjusting relative prices.* Financial programming can be described in terms of the underlying accounting framework that imposes *consistency* upon data and any prediction based on assumed behavioral relationships or projection rules.[11] The approach emphasizes the monetary dimension of the balance of payments and relates the monetary and fiscal accounts to the balance of payments.

The economy is divided into four institutional sectors: (1) the private sector, (2) the public (government) sector, (3) the foreign sector or the rest of the world, and (4) the domestic banking sector. Each sector in the economy is represented by a budget that constrains its behavior, and all variables are measured in nominal local currency. Within this framework, financial transactions are distinguished from those arising from the production or acquisition of goods and services (also known as income/expenditure transactions). It is assumed that the private sector owns all factors of production. The private sector gets nominal income from the sale of current output. This income is used to pay taxes to the government, purchase goods for consumption, and make investments. Any disposable income after expenditure is used to accumulate financial assets or liabilities in the form of money, foreign assets, and borrowing from the banking system.

The public sector collects taxes from the private sector and uses the proceeds for consumption. Any surplus or deficit is accounted for by the accumulation of financial assets or liabilities in the form of foreign assets and net borrowing from the banking system. The foreign sector gets revenues from the sale of imports to the domestic economy. It spends on domestic exports. In the case of a current account deficit, the revenues of the foreign sector exceed its expenditures. The foreign sector can buy back its liabilities from the domestic private and public sectors and acquires reserves from the domestic banking system. The financial sector functions as a financial intermediary among various actors. It obtains assets in the form of international reserves and claims on domestic actors and issues its own liabilities in the form of money to the private sector.

These budget constraints are not independent; they represent an overall resource constraint on the economy. This resource constraint can be expressed as follows: the difference between gross national disposable income and domestic absorption is equal to the current account balance.[12] The linkages among these sectoral accounts imply that a deficit in any sector must be financed by savings in other sectors. For the whole economy, excess spending is possible only if financing is available from the rest of the world. The relationship between excess absorption and the current account balance shows that an improvement in the latter may be achieved through an increase in the country's output or a reduction in absorption. Furthermore, the sum of the current account balance and net capital inflows is equal to the change in net official reserves. This identity connects excess absorption (over income) to two financing sources: capital inflows to the nonbanking sector and official international reserves. This clearly shows that *the current account balance acts as a resource constraint on the whole economy* (IMF 1987).

The basic structure of the financial programming model can be understood by focusing on the case of a small open economy with a fixed exchange rate, which is known as the Polak model (Agénor 2004a; Polak 1998; IMF 1987). In this context, the money supply is viewed as an endogenous variable that depends on changes in the balance of payments.

The core model contains four relationships. The first relationship is an *accounting identity* based on the balance sheet of the banking system.[13] Accordingly, the change in the money supply (a liability for the banking system) equals the sum of the change in net official reserves and the change in net domestic credit (that is, the sum of changes in the foreign and domestic assets held by the banking system). The second relationship defines the change in the nominal demand for money as the change in the nominal income multiplied by the inverse of the income velocity of money, which is assumed to be constant over time. The third relationship defines flow equilibrium in the money market. The last relationship restates the balance of payments identity as follows: the change in official reserves is equal to exports, minus imports, plus the change in net capital inflows to the nonbanking system. Exports are assumed to be exogenous, while imports are computed as national income multiplied by a constant marginal propensity to import.

The design of a financial program involves an iterative process based on the following five steps (IMF 1987): (1) Set the target for the change in the official reserves. (2) Use the last relationship (the balance of payments identity) to compute residually a value for imports that is consistent with the reserve target and the assumed level of the exogenous variables (exports and the change in net capital flows to the nonbanking sector). (3) Project nominal income and use the projection, along with the assumed values for the income velocity of money and the marginal propensity to import, to obtain the demands for money and imports. (4) Given a forecast of the money demand (equal to the money supply in equilibrium) and the target for official reserves, use the balance-sheet identity of the banking system (first equation) to infer the change in domestic credit that is compatible with the target for official reserves and the desired increase in nominal money balances. (5) Check for consistency by comparing the projected imports with the residual value computed from the balance of payments identity in step 2. If the two values are equal, stop the process; if not, make adjustments to the underlying assumptions and repeat the process until consistency is achieved.

Monetary and fiscal policy can be linked through the financial programming framework by distinguishing the expansion of credit to the private sector from that to the public sector (IMF 1987). Thus, the total change in the domestic assets of the banking system appearing in the balance-sheet identity must now include two components: (1) the change in domestic credit to the government and (2) the change in domestic credit to the private sector. Similarly, the total change in foreign capital inflows to the nonbanking sector has two components: public and private. Finally, a relationship must be added to reflect the fact that the government can finance its budget deficit through net borrowing either from abroad or from the domestic banking system.

The growth module

The growth module has two components. The first is a trivariate VAR model designed to capture an improvement or deterioration in the terms of trade or other short-run growth impact that is produced by a shock or a change in government expenditure or other short-run growth impact that is produced by a policy reform. The VAR model is a useful tool for analyzing interrelationships among different time series. In this framework, all variables are endogenous because of the assumption that the time path of each variable affects and is affected by current and past realizations of the other variables. A VAR model may be characterized by the number of variables (time series) and the longest lag length (Enders 1995). Thus, a first-order bivariate VAR would involve two variables and a lag length of at most one. The random disturbances in the VAR framework are known as innovations or shocks. A shock in one variable not only affects that variable directly, but is also transmitted to all the other variables, depending on the lag structure of the model. A VAR can be written as a vector moving-average of the shocks, from which one can derive *impulse response functions.* An impulse response function represents the behavior of time series in response to various shocks. The 123PRSP framework includes the following three variables: the growth rate, the real exchange rate, and either the terms of trade or government expenditure. *The parameter estimates based on impulse response functions are interpreted as short-run growth elasticities.*

The second component of the growth module is a cross-country regression model (Easterly 2001) designed to capture the impact of macroeconomic policies on long-run growth. The model involves three groups of independent variables. The first group includes policy determinants of growth: (1) a black market premium, (2) a measure of financial development (M2/GDP),[14] (3) inflation, (4) the real exchange rate, (5) secondary education enrollment, and (6) telephone lines per 1,000 individuals (a proxy for infrastructure stock). The second group of variables captures the impact of shocks such as: (1) the terms of trade as a percentage of GDP, (2) the interest on external debt as a percentage of GDP, and (3) growth among trading partners of the Organisation for Economic Co-operation and Development. Finally, variables measuring initial conditions include (1) initial income, (2) an intercept, (3) a dummy variable for the 1980s, and (4) a dummy variable for the 1990s.

The two-sector general equilibrium model

The mesolayer of the 123PRSP is represented by a two-sector general equilibrium model of a small open economy. The model is a generalization of the Salter-Swan framework, which provides a foundation for the study of the impact of macroeconomic imbalances and adjustment policies on the real sector of the economy. This single-country model (as opposed to a multicountry trade model) represents a significant improvement on both the standard neoclassical trade model and the Salter-Swan model. The neoclassical model often leads to implausible empirical results because of two basic assumptions. The first assumption states that all goods are tradable, while the second implies perfect substitutability between foreign and domestic goods. These two assumptions imply the law of one price, according to which the domestic prices of tradable goods and services are determined by the world market.

The Salter-Swan framework makes an important distinction between *tradable* and *nontradable* goods and services. Nontradables are goods and services the prices of which are determined by supply and demand conditions within domestic markets. Prices for tradable goods are determined by the world market. The fact that a good is nontradable may be due to its nature (such as public services or construction) or to prohibitive transport costs that keep the good off the world market. Thus, some policy changes may cause some goods to switch categories. Furthermore, the country under consideration is assumed to be small with respect to international trade and therefore faces a perfectly elastic excess supply from the rest of the world. In other words, it cannot affect the terms at which it is trading with the rest of the world. Exportable and importable goods can therefore be aggregated into a single class of good, tradables, using world prices as weights. The model still maintains the neoclassical assumption that domestic and foreign goods are perfect substitutes in consumption and focuses on the *effects of external shocks on the real exchange rate,* which ultimately directs resource allocation within the economy.

The extensions of this framework as implemented within the 123PRSP drop the assumptions about aggregation and perfect substitution and explicitly add government, savings, and investment.[15] These extensions allow the inclusion of policy instruments such as taxes, as well as the consideration of macroeconomic effects. These extensions are now briefly described. (See Devarajan, Lewis, and Robinson 1990 for a more detailed presentation.)

The small country assumption is maintained; thus, the country cannot affect its terms of trade with the rest of the world. There are two sectors of production. The first produces exports, and the second produces all other final goods, which are referred to as domestic (home) goods. Real GDP is an aggregation of exports and domestic goods based on a constant elasticity of transformation function.[16] The supply of exports relative to domestic goods is obtained by maximizing GDP, subject to the technical transformability constraint (above) and sales opportunities at home and abroad.

Consumption is expressed in terms of a composite good that is an aggregation of home goods and imports based on a constant elasticity of substitution function. The demand for imports and for domestic goods is derived by minimizing the cost of the composite good, subject to a substitutability constraint represented by the elasticity of substitution function. The representative household is assumed to save a constant fraction of its disposable income. Gross income is the sum of GDP, transfers from the public sector, and remittances from abroad.

The domestic prices of exports and imports are calculated from world prices, the exchange rate, and all applicable taxes. The GDP deflator is a weighted average of the domestic price of exports and that of home goods. The weights are the shares of each commodity in GDP. Similarly, the aggregate price of the composite consumption good is a weighted average of the domestic prices of imports and home goods.

Two types of equilibrium conditions are explicitly stated. The first group concerns commodity market equilibrium: (1) the supply of home goods equals the demand, and (2) the supply of the composite good equals the demand, which includes private consumption, investment, and government consumption (assumed to be fixed in real terms). The other group of conditions pertains to macroeconomic balances: (1) the current account balance is fixed; (2) total savings (the sum of private, public, and foreign savings) equals investment, and (3) government revenue from direct and indirect taxes is accounted for by government consumption, transfers, and savings. There are also implicit equilibrium conditions associated with the use of the constant elasticity of transformation production-possibility frontier. This assumption is a cover for the operation of factor markets (labor and capital). Indeed, *it is equivalent to assuming full employment in a single labor market within the economy.* In this static model, capital is assumed to be fixed and sector specific. Thus, there is an equilibrium wage rate associated with each equilibrium price for home goods. Returns to capital in each sector can be computed residually from the value of output.

The financial programming model and the growth module trace the macroeconomic implications of shocks and policies. In particular, these two submodules produce information on the evolution of GDP that is consistent with the underlying macroeconomic framework over the relevant horizon. The 1-2-3 model then takes this information and computes the structural implications induced by a change in relative prices. This is a key link in the chain of transmission from macroeconomic events to poverty. Based on the distinction between tradable and nontradable commodities, the *real exchange rate* is defined as the price of tradables relative to nontradable goods. An increase in domestic prices relative to world prices is known as an *appreciation* of the real exchange rate, while a decrease marks a *depreciation*. Real appreciation of the exchange rate, for instance, shifts incentives in favor of domestic goods relative to exports. The final outcome depends on the structural characteristics of the economy as revealed by the elasticity of transformation and of substitution.

The microlayer

The purpose of the microlayer is to translate the solution of the 1-2-3 general equilibrium model into changes in household welfare. For any macroeconomic event worked out within the macroeconomic framework, the general equilibrium model computes the corresponding changes in income (wages and profit) by sector (tradable and nontradable) and the changes in commodity prices (imports and home goods). The construction of the household module follows the envelope approach (discussed elsewhere above). Here, the indirect utility is a function of the *wage rate, sectoral profits,* and *commodity prices.* These are the *linkage variables* between the *meso-* and the *micro*layers. Thus, the first-order approximation of the welfare impact of a macroshock at the household level is equal to the sum of three components: (1) the initial level of labor income multiplied by the relative change in the wage rate, (2) the change in profit income, and (3) the sum over commodities of the product of the negative of the initial consumption and the relative change in the commodity price.[17]

For the empirical implementation, distributions of income and expenditure by deciles are derived from available household-survey data. There are three income sources: wages, profits from the home goods sector, and profits from the exports sector. Consumption expenditure is divided between imports and domestic goods. *Heterogeneity among households is thus reflected by differences in the sources of incomes and in the patterns of consumption.* This helps capture the differential impacts among households of shocks and policies.

Consider, for instance, a cut in public expenditure that falls mainly on nontradable goods. If there is sufficient structural flexibility, the induced fall in the price of nontradables will lead to a real depreciation in the exchange rate. The production of tradable goods will increase, while that of nontradables will decline. The welfare impact at the household level will depend on whether a household is a net seller or a net buyer of tradable goods. Net sellers would gain, while net buyers would lose. Once these differential impacts are computed, standard techniques can be used to derive the desired poverty and inequality measures. However, it is important to keep in mind that, *even when abundant and relevant household-level data are available, the ability of a modular framework such as 123PRSP to account for heterogeneity is constrained by the degree of disaggregation at the mesolevel.* By unifying the labor market and dividing the economy into only two sectors, the 123PRSP model achieves a great deal of transparency at a significant cost in terms of heterogeneity.[18]

The use of the 123PRSP model is illustrated in Box 7.7.

 The 123PRSP Model: Distributional Effects of Macropolicies and Shocks in Zambia

Devarajan and Go (2003) employ the 123PRSP model to examine the distributional impact of macroeconomic shocks and policies in Zambia.

Zambia is a landlocked economy that depends heavily on mineral exports, particularly copper. This renders the country very vulnerable to external price shocks. Over the 2001–3 period, two risk factors threatened macroeconomic stability in Zambia. The first shock stemmed from expenditure pressures associated with the presidential election in late 2001, and the second from the decline in the world price of copper (the major export for the economy) induced by a slowdown in world demand.

(continued)

BOX 7.7 **The 123PRSP Model: Distributional Effects of Macropolicies and Shocks in Zambia (Continued)**

One scenario assumes a 15 percent increase in government consumption in 2001 followed by another 10 percent increase in 2002. Assuming that foreign borrowing is kept at a constant fraction of GDP with respect to the base case and that investment adjusts to available total savings, model simulations show a small increase in GDP the first year that disappears the following year. The first-round multiplier effects of a rise in government consumption are offset by the crowding-out effect of high fiscal deficits in subsequent periods. The results also show small increases in consumption and household incomes.

Another simulation combines the expenditure shock with a decline in the copper price by 20 percent the first year, 15 percent the second year, and 10 percent the third year. The results (see Table 7.9) show that these shocks would lead to a significant drop in GDP growth of about 0.5 percent the first year, 1.4 percent the second year, and 1.3 percent the third year. Relative to the base case, household income falls about 2 percent the first year, cumulating to about 6 percent the last year. Even though all household groups are affected negatively, the results show that the poorest are the hardest hit.

TABLE 7.9. Impact of Shocks in Government Expenditures and Copper Prices
percentage deviation from the reference run, unless otherwise stated

	2001	2002	2003
Real GDP (% +/–)			
Expenditure shock	0.6	−0.1	0.1
Expenditure +TOT	−0.5	−1.4	−1.3
Real exchange rate of exports (depreciation>0)			
Expenditure shock	0	0	0
Expenditure +TOT	7.9	7.9	7.9
Household income (real), expenditure +TOT			
Decile 1 (poorest)	−4.6	−8.0	−9.8
Decile 2	−4.2	−7.4	−9.2
Decile 3	−4.0	−7.0	−8.8
Decile 4	−3.6	−6.4	−8.2
Decile 5	−3.4	−6.1	−7.8
Decile 6	−2.6	−5.0	−6.6
Decile 7	−2.4	−4.7	−6.3
Decile 8	−2.7	−5.1	−6.7
Decile 9	−2.5	−4.8	−6.4
Decile 10 (richest)	−1.7	−3.7	−5.3
Total	−2.1	−4.4	−5.8

Source: Devarajan and Go 2003.

The PAMS framework

PAMS is a simple simulation framework analogous to the 123PRSP to the extent that it is designed to help trace sequentially, in a *top-down* fashion, the poverty and distributional implications of macroeconomic shocks or policies. The original implementation of this framework (PAMS I) has three layers. The macroeconomic layer is represented by a standard macro-consistency model such as the World Bank's RMSM-X.

The second layer, which represents the mesolevel of analysis, is based on the idea that each household in the economy gets its means of livelihood both from the *government* (net public transfers) and from the *market*. The microlayer deals with household-level information organized on the basis of *policy-relevant characteristics* in a way that allows easy linkages with the mesoframework. Unit record data are used in a manner analogous to PovStat. The second generation of the framework is a reduced-form application that combines the macro- and mesolayers into a general equilibrium model and employs a parameterization of the Lorenz curve for poverty simulation.

This section first discusses the macroeconomic module within the RMSM-X framework. It then provides a brief description of the meso-module and the poverty simulator. It closes with a brief description of the essential features of the reduced-form version, which links a CGE model to a parameterized Lorenz curve.

The RMSM-X module

In essence, the RMSM-X framework may be viewed as an extension of a financial programming model that includes a growth model specified along the lines of the Harrod-Domar model.[19] In the basic formulation, there are four economic agents or sectors in the economy: (1) the central government, (2) the monetary system, (3) the private sector, and (4) the rest of the world (or the foreign sector). The underlying macroeconomic accounting framework is the same as the one described in the section on financial programming. It obeys the principles of flow-of-funds accounting: (1) a *source* of funds for one sector represents a *use* of funds by another sector, and (2) for each sector, the total amount of funds from all sources must equal the total disposition for all uses.

The structure of the model is characterized by (1) the budget constraints facing each sector and the overall economy, (2) market equilibrium conditions for goods and asset markets, and (3) behavioral and projection rules linking some variables to others. Consider, in particular, an economy with the four sectors and three assets above, including money, domestic lending by the banking system, and foreign debt.[20] A basic

RMSM-X model could then be specified along the following lines. The *growth equation* establishes a relationship among the growth of real output, investment, and the incremental capital output ratio (ICOR). A standard assumption is that the ICOR is constant over time, which implies a proportional relationship between growth and investment.[21] Next, one includes two equations describing changes in *nominal output* and changes in the *overall price index*. The change in the overall price index can be defined as a weighted average of the changes in the index of domestic prices and the changes in the exchange rate.

On the financial side of the economy, one would add the following relationships from the financial programming framework. A *money supply equation* would be derived from the balance sheet of the banking system. The equilibrium condition in the *domestic lending market* states that a change in domestic credit is the sum of the credit to the private sector and the credit to the public sector. The credit to the private sector could be expressed as a function of the change in nominal GDP. The change in official reserves is derived from the *balance of payments identity*. In this identity, *exports* are exogenous and computed on the basis of a simple projection rule. *Imports* can be computed as a function of real income and the real exchange rate (Agénor 2004a). The flow of foreign debt is given by the equilibrium condition on the *foreign asset market*, which states that the total flow is equal to the sum of the private and public flows. As before, the *demand for money* is a function of the velocity parameter and nominal income. Flow equilibrium prevails in the money market.

The budget constraints of both the public and private sectors can be written in a reduced form that shows the accumulation of the assets and liabilities associated with a surplus or deficit. In addition, to compute investment, the budget constraint of the private sector can be combined with the notion that private consumption is a linear function of disposable income (Agénor 2004a).

Adding up the four budget constraints in the model gives the fundamental national income identity. The model therefore contains eight core equations represented by the four budget constraints, the derived national income identity, and the three flow equilibrium conditions in asset markets (money, domestic credit, and foreign debt). These core equations are not mathematically independent due to the relationship between the sectoral budgets and the overall resource constraint. The system thus obeys Walras' Law and can be solved on the basis of only seven of the core equations. The solution of the remaining equation can be inferred from that of the other seven. However, the solution procedure depends on the closures chosen. There are three common closure rules

(World Bank 1995). In the case of *public closure,* one seeks values of government consumption and borrowing from both the monetary system and abroad that are consistent with projected growth, inflation, and other variables. In the case of *private closure,* one seeks a solution in terms of private consumption and borrowing. With respect to the *policy closure,* one is interested in the likely impact of alternative macroeconomic programs on target variables such as growth and inflation.

The policy closure seems more appropriate when the module is used to study the impact of macroeconomic policies on poverty and the distribution of income. In this context, one could solve the system recursively as follows (World Bank 1995). *Step 1:* identify and fix all foreign borrowing available to the country; then compute imports residually from the balance of payments. *Step 2:* use the value of imports derived from step one in the national income identity to solve for private investment.[22] *Step 3:* compute the value of the second target variable, the current price, from the money market equilibrium and the money demand equation.[23] *Step 4:* derive total domestic credit residually from the money supply equation. *Step 5:* given the change in government credit, compute private credit residually from the equilibrium condition of the domestic credit market.

The mesomodule

The main element of this component is the labor and wage-income module, which reconfigures the productive sector of the economy into a number of sectors equal to the number of socioeconomic groups. This effectively leads to a segmented labor market in the module. This segmentation is achieved as follows. First, the module divides the economy into two basic components, rural and urban. Then, within each component, one distinguishes the formal sector from the informal sector. Within each of these sectors, subsectors producing tradables are distinguished from those producing nontradables.

GDP, which is determined at the macro level, is an important linkage variable and must also be broken down according to the above categories. Here again, it will be necessary to determine residually the production of certain sectors (for example, the urban informal sector and the rural subsistence sector) in order to maintain overall consistency. The simplest way to model the rural economy is to represent its output as a constant elasticity function of rural labor. Within the urban economy, the production of the public sector is exogenous. Assuming that all private investment in the economy occurs within the formal sector, the output in that sector can be computed on the basis of an appropriate incremental capital output ratio. In such a case, the growth rate of output in the urban formal economy would stand in a fixed-coefficient relationship with the ratio of investment to output. For the sake of consistency, the output of the informal nontradable sector is determined residually.

Labor supply is seen as largely driven by demographic considerations and semi-exogenous migrations of labor and skill categories. Labor demand is broken down by socioeconomic categories, skill levels, and location (rural and urban) and is viewed as dependent on sectoral demand (output growth), as well as real wages. Hence, the new module determines wage income broken down by socioeconomic categories, skill levels, and location (rural and urban). Even though each sector in the reconfigured economy may employ both skilled and unskilled labor, the module relies on a simplifying assumption according to which each sector employs only one kind of labor. Thus, there is no substitution among types of labor in the production process except for semi-exogenous migration based on the Harris-Todaro process.

The excess of the total income generated in the economy with respect to the total wage bill distributed to all labor categories represents the profits that are distributed to a representative class of rentiers. The current version of the tool does not track down financial assets and returns on these assets. However, the interest revenue can conceivably be redistributed from the macroframework to various socioeconomic groups according to some rule. Average tax and transfer rates are used to compute the disposable income for each socioeconomic group. It is the percentage change in this disposable income that is transmitted to the poverty simulator in order to simulate the impact of shocks and policies on poverty and between-group inequality.

The poverty simulator

The poverty simulator in this version of PAMS (PAMS I) is analogous to PovStat. Intragroup distributions are represented by unit records pertaining to each socioeconomic group. To compute the impact of a macroeconomic shock or a policy on the welfare of a given household, the per capita income or expenditure of the household is multiplied by the induced growth rate of the disposable income of the representative group to which the household belongs. This growth rate is jointly determined by the macro- and the mesolayers.

As with any of the frameworks examined here, there are structural and, possibly, data constraints that can limit the reliability of the framework in predicting the poverty and distributional impact of macroeconomic shocks and policies. In the particular case of PAMS I, there is a data constraint stemming from the fact that most household surveys provide some information at the household level, such as expenditure and self-employment income, while other information, such as labor income and employment status, is given at the individual level. Choosing the household as the unit of analysis means that individual-level data must be aggregated up to the household level. Socioeconomic groups are thus created on the basis of the characteristics of heads of household. This obviously leads to results that are coarser than results based on relevant individual-level data.

In addition, the poverty simulator is bound to inherit the strengths and weaknesses of the top layers. It is well known, for instance, that the basic RMSM-X is a simple macroeconomic accounting framework and shows no behavioral relationships in the economic sense. Also, the use of a labor demand function that is defined by sector and skill level is equivalent to assuming a homogenous labor factor with different, sector-specific remuneration.

Operational support

PAMS I has seen battle in support of the design of Poverty Reduction Support Credits and the Poverty Assessment for Burkina Faso. Specifically, the framework was used to simulate the poverty implications of negative shocks to the cotton sector, as well as the impact of some patterns of growth. Assuming a permanent 20 percent decline in the price of cotton starting in 2004, the simulations reveal an increase of about 1.5 percentage points above the baseline. Naturally, cotton farmers (18 percent of the population) are the most affected. This impact would be exacerbated if it were accompanied by drop of 20 percent in output.

In the context of the analysis of the implications of different growth patterns, the simulation framework was used to study the impact of shocks to the agriculture sector outside cotton. A 20 percent increase in the output of the primary sector could lead to a 3 percentage point decline in poverty. One set of simulations concerns the implications of a pattern of growth wherein the overall growth rate remains unchanged, while the primary sector grows at a rate 2 percent higher than the baseline, along with a lower growth rate for the tertiary sector. In this case, poverty falls by 1 percent up to 2007 and by 4 percentage points by 2015.

Reduced-form implementation

The purpose of the mesolayer in the original PAMS is to model an extended functional distribution of the income generated by the upper-layer macroeconomic model based on the selected socioeconomic groups. In practice, several iterations are required in order to calibrate this module to available data. If a disaggregated SAM is available that is compatible with the selected socioeconomic groups, then it might be easier to compress the macro- and mesolayers into a general equilibrium model. As far as the poverty simulator is concerned, it should be noted that multiplying each observation (expenditure or income) in the unit record representation of a distribution by a scalar implies that the mean of the distribution is multiplied by the same scalar. Given that the within-group group distribution remains constant from one state to another, one might as well construct the poverty simulator on the basis of group means and Lorenz functions estimated from the available household data.

An example of the application of PAMS is supplied in Box 7.8.

This approach increases computational efficiency in a simulation environment. Thus, within the reduced-form version of PAMS (PAMS II) that runs in EViews (version 4.1 or later), poverty and distributional outcomes of shocks and policies are derived by linking recursively an appropriately disaggregated CGE model with a poverty and inequality simulator built upon a parameterization of the Lorenz curve. The approach underlying PAMS II is analogous to the ERH approach described elsewhere above. The main difference with other implementations of this approach stems from the fact that, in the PAMS framework, the within-group size distribution of income is derived from the assumed Lorenz distribution. Many other applications assume functional forms for the density function characterizing the within-group distribution.

A macro-micro simulation model for Brazil

In the context of this review, a macro-micro simulation model stands for any simulation framework that links in some fashion a representation of the macroeconomy to a model of the size distribution of income. In this fundamental sense, the 123PRSP model, PAMS, and even the ERH framework are members of the family of macro-micro simulation models. Two approaches commonly followed in the literature are to combine a CGE model either with an envelope model of welfare distribution or with an income and occupational model. The first approach is analogous to the way 123PRSP links a two-sector CGE model to the corresponding household module. Given this analogy and the fact that this chapter has already reviewed the structure of CGE models and income-occupational models, the focus here below is only on an approach followed by Ferreira et al. (2004) in a study of the distributional impacts of macroeconomic shocks

BOX 7.8 **PAMS II: A Reduced-Form Application of PAMS to Indonesia**

Essama-Nssah (2004) explains the implementation of a reduced-form version of PAMS using Indonesian data. The poverty outcomes of policies are analyzed by linking recursively the CGE model to a poverty simulator built upon a parameterization of the Lorenz curve. The aggregate formulation employs private consumption as the key linking variable, while the multisector interpretation relies on real disposable income. The poverty simulator of PAMS II is used to study the poverty implications of (1) terms-of-trade shocks, (2) changes in the balance of trade, and (3) changes in income tax or indirect taxes.

The reduced-form version developed for Indonesia (known as IndoPAMS) represents a significant improvement both computationally and in the modeling of the links between poverty and distributional outcomes and the macroeconomy. Furthermore, the version collapses the macro- and mesomodules of the original framework into a simple CGE model. This approach allows one to endogenize to some extent the growth process via factor accumulation. A stylized version of this framework is also described by Essama-Nssah (2005).

In the application, the key linkage variable is the mean of the distribution of income or expenditure, the changes of which are determined by the economy-wide model. These changes are then fed into the Lorenz framework to predict the corresponding changes in poverty. In accordance with the ERH approach that underlies it, PAMS II assumes constant intragroup inequality. Thus, it can only predict changes in between-group inequality. Various scenarios were simulated to examine the impact on poverty and inequality indicators. Table 7.10 shows, for instance, the poverty implications of an export boom in the form of a 20 percent increase in the world price of exports. It is clear that the extent of poverty reduction depends crucially on the structure of the economy as represented by the elasticities of output transformation and import substitution. The higher these elasticities, the greater the extent of poverty reduction.

TABLE 7.10. Poverty Implications of an Improvement in the Terms of Trade

Elasticity of output transformation	Import substitution elasticity	Head-count (base)	Head-count (20%)	Poverty gap (base)	Poverty gap (20%)
−0.20	0.20	0.161	0.145	0.023	0.019
−0.50	0.50	0.161	0.133	0.023	0.017
−0.75	1.26	0.161	0.128	0.023	0.016
−2.00	2.00	0.161	0.126	0.023	0.015
−5.00	5.00	0.161	0.121	0.023	0.014

Source: Essama-Nssah 2004.

in Brazil. They link an IS-LM model to a model of income and occupational choice. In what follows, only the macroeconomic model and the linkage variables are considered.

The IS-LM model

The basic IS-LM model is considered an expression of the Keynesian approach to macroeconomics[24] and is grounded on a key assumption: aggregate demand determines the equilibrium level of output. The model provides a framework for the study of the interaction between the real and the financial sides of the economy. This interaction is governed by two key variables: the real economy determines the level of *income*, which affects the demand for money (a financial variable), and the financial sector determines the *interest rate*, which affects investment in the real economy.

The Brazilian model reviewed here is a neo-Keynesian extension of the above basic framework; it has three key elements. The real economy block of the model determines the aggregate demand, production, and factor demand components. The second block models the determination of the price level and the wage rate. Finally, the interest rate is determined in the financial block of the model. The main transmission mechanism between the real and the financial sides of the economy relies on the specification of real private consumption and investment as functions of the interest rate. Private consumption is also a function of disposable income and the general price index. The model includes a disaggregated representation of the balance of payments.

In order to improve the ability of the model to handle the agent heterogeneity observed in the household survey, supply is divided into six sectors: (1) urban tradable formal, (2) urban nontradable formal, (3) urban nontradable informal, (4) rural tradable formal, (5) rural nontradable formal, and (6) rural nontradable informal. Production in each of these sectors is assumed to be an elasticity of substitution function of capital and a composite labor input with skilled and unskilled components. Labor demand by skill level (low, intermediate, and high) is determined by profit maximization.

Linkage variables

The solution of the model affords the linkage variables needed for impact analysis with the microsimulation module. In particular, it produces 18 wage rates (for three skill levels in six sectors), and 21 occupation rates (six employment levels and one value for unemployment for six sectors). Another set of linkage variables includes changes in output prices in the six sectors. The authors (Ferreira et al. 2004) use an algorithm to ensure consistency between the macroeconomic solution and the predictions of the microsimulation model.

The IMMPA framework

The IMMPA is a dynamic framework designed around some key characteristics of low-income countries. It focuses on issues relating to labor market segmentation, informal activities, credit market imperfections, and the composition of public expenditure. The macro- and mesoparts of the economy are represented by a financial CGE model with seven distinct blocks: (1) production and employment, (2) the demand side of the economy, (3) the price system, (4) external trade, (5) income formation, (6) the financial sector, and (7) the public sector. The specification of each of these blocks follows well-known principles in general equilibrium modeling. The focus is therefore the presentation here of some key, distinctive features of the IMMPA.

It should be noted at the outset that this framework is richer than any of those described above. The framework allows the analyst to consider the segmentation of the labor market induced by legislation or wage-setting practices, along with the role of informal employment in the transmission of the impact of shocks and policies to the poor. For highly indebted countries, one can analyze the effects of foreign debt on private incentives to invest. The integration of the real and financial sides of the economy in the context of credit market imperfections allows a realistic consideration of stabilization and structural policy issues. Finally, by distinguishing the components of public expenditure on infrastructure, health, and education, the framework permits a disaggregated impact analysis. However, while this structural richness is desirable for a proper accounting of heterogeneity, it may also prove to be a severe constraint to implementation in a data-poor environment.

The labor market

With respect to the modeling of the labor market, the IMMPA framework emphasizes the idea that the structure of labor plays a crucial role in the transmission of the impact of shocks and policies to economic activity, employment, and relative prices. This is especially important because, generally speaking, labor supply is a major source of income for the poor in many countries. The framework distinguishes between the rural and the urban sectors of the economy. The urban labor market has two components: the formal and the informal segments. Wages are assumed to be fully flexible in the informal economy. In the formal sector, labor is heterogeneous and comprises a skilled element and an unskilled element. Wages for skilled workers in the private sector are fixed on the basis of efficiency-wage considerations. The government determines the wages for public sector employees and unskilled workers in the formal private sector.

It is assumed that unskilled workers can work in the rural and urban sectors, while skilled workers are restricted to the urban sector. The labor force in rural areas grows at an exogenous rate equal to the population growth rate, minus the net migration to urban areas. According to the Harris-Todaro model, migration is governed by the differential between the expected income in the rural sector and the one prevailing in the urban sector.

The financial sector

The modeling of the financial sector is based on features of an archetypical poor economy with a limited number of financial assets. This component of the framework seeks to determine the structure of the portfolio held by households, the demand for credit by firms, and the behavior of commercial banks. Savings can be held only in the form of money or bank deposits at home and abroad. Financial intermediation is dominated by commercial banks. A key assumption states that firms are unable to issue tradable claims on their assets or future output. The framework also tries to capture the impact of interest rates on capital flows and the structure of agent portfolios, the real balance effects on expenditure, and the linkages between bank credit and the supply side of the economy through the demand for working capital by firms. In particular, the bank lending rate is incorporated in the effective price of labor faced by firms that must finance their working capital needs prior to the sale of output. This is one of the crucial ways in which the real and financial sides of the economy interact.

Public expenditure

The IMMPA framework is designed to account for the channels through which various components of public investment affect the economy. In particular, the stock of public capital in infrastructure (roads, power plants, and railroads) is assumed to have a direct effect on the level of production in the private sector and, hence, on the marginal productivity of primary factors employed in that sector.

Public expenditure on education consists of spending on items such as school buildings and other infrastructure and is assumed to have an impact if it assists unskilled workers to acquire skills. Similarly, public assets such as hospitals and health centers affect individual health outcomes.

Distributional analysis

For the purpose of distributional analysis, the IMMPA framework considers six categories of households: (1) workers in the rural traded sector, (2) workers in the rural nontraded sector, (3) unskilled workers in the urban informal sector, (4) unskilled workers in the urban formal sector, (5) skilled workers in the urban formal sector, and (6) capitalists. The macroeconomic model is linked to unit record data in a way that is analogous to impact analysis with PovStat. Following a shock to the model economy, the macromodel generates real growth rates in per capita consumption and disposable income for all six household categories and for each year in the simulation horizon (up to 10 years). These growth rates are then used to scale per capita consumption and disposable income appropriately in each group. New poverty and inequality indicators (the Foster-Greer-Thorbecke family, the Gini, and the Theil) are computed and compared to the baseline values. The difference is attributed to the shock. In this dynamic framework, short-term impact corresponds to the first two periods. Medium-term impact is supposed to occur between periods 3 and 5. Long-term impact is felt beyond period 6.

The IMMPA model is demonstrated by the case described in Box 7.9.

BOX 7.9   **The IMMPA Model: Adjustment Policies and the Poor in Brazil**

Brazil has made significant progress in controlling inflation and achieving stabilization since the Real Plan of 1994. Despite the 1999 currency crisis, which put pressure on the exchange rate and led to the adoption of a flexible exchange rate regime, inflation remained low. This stabilization was achieved through a prudent fiscal policy and the active management of short-term interest rates by the central bank.

Agénor et al. (2006) provide an interpretation of the IMMPA framework to analyze the impact of adjustment policies on poverty and income distribution in Brazil. The interpretation involves extensions to the prototype framework to capture important characteristics specific to the Brazilian economy. In particular, the Brazilian model allows for open unskilled urban unemployment, a distinction between product wage and consumption wage in the determination of skilled worker wages, the possibility of congestion effects linked to the use of public services in urban areas, and the bond financing of public sector deficits, while excluding borrowing from the central bank.

The poverty and distributional implications of a 10 percent increase in the interest rate are presented in Table 7.11. In the short run, the poverty headcount index increases only slightly

(continued)

BOX 7.9 | **The IMMPA Model: Adjustment Policies and the Poor in Brazil (Continued)**

TABLE 7.11. Brazil Simulation Results: Impact of a 10 Percentage Point Increase in the Interest Rate

Poverty and distributional indicators, consumption based	Period 1	Period 2	Period 3	Period 8	Period 9	Period 10
Poverty headcount						
Rural households	−0.1	0.1	0.2	1.5	2.6	3.0
Urban households	−0.6	0.0	−0.1	1.0	1.5	2.2
Informal	−0.1	0.0	0.1	2.5	3.3	4.9
Formal unskilled	−1.8	−0.1	0.0	0.5	0.8	0.9
Formal skilled	−0.1	−0.1	−0.4	0.0	0.2	0.3
Capitalists and rentiers	0.5	0.5	0.0	−1.0	−1.0	−0.7
Economy	−0.5	0.0	0.0	1.1	1.7	2.3
Distributional indicators						
Gini coefficient	−2.3	−0.3	0.0	3.8	4.6	5.3
Theil index	−1.2	−0.3	−0.1	3.7	4.9	6.2

Source: Agénor et al. 2006.

in both rural and urban areas. However, in the long run, the increase in the official interest rate would cause the headcount index to rise by 2 percent in urban areas and 3 percent in rural areas. The households engaged in urban informal activities are the group hit the hardest. Poverty among this group increases by about 5 percent. Income inequality increases as well. Overall, higher interest rates (a tight monetary policy) will lower inflation, but at the expense of greater poverty and income inequality.

CONCLUDING REMARKS

This chapter reviews some common approaches in modeling the poverty and distributional impact of macroeconomic shocks and policies. These include terms-of-trade shocks, fiscal adjustment, monetary policy, and trade liberalization. What is needed in these situations is a framework that adequately links a macroeconomic model to a model of the distribution of economic welfare at the individual or household level.

The approaches or specific models described in this chapter vary in the ways they specify the macroeconomy, the distribution of welfare, and the macro-micro linkages. Models that focus only on income distribution may be viewed as frameworks that keep the macromodel implicit. They can therefore be used in conjunction with assumptions about the response of the macroeconomy to shocks and policies. The second approach involves embedding distributional mechanisms within a general equilibrium framework. The third class of models adopts a modular approach in linking poverty and distributional outcomes to macroeconomic shocks and policies. An emerging approach known as Top-Down/Bottom-Up (Savard 2005) is worth mentioning. It tries to account for the feedback effect from the micromodule to the macro and back until convergence is achieved. Which approach to adopt depends, of course, on the problem at hand, the data, and other constraints imposed by modeling resources, such as skills.

The reliability of a model designed to predict the poverty and distributional outcomes of macroeconomic shocks and policies depends on how well the model handles three *fundamentals*. The first relates to the *heterogeneity* of socioeconomic agents in terms of endowments (assets and personal characteristics) and behavior. The availability of reliable household data is a key constraint in accounting for such heterogeneity. The second fundamental concerns the modeling of transmission channels in terms of *institutional arrangements* that control social interaction. A realistic representation of such arrangements allows one to estimate more accurately both the direct and the indirect effects of shocks and policies. Finally, the macroeconomic model should be designed to account for the interdependence among policy issues (stabilization, structural, and distributional). In a modular approach, the ability of the bottom layer to account for heterogeneity can be severely constrained by the top layers if they are not disaggregated in a way that is consistent with the bottom layer. It may therefore be said that the *whole framework is only as "strong" as its "weakest" module*.

NOTES

1. The review focuses on models dealing primarily with the income dimension of poverty. The Development Economics Development Prospects Group at the World Bank has established a framework known as MAMS or Maquette for MDG Simulation. This framework allows an economy-wide analysis of shocks and policies on income poverty and a set of Millennium Development Goals (MDGs) related to health, education, and infrastructure (see Löfgren and Diaz-Bonilla 2005).

2. Most economic models of behavior are based on the principle of optimization, according to which each agent attempts to implement the best possible action given her/his objective and the prevailing constraints. The maximum value function is the maximum attainable value of the objective function expressed in terms of the parameters characterizing the environment of the problem (see Dixit 1990).

3. POVCAL is programmed in Fortran 5.0 and uses the parametric specification of the underlying Lorenz curve. Currently, it supports the following specifications: (1) the general quadratic model (Villasenor and Arnold 1984) and (2) the Beta model (Kakwani 1980).

4. The ASCII data file must be in tabular form wherein each row of data corresponds to a record, and columns represent the variable for the subgroups. Variables must be organized according to the order of subgroups.

5. In other terms, the household is facing a linear budget constraint. The institutional underpinning of this assumption consists of efficient markets with negligible transaction costs (Deaton and Muellbauer 1980).

6. According to Lindblom (2001), social coordination aims at minimizing conflict and promoting cooperation viewed as an exchange of help. Lindblom also notes a fundamental distinction between the notions of market and market system. There are markets whenever people frequently pay others to do something. A market system is a collection of markets designed to organize and coordinate social interaction.

7. This is a record of the foreign exchange inflows and outflows associated with trade, factor and interest payments, and institutional transfers, including migrant remittances.

8. It is assumed here that indirect taxes are paid at the factory gate. That is why, in the SAM, they appear as a payment by the activity account to the government account. However, such taxes may also be paid out of the commodity account.

9. The parameters can be estimated using household-survey data. Alternatively, group density functions can be estimated using relevant parameterized Lorenz curves, as is done in the discussion of the PAMS framework.

10. Agénor, Chen, and Grimm (2004) consider the following categories: (1) rural workers, (2) urban workers in the informal sector, (3) urban unskilled workers in the formal sector, (4) urban skilled workers in the formal sector, and (5) capitalists-rentiers. This does not mean that any policy model should follow the same disaggregation. Disaggregation in terms of sectors, factor markets, institutions, and socioeconomic groups is dictated by the issues at hand, the availability and reliability of relevant data, and the adequacy of the resources for information processing.

11. This presentation of the accounting framework follows Khan, Montiel, and Haque (1990).

12. Absorption is taken to represent the sum of private consumption, domestic investment, and government expenditure (IMF 1987).

13. It is also possible to base the analysis on the balance sheet of the central bank instead of that of the banking system as a whole. The policy variable would then be changes in the net domestic assets of the central bank and not domestic credit expansion. The balance sheet identity would be stated in terms of reserve money (the currency held by the public and the reserves held by commercial banks). The total money supply would then be a function of the reserve money. See Polak (1998) and IMF (1987) for details.

14. In calculations of the quantity of money in an economy, M1 stands for currency, plus the demand deposits held by nonbank institutions. M2 is based on a broader concept and is equal to M1, plus savings and time deposits in commercial banks.

15. This extended Salter-Swan model is commonly known as the 1-2-3 model because it represents one country, two sectors of production (exports and domestic goods), and three commodities (exports, domestic goods, and imports).

16. The use of a constant elasticity of transformation production-possibility frontier may be viewed as a reduced-form interpretation of the framework. Devarajan, Lewis, and Robinson (1990) show how to specify the model as a standard CGE model with the explicit use of production functions and a consideration of factor markets.

17. There is an inverse relationship between the demand for a commodity and the price of the commodity.

18. It is important to keep in mind that the core model here is the 1-2-3 model that is used to derive the aggregate income and key relative prices. Nothing prevents the analyst from adopting a different configuration for the other components. For the macroframework, a government development plan can be used, or other growth regressions such as Barro's can be employed. For the poverty module, one could use POVCAL or PovStat or even a microsimulation model.

19. Easterly (1999) refers to the current version of the growth model employed at the World Bank as the "financing gap model"; its most important uses involve determining growth prospects and the associated financing shortfalls.

20. One could add a fourth asset: bonds issued by the government to borrow money from the general public. This addition would not alter the basic logic presented in the text.

21. In a critique of the use of this model in short-term growth analysis, Easterly (1999) notes that, in both the neoclassical and endogenous growth models, the ICOR can be constant in a steady state. In the neoclassical framework, this steady state ICOR is equal to the ratio of the investment rate to the sum of population growth and the rate of labor-augmenting technical progress. Furthermore, this constancy does not imply a causal and proportional relationship between investment and growth. Finally, he argues against viewing the ICOR as an indicator of the quality of investment.

22. This is possible because, once imports are known, all other components of this identity are determined except private investment. In particular, real GDP is determined from the ICOR and the total investment during the previous period. Exports are projected exogenously. Private consumption is specified as a fraction of disposable income, and government consumption and investment are each a fraction of GDP.

23. The current level of the overall price index is equal to the money supply multiplied by the velocity of money, divided by nominal income.
24. The simplest version presented in textbooks is commonly called the Keynesian cross.

BIBLIOGRAPHY

Agénor, P.-R. 2003. "The Mini-Integrated Macroeconomic Model for Poverty Analysis: A Framework for Analyzing the Unemployment and Poverty Effects of Fiscal and Labor Market Reforms." Policy Research Working Paper 3067, World Bank, Washington, DC.

———. 2004a. *The Economics of Adjustment and Growth.* 2nd ed. Cambridge, MA: Harvard University Press.

———. 2004b. "Macroeconomic Adjustment and the Poor: Analytical Issues and Cross-Country Evidence." *Journal of Economic Surveys* 18 (3): 351–408.

Agénor, P.-R., D. H. C. Chen, and M. Grimm. 2004. "Linking Representative Household Models with Household Surveys for Poverty Analysis: A Comparison of Alternative Methodologies." Policy Research Working Paper 3343, World Bank, Washington, DC.

Agénor, P.-R., R. Fernándes, E. Haddad, and H. T. Jensen. 2006. "Adjustment Policies and the Poor in Brazil." In *Adjustment Policies, Poverty, and Unemployment: The IMMPA Framework,* ed. P.-R. Agénor, A. Izquierdo, and H. T. Jensen. Oxford: Blackwell Publishing.

Agénor, P.-R., A. Izquierdo, and H. Fofack. 2003. "IMMPA: A Quantitative Macroeconomic Framework for the Analysis of Poverty Reduction Strategies." Photocopy, World Bank, Washington, DC.

Agénor, P.-R., A. Izquierdo, and H. T. Jensen, eds. 2006. *Adjustment Policies, Poverty, and Unemployment: The IMMPA Framework.* Oxford: Blackwell Publishing.

Avitsland, T., and J. Aasness. 2004. "Combining CGE and Microsimulation Models: Effects on Equality of VAT Reforms." Discussion Paper 392, Research Department, Statistics Norway, Oslo.

Bandara, J. S. 1991. "Computable General Equilibrium Models for Development Policy Analysis." *Journal of Economic Surveys* 5 (1): 3–69.

Barja Daza, G., J. Monterrey Arce, and S. Villarroel Böhrt. 2004. "Bolivia: Impact of Shocks and Poverty Policy on Household Welfare." Paper, Global Development Network, World Bank, Washington, DC.

Bourguignon, F, W. H. Branson, and J. de Melo. 1992. "Adjustment and Income Distribution: A Micro-Macro Model for Counterfactual Analysis." *Journal of Development Economics* 38 (1): 17–39.

Bourguignon, F., and F. H. G. Ferreira. 2005. "Decomposing Changes in the Distribution of Household Incomes: Methodological Aspects." In *The Microeconomics of Income Distribution Dynamics in East Asia and Latin America,* ed. F. Bourguignon, F. H. G. Ferreira, and N. Lustig, 17–46. New York: Oxford University Press.

Bourguignon, F., F. H. G. Ferreira, and N. Lustig. 2005. "Introduction." In *The Microeconomics of Income Distribution Dynamics in East Asia and Latin America,* ed. F. Bourguignon, F. H. G. Ferreira, and N. Lustig, 1–15. New York: Oxford University Press.

Bourguignon, F., A.-S. Robilliard, and S. Robinson. 2003. "Representative Versus Real Households in the Macro-Economic Modeling of Inequality." DELTA Working Paper 2003–5, Département et Laboratoire d'Economie Théorique et Appliquée, Paris.

Bourguignon, F., and A. Sapadaro. 2005. "Microsimulation as a Tool for Evaluating Redistribution Policies." Working Paper 2005-02, Paris-Jourdan Sciences Economiques, Paris.

Chen, S., G. Datt, and M. Ravallion. 1991. "POVCAL: A Program for Calculating Poverty Measures from Group Data." Photocopy, World Bank, Washington, DC.

Chen, S., and M. Ravallion. 2004. "Welfare Impacts of China's Accession to the World Trade Organization." *World Bank Economic Review* 18 (1): 29–57.

Coady, D., and R. Harris. 2001. "A Regional General Equilibrium Analysis of the Welfare Impact of Cash Transfers: An Analysis of Progresa in Mexico." Trade and Macroeconomics Division Discussion Paper 76, International Food Policy Research Institute, Washington, DC.

Cockburn, J. 2001. "Trade Liberalization and Poverty in Nepal: A Computable General Equilibrium Micro Simulation Analysis." Photocopy, Department of Economics, Laval University, Montreal.

Datt, G. 1992. "Computational Tools for Poverty Measurement and Analysis." Photocopy, World Bank, Washington, DC.

———. 1998. "Computational Tools for Poverty Measurement and Analysis." Food Consumption and Nutrition Division Discussion Paper 50, International Food Policy Research Institute, Washington, DC.

Datt, G., K. Ramadas, D. van der Mensbrugghe, T. Walker, and Q. Wodon. 2003. "Predicting the Effect of Aggregate Growth on Poverty." In *The Impact of Economic Policies on Poverty and Income Distribution: Evaluation Techniques and Tools,* ed. F. Bourguignon and L. A. Pereira da Silva, 215–33. New York: Oxford University Press.

Datt, G., and M. Ravallion. 1992. "Growth and Redistribution Components of Changes in Poverty Measures: A Decomposition with Applications to Brazil and India in the 1980s." *Journal of Development Economics* 38 (2): 275–95.

Datt, G., and T. Walker. 2002. "PovStat 2.12: A Poverty Projection Toolkit, User's Manual." Photocopy, World Bank, Washington, DC.

Davies, J. B. 2004. "Microsimulation, CGE, and Macro Modelling for Transition and Developing Economies." Discussion Paper 2004/08, United Nations University–World Institute for Development Economics Research, Helsinki.

Deaton, A., and J. Muellbauer. 1980. *Economics and Consumer Behavior.* Cambridge: Cambridge University Press.

Decaluwé, B., J.-C. Dumont, and L. Savard. 1999. "Measuring Poverty and Inequality in a Computable General Equilibrium Model." CREFA Working Paper 99–20, Research Center in Applied Economics and Finance, Department of Economics, Laval University, Montreal.

Decaluwé, B., A. Martens, and L. Savard. 2001. *La politique économique du développement et les modèles d'équilibre général calculable.* Montreal: Université Francophone–Presses de l'Université de Montréal.

Decaluwé, B., A. Patry, L. Savard, and E. Thorbecke. 1999. "Poverty Analysis within a General Equilibrium Framework." CREFA Working Paper 99–06, Research Center in Applied Economics and Finance, Department of Economics, Laval University, Montreal.

de Melo, J., and S. Robinson. 1980. "The Impact of Trade Policies on Income Distribution in a Planning Model for Colombia." *Journal of Policy Modeling* 2 (1): 81–100.

Demombynes, G., and J. G. Hoogeveen. 2004. "Growth, Inequality, and Simulated Poverty Paths for Tanzania, 1992–2002." Policy Research Working Paper 3432, World Bank, Washington, DC.

Dervis, K., J. de Melo, and S. Robinson. 1982. *General Equilibrium Models for Development Policy.* World Bank, Washington, DC.

Devarajan, S., and J. de Melo. 1987. "Adjustment with a Fixed Exchange Rate: Cameroon, Côte-d'Ivoire, and Senegal." *World Bank Economic Review* 1 (3): 447–87.

Devarajan, S., and S. D. Go. 2002. "A Macroeconomic Framework for Poverty Reduction Strategy Papers with an Application to Zambia." Africa Region Working Paper Series 38, World Bank, Washington, DC.

———. 2003. "The 123PRSP Model." In *The Impact of Economic Policies on Poverty and Income Distribution: Evaluation Techniques and Tools,* ed. F. Bourguignon and L. A. Pereira da Silva, 277–99. New York: Oxford University Press.

Devarajan, S., and J. D. Lewis. 1991. "Structural Adjustment and Economic Reform in Indonesia: Model-Based Policies vs. Rules of Thumb." In *Reforming Economic Systems in Developing Countries,* ed. D. H. Perkins and M. Roemer, 159–86. Cambridge, MA: Harvard University Press.

Devarajan, S., J. D. Lewis, and S. Robinson. 1990. "Policy Lessons from Two-Sector Models." *Journal of Policy Modeling* 12 (4): 625–57.

———. 1993. "External Shocks, Purchasing Power Parity, and the Equilibrium Real Exchange Rate." *World Bank Economic Review* 7 (1): 45–63.

Dinwiddy, C. L., and F. J. Teal. 1988. *The Two-Sector General Equilibrium Model: A New Approach.* Oxford: Phillip Allan; New York: St. Martin's Press.

Dixit, A. K. 1990. *Optimization in Economic Theory.* Oxford: Oxford University Press.

———. 1996. *The Making of Economic Policy: A Transaction Cost Politics Perspective.* Cambridge, MA: The MIT Press.

Drazen, A. 2000. *Political Economy in Macroeconomics.* Princeton, NJ: Princeton University Press.

Duclos, J.-Y., A. Araar, and C. Fortin. 1998–2004. "DAD: A Software for Distributive Analysis/Analyse Distributive." International Development Research Centre, Government of Canada, Ottawa; Research Center in Applied Economics and Finance, Department of Economics, Laval University, Montreal. www.mimap.ecn.ulaval.ca.

Easterly, W. 1999. "The Ghost of Financing Gap: Testing the Growth Model Used in the International Financial Institutions." *Journal of Development Economics* 60 (2): 423–38.

———. 2001. "The Lost Decades: Developing Countries' Stagnation in Spite of Policy Reform 1980–1998." *Journal of Economic Growth* 6 (2): 135–57.

———. 2004. "An Identity Crisis?: Examining IMF Financial Programming." Photocopy, Department of Economics, New York University, New York.

Emini, C. A., J. Cockburn, and B. Decaluwé. 2005. "The Poverty Impacts of the Doha Round and the Role of Tax Policy: A Case Study for Cameroon." Paper, Centre d'Etudes et de Recherches en Economie et Gestion, University of Yaounde II, Yaounde, Cameroon.

Enders, W. 1995. *Applied Econometric Time Series.* New York: John Wiley and Sons.

Essama-Nssah, B. 1997. "Impact of Growth and Distribution on Poverty in Madagascar." *Review of Income and Wealth* 43 (2): 239–52.

———. 2004. "A Reduced-Form Application of PAMS to Indonesia." Photocopy, World Bank, Washington, DC.

———. 2005. "Simulating the Poverty Impact of Macroeconomic Shocks and Policies." Policy Research Working Paper 3788, World Bank, Washington, DC.

Ferreira, F. H. G., and P. G. Leite. 2003. "Policy Options for Meeting the Millennium Development Goals: Can Microsimulation Help?" Policy Research Working Paper 2975, World Bank, Washington, DC.

Ferreira, F. H. G., P. G. Leite, L. A. Pereira da Silva, and P. Picchetti. 2004. "Can the Distributional Impacts of Macroeconomic Shocks be Predicted? A Comparison of the Performance of Macro-Micro Models with Historical Data for Brazil." Photocopy, World Bank, Washington, DC.

Fisher, S., and W. Easterly. 1990. "The Economics of the Government Budget Constraint." *World Bank Research Observer* 5 (2): 127–42.

Foster, J., J. Greer, and E. Thorbecke. 1984. "A Class of Decomposable Poverty Measures." *Econometrica* 52 (3): 761–66.

Gemmell, N., and O. Morrissey. 2005. "Distribution and Poverty Impacts of Tax Structure Reform in Developing Countries: How Little We Know." *Development Policy Review* 23 (2): 131–44.

Gomes, R., and M. Lawson. 2005. "Pro-Poor Macroeconomic Policies Require Poverty and Social Impact Analysis." *Development Policy Review* 23 (3): 369–84.

Grimm, M. 2004. "A Decomposition of Inequality and Poverty Changes in the Context of Macroeconomic Adjustment: A Microsimulation Study for Côte d'Ivoire." In *Growth, Inequality, and Poverty: Prospects for Pro-Poor Economic Development*, ed. A. F. Shorrocks and R. van der Hoeven, 197–221. Oxford: Oxford University Press.

Gunter, B. G., M. J. Cohen, and H. Löfgren. 2005. "Analyzing Macro-Poverty Linkages: An Overview." *Development Policy Review* 23 (3): 243–65.

Gunter, B. G., L. Taylor, and E. Yeldan. 2005. "Analyzing Macro-Poverty Linkages of External Liberalization: Gaps, Achievements, and Alternatives." *Development Policy Review,* 23 (3): 285–98.

Hertel, T. W. 1999. "Applied General Equilibrium Analysis of Agricultural and Resource Policies." Staff Paper 99-2, Department of Agricultural Economics, Purdue University, West Lafayette, IN.

Hertel, T. W., and J. J. Reimer. 2004. "Predicting the Poverty Impacts of Trade Liberalization." Policy Research Working Paper 3444, Washington, DC, World Bank.

Host-Maden, P. 1979. "Macroeconomic Accounts: An Overview." Pamphlet Series 29, International Monetary Fund, Washington, DC.

Howard, M., and N. Mamingi. 2002. "The Monetary Approach to the Balance of Payments: An Application to Barbados." *Singapore Economic Review* 47 (2): 213–28.

IMF (International Monetary Fund). 1987. "Theoretical Aspects of the Design of Fund-Supported Adjustment Programs." IMF Occasional Paper 55, International Monetary Fund, Washington, DC.

Ianchovichina, E., A. Nicita, and I. Soloaga. 2001. "Trade Reform and Household Welfare: The Case of Mexico." Policy Research Working Paper 2667, World Bank, Washington, DC.

Kakwani, N. 1980. *Income Inequality and Poverty: Methods of Estimation and Policy Applications.* Oxford: Oxford University Press.

———. 1993. "Poverty and Economic Growth with Application to Côte d'Ivoire." *Review of Income and Wealth* 39 (2): 121–39.

———. 1997. "On Measuring Growth and Inequality Components of Changes in Poverty with Application to Thailand." Discussion Paper 97/16, School of Economics, University of New South Wales, Sydney.

Khan, H. A. 2004. "Using Macroeconomic Computable General Equilibrium Models for Assessing the Poverty Impact of Structural Adjustment Policies." Discussion Paper 12, Asian Development Bank Institute, Tokyo.

Khan, M. S., P. Montiel, and N. U. Haque. 1990. "Adjustment with Growth: Relating the Analytical Approaches of the IMF and the World Bank." *Journal of Development Economics* 32 (1): 155–79.

King, D., and S. Handa. 2003. "The Welfare Effects of Balance of Payments Reform: A Macro-Micro Simulation of the Cost of Rent-Seeking." *Journal of Development Studies* 39 (3): 101–28.

Kraev, E., and B. Akolgo. 2005. "Assessing Modelling Approaches to the Distributional Effects of Macroeconomic Policy." *Development Policy Review* 23 (3): 299–312.

Lindblom, C. E. 2001. *The Market System: What Is It, How It Works, and What to Make of It*. New Haven, CT: Yale University Press.

Löfgren, H., and C. Diaz-Bonilla. 2005. "An Ethiopian Strategy for Achieving the Millennium Development Goals: Simulations with the MAMS Model." Photocopy, World Bank, Washington, DC.

Löfgren, H., R. L. Harris, and S. Robinson. 2002. *A Standard Computable General Equilibrium (CGE) Model in GAMS*. With M. El-Said and M. Thomas. Vol. 5 of *Microcomputers in Policy Research*. Washington, DC: International Food Policy Research Institute.

Löfgren, H., S. Robinson, and M. El-Said. 2003. "Poverty and Inequality Analysis in a General Equilibrium Framework: The Representative Household Approach." In *The Impact of Economic Policies on Poverty and Income Distribution: Evaluation Techniques and Tools*, ed. F. Bourguignon and L. A. Pereira da Silva, 325–37. New York: Oxford University Press.

Papageorgiou, D., A. M. Choksi, and M. Michaely. 1990. *Liberalizing Foreign Trade in Developing Countries: The Lessons of Experience*. World Bank, Washington, DC.

Pereira da Silva, L. A., B. Essama-Nssah, and I. Samaké. 2002. "Poverty Analysis Macro-Simulator or PAMS." Photocopy (February), World Bank, Washington, DC.

———. 2003. "Linking Aggregate Macro-Consistency Models to Household Surveys: A Poverty Analysis Macroeconomic Simulator, or PAMS." In *The Impact of Economic Policies on Poverty and Income Distribution: Evaluation Techniques and Tools*, ed. F. Bourguignon and L. A. Pereira da Silva. New York: Oxford University Press.

Polak, J. J. 1998. "The IMF Monetary Model at 40." *Economic Modelling* 15 (3): 395–410.

Powell, M., and J. I. Round. 2000. "Structure and Linkage in the Economy of Ghana: A SAM Approach." In *Economic Reforms in Ghana: Miracle or Mirage?*, ed. E. Aryeetey, J. Harrigan, and M. Nissanke, 68–87. Oxford: James Currey Press.

Pyatt, G., and J. I. Round, eds. 1985. *Social Accounting Matrices: A Basis for Planning*. World Bank, Washington, DC.

Quade, E. S. 1982. *Analysis for Public Decisions*. New York: North-Holland.

Rajcoomar, S., and M. W. Bell. 1996. *Financial Programming and Policy: The Case of Sri Lanka*. With J. Karlik, M. Martin, and C. Sisson et al. Washington, DC: IMF Institute, International Monetary Fund.

Ramadas, K., D. van der Mensbrugghe, and Q. Wodon. 2002. *SimSiP Poverty: Poverty and Inequality Comparisons Using Group Data*. World Bank, Washington, DC.

Ravallion, M., and M. Huppi. 1991. "Measuring Changes in Poverty: A Method-ological Case Study of Indonesia during an Adjustment Period." *World Bank Economic Review* 5 (1): 57–82.

Ravallion, M., and M. Lokshin. 2004. "Gainers and Losers from Trade Reform in Morocco." Policy Research Working Paper 3368, World Bank, Washington, DC.

Reimer, J. J. 2002. "Estimating the Poverty Impacts of Trade Liberalization." GTAP Working Paper 20, Center for Global Trade Analysis and Department of Agricultural Economics, Purdue University, West Lafayette, IN.

Reinert, K. A., and D. W. Roland-Holst. 1997. "Social Accounting Matrices." In *Applied Methods for Trade Policy Analysis: A Handbook,* ed. J. F. Francois and K. A. Reinert, 94–121. Cambridge: Cambridge University Press.

Robb, C. M. 2003. "Poverty and Social Analysis, Linking Macroeconomic Poli-cies to Poverty Outcomes: Summary of Early Experiences." IMF Working Paper WP/03/43, International Monetary Fund, Washington, DC.

Robilliard, A.-S., F. Bourguignon, and S. Robinson. 2001. "Crisis and Income Dis-tribution: A Micro-Macro Model for Indonesia." Photocopy, International Food Policy Research Institute, Washington, DC.

Robinson, S. 1989. "Multisector Models." In *Handbook of Development Eco-nomics,* Vol. 2, ed. H. Chenery and T. N. Srinivasan, 885–947. Amsterdam: North-Holland.

———. 2003. "Macro Models and Multipliers: Leontief, Stone, Keynes, and CGE Models." Paper, International Food Policy Research Institute, Washington, DC.

Robinson, S., and H. Löfgren. 2005. "Macro Models and Poverty Analysis: Theoretical Tensions and Empirical Practice." *Development Policy Review* 23 (3): 267–83.

Robinson, S., and L. D. Tyson. 1984. "Modeling Structural Adjustment: Micro and Macro Elements in a General Equilibrium Framework." In *Applied General Equilibrium Analysis,* ed. H. E. Scarf and J. B. Shoven, Chapter 6. Cambridge: Cambridge University Press.

Round, J. I. 2003. "Social Accounting Matrices and SAM-based Multiplier Analysis." In *The Impact of Economic Policies on Poverty and Income Distribu-tion: Evaluation Techniques and Tools,* ed. F. Bourguignon and L. A. Pereira da Silva, 301–24. New York: Oxford University Press.

Sadoulet, E., and A. de Janvry. 1995. *Quantitative Development Policy Analysis.* Baltimore: Johns Hopkins University Press.

Savard, L. 2005. "Poverty and Inequality Analysis within a CGE Framework: A Comparative Analysis of the Representative Agent and Microsimulation Approaches." *Development Policy Review* 23 (3): 313–31.

Sen, A. 1999. *Development as Freedom.* New York: Alfred A. Knopf.

Shorrocks, A. F. 1999. "Decomposition Procedures for Distributional Analysis: A Unified Framework Based on the Shapley Value." Draft, Department of Economics, University of Essex, Colchester, United Kingdom.

Shoven, J., and J. Whalley. 1992. *Applying General Equilibrium.* New York: Cambridge University Press.

Tarp, F. 1993. *Stabilization and Structural Adjustment: Macroeconomic Frameworks for Analysing the Crisis in Sub-Saharan Africa.* London: Routledge.

Tarp, F., D. W. Roland-Holst, and J. Rand. 2002. "Trade and Income Growth in Vietnam: Estimates from a New Social Accounting Matrix." *Economic Systems Research* 14 (2): 157–84.

United Nations. 2000. *United Nations Millennium Declaration.* Resolution adopted by the General Assembly, September. United Nations, New York.

Varian, H. R. 1984. *Microeconomic Analysis.* New York: Norton & Company.

Villasenor, J., and B. C. Arnold. 1984. "The General Quadratic Lorenz Curve." Technical report (photocopy), Colegio de Postgraduados, Mexico City.

———. 1989. "Elliptical Lorenz Curves." *Journal of Econometrics* 40 (2): 327–38.

Wodon, Q., K. Ramadas, and D. van der Mensbrugghe. 2003. "SimSIP Poverty Module." Photocopy, World Bank, Washington, DC.

World Bank. 1995. "Model Building: RMSM-X Reference Guide." Development Data Group, Development Economics, World Bank, Washington, DC.

———. 1998. "RMSM-X User's Guide." Development Data Group, Development Economics, World Bank, Washington, DC.

———. 2003. *A User's Guide to Poverty and Social Impact Analysis.* Washington, DC: Poverty Reduction Group and Social Development Department, World Bank.

———. 2004. "Kingdom of Morocco Poverty Report: Strengthening Policy by Identifying the Geographic Dimension of Poverty." Report 28223-MOR, Social and Economic Development Group, Middle East and North Africa Region, World Bank, Washington, DC.

Young, H. P. 1994. *Equity: In Theory and Practice.* Princeton, NJ: Princeton University Press.

Selected Tools for the Poverty and Social Impact Analysis of Macroeconomic Shocks and Policies

TABLE A7.1. Selected Tools for the Poverty and Social Impact Analysis of Macroeconomic Shocks and Policies

Tool Name	Social Accounting Matrices
What is it?	A SAM is a technique related to national income accounting that provides a conceptual basis for examining growth and distributional issues within a single analytical framework. It can be seen as a tool for the organization of information in a single matrix of the interaction between production, income, consumption, and capital accumulation.
What can it be used for?	SAMs can be used for some simple policy simulations.
What does it tell you?	SAMs can be applied to the analysis of the interrelationships between structural features of an economy and the distribution of income and expenditure among household groups.
Complementary tools	SAMS would complement and be complemented by the use of household surveys to map impacts in distributional changes. Stakeholder analysis can be useful in identifying different groups of interest.
Key elements	A typical SAM contains entries for productive activities, commodities, factors, institutions, the capital account, and the "rest of the world." An activity produces (and receives income from) commodities, buys commodities as production inputs, and pays wages to labor, rents to capital, and taxes to the government. Factor income accrues to households as owners of the factors. The SAM can be constructed to distinguish household groups by, for example, sources of income. SAM techniques select some accounts as exogenous and leave the remaining accounts endogenous. In part, this selection can be made on a sound theoretical basis, but it is often arbitrary. For example, if the SAM contains an account for agricultural production and one for transportation, an experiment can be run by imposing some exogenous change (a "shock") to agriculture, while leaving the transport sector fixed or while allowing the transport sector to adjust endogenously as a result of the shock.

Requirements

Data/information	The data sources for a SAM come from input-output tables, national income statistics, and a household survey with a labor module.
Time	About three months for a moderately detailed SAM.
Skills	Working with household-data sets, strong knowledge of national accounts, and use of Excel and, maybe, the General Algebraic Modeling System (for using dedicated software).

Tool Name	Social Accounting Matrices
Supporting software	Excel and dedicated software based on the General Algebraic Modeling System, and Stata, SAS, or Statistical Package for the Social Sciences for working with household-data sets.
Financial cost	$25,000 when the data are available. This does not include the cost of developing a new household survey.
Limitations	SAM models have at least two major drawbacks. First, prices are fixed and do not adjust to reflect changes in, say, real activity. As a result, supply is either perfectly elastic (if chosen to be endogenous) and entirely demand driven or perfectly inelastic, that is, supply is constant. Second, the results of the simulations vary greatly depending on the assumptions made about which accounts are exogenous and which accounts are endogenous.
References and applications	• For an overview of the technique, see Round (2003). • Pyatt and Round (1985). • Powell and Round (2000). • Reinert and Roland-Holst (1997). • Sadoulet and de Janvry (1995). • Tarp, Roland-Holst, and Rand (2002).

(continued)

TABLE A7.1. Selected Tools for the Poverty and Social Impact Analysis of Macroeconomic Shocks and Policies (*Continued*)

Tool Name	Computable General Equilibrium Models
What is it?	CGE models are completely specified models of an economy or a region, including all production activities, factors, and institutions. The models therefore include the modeling of all markets (in which agent decisions are price responsive, and markets reconcile supply and demand decisions) and macroeconomic components, such as investment and savings, balance of payments, and government budget.
What can it be used for?	CGE models can be used to analyze the poverty and social impacts of a wide range of policies, including exogenous shocks (exchange rate, international prices, and so on), changes in taxation, subsidies, and public expenditure (including changes in trade policies), and changes in the domestic economic and social structure (including technological changes, asset redistribution, and human capital formation).
What does it tell you?	CGE models are best chosen for policy analysis when the socioeconomic structure, prices, and macroeconomic phenomena all prove important for the analysis. They allow one to take into account all sectors of the economy, as well as the macroeconomy, and, hence, permit the explicit examination of both the direct and the indirect consequences of policies. This is particularly important for those policy reforms that are likely to play a large role in the economy and might have important impacts on other sectors or on the flow of foreign exchange or capital.
Complementary tools	Other tools described here belong to this class of models, with an additional model to take distribution into account: the 123PRSP, IMMPA, and the augmented CGE model with a representative household approach. See the respective tables in this annex.
Key elements	A CGE can be described by specifying the agents and their behavior, the rules that bring the different markets in equilibrium, and the macroeconomic characteristics. CGE models are based on SAMs (see the table on social accounting matrices) and can be distinguished by the complexity and the level of disaggregation of productive activities, factors, and institutions, including households.
Requirements	
Data/information	CGE models are data intensive. They are constructed from combined national accounts and survey data. These are first compiled into a SAM, which is then used as the foundation of the CGE.
Time	A few months to a year, depending on the existence of a SAM or of another CGE model built to address a different question. Even these simple CGEs can be complex and time consuming. An alternative is to use a previously constructed CGE. For example, Ianchovichina, Nicita,

Tool Name	Computable General Equilibrium Models
	and Soloaga (2001) use a CGE model constructed through the Global Trade and Analysis Project to examine the impact of the North American Free Trade Agreement on household welfare in Mexico. However, the use of a previously constructed, simple CGE can limit the number of policy changes that can be simulated. (In the Mexico example, the model was constructed to examine trade policy and did not cover domestic taxes or public expenditure.)
Skills	Experienced modelers with substantial prior exposure to CGE models.
Supporting software	Excel, EViews, Gauss.
Financial cost	$25,000–75,000 depending on the existing data.
Limitations	The results of CGE simulations depend at least partly on the assumptions made in the model, such as the "closure" rules. These ensure that macroeconomic accounts (fiscal, trade, savings-investment) balance. Whether they are fixed exogenously or allowed to balance endogenously, as well as how they balance, can have a significant impact on the outcomes. In addition, the production accounts specified in most available CGEs are too aggregated for the identification of the impact of policy changes in one component of one account. Many CGEs have at most two agricultural activities, one each for tradable and nontradable crops or food crops and cash crops.
References and applications	• Dervis, de Melo, and Robinson (1982), Decaluwé et al. (1999), and Shoven and Whalley (1992) for summaries of the CGE models used. • Ianchovichina, Nicita, and Soloaga (2001). Global Trade and Analysis Project models, at www.gtap.agecon. purdue.edu.

(continued)

TABLE A7.1. Selected Tools for the Poverty and Social Impact Analysis of Macroeconomic Shocks and Policies (*Continued*)

Tool Name	PovStat
What is it?	An Excel-based software program that simulates the changes in poverty and inequality resulting over time from changes in growth in output and employment.
What can it be used for?	PovStat may be used to simulate the poverty and inequality impact of policies affecting sector-level output and employment growth rates.
What does it tell you?	PovStat simulates poverty and inequality measures under alternative growth scenarios. Forecasts of varying levels of complexity may be computed, depending on the availability of reliable data and the extent to which factors influencing poverty levels are incorporated. The simulations vary according to optional projection parameters.
Complementary tools	Other software programs that provide poverty and inequality forecasts include SimSIP Poverty (see this annex on SimSIP) and DAD (a software for distributive analysis).
Key elements	On the basis of household-level data, the software translates differential output and employment growth across sectors into differential growth in the per capita income or consumption of households across those sectors. The tool simulates the impact on poverty of policies affecting output. It does this by using the fact that poverty changes can be decomposed into two parts: a component related to the uniform growth of income and a component linked to changes in relative income. The simulations are made under the assumption that the policy analyzed will be distribution neutral or, conversely, that there is a specific, quantifiable form for the distributional change. Changes in employment distribution are accommodated by reweighing the sample households.
Requirements	
Data/information	This program requires unit record household-survey data. Also, a poverty line, survey year, and forecast horizon are parameters that must be provided by the user. Macroeconomic variables at the nationally aggregated or sectorally disaggregated level and growth rates of income, employment, and population are also required. In addition, the user can input changes in the CPI and GDP deflator, changes in the relative prices of food and the shares of food in CPI, and changes in the poverty-line-consumption bundle. This allows one to generate different types of forecasts and optional projection parameters such as

Tool Name	PovStat
	employment shifts across sectors. The software can be adapted for grouped data.
Time	One or two days to format the household-survey data, collate and check exogenous economic variables, and enter everything into PovStat.
Skills	Familiarity with Excel and appropriate household-data-handling software (such as Stata). Also, familiarity with POVCAL if synthetic data from a grouped distribution are to be used.
Supporting software	Excel.
Financial cost	—
Limitations	PovStat does not capture second-round effects. These may be captured by CGE models.
References and applications	• For an overview of the technique, see Datt et al. (2003). • Datt and Walker (2002). • Software available at www.worldbank.org/psia, "Tools and Methods."

(continued)

TABLE A7.1. Selected Tools for the Poverty and Social Impact Analysis of Macroeconomic Shocks and Policies (*Continued*)

Tool Name	SimSIP Poverty
What is it?	SimSIP Poverty is a generic Excel-based simulator that allows one to estimate the changes in poverty and inequality over time resulting from changes in output and employment growth.
What can it be used for?	This tool may be used to simulate the poverty and inequality impact of policies affecting sector-level output and employment growth.
What does it tell you?	It simulates poverty and inequality measures nationally and within sectors (urban and rural, agriculture, manufacturing, and services). It may simulate the impact that various sectoral growth patterns and population shifts between sectors will have on future poverty and inequality.
Complementary tools	Other tools for poverty forecasting include PovStat (see this annex on PovStat) and DAD (a software for distributive analysis).
Key elements	On the basis of existing information on group-level household-survey data (typically by deciles or quintiles), the software translates differential output and employment growth across sectors into differential growth in per capita income or household consumption across these sectors. The tool simulates the impact on poverty of policies affecting output by using the fact that poverty changes can be decomposed into two parts: a component related to the uniform growth of income and a component linked to changes in relative income. The simulations are made under the assumption that the policy analyzed will be distribution neutral or, conversely, that there is a specific, quantifiable form for the distributional change. Changes in employment distribution are accommodated by reweighing the sample households.
Requirements	
Data/information	SimSIP Poverty uses grouped household data, typically grouped by income; the mean income or consumption by group and the share of these groups are required. In addition, SimSIP Poverty requires macroeconomic data at a nationally aggregated or sectorally disaggregated level. This includes, for example, past or expected growth rates of output, employment, and population by sector. Finally, population size and growth and a poverty line are necessary for calculating poverty incidence.
Time	One day to gather the data on population shares and mean income or consumption by group, check the credibility of scenarios, and enter the data into the software.
Skills	Familiarity with Excel.
Supporting software	Excel.

Tool Name	SimSIP Poverty
Financial cost	—
Limitations	SimSIP does not capture second-round effects. These may be captured by CGE models.
References and applications	• For an overview of the technique, see Datt et al. (2003). • Wodon, Ramadas, and Van der Mensbrugghe (2003). • Ramadas, Van der Mensbrugghe, and Wodon (2002). • Software available at www.worldbank.org/simsip.

(continued)

TABLE A7.1. Selected Tools for the Poverty and Social Impact Analysis of Macroeconomic Shocks and Policies (*Continued*)

Tool Name	123PRSP
What is it?	123PRSP (one country, two sectors, and three goods) is a static CGE model.
What can it be used for?	123PRSP can be used to analyze the impact of macroeconomic policy and external shocks on income distribution, employment, and poverty.
What does it tell you?	It allows for a forecast of welfare measures and poverty outcomes that is consistent with a set of macroeconomic policies in the context of a very simple general equilibrium model. For a given set of macroeconomic policies, 123PRSP generates a set of wages, sector-specific profits, and relative prices that are mutually consistent. The projected changes in prices, wages, and profits are then inputted into household data on wages, profits, and commodity demand among representative groups or segments of the distribution. In principle, 123PRSP can calculate the policy impact on each household in the sample so as to capture the effect on the entire distribution of income. For a given poverty line, 123PRSP can also compute the effect of different poverty measures.
Complementary tools	Analysis of impacts on income distribution could be complemented by social impact analysis and institutional analysis, which look at variables that would affect household participation in growth. Scenario analysis, which helps policy makers assess the effects of major discontinuities on economic projections, could complement CGE models operating on a long-time horizon.
Key elements	123PRSP can be viewed as a middle ground between consistency models such as RMSM-X and more sophisticated approaches such as disaggregated CGE models. The former are simple to estimate and use, but consider the two most important determinants of poverty—economic growth and relative prices—as exogenous. The latter are useful for capturing the poverty impacts of policies, but are too data intensive and difficult to master. One salient feature of 123PRSP is its modular approach; by linking several existing models together, it can make use of individual modules that already exist. Furthermore, if a particular module is not available because of data-related reasons or other reasons, the rest of the framework can be implemented without it.

Tool Name	123PRSP
Requirements	
Data/information	The 123PRSP model requires national accounts, a SAM, and some basic distributional data or a household survey. The model builds on an existing static aggregate model, such as the International Monetary Fund's Financial Programming Model (containing a consistent set of national accounts that are linked with fiscal balance of payments and monetary accounts). Macroeconomic policies are then fed into the "get real module" or an alternative country-specific model of long-run growth determination and into a trivariate VAR module of short-run fluctuations. This trivariate module would require historical national account data. Both long-run and short-run projections would then feed into the 1-2-3 model to generate projections on changes in wages, profits, and the prices of the three goods, which, in turn, are fed into a household-data module to capture the effects of macroeconomic policies on poverty.
Time	About three months if a household survey and the macromodel are available.
Skills	Experienced modelers with expertise in financial programming and advanced time-series econometrics.
Supporting software	EViews, Excel.
Financial cost	Aside from any cost for the development of the macromodel or the household survey, about $25,000 to set out a new model.
Limitations	As noted above, 123PRSP adopts several strategic simplifications in order to make the model user friendly. The disadvantage of adopting this approach is that the causal chain from macroeconomic policies to poverty is in one direction only. In this regard, the model does not capture the feedback effect of changes in the composition of demand (due to shifts in the distribution of income) on macroeconomic balances.
References and applications	• For an overview of the technique, see Devarajan and Go (2003).

(continued)

TABLE A7.1. Selected Tools for the Poverty and Social Impact Analysis of Macroeconomic Shocks and Policies (*Continued*)

Tool Name	Poverty Analysis Macroeconomic Simulator
What is it?	PAMS is an econometric model that links a macroconsistency model or macroeconomic framework to a labor-poverty module.
What can it be used for?	PAMS can be used to address the impact of macroeconomic policies and exogenous shocks (such as an exogenous rise or fall in output growth or a change in the sectoral composition of output) on individual households.
What does it tell you?	PAMS can produce historical or counterfactual simulations of (1) alternative growth scenarios with different assumptions for inflation and fiscal and current account balances; these simulations allow trade-offs within a macrostabilization program to be tested; (2) different combinations of sectoral growth (agricultural or industrial, tradable or nontradable goods sectors) within a given aggregate GDP growth rate; and (3) tax and budgetary transfer policies.
Complementary tools	Stakeholder analysis may be useful for identifying groups to inform the process of selecting microcategories.
Key elements	PAMS has three main components. First is a standard aggregate macroframework that can be taken from any macroconsistency model (for example, RMSM-X, 123) to project GDP, national accounts, the national budget, the balance of payments, price levels, and so on, in aggregate consistent accounts. Second is a labor market model that breaks down labor categories by skill level and economic sectors in which the production total is consistent with that of the macroframework. Individuals from the household surveys are joined in representative groups of households defined by the labor categories of the heads of household. For each labor category, labor demand depends on sectoral output and real wages. Wage-income levels by economic sector and labor category can thus be determined. In addition, different income tax rates and different levels of budgetary transfers across labor categories can be added to wage income. Third is a model that uses the labor-model results for each labor category to simulate the income growth for each individual inside a group, which is assumed to be a representative group. After projecting individual incomes, PAMS calculates the incidence of poverty and the intergroup inequality.

Requirements

Data/information	The model requires national accounts with a breakdown by sector, household-survey data with income or expenditure data by unit, and a wage and employment breakdown by sector.

Tool Name	Poverty Analysis Macroeconomic Simulator
Time	With a macromodel, the time needed to build a PAMS would be about three months: (1) one month to select or extract categories of households from the household survey and match the economic sectors from the macromodel, (2) one month to link the macromodel to the household-survey data, and (3) one month to run the macromodule and household module together and adjust.
Skills	Knowledge is required of (1) national-accounts-based macroeconomic models, (2) basic labor demand models, and (3) the structure of household surveys.
Supporting software	EViews, Excel.
Financial cost	$25,000 if the data are available. This does not include the cost of developing a macromodel or a new household survey.
Limitations	The main limitation is the lack of feedback of the micromodel into the macromodel.
References and applications	• For an overview, see Pereira da Silva, Essama-Nssah, and Samaké (2003). • Pereira da Silva, Essama-Nssah, and Samaké (2002).

(continued)

TABLE A7.1. Selected Tools for the Poverty and Social Impact Analysis of Macroeconomic Shocks and Policies (*Continued*)

Tool Name	Integrated Macroeconomic Model for Poverty Analysis
What is it?	IMMPA is a dynamic CGE model.
What can it be used for?	IMMPA can be used to analyze the impact of macroeconomic policy and external shocks on income distribution, employment, and poverty.
What does it tell you?	One of the main features of IMMPA is that it integrates the real and financial sides of the economy; in this regard, IMMPA is useful for analyzing both the impact of structural reforms (such as changes in tariffs or the composition of public expenditure) and the effects of short-term stabilization policies (such as a cut in domestic credit or a rise in deposit interest rates). The detailed treatment of the labor market is key for the assessment of the poverty reduction impact of macroeconomic policies. Also, it is useful for drawing the distinction between rural and urban sectors by completing separate projections on output and employment fluctuations for both areas; it is therefore also useful for studying poverty in different geographic areas.
Complementary tools	IMMPA would complement and be complemented by the use of household surveys to map impacts into distributional changes. Stakeholder analysis can be useful for identifying different groups that are of interest.
Key elements	The main features that distinguish IMMPA from other CGE models are as follows. First, IMMPA offers a very detailed specification of the labor market, which is the main transmission channel of macroeconomic shocks and adjustment policies to economic activity, employment, and relative prices. The labor market specification permits a disaggregation at the urban and rural levels and, within each level, in the formal and informal sectors. Second, IMMPA links real and financial sectors through an explicit treatment of the financial system. Third, the model emphasizes the negative effect of external debt on private investment and therefore incorporates the possibility of debt overhang. Finally, IMMPA accounts explicitly for the channels through which various types of public investment outlay affect the economy.
Requirements	
Data/information	The greatest drawback of any fully specified CGE model is the time and data required to construct it. The model must be constructed from combined national accounts and survey data. These are first compiled into a SAM, which is then used as the foundation for the model. IMMPA, for example, consists of 131 equations, more than 30 exogenous variables, and more than 200 endogenous variables.

Tool Name	Integrated Macroeconomic Model for Poverty Analysis
Time	The process can take more than a year and rarely less than a few months.
Skills	Experienced modelers with substantial prior exposure to CGE models.
Supporting software	EViews, Excel.
Financial cost	$75,000 to develop the IMMPA general equilibrium model.
Limitations	CGE simulations depend to a large extent on the assumptions made in the model, especially those that are required to close the model. They are also data intensive and difficult to master, which could limit the usefulness of the model under tight deadlines or significant capacity constraints.
References and applications	• Agénor, Izquierdo, and Fofack (2003).

(*continued*)

TABLE A7.1. Selected Tools for the Poverty and Social Impact Analysis of Macroeconomic Shocks and Policies (*Continued*)

Tool Name	Augmented CGE Model with the Representative Household Approach
What is it?	This technique is based on a CGE model with representative households that are linked to a household module.
What can it be used for?	RH models can be used to analyze the impact of macroeconomic policy and external shocks on income distribution, employment, and poverty.
What does it tell you?	RH models allow for a forecast of welfare measures and poverty outcomes consistent with a set of macroeconomic policies in the context of a general equilibrium model.
Complementary tools	—
Key elements	The key features of the RH approach are, first, a CGE model that incorporates markets for factors and commodities and their links to the rest of the economy and that generates equilibrium values for employment, wages, and commodity prices, as well as "extended" functional distributions (that is, labor differentiated by skill, education, gender, region, and sector of employment) and, second, a mapping from the extended functional distribution into the "size" distribution (the distribution of income across different households). In this approach, the representative households that appear in the CGE (corresponding to aggregates or averages of groups of households) play a crucial role: the "size" distribution is generated by feeding data on the simulated outcomes for the representative households into a separate module that contains additional information about each household.
Requirements	
Data/information	RH models require a SAM and distributional data describing the representative household groups or, more specifically, a household survey.
Time	Only a few days to generate a base solution if data and skills are available. Between six months and a year to collect data and work with the simulations.
Skills	Experienced modelers with substantial prior exposure to CGE models.
Supporting software	Excel, EViews, Gauss.
Financial cost	$25,000–75,000 depending on the data that exist.

Tool Name	Augmented CGE Model with the Representative Household Approach
Limitations	In the absence of a CGE model to feed into the RH module, the model is data intensive and difficult to master.
References and applications	<ul><li>For an overview, see Löfgren, Robinson, and El-Said (2003).</li><li>Robilliard, Bourguignon, and Robinson (2001) on Indonesia.</li><li>Coady and Harris (2001) on Mexico.</li><li>Löfgren, Harris, and Robinson (2002).</li></ul>

Source: World Bank 2003.